3/04

THE MIGHTY NIAGARA

THE MIGHTY NIAGARA

ONE RIVER—TWO FRONTIERS

JOHN N. JACKSON

WITH JOHN BURTNIAK AND GREGORY P. STEIN

Prometheus Books

59 John Glenn Drive
Amherst, New York 14228-2197

Photo on half-title page: Crest of the Falls (John N. Jackson)

Published 2003 by Prometheus Books

Inquiries should be addressed to

Prometheus Books
59 John Glenn Drive
Amherst, New York 14228–2197

VOICE: 716–691–0133, ext. 207; FAX: 716–564–2711
WWW.PROMETHEUSBOOKS.COM

07 06 05 04 03   5 4 3 2 1

Library of Congress Cataloging-in-Publication Data

Jackson, John N.
    The mighty Niagara : one river, two frontiers / John N. Jackson, with John Burtniak and
Gregory P. Stein.
        p. cm.
    Includes bibliographical references and index.
    ISBN 1–57392–980–8 (cloth : alk. paper)
    1. Niagara River (N.Y. and Ont.)—History. 2. Niagara River Valley (N.Y. and Ont.)—
History. 3. Niagara River Valley (N.Y. and Ont.)—Geography. 4. Frontier and pioneer life—
Niagara River Valley (N.Y. and Ont.) 5. Landscape—Niagara River Valley (N.Y. and Ont.)—
History. 6. Human geography—Niagara River Valley (N.Y. and Ont.)—History. 7. Niagara
River (N.Y. and Ont.)—Environmental conditions. 8. Niagara River Valley (N.Y. and Ont.)—
Environmental conditions. I. Burtniak, John. II. Stein, Gregory P. III. Title.

F127.N6 J33 2002
971.3'38—dc21

                                                                                    2002072746

Printed in the United States of America on acid-free paper

A century ago there were no skyscraper offices, no automobile-dependent suburbs, no streets bathed at night in the glare of electric lights, no airports, parking lots, expressways or shopping malls; there were no microwave transmission towers or huge concrete convention centres or international chains of fast food restaurants. These, and most of the other familiar features of modern cities, had yet to be invented and built. Slowly at first, then increasingly rapidly in the second half of the twentieth century, they have been put together to create an urban landscape that bears little resemblance to any of its industrial, renaissance or medieval predecessors, even though it has sometimes been built on their footprint of street and lot patterns. For anyone living in a city this new landscape is omnipresent, and even for those who live in quaint old towns and remote hamlets it is an unavoidable, encroaching reality. It is encountered wherever we see skyscraper skylines, electrical signs, concrete buildings or parking lots, and whenever we eat an international hamburger in the climate-controlled gloss of an indoor shopping centre, or look up at the cloud reflections in the mirror glass of an office building, or suffer the multiple indignities of the frantic spaces of an airport, or, most frequently of all, whenever we drive a car.

—E. Relph, *The Modern Urban Landscape* (1976)

CONTENTS

CONTENTS

CONTENTS

CHAPTER 10. QUALITY AND DISGRACE IN THE REGIONAL ENVIRONMENT

353

CHAPTER 11. THE EXPANDING TOURIST INDUSTRY

383

CHAPTER 12. THE FALLS AND THEIR VICINITY: A CHANGING LANDSCAPE

417

CHAPTER 13. THE NIAGARA BOUNDARY: A RETROSPECTIVE APPRECIATION   451

INDEX   461

MAPS, DIAGRAMS, AND TABLES

PREFACE AND ACKNOWLEDGMENTS

This book began when two urban geographers with interests in the changing character of cities, John N. Jackson from Brock University, St. Catharines, Ontario, and Gregory P. Stein from Buffalo State University College, Buffalo, New York, raised questions about the international boundary along the Niagara River. Why was our knowledge of the other side so limited and selective when that side was so near in access, time, and distance? What could we and our students learn by searching for comparisons and contrasts between the Canadian and the American Frontiers?

Our studies began with fieldwork, and we organized field trips across the river for our students and those from the other side. We soon realized that we were hard pressed to explain the many differences that existed, that our students in most instances had rarely ventured to the other side except for the occasional recreational or shopping visit, and that very few of our friends and colleagues were informed about the opposite set of circumstances. We ventured therefore into a complex geographical field, not just the historic and modern interpretation of the Frontier landscape, but the need to explain similarities and differences between the two national entities.

Our intention is to understand and explain the features and characteristics of space and place on both sides of the Niagara River, and the differences between the Canadian Frontier in Ontario and the American Frontier in New York State. The emphasis is on the major stages in the evolution of settlement, the changes in landscape as the international boundary is crossed, and the respective impact and significance of the various periods of technological advance.

An analogy might be that of a series of tracing overlays, with each new sheet blurring the previous set of circumstances. The base map introduces the qualities of the physical background with their ongoing ramifications up to the present for the use and development of land. The first overlay adds the Native groups with their trails, settlements, and economic activities, and the amazing fact that, although now blurred by the subsequent overlays, certain Native features remain an intrinsic part of the modern landscape. The past has become part of the present. The next overlay recognizes that the previous human landscapes, once continuous across the Niagara River, have become an acute discontinuity with the creation of an unseen but divisive international boundary. There is then the arrival of pioneer settlers, their contrasting responses to the preexisting physical and human circumstances, and again their use and modification to the landscape as roads, lots, and concessions change former communal territories.

This cumulative and additive process of using and changing previous circumstances recurs again and again, as new developments take place. Canals, bridges, railways, harnessing the river for water power, the emergence of village then town centers, the advance of service and manufacturing industries, immigration, and highways, among other things, have to be added through successive overlays. These features have each exerted a steady and continuous influence over the landscape that previously existed. The modern environment with its multitude of decisive roots from the past is the cumulative outcome from that past. As Disraeli noted, "Change is inevitable. In a progressive country change is constant."

The process by which something becomes new and unlike what it was before begins with an appreciation of the terminology that is used, discussing the meaning of boundary, frontier, and regional situation, and then introducing the physical and human features that exist in a journey taken along the Niagara River. Chapter 1 takes us into the physical background of the Niagara Frontier, reviewing terrain, drainage, climate, and soils, and introduces both the first Native inhabitants and the centuries of French-British rivalry to control the Niagara River for the access that it provided to the interior of the North American continent.

The approach is then chronological. Chapter 2 starts with the creation of an international boundary in 1783 and then examines the pioneer prelude to settlement, the division of the land into lots and concessions, and the rudimentary framework of roads and government which have survived to this day. In chapter 3 this landscape is then changed and advanced by the arrival of canals, which transformed the transportation system, added new economic opportunities, and radically changed the rural scene.

The accounts are then of the railway era of development in chapter 4, the transition to hydroelectric power from the Falls in chapter 5, the arrival and then assertive dominance across the landscape of the motor vehicle in chapter 6, and the impact of these transportation and technological advances on the two established canal systems in chapter 7. Chapter 8 adds the development of manufacturing and service activities, with noted similarities yet also remarkable differences between the two sides at the Niagara boundary.

Against this steadily expanding and changing background in the basic supporting structure of facilities, equipment, services, and installations, the contemporary scene up to the end of the twentieth century is then examined through the settlement pattern, its government, and population structure and character in chapter 9. This material is followed by an interpretation of the various parts that comprise the modern landscape: open space, agriculture, and the quality of the environment in chapter 10, the tourist industry in chapter 11, culminating in an appreciation of the Falls and their vicinity in chapter 12 as the fulcrum around which the Niagara Frontier has developed. The concluding chapter 13 interprets the scene as it might have been, as it is, and offers thoughts about the changing role of the Niagara boundary over time.

The text as a whole is an expression of historical, urban, and regional geography in order to understand a significant region astride an international Frontier that connects and separates, unites and divides Canadian and American territories bordering the Niagara River. This work could not have been undertaken without the kind assistance of many people and their organizations who helped and contributed enormously to the final work.

Particular thanks are expressed to Dr. Gregory P. Stein, Professor Emeritus (Geography and Planning), Buffalo State University College, Buffalo, New York, who helped to initiate the project and who has been involved closely in the necessary research, especially of the American scene; and to John Burtniak, retired Head, Special Collections, and University Archivist, Brock University, St. Catharines, Ontario, for his understanding of the Frontier scene, his introductions to its library resources, and for reading draft, intermediate, and final manuscripts.

The research of previous scholars is respected in the notes at the end of each chapter. Considerable thanks are also due to the staff in libraries, archives, and museums on both Frontiers who have introduced us to evidence, and the range of authoritative materials in their respective collections.

A tremendous debt of gratitude is also owed to colleagues in our respective universities who have provided advice when consulted. Officers, officials, and appointed members at all levels of government and in their several agencies have also provided a considerable range of data. To them must be added many nongovernment employees who have added worthwhile comments and advice when asked.

The Social Science and Humanities Research Council of Canada supported aspects of the research through a grant to Jackson to examine the evolution and characteristics of urban settlement in the Niagara Region, and the New York State University Foundation provided a grant to Stein to research the ethnic nature of settlement on the New York Frontier.

Loris Gasparotto, Cartographer, Brock University, has drawn the maps that are acknowledged as prepared by the Department of Geography, Brock University; and Divino Mucciante, Photographer, Brock University, has assisted with the photographic work, as has Black's Photography, St. Catharines. Parts of earlier manuscripts have been typed and retyped by secretaries in our respective Departments of Geography, and the final materials have been processed by Temporary Employment Services, Brock University, through Joyce Samuels and Jenny Gurski.

For reviewing earlier draft manuscripts, we owe considerable thanks to Dr. John S. Adams, Professor of Geography, University of Minnesota, Minneapolis; Suzanne Kirkland, a retail manager in Buffalo, and Modesto Argenio, then a writer for the *Buffalo News*; Donald E. Loker, Local History Specialist, Earl W. Brydges Public Library, Niagara Falls, New York; Dr. Richard Mitchell, Professor of Geography, State University of New York at Buffalo; and Dr. John Warkentin, Professor of Geography, York University, Downsview, Ontario. Dr. William C. Noble, Professor Emeritus (Anthropology), McMaster University, has reviewed the Native background in chapter 1. John Percy, Western New York Heritage Institute, Buffalo, has kindly provided the author with a prepublication draft of his book, *The Niagara Link: The Niagara Region's Special Connection*.

Prior work on the manuscript was undertaken by the University of Toronto Press, Vanwell Publishing in St. Catharines, the Western New York Heritage Institute in Buffalo, and the Center for Urban Places in Virginia. In each instance the manuscript was reviewed and favorably assessed, but was eventually withdrawn because of vicissitudes in the publishing industry.

In the final stages of this publication, there has been the encouraging support and help of Steven L. Mitchell, Editor-in-Chief, Prometheus Books, Amherst, New York, with his valuable knowledge and interest in the Frontier Region. Senior Editor Mary A. Read is in particular to be thanked for her copyediting abilities, including the translation of the submitted manuscript from the Canadian to the American language. Although two nations are involved, American words and spellings are used in this text. Especial thanks are given to typesetter Bruce Carle and artist Jacqueline Cooke.

The above have each left their stamps of authority on the pages of this book, and all are warmly thanked for their respective contributions. It has been a privilege and a pleasure to work with them, and to receive their excellent and welcome advice, but tradition states that the final responsibility for the text, its interpretations, and the illustrations rests with the author.

John N. Jackson
Professor Emeritus (Applied Geography)
Brock University
St. Catharines, Ontario

15 June 2001

INTRODUCTION

BOUNDARIES AND FRONTIERS

Because neither space nor place is continuous and because geographers are concerned with the areal differentiation of the earth's surface as the home of man, boundaries as the actual line of demarcation separating one political or administrative unit from another take on considerable importance. The longer they have existed, the stronger are likely to be their cumulative impressions.

The Niagara boundary, established in 1783, has more than two centuries of history. Among the most enduring of the world's political boundaries, it contrasts with many European boundaries where nations were restructured during the nineteenth century, and again after the Peace of Versailles in 1919. By world standards the boundary at Niagara has proved to be stable, long-term, and persistent.

Geometric boundaries follow straight lines between known points, often lines of latitude or longitude. Their nongeometric equivalents follow the irregular course of natural features such as rivers and watersheds. At Niagara the boundary is nongeometric. It follows the midline of the Niagara River's deepest channel, and differs markedly in type from the more extensive international division that follows the 49° N parallel between western Canada and the United States. Lakes Erie and Ontario are also divided between the two nations by an invisible boundary along the center of their waters.

Antecedent boundaries precede settlement. Subsequent boundaries are drawn after the population has become established. The boundary at Niagara is antecedent in the limited sense that, when it was created, the Niagara portage and a line of forts guarded a British route of entry to the continental interior. Permanent settlement followed when the boundary divided the length of the Niagara River. All later developments had then to accord with the presence of this boundary, and with the dictates of the various laws, regulations, and attitudes that emerged on its two sides. As both nations are major decision-making units controlling their own interests, inevitable differences have arisen, overlaid by technological and cultural similarities. Boundaries in this sense are mirrors; McGreevy (1988) has referred to the boundary at Niagara as a "wall of mirrors, reflecting back different meanings to Canadians and Americans, meanings that in turn reflect ideologies of nationalism."[1]

Boundaries are positioned precisely by statute. They provide the administrative "edge" for the various levels of government business, industry, and social organizations. They separate social, economic, and administrative differences in adjacent territories, and they integrate because a boundary provides the point of contact where these different powers meet and interact. Though the boundaries of nation-states divide the world, many characteristics of modern society transcend their confines. A boundary is overridden physically when crossed by bridges, pipes, wires, and cables; administratively when multinational acts regulate trade, water flow, and transportation; and socially when recreational, shopping, and leisure activities link the two adjoining cultures. Religion, ethnicity, and language may also extend across such territorial divisions. The boundary at Niagara is permeable, and open, not closed. It is crossed regularly in both directions and at all hours, for numerous commercial and private purposes, and by bus, rail, and highway modes of transportation.

The international boundary at Niagara defines the federal limits of Canada, the provincial limits of Ontario, and the extent of the present Regional Municipality of Niagara. In the United States it defines the state limits of New York, the counties of Erie and Niagara, and the Buffalo-Niagara Falls metropolitan area. In both nations the boundary also demarcates the extent of all local municipal units, special-purpose bodies, and the legion of public and private social, business, and group agencies that have been formed as modern society has expanded on both sides at the boundary.

It is a fluid boundary, crossed by Canadians to shop, to ski in the hills south of Buffalo, and in transit to distant destinations. Americans have monopolized the eastern shoreline of Lake Erie with their summer cottages, and the Shaw Festival Theatre in Niagara-on-the-Lake is patronized by Americans as is Artpark in Lewiston by Canadians. Heavy flows of trade and private traffic across the boundary testify to this regular inter-

The boundary, unseen in the river below, is marked by controls, and by differences in rules, regulations, laws, and attitudes between the two nations when crossed. (John N. Jackson)

change, as do the bank accounts in American dollars on the Canadian Frontier and vice versa in Buffalo and Niagara Falls, New York.

The boundary at Niagara, born out of war, has endured through both war and peace. The area was the scene of incessant French-British conflict until the British took control of North America in 1763. After the Niagara River was established as the boundary in 1783, the Canadian Frontier was invaded from the American side during the War of 1812, and in retaliation for the burning of Niagara-on-the-Lake, the British burned Buffalo. During the Canadian Rebellions of 1837–1838, raids across the boundary nearly caused the renewal of war, and Buffalonians resented the tolerance of Confederate spies on the Canadian Frontier during the American Civil War, 1861–1865.[2] Tensions rose again in 1866 when Fenians seeking to destroy the British Crown crossed the Niagara River from Buffalo. Finally, after Canada achieved Dominion status in 1867, the Treaty of Washington in 1871 required the withdrawal of opposing fleets on the Great Lakes. Even so, during the Prohibition period of the 1920s and the 1930s, armed American vessels attempted to stop the transportation of illicit booze into the United States, and Canadian vessels were fired on. During the First and Second World Wars, the Welland Canal had to be defended from possible sabotage by the German population in Buffalo, and in the 1990s illegal immigration, the fears of sabotage, and the drug trade caused tightened security on the American side at the border crossings.

People living on either side of the Niagara Frontier have generally been able to cross into each other's country without difficulty and with a minimum of restrictions. The boundary may indeed be of little concern when one crosses the Niagara River on routine occasions: after all, the two countries share the same language, enjoy a common background of west European culture, and both take full advantage of advanced technology. When problems have arisen, they are generally settled by arbitration and negotiation. The Niagara Frontier, established in a period of distrust and animosity, has been the scene of international toleration and under-

standing, perhaps epitomized by the name for the Peace Bridge that crosses the Niagara River between Fort Erie and Buffalo.

The differences that remain between Canada and the United States are relative rather than absolute. Both nations form part of the prosperous Western world. Both have populations that are healthy, long-lived, literate, and capable. Both sides at Niagara have universities, hospitals, retail centers, transportation systems, extensive industrial achievements, and a galaxy of professional, technological, and artistic talent in every conceivable field. Differences across the boundary may indeed be less significant and important than differences between the various regions within each country.

Frontier and its substitute "the border" are more difficult to define than boundary. Now a seam and not an edge faces a neighboring country. Unlike the boundary, no precise limits are defined for the Frontier concept in statutes. At Niagara, this concept includes the sub-units of both a Canadian and an American Frontier. Porter (1914) defined this extent as the strip of land along the American side of the Niagara River ceded by the Seneca Indians to the British Crown in 1764.[3] Whittemore (1966) suggested a more extensive area adjoining the Niagara River that included the Canadian and the American sides.[4] In this book, the Niagara Frontier is defined to include the fortifications, the portages, and the canals constructed to avoid the turbulent midsection of the Niagara River, and the patterns of settlement in association with these features. Such criteria extend the concept of the Niagara Frontier inland from the river to settlements along the Welland Canal between Port Dalhousie and Port Colborne, and along the Erie Canal from Lockport to Buffalo.

Tensions exist. The determination to resist and the desire to benefit from the American presence have been conflicting themes in Canadian history.[5] Canada worries when it is treated as an economic, cultural, or political satellite by the United States; at the penetration of American culture; and through the American ownership of much Canadian industry and the country's natural resources. Local concerns include severe pollution of the Niagara River by industries and chemical dumps, mainly on the American side. Anxieties are that the "buy American" policies of American states will have adverse effects on Canadian industrial production, and that free trade agreements between the two nations will diminish or end Canadian sovereignty. Local retailers on both sides have suffered significantly and alternatively in the past twenty years because of tax, price, and dollar-value differences, which have been sufficient to cause well-publicized movements of trade to the opposite side of the easily crossed boundary.

The term "friendly rivals" may usefully be applied to the overall situation at the Niagara Frontier. Although both Frontiers are parts of independent nations, the United States has the advantages of greater economic and political influence, a larger population, and resources. The distinction between the two entities has been described as the Canadian mouse next to the American elephant, or the shy Canadian chipmunk versus the soaring American eagle. The United States is the larger, wealthier, and more visible neighbor. The two facing nations are thereby unequal but peaceful partners, rivals rather than foreigners to each other. Common interests include an educated democratic society, an integrated economy, a mass culture, and a common lifestyle that the two peoples increasingly share. As President John F. Kennedy remarked in Ottawa in 1961: "Geography has made us neighbors. History has made us friends. Economics has made us partners. And necessity has made us allies."[6]

THE LANGUAGE OF LANDSCAPE

Landscape, meaning at first the rural scenery depicted by artists, has come to mean the sum total of all aspects of the scene, rural and urban, physical and human, townscape and farmscape. It is the surface of the earth as modified by human activity, expressed visually in urban and rural regions, and in the processes whereby people have chosen specific courses of action from among alternatives to modify and change the natural scenery. It is what we see about us every day of the week, and when we drive the car. It is the context of daily existence. It is what we photograph, at home and abroad. It has many components: transportation networks, buildings and roads, street scenes, and the natural background. It is the totality of what we observe, much more than its many parts, an entirety composed of many different items and features.

To Hoskins (1955): "The . . . landscape itself, to those who know how to read it aright, is the richest historical record we possess."[7] Created slowly over the years by a multitude of small events and major acts, the present has emerged gradually from the past, and can be understood only in those terms as a cumulative process of continuity and change. Land and water have been used, reused, and used again as new circumstances have arisen. The outcome is an "intricately organized expression of causes and effects, of challenges and responses, of continuity and, therefore, of coherence."[8]

Periods of change and their distinctive expressions have to be identified to suggest how new patterns and relationships have emerged. As something new is added, the old is either retained, amended, or deleted. If geography be perceived literally as "geographos," writing on the surface of the earth, humans record their actions in a "palimpsest":[9] the Indian trail used as a modern street, the survey lines that crisscross the landscape, and the Niagara boundary itself provide examples of human impressions upon the land that have survived.

Landscape, never static, is subject to the dynamic processes of continued change as its many components respond to the dictates of society. We may be impressed or not by visual features, but to read and understand these features should be as much a part of everyone's education as literature. Every visible urban and rural landscape has been used in different ways, again and again. The center of every place at the Niagara Frontier was once forest, then agricultural land. Drastic changes in land use have taken place and, as new technologies have arisen, the urban periphery has expanded to place new imprints on the landscape.

Clay (1973) has suggested that "no true secrets are lurking in the landscape . . . only undisclosed evidence . . . patterns and clues waiting to be organized."[10] He has stated that, "Only when we manage to break loose from the old fixes and look with new vision will the city fully come alive to our presence in it. Only then can we fully recognize functions, goings-on, competition, cooperation—the energetic process of city life."[11]

There is no one "correct" interpretation of landscape.[12] A factory may be perceived as an unattractive building belching smoke; as industry that is advancing, or declining; part of the chain in the manufacturing process; a traffic generator; a place of employment; a taxpaying resource; a site that requires complex waste disposal facilities; or as an investment for its shareholders. Each response is valid, and the plant will be appraised differently by its many viewers. The same argument applies to all elements of the landscape: we see the same things, but our eyes and our minds see and interpret the various features differently.[13] Ideas about the character of landscape are important; not necessarily incorporating that which is either good, beneficial, or beautiful, they present the roots and prejudices through which successive developments have gradually but steadily created the present.[14]

Landscape has three-dimensional architectural, aesthetic, and qualitative components. Lynch has developed the concept of "imageability," being that quality in a physical object which gives it a high probability of evoking a strong image in any given observer. Shape, color, height, and arrangement each contribute to the mental image of an environment. This might be called "legibility," or perhaps "visibility" in a heightened sense, where objects are not only seen but presented sharply and intensely.[15] Carver, landscape architect for the Canadian Queen Elizabeth Way (QEW) from Toronto to Fort Erie, used the word "inscape" to describe "the intrinsic and inherent qualities in those assemblies of buildings and landscapes that peculiarly command our attention and devotion."[16] More is involved than architecture or building materials. It is the appreciation of streetscape, the relationship of objects in space, and the values of scale and composition in the landscape as applied to residential, commercial, and industrial buildings, and to transportation facilities and open space.

Understanding the modern landscape is the starting point for the future. Neither the past nor the present can be changed. It is only as the present moves into the future that the challenges of retention or change are posed. We may then formulate policies, suggest improvements, and praise or criticize present conditions. We can act only to influence future events.[17] All else is beyond recall. The modern landscape, the canvas of interface between past and future, has to be understood for its own varied qualities. It may then be used as the basis for future actions.

There is also an important distinction between reality and perceived reality. Here, terminology may confuse rather than enlighten. The Niagara Peninsula is a promontory of Southwest Ontario, but it is a "peninsula" that neither penetrates into water nor is it an extent of land almost surrounded by water—an impression perpetuated when maps end at the boundary and leave the other side blank. The peninsula is more readily viewed as the continuity of a "land bridge," crossed by a series of interlinking railways and highways, with substantial travel and the movement of people and goods between the two countries.

Directions at the Niagara Frontier may confuse, as local detail varies from the generalized Canadian-American situation. Most of Canada lies north of the United States, but the Canadian north shore of Lake Erie lies south of the American shore of Lake Ontario. Canadian Fort Erie lies south of Grand Island, New York. Canada generally lies north of the Great Lakes, but the Niagara Peninsula is south of Lake Ontario. Climate is unusual: it is colder to the south on the Erie Plain and south of Buffalo, and growing peaches in the Niagara Fruit Belt is an anomaly not repeated until the southern states of the United States are reached.

Americans often perceive the Niagara Peninsula to be a continuation of their national estate. Yankee investors and craftsmen perceived the Niagara and Gore Districts at the Head of Lake Ontario to be "a virtual extension of the land mass of New York State."[18] The American invasion during the War of 1812, American railways between the Detroit and the Niagara Frontiers, the American harnessing of the Canadian power resource at the Falls, American cottages along the north shore of Lake Erie, and the extensive American ownership of industrial activities on the Canadian Frontier provide vivid examples for the American penetration of Canadian space.

Response to the major physical features of the Niagara Escarpment differs between the two Frontiers. Canadian residents have a greater awareness of this feature than Americans. It is a more visible part of their daily environment and St. Catharines, the largest population center, lies under its brow. The escarpment, crossed by the busy Queen Elizabeth Way, clearly visible to the south when traveling across the Niagara Peninsula, can be perceived directly for its striking impact, with differences in climate, settlement, and agriculture as its brow is crossed; for its direct significance where the locks of the Welland Canal "climb the mountain"; and in the route alignment of several railways and highways across its abrupt slope.

On the American Frontier, where the population centers of Niagara Falls and Buffalo lie to the south, the Niagara Escarpment is not so appreciated as a significant factor in daily life. The locks at Lockport on the Erie Canal entice fewer visitors than do their counterparts along the Welland Canal. American appreciation is more likely to recognize the escarpment as only a Canadian feature that parallels the first half of the route to Toronto, and this visitor is unlikely to understand the relationship between the Welland Canal and the escarpment when arching over this waterway in St. Catharines.

To appreciate the character and the potential of the Frontier has often required the challenge of tremendous mental ability. During the early days of canal construction with only primitive measuring instruments and before contoured maps, it was a thought-provoking idea that the Grand River might be dammed and its waters diverted to the Welland River at Port Robinson. Heroic vision also applied to the creation of Buffalo as a port on Lake Erie, to the design of this small village in the baroque spirit of Washington, D.C., and to the conversion of Buffalo Creek into a harbor. Ontario's Niagara River Parkway, the rescue of Goat Island and the banks next to the American Falls from industry, the addition of a park system designed by Frederick Law Olmsted to Buffalo's expanding urban area, and Canadian attempts to preserve the Niagara Fruit Belt and to safeguard the Niagara Escarpment have also required tremendous foresight to steer the emerging landscape in positive new directions. The Frontier has also been prolific in its industrial inventions and advances, with the generation of hydroelectricity from the Falls being in the forefront of these adventurous changes to the landscape.

Geography studies what is there, or has been there, on the ground. Always, something else might have been achieved. There is no certainty about the evolution of landscape. It involves the whims and not just the successes of human nature. Had Louis XIV of France spent less on his clothes, Versailles, and court opulence and diverted more wealth to his French empire overseas, then the Niagara area might well have been French rather than British by the time of the American

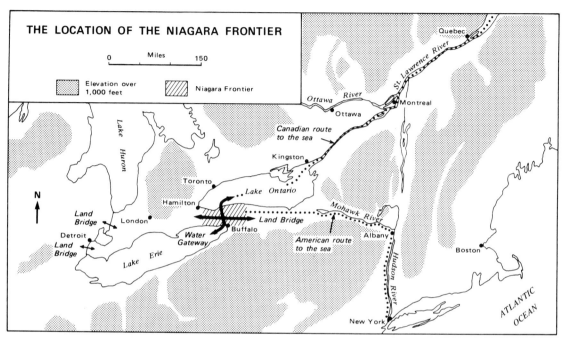

Fig. I. The Niagara Frontier includes a Canadian and an American Frontier. Regional setting in North America reflects both a "water gateway" to the continental interior and a "land bridge" between two of the Great Lakes. (Prepared by the Department of Geography, Brock University)

Revolution. The War of 1812 involved serious miscalculation that British territories would soon fall into American hands, as did the subsequent Mackenzie Rebellion and the Fenian Raids that presumed British rule in Canada would soon fall to invasion. Only a series of unanticipated accidents permitted the achievement of the First Welland Canal.

This study presents landscape as a process of historic change, created over the centuries and incorporating events large and small. It probes the similarities and the differences that have evolved over the past two centuries and studies the Niagara Frontier in terms of its vital opposites: in strife and harmony, divergence and convergence, the transition from pioneer economies to the advanced status of world powers on both sides of the boundary at

Niagara, and with Canada as the smaller state both resisting and encouraging American cultural and economic overtures. The Niagara Frontier emerges as a landscape that is diverse yet similar, contradictory and consistent, full of conflict yet having survived longer than most other world boundary locations.

REGIONAL SITUATION

The two Frontiers enjoy different national contexts within North America.[19] Canada, perceived as the "attic" of North America, occupies the northern part of the continent. Even so, the Niagara Frontier lies further south than the states of Washington or Maine in the United States. Niagara Falls, Ontario, at 43.05′ N, lies south of Seattle, Washington (47.36′ N), and Portland, Maine (43.40′ N). The Niagara Fruit Belt is at about the same latitude as northern Spain, southern France, or Italy north of Rome.

The shortest overland routes between New York City and the American West cross the Canadian Frontier, providing the most direct route between Buffalo and Detroit or between New York City and Chicago (fig. 1). Canal, rail, and highway developments on the Canadian Frontier strongly reflect this axis of movement, as does the growth of Buffalo.

The Canadian Frontier lies astride the Welland Canal, the primary route of water travel between the Upper Great Lakes and the Atlantic Ocean via the St. Lawrence River and Montreal.[20] The American Frontier in its contrasting regional setting provides the eastern terminal for water navigation on Lake Erie and links the Upper Great Lakes via the Erie Canal to New York City. With the division of the Niagara River between two nations after the American Revolution, the Canadian outlet to Montreal then vied commercially for supremacy with the American outlet to New York City. Both sides of the Niagara Frontier have grown where the rival hinterland areas of Montreal and New York overlapped for control of the continental interior.[21]

Other competing outlets between the Atlantic Ocean and inland North America presented alternative possibilities (fig. 1). The St. Lawrence River via Lake Champlain and the Hudson River, and the Hudson-Mohawk Rivers via Lake Ontario and Oswego both connected through to the Atlantic Ocean at New York. Trade might flow from the hinterland of Lake Erie south to the Ohio and Mississippi Rivers and the Gulf of Mexico. The Ottawa Valley and Georgian Bay provided an alternative route between Montreal and the Upper Great Lakes. The Niagara Frontier is a marine crossroad of continental importance as a "water gateway" to the inland heart of the North American continent, a fact that has flavored the development of overland portages around the tumultuous middle length of the Niagara River, and subsequent canals on both Frontiers to this day.

The Niagara Frontier also functioned as a "land bridge" across the Great Lakes water system, a concept that emphasizes the Niagara River as only a short span of water between two almost-continuous masses of land. The channel could be crossed by canoe, Conestoga wagon, ferry, and railway and highway bridges. To stress the continental importance of these crossings, the nearest similar crossings are over 563.3 kilometers (350 miles) distant at Windsor-Detroit upstream and Kingston-Cape Vincent downstream.

With Niagara's water gateway and land bridge routes divided between two competing countries, the combination of regional situation and the rival and contrasting patterns of transportation linkage are of critical importance in explaining the comparative evolution of settlement across the two Frontiers and the location and intensity of economic and urban activities that have emerged. The portages to bypass the Falls on the Niagara River introduced villages at both ends on both banks. Ports, harbors, and

wharves arose along the Welland and the Erie Canals. Buffalo became an important port city where canal barges met lake vessels, and grew immensely when railways arrived on the scene. Ferries, then bridges, across the Niagara River created urban centers on both banks. Where these railways crossed the Welland Canal, further urban-industrial advances took place. As the automobile-truck era of transportation advanced, first paved and then multilane highways transformed almost every aspect of settlement and development throughout the Frontier.

The classic nineteenth-century understanding of urban growth has indeed been in full operation at the Niagara Frontier: "Transportation . . . is the main cause of the location of cities in an industrial society. The mode of its action is that population and wealth tend to collect at a break in transportation; the reason being in the first place the necessity for the material and symbolic machinery of transfer at breaks, and in the second the tendency of other activities to collect where the machinery exists."[22]

Both nationally and at Niagara the population is and has been since the early nineteenth century greater on the American than the Canadian Frontier. Even so, a curious anomaly exists: the Canadian Frontier is now less isolated within its national situation than

The overall picture presented by a satellite air photograph indicates the concept of an east-west land bridge across the great lakes system of inland waterways, with Lake Ontario (top) and Lake Erie (below) and Buffalo at the eastern end of Lake Erie. The function of the Niagara Frontier as a water gateway to the continental interior is also depicted by the Niagara River at the center of this photograph and with the Welland Canal being left center also connecting the two lakes. Where major land and water routes meet and cross has proved to be a major factor in the gradual evolution of the settlement pattern at the Frontier. (This Satellite Imagery [Niagara River] © Her Majesty the Queen in Right of Canada, reproduced from the collection of the National Air Photo Library, Ottawa, with permission of Natural Resources Canada)

the American Frontier. The Canadian side is an integral part of the "Golden Horseshoe" of Southwest Ontario which, centered on Toronto, extends around the head of Lake Ontario from Niagara-on-the-Lake to Oshawa. This expanding metropolitan region, the largest and most prosperous in Canada, contrasts with recent economic decline in the Buffalo metropolitan area, an almost complete reversal from when Buffalo was expanding rapidly at the turn of the twentieth century and Toronto was the second largest city after Montreal in a small country.

Another aspect of the contrasting regional circumstances is that Canada's Niagara Fruit Belt has replaced its former American equivalent. In the United States products grown on the American Frontier now have to compete with produce from the southern states, but in Canada provincial measures have been taken to protect its famous fruit-growing areas.

THE NIAGARA RIVER AND ITS UPPER LENGTH

The Niagara River, the keystone around which the Canadian and American Frontiers have developed, provides a pronounced physical barrier to human interaction across its often turbulent waters. There are rapids to be overcome at the entrance to the river from Lake Erie, the middle section of the river carries the world-famous Falls with rapids above and the gorge below, and strong currents prevail at the Lake Ontario entrance. In the east-west direction the land bridge concept of crossing the river included both spanning the gorge in the middle length of the river and the need to place piers for bridge construction in the bed of the fast-flowing river at its point of departure from Lake Erie. In both instances, the human approach to problems created by the physical environment has involved the policies of the two bordering nations and the provincial/state regional jurisdictions next to the river.

The river itself is an atypical natural feature. It rises not in the mountains and it sets not in the sea. A river typically has headwaters of many smaller streams, but the Niagara River pours out from Lake Erie. A normal river is set within either an observable valley or it meanders across a floodplain, but neither characteristic is visible along the Niagara River. Nor does the usual river profile, steepest at the beginning, prevail along the Niagara River where the fall is most abrupt along its central length. Furthermore, the river with its complex physical origins and its lengthy human history can be appreciated only as an integral part of the extensive, inland drainage system described as "The River of Canada" by both Jacques Cartier and Samuel de Champlain, a continuity that includes Lake Erie, the Niagara River, and Lake Ontario.

The river drops 99.4 meters (326 feet) over the short distance of 53.1 kilometers (33 miles).[23] This impressive fall, the most dramatic along the St. Lawrence–Great Lakes system, is concentrated in the midsection where the river has cut back into the brow of the Niagara Escarpment and created the world-famous sequence of the rapids, the Falls, and the gorge.

Described as a "strait" by early writers,[24] the Niagara River begins with an average flow of about 5,805 m^3/sec (205,000 cfs [cubic feet per second]) from the Upper Great Lakes. This consistent, year-round flow is affected by diversions into and from the Upper Great Lakes and by diversions from within the river to hydroelectric power stations and to the New York Barge (former Erie) Canal (fig. 2). This flow has been changed considerably over the years by the activities of man, and is now subject to international dictates.[25]

The principal features along the river are depicted in figure 5.[26] The narrow outlet from Lake Erie, the "débouchure" in early descriptions,[27] is controlled by a natural rock weir where the river crosses the submerged outcrop of the Onondaga Escarpment. Here at the Rapids, the river narrows to a width of about 457.2 meters (1,500 feet), then falls 1.5 meters (5 feet) in its first 6.4 kilometers (4 miles). The Peace Bridge, a major link between the highway system of the two nations, crosses the Niagara River close to this point of departure from Lake Erie.

Winter ice across the head of Lake Erie has caused the destruction and successive relocation of the fortification known as Old Fort Erie. Late spring ice shortens the navigation season, a disadvantage for Buffalo and the Erie Canal, but favoring the more westerly location for the entrance to the Welland Canal at Port Colborne. Since 1964 a 3-kilometer (2-mile) ice boom of floating beams has been built each winter across the eastern end of Lake Erie to prevent ice from blocking the intake systems of the downstream power plants. Controversy exists over whether ice piling up behind the boom and extending for miles into Lake Erie, coupled with westerly winds from off this lake, aggravates Buffalo's winter climatic conditions and delays the spring thaw.

Despite swift currents, the Upper River is navigable north to Chippawa and Fort Schlosser. Boats were once hauled upstream by a "breeze of oxen," an arduous task offset by the inland construction of the Welland Canal and by the Erie Canal along the bank

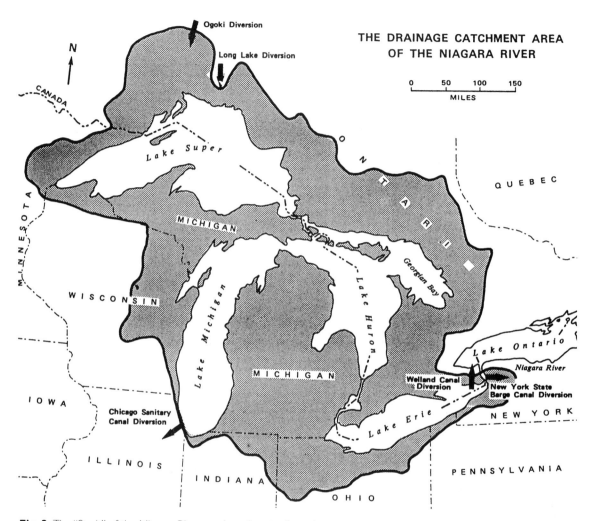

Fig. 2. The "Strait" of the Niagara River receives all water from the Upper Great Lakes and their catchment areas in both Canada and the United States, plus and minus diversions into and out of this basin. (Prepared by the Department of Geography, Brock University)

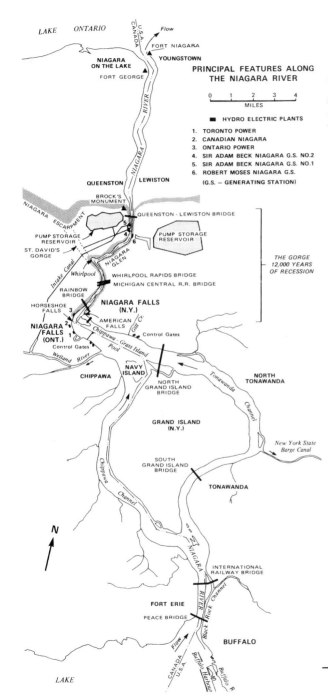

LAKE ONTARIO

Flow

FORT NIAGARA

YOUNGSTOWN

NIAGARA
ON THE LAKE

FORT GEORGE

**PRINCIPAL FEATURES ALONG
THE NIAGARA RIVER**

0   1   2   3   4
MILES

■ HYDRO ELECTRIC PLANTS

1. TORONTO POWER
2. CANADIAN NIAGARA
3. ONTARIO POWER
4. SIR ADAM BECK NIAGARA G.S. NO.2
5. SIR ADAM BECK NIAGARA G.S. NO.1
6. ROBERT MOSES NIAGARA G.S.
   (G.S. — GENERATING STATION)

QUEENSTON   LEWISTON

BROCK'S
MONUMENT

NIAGARA ESCARPMENT

QUEENSTON - LEWISTON BRIDGE

PUMP STORAGE
RESERVOIR

PUMP
STORAGE
RESERVOIR

ST. DAVID'S
GORGE

NIAGARA
GLEN

THE GORGE
12,000 YEARS
OF RECESSION

Intake Canal   *Whirlpool*

WHIRLPOOL RAPIDS BRIDGE
MICHIGAN CENTRAL R.R. BRIDGE

RAINBOW
BRIDGE

HORSESHOE
FALLS

**NIAGARA FALLS
(N.Y.)**

AMERICAN
FALLS

**NIAGARA
FALLS
(ONT.)**

Chippawa   Grass Island

Control Gates

Control Gates

Welland River

CHIPPAWA

**NAVY
ISLAND**

NORTH
GRAND ISLAND
BRIDGE

**NORTH
TONAWANDA**

Tonawanda Channel

**GRAND ISLAND
(N.Y.)**

New York State
Barge Canal

SOUTH
GRAND ISLAND
BRIDGE

TONAWANDA

Chippawa Channel

N

NIAGARA RIVER

INTERNATIONAL
RAILWAY BRIDGE

Black Rock Channel

FORT ERIE

PEACE BRIDGE

BUFFALO

CANADA
U.S.A.

Flow

Buffalo Harbour   Buffalo R.

LAKE

Fig. 3. Principal features along the Niagara River. (Prepared by the Department of Geography, Brock University)

on the American side. All islands in the river lie between the Peace Bridge and the Falls. Squaw Island on the American side, the first of the larger islands, is located across the mouth of Scajaquada Creek. This island, once a recreational center, provided a foundation for the eastern piers of the International Railway Bridge and now houses the treatment plants of the Buffalo Sewer Authority.

At the much larger Grand Island, the deep Chippawa Channel on the Canadian side carries about 60 percent of the river's flow; the longer Tonawanda Channel on the American side carries the rest. Tonawanda Creek, the former route of the Erie Canal and now with a reversed drainage from the Niagara River to serve the canal, previously entered the eastern channel opposite Grand Island. Tonawanda Island downstream from the creek's mouth has attracted railroad tracks, oil tanks, and large-scale industry, but recreational boating facilities are increasing, and popular bicycle and walking trails follow both shores of the river.

Grand Island covers about 45.1 square kilometers (28 square miles). Short, steep bluffs face the surrounding channels. The island, connected to the American mainland by early ferries, received its first highway bridge in 1935. The bridge, later duplicated, attracted a suburban population and light industrial developments; Buckhorn and Beaver Islands at opposite ends of the island became state parks. A highway encircles the island, the West River Parkway faces the Canadian Niagara River Parkway, and the East River Road faces the mainland United States.

The smaller Navy Island, named after a British shipyard of the 1760s, is Canadian territory. Once occupied by insurgents, mostly Americans for an attack on Canada during the Canadian Mackenzie Rebellion of 1837–1838, the island covers 127.9 hectares (316 acres). With no connecting bridge to either mainland, the island was promoted for the site of the United Nations Headquarters until New York received this distinction.[28] Though once farmed and the site of a resort hotel and docks, the island has become an uninhabited wildlife preserve and a camping site managed by the Ontario Niagara Parks Commission.

A remarkable contrast exists between the two banks of the Upper River. The Canadian side carries the two-lane Niagara River Parkway, one of the finest landscaped routes in the world, backed by upper-income homes and agricultural land. The American bank, in stark contrast, is heavily industrialized, with the river frontage occupied by the multilane I-190 known locally as the Niagara Section of the New York State Thruway.

North of Navy Island and Grand Island, the Niagara River is broadest when crossing the Chippawa-Grass Island Pool. Ferries once crossed these waters, 1.5 kilometers (1 mile) in width, connecting Chippawa on the Canadian Frontier with Fort Schlosser on the American Frontier. Both centers lay at the southern end of the portages that bypassed the middle section of the river, both grew in conjunction with portages from Queenston and Lewiston on the Lower Niagara River, and both had forts in conjunction with the military and trading importance of the river as a major route to inland North America.

The Welland River, the major west-bank tributary, joins the Niagara River at Chippawa. This broad slow-flowing river, an inland route used for Indian, French, and pioneer travel, became part of the Welland Canal in 1829. A channel was cut through the southern bank at Chippawa where a headland extended into the Niagara River. The flow in this channel was later reversed to serve the downstream Sir Adam Beck power complex at Queenston Heights, and the former mouth of the river was filled in to become King's Bridge Park managed by the Niagara Parks Commission.

The International Control Dam projects into midchannel from the Canadian bank at the Chippawa-Grass Island Pool. Its movable gates control the flow of water in the Niagara River, which reduces erosion at the Horseshoe Falls by diverting some water past Goat Island to the American Falls, and controls the level of water in the pool for diversion to downstream power plants at Queenston and Lewiston. Tunnels on both banks, guarded by massive intake gates, can divert up to three-quarters of the river's volume to reservoirs located close to the Niagara Escarpment. Whether to divert water from the river for power or to use its natural flow for tourist advantage at the Falls became a controversial issue at the turn of the nineteenth century when the river's flow was diverted to an expanding number of power plants on both banks.

THE MIDDLE LENGTH OF THE NIAGARA RIVER

Closer to the Falls, a series of small islands was changed by hydroelectric development. Cedar Island next to the Canadian bank disappeared in 1904 when the Canadian Niagara Power Company constructed its power station, and small islands next to the American bank were obliterated when the Robert Moses Parkway was constructed on material excavated from the power tunnels.

Upstream from the Falls on the Canadian Frontier, open space and high-quality residential areas line the Niagara River Parkway. The American scene above the Falls is dominated by an industrial-chemical complex that developed using hydroelectric power from the river. Both banks have marinas and boat slips, and the river is used extensively for recreational boating.

The Niagara River is spectacular as it narrows and gathers momentum for its scenic climax. The Cascades, the succession of rock ledges or "chutes" over which the river plunges with increasing rapidity for 1.5 kilometers (1 mile) above the Falls, are viewed with more pleasure than the Falls by some visitors.[29] The river is divided into two channels; Goat Island in the middle and once partially industrialized, but now landscaped with trees and trails, provides noted views over the white water of the Cascades. Channels, dotted with small islands, intervene between Goat Island and the mainland; bridges have crossed this speeding flow since 1817.

Ninety percent of the river's flow is carried over the Horseshoe Falls and about 10

To many, the rapids above the Falls are more visually exciting than the Falls. The rapids can be comprehended; the Falls may awe. (John N. Jackson)

percent passes over the American Falls. As the rock strata under the riverbed dip gently toward the Canadian side, water is thrown toward the west bank. This fact, important scenically and for the diversion of water to power plants, explains the embayment of Dufferin Islands caused by the sloping "weirs" of the first and second cascades in the river. The dip in the strata also produced the highest rate of erosion in the notch of the Horseshoe Falls and led to the erosion-control measures in the Chippawa-Grass Island Pool that have been described.

The Horseshoe Falls, larger and higher than the American Falls, have a direct width of some 304.8 meters (1,000 feet). The actual length (following the curving and indented crestline is about 762 meters [2,500 feet]) presents an uninterrupted arc of white and green water tumbling some 53.6 meters (176 feet).[30]

This noteworthy spectacle has captured the imagination of innumerable artists, writers, travelers, and visitors since their "discovery" at the end of the seventeenth century.[31] The scene is "on a scale which baffles every attempt of the imagination...the ordinary means of description, I mean analogy, and direct comparison, with things that are more accessible, fail entirely in the case of that amazing cataract, which is altogether unique."[32]

At the American Falls, Luna Falls and Luna Island are named after the rainbow once visible in the mist in full moonlight; the illumination of the Falls ended that phenomenon. The American Falls, 55.5 meters (182 feet) high in summer, have a free drop of 21.3 to 36.6 meters (70 to 120 feet),[33] and the length of the crestline is about 323.1 meters (1,060 feet). The water then flows over boulders into the Maid of the Mist Pool. As these rocks at the base of the Falls are accumulating faster than their removal, the long-term expectation is for a sloping cascade rather than a vertical fall (fig. 4).

The combined flow over the two Falls varies from a summer daytime maximum of 2,832 m^3/sec (100,000 cfs) to half that amount during the winter period. Because of power, canal, and municipal diversions, the summer flow is now approximately half the volume that enters the Niagara River. Even so, the spectacle at the Horseshoe and American Falls remains a breathtaking scene of world acclaim. Streams of visitors observe the scene, with Table Rock on the Canadian side being the most favored viewpoint. As public open space has been provided on both sides, tourism on a grand scale has been attracted to the landscape.

Canada's Queen Victoria Park is backed by a ridge 30.5 meters (100 feet) high, which curves around the Falls to become the site for high-rise hotels and commercial-recreational developments such as the Skylon Tower. This ridge, physically and visually, separates parkland along the river from the residential areas of the City of Niagara Falls. Below this ridge the "scenic ledge" of Queen Victoria Park has no American counterpart. Here the land, flat back from the rim of the gorge, has no distinguishing physical characteristics. The scenic advantages of the park system on the Canadian side in part stem from specific natural features that are not repeated on the American bank.

The Falls offer a special winter allure. Although the ice boom across Lake Erie has reduced the volume of ice, the winter scene remains one of particular interest as freezing spray transforms vegetation, walls, and lampposts into ice sculpture. The Falls do not freeze, but ice accumulates in the Maid of the

THE HORSESHOE AND THE AMERICAN FALLS

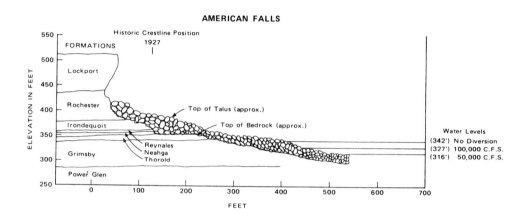

AMERICAN FALLS

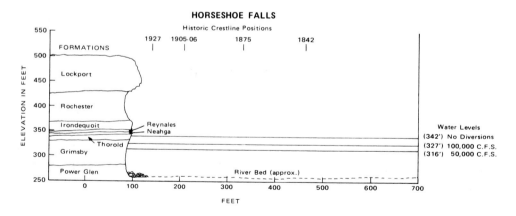

HORSESHOE FALLS

Fig. 4. The Falls provide the climactic landscape feature on the Niagara River and at the Niagara Frontier. The Horseshoe Falls are larger, higher, and broader than the American Falls. Taken together, they are some twenty times as broad as they are high. (Prepared by the Department of Geography, Brock University)

Mist Pool, extends downstream through the gorge, and an ice bridge usually forms from bank to bank below the Falls. The river flows under this ice, which may rise some 24.4 meters (80 feet) above the water surface. For many years people walked across this "bridge," a frolic banned in 1912 when the ice broke apart and three people drowned. Pressure from ice also removed the abutments of the Upper Steel Arch Bridge (Honeymoon Bridge) below the Falls in 1938, causing this structure to collapse.

At the Falls, it is important to note that the Niagara River changes its direction of flow by some 90° from west to north, which favors the American side with the shortest route to bypass the Falls (fig. 5). This inner elbow of turn was followed by the original portage routes, and later by the first hydraulic canals that diverted water from the river to hydroelectric power stations. The greater concentration of settlement and industry on the American side can in part be attributed to this change in direction of the river's flow.

The Falls as an erosional feature have cut back for 11 kilometers (7 miles) from the edge of the Niagara Escarpment over the past 12,000 years.[34] When viewed by Father Hennepin in 1678, the predecessor Horseshoe Falls were located at about the upstream end of the Ontario Power Plant. The Falls have receded as spray and falling water attacked the underlying shale, and were further undermined as water from upstream moved under pressure into cracks in the top layer of the hard Lockport dolomite (fig. 6).

Below the Falls, the Maid of the Mist Pool, with a width of from 304.8 to 518.2 meters (1,000 to 1,700 feet) and a depth of about 42.7 meters (140 feet), can be crossed by boat. The name Ferry Street on the Canadian side recalls the rowboat ferry and the road constructed down the gorge to its landing point. Since 1846 the *Maid of the Mist* tourist boats have provided visitors with an exciting close view of the Falls from the river. As the river enters the Whirlpool Rapids, the sheer walls are crossed by the Rainbow Bridge, which carries a considerable volume of highway traffic and serves as a pedestrian viewing platform for visitors. On the Canadian side are the formal gardens of the Oakes Garden Theatre. The American side once carried an extensive industrial complex on the crest of the gorge, and the remains of the Schoellkopf hydroelectric power plant, destroyed in 1956, can still be seen down the side of the gorge.

Water velocity increases to over 48.3 kilometers (30 miles) per hour through the Whirlpool Rapids where the gorge narrows. As the depth of the gorge increases to the

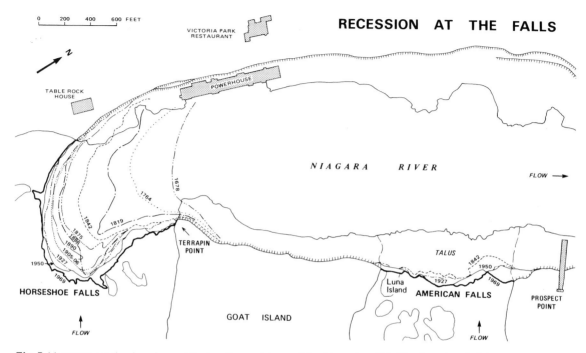

Fig. 5. Upstream erosion has changed the location and shape of the Horseshoe Falls. The American Falls have also been modified, but to a lesser extent. (Prepared by the Department of Geography, Brock University)

north, more of the lower rock strata are exposed and the river gradient combined with its narrow width creates white-crested breakers and standing waves. A boardwalk on the Canadian side and a walking trail along a former streetcar right-of-way at the base of the gorge on the American bank overlook this grandiose scene.

Where the Niagara Gorge is at its narrowest and the river most turbulent, a railway bridge and a combined railway-highway bridge cross the gorge, in turn attracting hotels, stations, freight yards, industrial establishments, and miles of track to the twin cities of Niagara Falls. Both urban complexes declined after the automobile arrived on the scene, leading to obsolescence and extensive renewal on both banks.

Downstream from these bridges the river enters the elliptical Whirlpool Basin from the

Fig. 6. The Falls have eroded from the edge of the Niagara Escarpment over the past 12,000 years. This process, delayed through controlling the volume and speed of water, has continued into the modern era. (Prepared by the Department of Geography, Brock University)

THE PROCESS OF EROSION AT THE FALLS

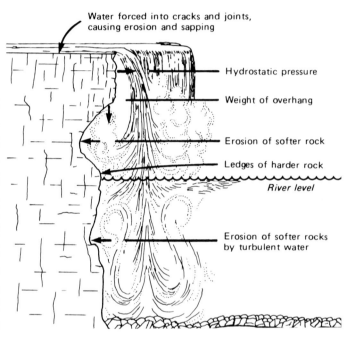

Water forced into cracks and joints, causing erosion and sapping

Hydrostatic pressure

Weight of overhang

Erosion of softer rock

Ledges of harder rock

River level

Erosion of softer rocks by turbulent water

southeast through a narrow gap at high speed. It crosses this basin counterclockwise before flowing northeast into the Lower Niagara Gorge beneath its own entering flow. This circuit reverses direction at night, a phenomenon created through both a diminished flow of water in the river and the physical configuration at the Whirlpool. The Whirlpool is crossed by the Spanish Aero Car, a "to and fro" aerial cableway, from Canadian bank to Canadian bank, in part over mid-river American territory. On the Canadian side a pioneer water-hoist system brought water to the top of the bank where the power was used in a mill and quarry operation, and an incline railway served by this waterpower brought tourists to the water's edge and trails along the riverbanks. Both decayed, and neither have been reconstructed.

The buried St. David's Gorge, an ances-tral Niagara River whose channel was plugged by glacial deposition, is notched into the northeast banks of the Whirlpool. When the last glacier retreated, the present river cut back along the line of the Lewiston Spillway until it met the buried gorge and created the river's significant right-angle turn at the Whirlpool.

Leaving the Whirlpool through Niagara

The Falls on the Niagara River have always provided the major point of scenic grandeur for both sides of the Niagara Frontier. Access to the river was at first by private stairways, the "thrill of the day" being to venture behind the Falls on both sides of the river. (*Picturesque America*, 1872)

Glen, the river's gradient is steep, 13.7 meters over 3.2 kilometers (45 feet over 2 miles). Erosion has exposed former potholes, rounded rocks, and ledges next to the river. Wintergreen Terrace near the top of the gorge on the Canadian side is the bed of an earlier river, before a deeper channel to the east captured its waters and cut the modern gorge. Devil's Hole, a notch on the American side and an outlet from former glacial Lake Tonawanda, was the scene of a Native ambush of a British wagon train during the early colonial period. On the Canadian bank are a golf course, horticultural gardens, and the butterfly conservatory of the Niagara Parks Commission, with Niagara University on the American bank. The rapids in the river can be approached by footpath on both sides through wooded scenery with rock overhangs and talus slopes.[35]

Downstream the Canadian Sir Adam Beck and the American Robert Moses power plants, with generating stations, penstocks, and reservoirs, have replaced the former hydroelectric plants at the Falls and together comprise one of the largest hydroelectric installations in the world. Marching lines of steel towers and high-tension power lines provide further evidence for the substantial hydroelectric power base that has developed at the Niagara Frontier. Nearby the Queenston-Lewiston Arch Bridge, named the Lewiston-Queenston Arch Bridge on the American side, was once the largest single span arch in the world. This bridge replaced a former highway suspension bridge between Queenston and Lewiston at the foot of the Niagara Escarpment.

The bridges across the gorge,[36] together with the two bridges between Fort Erie and Buffalo, exemplify the "land bridge" function of the Frontier. The bridges cross the two narrowest points of the river. By contrast the earlier ferries crossed at the river's widest points where the current was less turbulent, a change in location of significance for the form and evolution of their associated settlements which grew as interrelated features of the landscape and which today are major connecting elements in the national systems of transportation that have emerged on both sides of the intervening river. The bridges with their converging routes are important hubs in the landscape, and their structures are both renowned engineering feats and noted landmarks.

At the northern end of the Niagara Gorge in Queenston Heights Park are the earthworks redoubt of Fort Drummond, where the imposing monument to the British commander at the Battle of Queenston Heights, Major General Sir Isaac Brock, dominates the scene. Another monument is dedicated to

The Niagara River, generally flowing from south to north between Lake Erie and Lake Ontario, makes two significant right-angle turns: at the Falls (**left**), and at the Whirlpool (**below**). (Left: John N. Jackson; below: W. H. Bartlett print, 1840, John H. Jackson collection)

Laura Secord, the heroine of the War of 1812 who informed the British at Beaverdams about an impending American attack. Both monuments are surrounded by picnic grounds, formal gardens, and informal public open space managed by the Niagara Parks Commission. On the American bank the theater and arts complex of Artpark is located at the northern end of the original Niagara Portage on land filled in with debris from the upstream Robert Moses power plant. Opened in 1974 to combine the performing arts with workshops, performances, and demonstrations, these facilities are well patronized by both sides of the river to provide an excellent example of the permeable boundary for cultural and recreational pursuits.

THE LOWER NIAGARA RIVER

Where the river widens and leaves the gorge, the villages of Queenston and Lewiston developed at the head of navigation for the Lower River, where portages to the south carried trade to and from the Upper River. A ferry, then a bridge, linked the roadways that followed the raised shoreline of glacial Lake Iroquois east and west from the Niagara River. Both villages are now primarily residential localities.

As the river flows across the Ontario Plain, between the Niagara Escarpment and Lake Ontario, the channel broadens out to about 609.6 meters (2,000 feet), the river's gradient is gentle, and steep banks are cut 10.5 meters (35 feet) into soft glacial materials. The Canadian side, with almost continuous riverside open space and fringing homes, is followed by the Niagara River Parkway and contrasts with an American side lined with residential development and limited riverside parkland. The Niagara Fruit Belt that developed on both banks now persists only on the Canadian side.

Where the river enters Lake Ontario, the former military importance of the Niagara River as a water gateway is reflected in Forts George and Mississauga on the Canadian bank and by the older French, then British, Fort Niagara on the American bank. Decades of hostility and destiny are manifest in these fortresses. Niagara-on-the-Lake (formerly Newark) became the first capital of Upper Canada, and much of the community's original open character and plan has been retained. The town faces the smaller American village of Youngstown, also with many buildings of historical and architectural interest. Active ferries once connected these two Frontier outposts; today only a seasonal summer ferry for use by tourists shuttles between the two communities.

The villages of Queenston on the Canadian Frontier and Lewiston on the American Frontier developed where the broad Lower Niagara River could be crossed with dry sites on both banks, at the head of navigation from Lake Ontario and at the foot of portage routes from the Upper River. **Above:** The engraving of 1840 depicts the view south to the Niagara Gorge, with the first monument to General Brock crowning the heights above the village of Queenston. (W. H. Bartlett print, John N. Jackson collection) **Right:** A modern scene of the Lower Niagara River. (John N. Jackson)

Lakeshore bluffs, 9.1 to 12.2 meters (30 to 40 feet) high, edge Lake Ontario. Composed of unconsolidated glacial clays and sands, they are subject to wave erosion and slumping despite a downstream dam that now controls water levels. The Niagara River cuts through these bluffs with a midchannel depth of 21.3 meters (70 feet). Offshore bars, shoals, and sandbanks presented an early hazard to navigation. Here, with severe constraints posed by the middle length of the river, lay a major route of entry to the inland heart of North America—a fact that flavors much of the ensuing narrative.

Marine links at the northern entrance to the river, traditionally via Lake Ontario and the St. Lawrence River to Montreal, changed from Niagara-on-the-Lake to Port Dalhousie when the First Welland Canal opened in 1829. After Toronto grew on the opposite side of Lake Ontario, cross-lake steamer traffic from both ports was added, mostly of tourists en route to Niagara Falls. The SS *Cayuga* last sailed between Queenston and Toronto in the 1950s. These journeys were faster than in the modern automobile era via the circuitous Queen Elizabeth Way around the head of Lake Ontario.

NOTES

1. P. McGreevy, "The End of America: The Beginning of Canada," *Canadian Geographer* 32, no. 4 (1988): 307. A discussion of selected boundaries, but excluding Niagara, is D. Rumley and J. V. Minghi, eds., *The Geography of Border Landscapes* (London: Routledge, 1991).

2. A. A. Corey, *The Crisis of 1830–1842 in Canadian-American Relationships* (New Haven, Conn.: Yale University Press, 1941).

3. P. A. Porter, *Landmarks on the Niagara Frontier: A Chronology* (Niagara Falls, N.Y.: n.p., 1914), p. 10.

4. K. T. Whittemore, "Buffalo," in *Geography of New York State*, ed. J. H. Thompson (Syracuse, N.Y.: Syracuse University Press, 1966), p. 410.

5. J. Morchain, *Sharing a Continent: An Introduction to Canadian-American Relations* (Toronto: McGraw-Hill Ryerson, 1973), p. 4. See also S. E. Moffett, *The Americanization of Canada* (1907; reprint, Toronto: University of Toronto Press, 1972); and F. Landon, *Western Ontario and the American Frontier* (Toronto: Ryerson Press, 1941), pp. ix–x.

6. President Kennedy to Members of Parliament, Ottawa, 17 May 1961, in Morchain, *Sharing a Continent*, p. 1.

7. W. G. Hoskins, *The Making of the English Landscape* (London: Hodder and Stoughton, 1955), p. 14. See D. W. Meinig, "Reading the Landscape: An Appreciation of W. G. Hoskins and J. B. Jackson," in *The Interpretation of Ordinary*

Landscapes, ed. D. W. Meinig (New York: Oxford University Press, 1979), pp. 195–244.

8. G. Clay, *Close-up: How to Read the American City* (New York: Praeger, 1973), p. 14. See also J. B. Jackson, *Discovering the Vernacular Landscape* (New Haven, Conn.: Yale University Press, 1984), p. 8.

9. The *Palimpsest*, the title of a journal published by the Iowa State Historical Department, is thought to be based on the use of this word in F. J. Turner, "The Significance of the Frontier in American History," *Annual Report of the American Historical Association* (Washington, D.C., 1894), p. 207. F. A. Maitland described the topographic maps of England as "palimpsests" and used them to interpret the Domesday Book of 1086; S. W. Wooldridge and W. G. East, *The Spirit and Purpose of Geography*, 3d ed. (London: Hutchinson, 1966), p. 73. The word is also used by G. H. Martin, "The Town as Palimpsest," in *The Study of Urban History*, ed. H. J. Dyos (London: Arnold, 1968), p. 155.

10. Clay, *Close-up*, p. 11.

11. Ibid., pp. 29, 31.

12. D. W. Meinig, "The Beholding Eye: Ten Versions of the Same Scene," in Meinig, *The Interpretation of Ordinary Landscapes*, pp. 33–47. See also F. Lukermann, "Geography as a Formal Intellectual Discipline and the Way in which It Contributes to Human Knowledge," *Canadian Geographer* 8 (1964): 167–72.

13. Yi-Fu Tuan, "Thought and Landscape: The Eye and the Mind's Eye," in Meinig, *The Interpretation of Ordinary Landscapes*, pp. 89–102; and Yi-Fu Tuan, *Topophilia: A Study of Environmental Perception, Attitudes and Values* (Englewood Cliffs, N.J.: Prentice-Hall, 1974), pp. 5–12.

14. P. F. Lewis, "The Geographer as Landscape Critic," in P. F. Lewis et al., *Visual Blight in America*, Association of American Geographers, Commission on College Geography, Resource Paper 23 (Washington, D.C., 1973), p. 2; and E. Relph, *The Modern Urban Landscape* (Baltimore: Johns Hopkins University Press, 1987), p. 117.

15. K. Lynch, *The Image of the City* (Cambridge, Mass.: Technology Press, 1960), p. 9; and *A Theory of Good City Form* (Cambridge, Mass.: MIT Press, 1981).

16. H. Carver, *Cities in the Suburbs* (Toronto: University of Toronto Press, 1962), p. 20.

17. B. de Jouvenel, *The Art of Conjecture* (London: Weidenfeld and Nicholson, 1967), p. 6.

18. J. C. Weaver, "The Location of Manufacturing Enterprises: The Case of Hamilton's Attraction of Foundries, 1830–1890," in R. A. Jarrell and A. E. Roos, *Critical Issues in the History of Canadian Science, Technology and Medicine* (Thornhill, Ont.: HSTC Publications, 1983).

19. Contrasting studies include J. Spelt, *Toronto* (Don Mills, Ont.: Collier-Macmillan, 1973); and J. H. Thompson, ed., *Geography of New York State* (Syracuse, N.Y.: Syracuse University Press, 1966).

20. D. Creighton, *The Empire of the St. Lawrence* (Toronto: Macmillan, 1970), first published as *The Commercial Empire of the St. Lawrence, 1760-1850* (Toronto: Macmillan, 1937).

21. Spelt, *Toronto*.

22. C. H. Cooley, *The Theory of Transportation*, vol. 9, no. 4 (Baltimore: American Economic Association, 1891), p. 3.

23. The geological history of the river is covered by K. J. Tinkler, "Entre-Lacs: A Post Glacial Peninsula Physiography" and "Déjà Vu: The Downfall of Niagara as a Chronometer, 1845–1941," in *Niagara's Changing Landscapes*, ed. H. J. Gayler (Ottawa: Carleton University Press, 1994). A summary is W. M. Tovell, *The Great Lakes* (Toronto: Royal Ontario Museum, 1979). The distance is 57.9 kilometers (36 miles) along the eastern channel around Grand Island. As Canada has converted to the metric system, and the United States retains the imperial system, both imperial and metric measurements are provided throughout the text.

24. "Strait" was used by Joseph Ellicott; see R. W. Bingham, ed., *Holland Land Company's Papers: Reports of Joseph Ellicott* (Buffalo, N.Y.: Buffalo Historical Society, 1937), 1:6, and by J. W. Orr, *Pictorial Guide to the Falls of Niagara* (Buffalo, N.Y.: Salisbury and Clapp, 1842), p. 16.

25. International Joint Commission, *Further Regulation of the Great Lakes* (Ottawa and Washington, D.C.: International Joint Commission, 1976), p. 11. Cf. data from American Falls International Board, *Preservation and Enhancement of the American Falls at Niagara—Final Report to the International Joint Commission*, Appendices C, D, and G (Ottawa and Washington, D.C.: International Joint Commission, 1974).

26. For the Canadian Frontier see G. A. Seibel, *The Niagara Portage Road: A History of the Portage on the West Bank of the Niagara River* (Niagara Falls, Ontario: City of Niagara Falls, 1990). For American detail see N. F. Stafford, *Niagara Trail: Your Official Bicentennial Publication from Niagara County, New York* (Lockport, N.Y.: Niagara County Economic Development and Planning Department, 1976). An overall appreciation is H. W. Reynolds, ed., *Urban Characteristics of the Niagara Frontier: An Inventory* (Buffalo, N.Y.: Committee on Urban Studies, State University of New York at Buffalo, 1996).

27. An example is provided by *Black Rock Land and Railroad Company: A Concise View of Black Rock* (Black Rock, N.Y.: n.p., 1836).

28. International Committee to Promote Navy Island as Permanent Headquarters for the United Nations, *Proposed United Nations Headquarters: Navy Island at Niagara Falls on the International Boundary Between Canada and the United States* (Buffalo, N.Y.: Baker, Jones and Hausauer, 1945).

29. W. Barham, *Description of Niagara* (Gravesend, Eng.: The Compiler, 1847), p. 21.

30. In winter when more water is taken for power, the crest is lower. The height is then 54.9 to 56.7 meters (180 to 186 feet) for the Horseshoe Falls; D. E. Loker, *Guide to Niagara Falls* (Buffalo, N.Y.: Stewart and Spitalny, 1969).

31. C. M. Dow, *Anthology and Bibliography of Niagara Falls*, 2 vols. (Albany: State of New York, 1921); and G. A. Seibel, Project Co-ordinator, *Three Hundred Years Since Hennepin: Niagara Falls in Art, 1678–1978* (Niagara Falls, Ontario: Niagara

Falls Heritage Foundation, 1978). Appreciations of the quality and changing landscape at the Falls include W. Irwin, *The New Niagara: Tourism, Technology, and the Landscape of Niagara Falls, 1776–1917* (University Park, Pa.: Pennsylvania State University Press, 1998). P. McGreevy, *Imagining Niagara: The Meaning and Making of Niagara Falls* (Amherst: University of Massachusetts Press, 1994), and "Visions at the Brink: Imagination and the Geography of Niagara Falls" (Ph.D. diss., University of Minnesota, 1984); and E. R. McKinsey, *Niagara Falls: Icon of the American Sublime* (New York: Cambridge University Press, 1985). See also P. Berton, *Niagara: A History of the Falls* (Toronto: McClelland and Stewart, 1992) and *A Picture Book of the Falls* (Toronto: McClelland and Stewart, 1993).

32. Barham, *Description of Niagara*, p. 21.

33. Loker, *Guide to Niagara Falls.*

34. Studies include I. H. Tesmer, ed., *Colossal Cataract: The Geological History of Niagara Falls* (Albany: State University of New York, 1981); W. M. Tovell, *Niagara Falls: Story of a River* (Toronto Royal Ontario Museum, 1966) and *The Niagara River* (Toronto: Royal Ontario Museum, 1979); and K. J. Tinkler, "Canadian Landform Examples—Niagara Falls," *Canadian Geographer* 30 (1986): 367–71.

35. Access is from Whirlpool Glen and Wintergreen Terrace, Ontario, and from Devil's Hole State Park and north of Whirlpool State Park, New York.

36. G. A. Seibel, *Bridges Over the Niagara Gorge: Rainbow Bridge—Fifty Years 1941–1991* (Niagara Falls, Ont.: Niagara Falls Bridge Commission, 1991).

CHAPTER ONE

THE FRONTIER'S PHYSICAL BACKGROUND AND ITS HUMAN PRELUDE

THE PHYSICAL BACKGROUND OF ESCARPMENTS AND PLAINS

Landscape at the Frontier rises gently through a series of distinct physical regions from Lake Ontario to the Allegheny Plateau (fig. 1.1), that is from some 75 meters (246 feet) to over 457 meters (1,000 feet).[1] The Ontario Plain between the shore bluffs and the Niagara Escarpment is divided in two by the low but well-marked Lake Iroquois shoreline, a glacial predecessor of Lake Ontario. This former shoreline rises 7.5 meters (25 feet) and separates soils which are usually lighter, better drained, and more fertile than south of the Niagara Escarpment.

Before permanent settlement, these soils supported heavy forests of oak, maple, pine, elm, black ash, and chestnut.[2] The land then became important for wheat production and now supports grapes and tender fruit crops. This former shoreline provided a continuous east-west, dry site across the two Frontiers. Followed by an important Native trail now referred to as the Iroquois Trail, it became a significant route of pioneer movement and then a wagon and stagecoach route in both directions inland from the Queenston-Lewiston crossing of the Niagara River. This route graduated to provincial Highway 8 (now regional Highway 81) on the Canadian Frontier and to Highway 104 on the American Frontier. Downtown St. Catharines was built on the associated lakeshore sandbar known as the Homer Bar, and the villages of

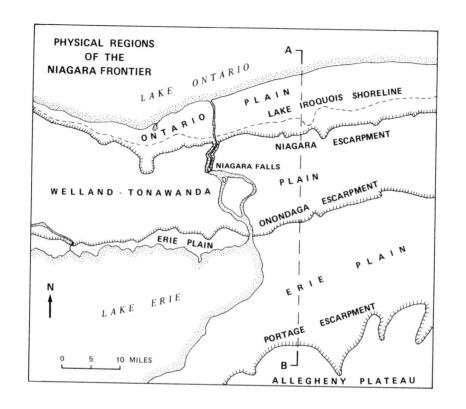

PHYSICAL REGIONS
OF THE
NIAGARA FRONTIER

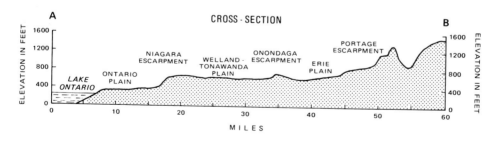

Fig. 1.1. The Niagara Frontier rises south from Lake Ontario across a series of plains separated by two escarpment edges. It is a stepped physical landscape on a grand scale. (Prepared by the Department of Geography, Brock University)

The low rise of the former Lake Iroquois shoreline provides a noted landscape feature across the Ontario Plain on both Frontiers. This slender rise was followed by a significant Native trail and became a major pioneer route of entry. (John N. Jackson)

Queenston and Lewiston are located on this shoreline.

Streams flow across the Ontario Plain from south to north in deeply incised valleys. Where these crossed the Iroquois shoreline, the potential of mill sites for the pioneer settler helps to explain the concentration of settlement along this physical feature. Gorges and waterfalls occur where the Niagara Escarpment is crossed, and most of the lower river valleys are ponded next to Lake Ontario behind sandbars. Named in both directions by their distance in miles from the mouth of the Niagara River, these streams offered substantial waterpower advantages for mills and most afforded harbors for small vessels. The First and Second Welland Canals used Twelve Mile Creek to cross the Ontario Plain, the first three canals used the natural outlet of Twelve Mile Creek at Port Dalhousie as the northern entrance to the canal system, and the Fourth Welland Canal followed the valley of Ten Mile Creek. Eighteen Mile Creek in New York was used as the tail-race for mill water obtained from the Erie Canal at Lockport, and in turn attracted mills along its route to Lake Ontario at Olcott.

The Niagara Escarpment separates the Ontario Plain from the higher plain to the south. Part of an extensive outcrop that extends east and west across the Niagara Frontier, the escarpment is sharply incised to the south along the gorge of the Niagara River. The height of the escarpment rises west toward Hamilton and diminishes east toward Rochester. Composed of nearly horizontal layers of sedimentary rock and capped by the resistant Lockport dolomite (fig. 1.2), the escarpment results from erosion and recession; it is not a fault line.[3]

Undoubtedly the major topographical, geological, and human feature of the Niagara Frontier, considerable variations in form, appearance, and character exist along the line of the steep escarpment slope. It may be almost perpendicular, as at Queenston Heights. It becomes ledged with terraces at Lockport and Lewiston, mantled by glacial deposits at St. Davids and St. Catharines, and recessed with sand deposits in the Short Hills southwest of St. Catharines. The escarpment has promontories, as where the brow is crossed by the Queen Elizabeth Way west of St. Davids. Its role as a divide is well expressed in local phraseology; on both Frontiers the edge of the escarpment is commonly referred to as "The Ridge" or "The Mountain" and the plateau to the south as "The Land above the Mountain."

The escarpment, the major barrier to be overcome by the Welland and the Erie Canals, influenced strongly the location of the channel and the succession of locks that have crossed this slope between Merritton and St. Catharines on the Canadian Frontier and between Pendleton and Lockport on the American Frontier. The rivers and canals that crossed its brow have been harnessed for mills, and for hydroelectric power as technology advanced. Its timber has been harvested as a resource, the edge has been quarried for limestone by a sequence of generations, and the crest has attracted up-scale residential developments. The Bruce Trail follows the crest west from Queenston Heights and, established by Ontario legisla-

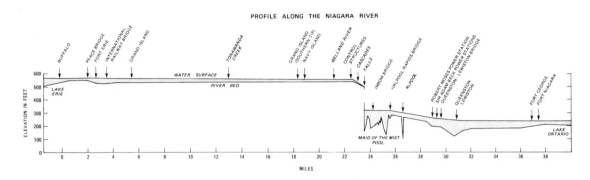

Fig. 1.2. The difference in height between Lake Ontario and Lake Erie is reflected most markedly at the Falls, in the rapids above and through the gorge, and to a lesser extent at the Peace Bridge where the Niagara River leaves the bridge. (Prepared by the Department of Geography, Brock University)

tion in 1973, the Niagara Escarpment Commission was provided with the authority to preserve the escarpment's scenic and ecological attributes against the pressures of expanding urbanization.

To the south, the Welland-Tonawanda Plains are located between the Niagara and the Onondaga Escarpments. Here the topography is flat or gently undulating, with low moraines, eskers, drumlins, and former lake beaches providing modest contrasts. Soils are mainly heavy clay with poorly drained marshy tracts at the Humberstone and Wainfleet peat bogs in Ontario, and in New York State at the low-lying Lake Tonawanda Plain with Tonawanda Creek, and Grand Island.

At Fonthill, Ontario, a glacial kame, a delta built out into a glacial lake with sand and gravel deposits, rises 61 meters (200 feet) above the plain. These sediments, laid down as the ice sheet melted, provided the highest point on the Canadian Frontier; they have been quarried extensively, attracted high-quality residential areas, and a part of the Short Hills to the north has become a conservation area and a provincial park. On the American Frontier a contrasting situation exists; the highest elevations are south of Buffalo in the Allegheny Plateau.

Lake Tonawanda, an intermediate stage in the glacial retreat process, extended some 53.1 kilometers (33 miles) from Lockport in the east to the Niagara River, and about 16.1 kilometers (10 miles) south from the Niagara

Sandbars on Lake Ontario indicate the direction of the prevailing current and temporarily hold back the streams that cross the Ontario Plain to create lakes. This scene at the entrance to Jordan Harbour on Twenty Mile Creek, Ontario, typifies the scene at Port Dalhousie before the First Welland Canal cut through the sandbar to provide a navigable channel for the passage of vessels. (John N. Jackson)

Escarpment. When the lake drained, a glacial outflow channel at Lockport later attracted the locks of the Erie Canal, and another and later outlet at Lewiston initiated the middle section of the Niagara River. This shallow lake bed of poorly drained, heavy soils extends across the boundary where, at one stage of glacial retreat, it was formerly coterminous with the Wainfleet and Willoughby Marshes.

The low Niagara Falls Moraine extends from Niagara Falls, Ontario, across Grand Island and east to former Lake Tonawanda.

The Niagara Escarpment presents a sharp east-west barrier that separates the Ontario and the Erie Plains. Contrasting patterns of agriculture, land use, and development occur as the escarpment is crossed, its steep slope has deterred north-south roads, and woodland along the slope contrasts with agricultural land on the two adjacent plains. (This aerial photograph, A19358-34 © 1965/09/06 Her Majesty the Queen in Right of Canada, reproduced from the collection of the National Air Photo Library, Ottawa, with permission of Natural Resources Canada)

The Barre Moraine follows the crest of the Niagara Escarpment, and the Fort Erie Moraine becomes the Buffalo Moraine east of the Niagara River where it underlies Porter Avenue and High Street. Although slender and low, the moraines provided dry ridge sites for pioneer roads and settlements above adjacent land, a point well illustrated by Lundy's Lane in Niagara Falls, Ontario. American examples include Beach Ridge and Bear Ridge Roads in Pendleton and the series of gravel-till ridges that trend across the Towns of Lewiston, Porter, and Newfane to provide a corrugated terrain.

Drainage in broad, shallow valleys parallels the main rock outcrops. Cayuga, Buffalo, and Cazenovia Creeks enter the Buffalo River, and together with Scajaquada, Tonawanda, and Ellicott Creeks meander through Erie County. They are matched by Lyons, Black, Usshers, Miller, and Frenchman's Creeks, together with the broad, slow-flowing Welland River on the Canadian side. These creeks and rivers provided routes of Native travel, encouraged the inland penetration of pioneer settlers, and their flow of water sometimes presented opportunities for mill sites. Further opportunities arose when canals were constructed. The Welland River and Tonawanda Creek were critical for the achievement of the Welland and the Erie Canals, and the Buffalo River and Little Buffalo Creek for Buffalo Harbor.

The Onondaga Escarpment crosses the south section of the Niagara Peninsula, inland from and parallel to Lake Erie. Composed of limestone bedrock, this low escarpment feature is more gentle and lower than the Niagara Escarpment. It crosses the Niagara River between Fort Erie and Black Rock, and caused the rapids at the entrance to the river. Rising from 6.1 to 30.5 meters (20 to 100 feet) above the Welland-Tonawanda Plain, the Onondaga slope is recognized in Canada by place names such as Ridgeway and Ridgewood, and Ridge Road in Fort Erie. Across the Niagara River the crest is followed by Main Street (Highway 5) in Buffalo to Clarence and Akron where the Onondaga Escarpment is at its highest. Chert in its strata at Port Colborne and Fort Erie was worked intensively by Native groups in the precolonial period and provided an important product in their trading network. Stone from this escarpment, often crushed and exported to American markets, has left behind large quarries. Some, when filled with seeping water, have become recreational areas as at Sherkston next to Lake Erie.

On the Canadian Frontier between the Onondaga Escarpment and Lake Erie the low-lying, marshy areas flood when their slender streams are backed up by high water levels on Lake Erie. This productive farmland is lined by high sand dunes along the lakeshore, and the dunes are capped with upscale, American-owned, summer cottage properties. The lakeshore of alternating low limestone headlands and sandy bays now provides a summer recreational experience. Gravelly Bay became the southern entrance for the First Welland Canal, and has retained this function since the early 1830s.

Canal and rail systems of transportation converge to cross the Niagara Escarpment in St. Catharines. (Hugh J. Gayler)

On the American Frontier where the Lake Erie Plain is broader, the terrain is drained by Buffalo Creek (now River) and Cazenovia Creek to Lake Erie. Height above sea level is now some 182.9 meters (600 feet), about twice that of the Ontario Plain. An eastern marshy area of Lake Erie has been reclaimed for industry in Buffalo and Lackawanna.

Buffalo itself has spread out over generally flat land and across several municipal jurisdictions to the south and east and along the south shore of Lake Erie. This city grew through its location at the head of Lake Erie, its lake traffic, and then in conjunction with the Erie Canal and as a railroad center with industrial and commercial facilities. The

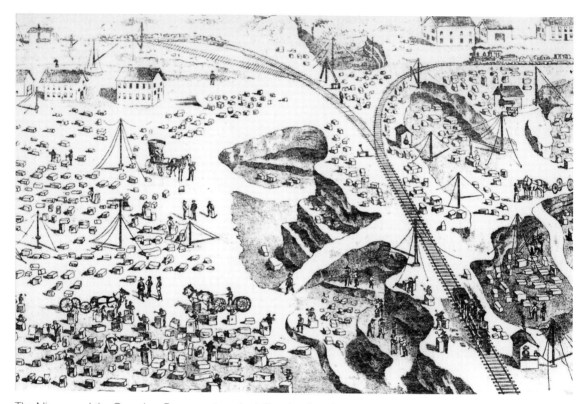

The Niagara and the Onondaga Escarpments on both Frontiers have been worked extensively for stone. This scene is the Queenston Quarry on the Niagara Escarpment at Queenston Heights, Ontario. (From H. R. Page, *Illustrated Historical Atlas of the Counties of Lincoln and Welland, Ontario*, 1876)

aftermath of severe pollution from former coal-based manufacturing activities continues to hamper the use of the lakeshore and the reuse or renewal of many former industrial localities. Severe problems exist as the port, canal, and railways have declined severely from their glory days of the late nineteenth and early twentieth centuries, and urban government uses the same boundaries as the 1850s despite massive suburban expansion.

To the south again are the Portage Escarpment, the rise to the Allegheny Plateau, and a series of long, steep-sided valleys separated by ridges. Light soils have encouraged good farmland south of Buffalo, and the Boston Hills and the Allegheny Plateau south of Buffalo have more recently proved attractive for suburban residential developments and winter skiing on the north-facing slopes.

CLIMATE AND SOILS

Climate is of special importance for the development and current practice of agriculture, for the season of inland navigation on the canals and ports on the Frontiers waterway systems, and now likewise for the restricted summer period of tourism from May to October. The current situation is compounded by the potential of global warming, with the expected adverse impact on the levels in the two bounding lakes aggravated by the further U.S. demand for the diversion of water from the Great Lakes to supply certain of its parched southern areas.

The overall situation is that the Frontier has a humid continental climate with moderate winters, and long warm-to-hot summers, mitigated seasonally by Lake Ontario to the north and Lake Erie to the south (fig. 1.3).[4] The east-west alignment of the Niagara Escarpment, its elevation, and prevailing winds from the southwest moderate the climate further, as does the drainage of cold air from the Niagara Escarpment, the Fonthill Kame, and the Boston Hills south of Buffalo.

Great variation in local weather and microclimate are common within short distances, both seasonally and over brief periods. Hurricanes with heavy rain cross the region several times a century, causing severe damage to buildings and crops and extensive erosion along streams, rivers, and lakeshores. The winters, though cold, generally do not have lengthy periods of severe subzero temperatures. Spring is slow to arrive but, with four distinct seasons, climate provided an attraction for the early agricultural settlers, and has remained important for farming, agribusinesses, tourism, and the seasonal operation of the Welland and Erie Canals. More recently, the favorable climate has resulted in the promotion of the Frontier as a retirement locale, and communities designed for the elderly have developed, particularly on the Canadian Frontier.

Buffalo and both shores of Lake Erie bear the brunt of storms off this lake, including the possibility of severe winter snowstorms such as the widely publicized "Blizzard of '77," when high winds off frozen, snow-covered Lake Erie blanketed the city with dense swirling snow and zero temperatures. While

AVERAGE CLIMATIC CONDITIONS
AT THE DISTRICT NIAGARA WEATHER OFFICE

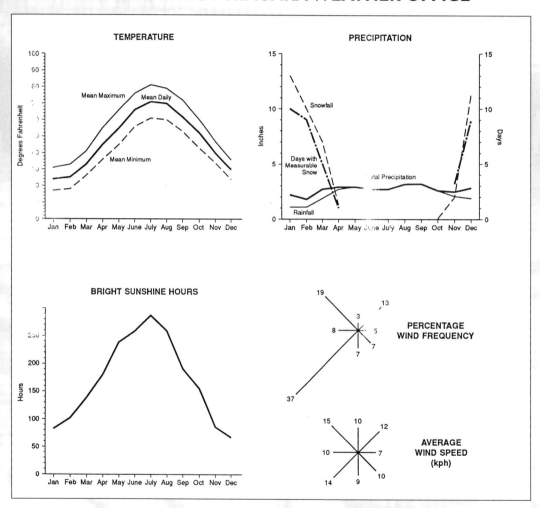

Fig. 1.3. The distinctive climate of the Niagara Frontier is influenced strongly by the presence of Lake Ontario, Lake Erie, and the alignment of the Niagara Escarpment. (Prepared by the Department of Geography, Brock University)

The ice bridge at the Falls and ice accumulation on the surrounding vegetation provide a major winter tourist attraction. (John N. Jackson)

Buffalo was crippled and virtually isolated for several days,[5] the Ontario Plain north of the Niagara Escarpment was relatively untouched. Lake Erie provides Buffalo with an extended winter, cooler summers, and high wind velocities.[6] The average annual precipitation at Buffalo is 25.4 centimeters (10 inches) more than on Lake Ontario, and southern Erie County in most years earns its reputation as "snowbelt." The annual snowfall in Buffalo can be 76.2 centimeters (30 inches) more than at St. Catharines, only 48 kilometers (30 miles) away. Short, gusty but hectic thunderstorms reflecting the influence of Lake Erie occur in summer. Temperatures decrease southward from Buffalo in the higher lands away from the lake. Even so, milder winters are experienced than farther west in similar mid-continental areas at comparable latitudes, and Buffalo has more days of sunshine than any other city in New York State.

The Ontario Plain has less rainfall and a longer,

warmer growing season than areas south of the Niagara Escarpment.[7] This escarpment confines the warming effect from Lake Ontario to this plain in winter. In spring it has the opposite effect, retarding blossoming until the danger from late frost is past. The Ontario Plain has therefore become a favored agricultural locality sustaining the production of grapes, tender fruits, and vegetables.[8] Deep-rooted peach, apricot, and cherry trees survive winters that are less severe than to the south and draw on subsoil moisture during the summer growing season. The type and mixture of crops is not repeated in the United States until the vicinity of the Carolinas.

Grapevines, more hardy than these fruit trees, extend above and to the south of the Niagara Escarpment where air drainage and soil permit. A similar lake effect permits fruit growing southwest of Buffalo in the Town of Eden. The mild climate and the long hours of sunlight have also contributed to the extensive recent expansion of greenhouse operations in the traditional farming areas on the Ontario Plain.

Spring and autumn are well-defined seasons characterized by variable, often cloudy weather and storms from rapidly moving air masses. Late autumn storms provide a dangerous period for shipping on both lakes, with many shipwrecks during the era of sail and still exerting some toll on navigation and at the marinas. A period of warm, often hazy weather usually prevails in October, postponing the first frosts, extending the growing season, and providing scope for an extended autumnal tourist season that has yet to be fully recognized.

Soils, locally varied because of geological circumstances, consist of glacial drift, lake deposits, and outwash sheets of sand and gravel, varying in composition from sand, peat, and clay to silt and sand loams. Both drainage and water supply can present problems to local agriculture. The heavy soils may require drainage ditches, and irrigation may be necessary for crops grown on permeable soils.

Soils, climate, and access to expanding urban markets abroad, locally in Buffalo, and in urban Southern Ontario made much of the Niagara Frontier and in particular the Ontario Plain suitable for high-quality, intensive agriculture from the pioneer period onward. These favorable conditions attracted settlers, encouraged farming, and promoted the Niagara Fruit Belt on both sides of the boundary. Despite extensive industrialization and urbanization, agriculture remains an important facet of the economy, especially on the Canadian Frontier. The current problem is neither climate nor soil but urban encroachment, which has led to campaigns to protect agricultural land by conservation groups on both sides of the Niagara River, whereas the municipalities encourage expansion. The conservation ethic is weaker than the wish to expand and grow.

Microclimatic conditions at the Falls, where spray and ever-present mist from the tumbling waters nurtured a luxuriant and unique vegetation, encouraged a natural nursery with many indigenous wildflowers, shrubs, and trees. Queen Victoria Park on the Canadian Frontier did not install a significant irrigation system for almost one hundred years. On American Goat Island this quality of forest beauty stimulated Frederick Law Olmsted in his crusade to preserve nature at the Falls. Vegetation has changed drastically before the advance of tourism, but the rainbow, the clouds of spray, and winter ice sculptures remain as evidence for the moist conditions that exist.

THE NATIVE OCCUPANTS

As climate changed and as the Laurentide ice sheet that covered the Niagara Frontier retreated, the meltwaters of the postglacial period created lakes and river channels that soon encouraged vegetation, animals, and a habitat that could be used by humans. Per-

haps by about 9,000 B.C.E. the Niagara area was occupied by Stone Age humans hunting migrating caribou for food and hides.[9] Small groups established temporary camps, used the caves along the edge of the Niagara Escarpment for protection, and fished around the edge of the marshy tracts that remained from the former glacial lakes. There was also much working of chipped stone from layers of chert in the Onondaga Limestone to produce tools and fluted arrowheads, one of the highest-quality toolstones to be found in the Great Lakes region.

By about 7000 B.C.E. a deciduous forest of oak, white pine, birch, and hemlock began to cover the area. The transition is from the Palaeo-Indian culture to the subsequent Archaic period. There were lower water levels in the Great Lakes and the expansion of more temperate forests. The transition favored nomadic, hunter-gather groups, who could make use of a wider variety of plants, nuts, fish, and animals. Still with small camps, the Niagara River and the Lake Erie shore were important areas for settlement.

In the subsequent Woodland Period from about 1000 B.C.E. the most significant development was the introduction of agriculture, a radical shift from the previous hunting and gathering economies. Perhaps introduced by people from the south, it is also feasible that crop-tending activities emerged locally. In about 500 C.E. corn (maize) production was added to the previous subsistence economies, followed by tobacco, beans, squash, and sunflowers. By the seventeenth century life was based on these storable crops, supplemented by hunting for white-tailed deer, black bear, and smaller animals as well as geese, turkeys, and waterfowl; fishing in the lakes and rivers and the gathering of fruit, nuts, and berries also provided food.[10]

Small agricultural villages were now located on the lighter, sandy soils and around the low-lying marshy areas where deer, wild berries, and fish were plentiful. The dead were buried in the sand dunes along Lake Erie. Flint from the Onondaga Escarpment was used extensively for making a variety of tools, scrapers, and blades, with Fort Erie at the present western entrance to the Peace Bridge and where the Onondaga Escarpment edged a former glacial lake north of Port Colborne being important sites for manufacture and trading.

The Iroquois, who shared a common language and culture and who occupied the region of the Lower Great Lakes and the St. Lawrence River corridor, lived in communal longhouses, which might be over 30.5 meters (100 feet) long and 5.5 meters (18 feet) in height and width. Fireplaces extended down the middle, sleeping platforms were built along the side, the rafters were used for storage, and dried foods were kept in bark-lined pits in the ground. Each building contained several nuclear families of father, mother, and children. Together with a longhouse that might be used for special purposes such as a council meeting, they together occupied palisaded agricultural villages of several hundred people, up to 6.1 hectares (15 acres) in size. It was a shared matrilineal culture, that is, the men hunted, the women worked the fields, and upon marriage a man joined his wife's longhouse and his children belonged to that clan. The villages were ephemeral features of the landscape as land around each village became exhausted after some ten to thirty years. Wood was cut for palisades, longhouses, and cooking fires, and elm bark covered the longhouses. Maize cultivation exhausted the soil, hunting depleted the forest, and midden (refuse) pits had to be replaced. The tribes also followed the seasons, sometimes moving to temporary hunting and fishing camps. These Native peoples traded with neighboring tribal groups and ranged over long distances to obtain seashells, stone for tools, feathers, metals, and minerals. The Niagara River was both a bridge across the Great Lakes and a passageway along this water route.

Palisaded Iroquoian villages with long-houses located on both sides of the Niagara River prior to the European period of settlement. These replicas are from a recreated seventeenth-century Iroquoian village at Kenata, near Brant-ford, Ontario. (John N. Jackson)

To avoid incessant conflict, the League of the Five Nations (alternatively the League of the Iroquois) was formed about 1500 C.E. by the Seneca, Cayuga, Onondaga, Oneida, and Mohawk groups.[11] Later, around 1720, the southerly Tuscaroras were admitted to become the Six Nations. The Petun, Huron, and Neutral Indians were not part of the League, but had their own confederacies. The purpose of the democratic League was to secure peace and avoid debilitating warfare between the Iroquois-speaking nations. The League was followed and strengthened by the Covenant Chain, a confederation established at Albany in 1677 between the British colonies and the Five Nations.[12]

The Neutrals, a French name signifying their neutrality and peace with both the Huron and the Five Nations Iroquois, occupied semipermanent fortified villages on both sides of the Niagara River during the early seventeenth century. Three to four villages under the same Native authority are described in the *Jesuit Relations* in this locality. Neutral villages are also probable along the Niagara River between present-day Fort Erie and Niagara-on-the-Lake, perhaps including Grand Island and the Ontario Plain to the north. The Niagara River is indeed described as "their" river, they moved across it freely,[13] and the same interrelated cultures existed on both sides. To the north were the Huron and Petun, to the south the Erie and the Wenro, and to the east successively the Seneca, Cayuga, Onondaga, Oneida, and Mohawk Nations in the present area of Western New York State. The main concentration of Neutral Iroquois settlements lay in the Hamilton-Brantford area, east of the Grand River.

The Neutrals commanded an important intermediary position at the end of two major trade routes, the French fur trade to the north and the routes south to Chesapeake Bay and the Ohio River to the Mississippi. The Niagara area was a crossroads center with north-south and east-west trading links. A description in 1626 by Joseph de la Roche Daillon, a Recollect missionary who spent three months among the Neutrals and visited a number of their villages, noted twenty-eight towns, cities, or villages, and small hamlets with seven or eight cabins in locations convenient for fishing, hunting, or agriculture.[14] The fish were described as excellent; hunting included vast numbers of deer, elk, beaver, and squirrels; and as regards agriculture he mentioned beans, corn, pumpkins, and tobacco. Hunting practice was to encircle a herd of deer, and in winter snowshoes were used to drive these animals into deep snow where they might more easily be killed.

There is also some evidence for the management of white-tailed deer at some historic Neutral Iroquois sites.[15]

By the late seventeenth century the Seneca were described as "The Keepers of the Western Gate," their function being to protect land east of the Niagara River from Native invaders. These aboriginal cultures began to change significantly with the arrival of the Europeans on the east coast. The Natives were viewed by many new immigrant arrivals as "ignorant savages" despite their rapport with the land. They were "pagans" who worshiped the Great Spirit, not the Christian God, and both clashes and friendships arose between the dark-skinned native peoples and the new, white European arrivals. The Natives with their long-established trade network were more than anxious to trade pelts for European goods, particularly ironware, and to carry these precious items inland. The Iroquois functioned as a buffer between the French colonies and the English settlements along the north Atlantic coast and effectively resisted European access to the west from Albany through the Mohawk Valley for about a century.[16]

Considerable change resulted in daily life as European wares became available. Clay pots were replaced by metal kettles and cooking vessels with handles, and woolen blankets took over from fur robes. Steel needles displaced the earlier bone ones, wampum beads were replaced by buttons or glass, and axes and knives of iron supplanted the stone tools. The musket superceded the bow and arrow. Rather than being self-sufficient and dependent on the natural environment for their requirements, the Iroquois now trapped fur-bearing animals to meet their need for European trading goods, and as trade expanded European diseases such as smallpox, measles, and influenza exacted a severe toll upon the Native inhabitants. Artifacts found in a Neutral village dated 1615–1630, on the crest of the escarpment next to Brock University in present-day St. Catharines, illustrate this transition.[17] Trade goods of French origin included iron axes, knives, iron spearheads, parts of copper kettles, and glass beads. Native products included molded clay pipes, decorated pottery, arrows, and shell beads. Though not converted to Christianity, the Neutral villages were visited by early French explorers and French missionaries, both Recollect and Jesuit.[18]

Increasing reliance on the fur trade with Europeans led to the depletion of local fur resources. To remedy this, the Seneca looked west to obtain new fur-trapping areas. They invaded Huron territory in 1649, destroyed its villages and broke its trading circuit with

Quebec. During this period, known as the Beaver Wars, the Seneca and Mohawk also struck at the Petun. In 1651 they turned on the Neutral villages of the Niagara Frontier. As the Neutrals were killed or dispersed and their villages laid waste, the Frontier area became generally depopulated except for seasonal hunting and fishing groups that included a seasonal fishing settlement at the mouth of the Niagara River where Seneca greeted the French explorer Cavelier de La Salle with gifts of fish in 1678.

Although the natural environment around the village sites was depleted, permanent ecological damage did not result from the Native periods. The resources from the forests and streams were "renewable" and, with low levels of technology and a small population, it was not an exploitive economy as became the norm after the arrival of European groups. The Neutrals, who numbered about forty thousand people in 1615–1650, were the largest Native group in the Northeast at that time.[19]

THE FRENCH PRESENCE

Overlapping with the Native heritage, the French colonized the St. Lawrence, penetrated the Great Lakes, and linked south to the Mississippi. The first to visit the Niagara area were Catholic traders and missionaries, including Etienne Brûlé in the early seventeenth century.[20] In the meantime, the English took over the Dutch settlements along the Hudson River in 1664 and promoted fur trading from Hudson Bay after 1670. The Niagara River, central to both French and British interests, became the object of their intense rivalries (fig. 1.4).[21]

In 1673 Count Frontenac, governor of New France, urged that land be "possessed" at the mouth of the Niagara River "in order to obtain firm control of the Indian trade."[22] La Salle had arrived there in 1669. He returned to construct the *Griffon*, a 36.3-tonnes (40-ton) sailing vessel at the mouth of Cayuga Creek, the first manufacturing enterprise at the Frontier and the first ship to sail the Upper Lakes. This enterprise required supplies from Fort Frontenac (now Kingston, Ontario) that were brought across Lake Ontario to a stockaded storehouse at the northeastern entrance to the Niagara River. Known as Fort Conti after a French prince, this stockade was abandoned toward the end of 1679.

In 1678 Father Louis Hennepin canoed up the Lower River to reach the Falls on the American side. Previous missionaries may have viewed the scene, but they have left no written record. Hennepin's classic description is: "a vast and prodigious Cadence of

Water, which falls down after a surprising and astonishing manner, in so much that the Universe does not afford its Parallel."[23]

The portage on the east side of the river was used to transport goods overland, an arduous task reflected in the Seneca description *Duh-jin-heh-oh*, meaning "to crawl on all fours," which aptly portrays the arduous climb up the Niagara Escarpment carrying a heavy load on the back.[24] Here was the "carrying place" around the major obstacle to water transport on the Great Lakes system, and the point where waterborne commerce might best be controlled. To the French the portage meant control over the St. Lawrence hinterland of Quebec City, access to Lake Erie and the Upper Lakes, and then control over watersheds and portages to the Ohio and Mississippi water systems. As stated by Dunnigan (1985): "The early importance of the Fort Niagara site derived almost solely from the portage around Niagara Falls";[25] the resources of the vicinity were of secondary importance.

Fort de Nonville, a substantial log structure with a stockade and ten log buildings, was constructed on the site of Fort Conti in 1687. Named after the governor of New France, Fort de Nonville was built to control the portage and subdue the Iroquois. Through cold, starvation, and siege by the Seneca, only twelve out of a garrison of one hundred men survived the first winter. Although new troops were stationed in the fort, it was abandoned in late 1688 before another winter threatened survival.[26]

The Niagara River, considered an "unguarded gateway, open both ways," was used by the Seneca, the French, and the British.[27] Louis Thomas de Joncaire, a French trader captured and adopted by the Seneca, constructed a trading house about 1700 on the east bank of the Niagara River just below the Niagara Escarpment.[28] By 1708 a thousand pelts annually were described as passing over the portage.[29] During the Queen Ann's War, 1702–13, between the French and the English, Joncaire retained the neutrality of the Seneca.

In 1720, to protect the portage the French constructed a "Magazin Royal" or Royal Store, a fortified blockhouse, which extended the importance of the original trading house.[30] The British, greatly angered, demanded its demolition as the Treaty of Utrecht in 1713 had assigned to them the lands of the Iroquois. The French argued their rights to Niagara on the basis of discovery, its early occupation by La Salle and de Nonville, and their employment of the Seneca on the portage.[31]

The Niagara River had become a field of intense contest between the British and the

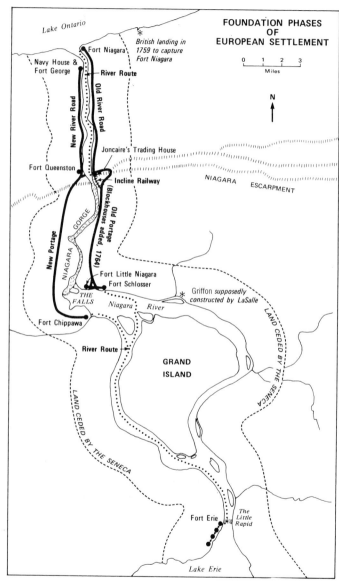

FOUNDATION PHASES
OF
EUROPEAN SETTLEMENT

Fig. 1.4. The French and the British used the Niagara River for entry to the continental interior. Decades of rivalry introduced forts at both entrances to the river and a defended portage around the Falls. (Prepared by the Department of Geography, Brock University)

French, with both seeking to control the fur trade and access to the continental interior. To consolidate their position on Lake Ontario, the British erected a trading post at Oswego east of the Niagara River in 1720 and tried to purchase land from the Seneca for a fort at the mouth of the Niagara River. Beaten in this attempt by the French, who feared the loss of the profitable fur trade, Joncaire persuaded the Seneca to allow the construction of another fort on the site of Fort de Nonville. The British built a rival fort at Oswego in the same year.

The fort at the mouth of the Niagara River, now the "trader's post" in Fort Niagara, was designed to look like an elegant French country house, but it had thick stone walls, a fireproof construction, gun batteries on the upper floors, quarters for the garrison, and a surrounding palisade. The Natives were informed that it was a "House of Peace" for their protection. Completed in 1727, the fort, constructed inland from the lakeshore, contained a well, chapel, and storerooms. It could house a garrison of about thirty men, resist attack, and control the trade route along the Niagara River. About 1745, with increasing trade, a secondary fortification, Fort Erie, was constructed at the southern end of the portage next to the rapids at the entrance to the river.

Fort Niagara served as the center of French influence for an extensive hinterland reaching to New Orleans. It protected French and Indian movements over the portage, intercepted the flow of furs to the British at Oswego, and deterred British penetration to the Upper Lakes. It impressed the Seneca by a powerful and visible French presence. A Seneca chief was appointed to Fort Erie to settle quarrels and to ensure that an Indian labor force worked on the portage.[32] A sawmill served by waterpower from the river was built at the upper end of Goat Island, and trading outposts were added on both banks close to the river's southern entrance.

Fort Niagara, built to withstand an Indian attack, became unsuitable for colonial wars between French and British troops armed with cannon. Enlarged eightfold in 1755 to the exacting standards of Sebastian Vauban, the French military engineer, and strengthened against artillery with earthworks and external bastions,[33] the fort was the largest French fortification west of Quebec City. Twenty buildings and space for over one thousand men were provided inside the walls.[34]

Captain Pouchot, the fort's commander, provides significant details about the fort, the resources of the vicinity, and how they were used.[35] Because of winter ice, vessels were then sheltered on the west side of the river where Navy Hall in Niagara-on-the-Lake now stands. Local resources used at the fort included stone from the foot of the Niagara Escarpment, lime from its crest, and pines from the areas around the mouths of Twelve, Fifteen, and Sixteen Mile Creeks. The pine tree is described as "rare in the region, where the trees are normally several species of oak, walnut, chestnut, bois jaune (whitewood or tulip tree), which is excellent for panelling in construction. One also finds a type of black walnut which makes very fine furniture, beech, plane-trees and maple. The two latter trees make very good sugar, which is less acidic than cane sugar."

With a sandbar in Lake Ontario in front of the fort, a hawser was used to haul vessels into the anchorage on the present site of the U.S. Coast Guard Station. The Lower Niagara River was stated to have a gentle current

Fort Niagara, perched on a bluff above Lake Ontario at the northern entrance to the Niagara River, has become a major tourist attraction with military drills. Now located within the United States and the oldest building at the Frontier, it recalls the long periods of the French presence and of French-British conflict at the Frontier. (John N. Jackson)

and a sufficient depth for frigates to reach the Niagara Escarpment. The gorge could not be navigated, but navigation resumed along the Upper River which Pouchot described as "no more than a swift current" against the terminology of a "gentle current" for the Lower River.

The portage is described as "the most frequented of [on] the American continent because this tongue of land [the Niagara Peninsula] links up with three great lakes & because the ease of the journey brings all the Indians that way. . . . Niagara is in some sense the center for trade between Indians and

Europeans and as a result they gladly make their way there from all parts of the continent."

The route between the fort and the foot of the Niagara Escarpment is described as a "cart track. . . . In the summer the journey is usually by water. In winter it is always necessary to take the land route because of the ice." About the portage: "since takes three hours to make the journey it traverses a forest, the going is sometimes muddy. If it were well maintained, it would be a fine road. . . . At the [foot of the escarpment] . . . there are three sheds which act as storehouses for goods that have arrived. The bank where they are unloaded is a good 60 feet [18.3 meters] high, which creates great difficulties. . . . To ascend, there are two tracks. One of them, for vehicles . . . [has] two ramps, which are fairly gentle. The other is a footpath, which runs straight down the hill. It is very steep. Travellers, & others who are heavily laden, always use this path. However, it never takes more than half an hour to walk up it. . . . At the top of the hill, there is a storage shed."

The Welland River is described as "a pleasant little river . . . on its banks of which are some fine woods. It is from this forest that wood was taken for building the bateaux for navigating in the area as well as boards & joists for the use of the fort." On the opposite bank: "The Five Nations use this water [Tonawanda Creek] to join up with the main river. Its current is extremely gentle and several sites along it are cultivated by the Indians. The surrounding land is very fine and the river is full of fish."

At the entrance to the Niagara River, "The small rapids . . . consist of reefs over which the current flows uniformly but with force. . . . There are channels where, if special vessels were built, they could sail against the current given a brisk wind. Bateaux can be poled or hauled up it."

The Lake Ontario Plain in the vicinity of Fort Niagara is described as "a very fine plain covered with trees," with pines in the vicinity of Twelve Mile Creek and at the junction of Fifteen Mile and Sixteen Mile Creeks, "which are convenient for use at Fort Niagara."

Early in the 1750s some two hundred Seneca worked the portage. There were camps, cabins, and storehouses from the landing above the Falls to Fort Niagara,[36] but for the lack of horses, equipage, and the right type of food, nearly four hundred men died from scurvy or the fatigue of portage work.[37] The portage road was improved in 1752 by easing gradients at the Lower Landing (now Lewiston), and goods could then be hauled over the whole distance in wagons.

And then came the finale for the active and exciting military history of Fort Niagara. In

1759, with support from Iroquois warriors, British regular troops from Oswego commanded by General John Prideaux landed from Lake Ontario east of the fort. The land approaches were cut off, the fort bombarded, and a French relieving force defeated on the portage road south of Fort Niagara.[38] Captain Pouchot surrendered on 25 July 1759. Fort Ticonderoga and the citadel at Quebec followed in the same year. With the capture of Montreal in 1760, the portage, its defenses, and its routes of approach were in British hands. The French lifeline to the interior had been cut, and the French era along the Niagara River ended when France relinquished her claims to lands in British North America in 1763.

BRITISH RULE

Lost to the French, Fort Niagara obtained a new role as a British supply and staging depot for troops moving west and as a gathering point for Indian-British councils. As trade returned to the portage, Fort Niagara was repaired and expanded, a military reserve of 115 hectares (284 acres) was added in 1760, and British traders built warehouses between the Niagara River and the fort. The portage was defended by blockhouses, and a fort (later Fort Schlosser) was established at the southern end of the portage, and another at the Lower Landing (later Lewiston). Two sloops and three schooners were constructed at a shipyard on Navy Island.[39]

The portage was improved by grading the steeper sections and laying logs across the muddy road so that the whole could be used by wagons hauled by horses or oxen. The "corduroy road" meant unemployment for the Seneca, who in 1763 attacked a wagon train traveling from Fort Schlosser to Fort Niagara at Devil's Hole, killing most of the drivers and soldiers and then throwing the wagons, their animals, and the dead into the gorge. A relief party from Fort Niagara met the same fate.

In retribution, the Natives were forced to cede a 3.2-kilometer (2-mile) strip on each bank of the Niagara River to the British Crown (fig. 1.4). This land, "Surrendered to His Majesty for His sole use, and that of the garrisons," could not be used for other purposes, but the acquisition enabled the portage to be made stronger, commercially and militarily.[40] A provisions warehouse constructed at Fort Niagara in 1762 could store 7,000 barrels on three levels. The difficult climb up the Niagara Escarpment was eased in 1764 by installing a three-stage wooden hoist system of cradles known as "the Montresor incline" by which "goods are drawn up the side of the bank about 50 feet (15.2 meters) high upon

INDIAN TERRITORY, 1774 AND 1791

1774

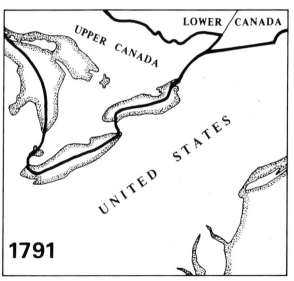

1791

Fig. 1.5. When the boundary along the Niagara River was confirmed by the peace treaty of 1783, a Native state east of the Niagara River was anticipated. However, the Native groups were ignored when British colonial territory was divided between the national entities that became Canada and the United States. (Prepared by Department of Geography, Brock University)

ways [wooden rails] on an easy slope by a capstan fixed on the top."[41] Eleven blockhouses were constructed along the portage, and a wharf, barracks, and a log fort were built on the west bank of the river at Fort Erie. The portage had become "the best protected highway in all America."[42]

When British rule in Canada was consolidated by the Quebec Act of 1774, the area astride the Niagara River was included in the new boundaries of Quebec (fig. 1.5) which attached the midcontinental fur area to its natural trading outlet at Montreal. This act also forestalled the ambitions and claims of the older American colonies to lands west of the mountains, and can be seen as one underlying cause of the American Revolution.[43] In 1775 Fort Niagara became a rallying point for the British cause and a haven for Loyalists fleeing from the terror of this war. Most of the Iroquois allied themselves with the British Crown, and Indian parties under Chief Joseph Brant and the Butler's Rangers raided to the east and south.[44] The war itself did not reach Niagara, but while it raged Fort Niagara and the portage provided part of the lifeline for supplies from the St. Lawrence to inland British forts such as Detroit and Michilimackinac.

Settlement on the Canadian Frontier was advanced in 1780 when General Haldimand, governor of Canada, advocated raising grain and stock to supply the garrison, Loyalist refugees, and Natives who had lost their former territories. A 6.4-kilometer (4-mile) strip of land west of the river was purchased for agriculture from the Chippawa and Mississauga in 1781.[45] Settlement at Butlersburg (now Niagara-on-the-Lake) therefore arose as an adjunct to Fort Niagara on the east bank. Barracks were constructed for the Butler's Rangers and for the distressed families sheltering at Fort Niagara.[46] A survey of 1782 described 16 households, a total of 84 people, 243 livestock, and 95.5 hectares (236 acres) of cleared land that produced Indian corn, potatoes, wheat, and oats. The surplus had to be sold to the commandant at Fort Niagara, and tenancy was on an annual basis; produce, not the land, provided the wealth of the farmers.

NOTES

1. For the Canadian Frontier see L. J. Chapman and D. F. Putnam, *The Physiography of Southern Ontario* (Toronto: University of Toronto Press, 1966); H. J. Gayler, ed., *Niagara's Changing Landscape* (Ottawa: Carleton University Press, 1994), pp. 13–104; J. N. Jackson, *St. Catharines, Ontario: Its Early Years* (Belleville, Ont.: Mika, 1976), pp. 21–46; and J. Menzies and C. M. Taylor, "Urban Geology of St. Catharines and Niagara Falls," in P. S. Tarrow and E. M. Taylor, eds., *Urban Geology of Canadian Cities*, Geological Association of Canada, Special Paper 42, 1999. For the American Frontier see G. B. Cressey, "Land Forms," in *Geography of New York*, ed. J. H. Thompson (Syracuse, N.Y.: Syracuse University Press, 1966), pp. 19–53; L. M. Kindle and F. B. Taylor, *Geologic Atlas of the United States: Niagara Folio*, United States Geological Survey (Washington, D.C., 1914); R. H. Pegrum, "Geology on the Niagara Frontier," in *Urban Characteristics of the Niagara Frontier: An Inventory*, ed. H. W. Reynolds (Buffalo: State University of New York at Buffalo, 1964); and I. H. Tesmer, *A History of Geology in Western New York* (Buffalo: State University of New York at Buffalo, 1984). A cartographic source for the Frontier in its Great Lakes context is Environment Canada, United States Environmental Protection Agency, Brock University, and Northwestern University, *The Great Lakes: An Environmental Atlas and Resource Book*, Environment Canada and United States Environmental Protection Agency (Toronto and Chicago, 1987).

2. M. R. Moss, "Forests in the Niagara Landscape: Ecology and Management," in Gayler, *Niagara's Changing Landscape*, pp. 139–75. R. Gowlay, *Statistical Account of Upper Canada* (London: Simkin and Marshall, 1822), describes the vegetation that then existed in each township.

3. T. E. Bolton, *Silurian Stratigraphy of the Niagara Escarpment in Ontario*, Memoir 289 (Ottawa: Geological Survey of Canada, 1957); W. M. Tovell, *The Niagara Escarpment* (Toronto: Royal Ontario Museum, 1965); and *Guide to the Geology of the Niagara Escarpment* (Georgetown: Niagara Escarpment Commission, 1992). For biological studies and inventories, see J. Riley, J. Jalava, and S. Varga, *Ecological Survey of the Niagara Escarpment Biosphere Reserve*, 2 vols. (Toronto: Minister of Natural Resources, 1998), financed by the Ontario Heritage Foundation and the Ministry of Natural Resources.

4. C. D. Ahrens, *Meteorology Today* (St. Paul, Minn.: West Publishing, 1994), pp. 486, 498–503. See also F. K. Hare and M. K. Thomas, *Climate Canada* (Toronto: Wiley, 1974); Environment Canada et al., *The Great Lakes*, pp. 8–9; A. Saulesleja, *Great Lakes Climatological Atlas* (Ottawa: Atmospheric Environment Services, 1986); and T. B. Shaw, "Climate of the Niagara Region," in Gayler, *Niagara's Changing Landscape*, pp. 287–321.

5. P. Beaudet and J. Amato, "Adjustment to the Snow Environment in a Metropolitan Area: A Case Study of Buffalo, New York" (paper presented at the annual meeting of the Association of American Geographers, Salt Lake City, Utah, 1977); K. Kline and C. Nash, *Buffalo Buried: The Blizzard of '77* (Buffalo, N.Y.: Thorner-Sidney Press, 1977); and E. Rossi, *White Death—Blizzard of '77* (Port Colborne, Ont.: 77 Publishing, 1978), pp. 5–6.

6. H. Jones and R. H. Pegrum, "The Geographic Portrait of Western New York," in Reynolds, *Urban Characteristics of the Niagara Frontier*, pp. 18–52. Climatic data from Atmospheric Environment Service, *Temperature and Precipitation, 1941–1970* (Downsview, Ont.: Environment Canada, n.d.); and U.S. Weather Bureau, *Climatic Summaries for New York State* (Washington, D.C.: Government Printing Office, various dates). See also D. W. Phillips and J. A. W. McCulloch, *The Climate of the Great Lakes Basin*, Climatological Studies No. 20 (Toronto: Atmospheric Environment Services, 1972).

7. For Canada see R. E. Wicklund, *The Soil Survey of Lincoln County*, Report No. 34, Ontario Soil Survey, Research Branch, Canada Department of Agriculture and the Ontario Agricultural College (Ottawa, 1963). Welland County was surveyed in 1935; a map, but no report, was published. M. S. Kingston and E. W. Presant, *The Soils of the Regional Municipality of Niagara*, vols. 1–2 (Guelph: Ontario Institute of Pedology, Guelph University, 1989). For the American Frontier see A. E. Taylor et al., *Soil Survey of Erie County, New York*, Bureau of Chemistry and Soils, U.S. Department of Agriculture, series 1929, no. 14 (Washington, D.C., 1929); and C. S. Pearson et al., *Soil Survey of Niagara County, New York*, Agricultural Research Administration, United States Depart-

ment of Agriculture, series 1937, no. 20 (Washington, D.C., 1947). Soil types mapped by the United States Soil Conservation Service are available at the County Extension Agencies; see also D. H. Cadwell, *Surficial Geologic Map of New York* (Albany: New York State Museum, 1988).

8. Shaw, "Climate of the Niagara Region," p. 111.

9. Dates vary between authorities. This account uses R. C. Harris, ed., *Historical Atlas of Canada*, vol. 1, *From the Beginning to 1800* (Toronto: University of Toronto Press, 1987). For the local detail of arrow-point types and pottery styles, see J. Pengelly and W. Fox, *The Native Occupation of the Northeastern Erie Shore* (manuscript in Department of Geography, Brock University, St. Catharines, c. 1990). For excavations at Fort Erie and Niagara-on-the-Lake, see R. F. Williamson and R. I. Mac-Donald, *Legacy of Stone: Ancient Life on the Niagara Frontier* (Toronto: Eastendbooks, 1998). Terminology is difficult; popularly referred to as "Indians" as in the various Indian Acts; "Natives," "Aboriginal Peoples," "First Nations," and "Native Americans" are also used. Words such as "bands," "clans," "tribes," and "nations" also carry different meanings, and it is a Canadian "reserve" but an American "reservation."

10. G. I. Quimby, *Indian Life in the Upper Great Lakes: 1,000 B.C. to A.D. 1800* (Chicago: University of Chicago Press, 1960); J. V. Wright, *Ontario Prehistory: An Eleven-Thousand-Year Archaeological Outline* (Ottawa: National Museum of Canada, 1972); W. A. Ritchie, *The Archaeology of New York State* (Garden City, N.Y.: Natural History Press, 1965);

and R. L. McCarthy and H. Newman, *Prehistoric People of Western New York*, Adventures in Western New York History, vol. 7 (Buffalo, N.Y.: Buffalo and Erie County Historical Society, 1961). Important works include W. J. Kubiak, *Great Lakes Indians: A Pictorial Guide* (Grand Rapids, Mich.: Baker Book House, 1970); H. H. Tanner, ed., Atlas of Great Lakes Indian History (Norman: University of Oklahoma Press, 1987); B. C. Trigger, ed., *Handbook of North American Indians*, vol. 15, *Northeast* (Washington, D.C.: Smithsonian Institution, 1978); and M. E. White, *Iroquois Culture History in the Niagara Frontier Area of New York State*, Anthropological Papers, No. 16, Museum of Anthropology (Lansing: University of Michigan, 1961). A Native interpretation is S. Baird, "Life in an Iroquois Longhouse," in *Villages in the Niagara Peninsula*, ed. J. Burtniak and W. B. Turner, Proceedings Second Annual Niagara Peninsula History Conference (St. Catharines: Brock University, 1980), pp. 57–64; R. F. Wiliamson and M. S. Cooper, "Prehistory and Archaeology," and M. S. Cooper, "A Study of the Neutrals," in *Many Voices: A Collective History of Greater Fort Erie*, ed. J. Davies and J. L. Felstead (Ridgeway, Ont.: Fort Erie Museum Board, 1996). W. C. Noble has contributed "The Neutral Indians," in *Essays in Northeastern Anthropology in Memory of Marian E. White*, Occasional Publications in Northeastern Anthropology, vol. 5., pp. 152–64; "Historic Neutral Iroquois Settlement Patterns," *Canadian Journal of Archaeology* 8, no. 1 (1984): 3–28; "Tsouharissen's Chiefdom: An Early Historic Seventeenth Century Neutral Iroquoian

Ranked Society," *Canadian Journal of Archaeology* 9, no. 2 (1985): 131–46; and "Frenchmen in Neutralia: Inter-Ethnic and Inter-Tribal Policies, Politics, and Practices of Contact," *Proceedings of the 1992 People to People Conference: Selected Papers*, Rochester Museum and Science Center, Research Records, 1994, no. 23, pp. 25–36.

11. A classic study is L. H. Morgan, *League of Iroquois* (Corinth, N. Y.: n.p., 1962; first published as *League of the Ho-de-no-sau-nee* (New York: Dodd, Mead, 1922). See also G. Beaver, "Early Iroquoian History in Ontario," *Ontario History* 85, no. 3 (1993); J. H. Coyne, *The Country of the Neutrals* (St. Thomas, Ont.: Times Print, 1985); R. L. McCarthy and H. Newman, *The Iroquois*, Adventures in Western New York History, vol. 4 (Buffalo, N.Y.: Buffalo and Erie County Historical Society, 1960); and E. Tooker, "The League of the Iroquois: Its History, Politics and Ritual," in *Handbook of North American Indians*, pp. 418–41.

12. A trilogy by F. Jennings is *The Invasion of America* (Chapel Hill: University of North Carolina Press, 1975); *The Ambiguous Iroquois Empire* (New York: Norton, 1984); *Empire of Fortune* (New York: Norton, 1984). See also F. Jennings et al., *The History and Culture of Iroquois Diplomacy* (Syracuse, N.Y.: Syracuse University Press, 1985).

13. F. Jennings, *The Ambiguous Iroquois Empire*, p. 30; and W. C. Noble, "The Neutral Indians."

14. G. K. Wright, *The Neutral Indians: A Source Book*, New York State Archaeological Association, Occasional Papers, no. 4 (Rochester, N.Y.: n.p., 1963); and W. C. Noble, "Frenchmen in Neutralia."

15. W. C. Noble and J. E. M. Crerar, "Management of White-Tailed Deer by the Neutral Iroquois, A.D. 999–1651," *Archaeozoologia* 5, no. 6 (1993): 19–70; and J. E. M. Crerar, "Assets and Assemblages: The Neutral Economic Approach to Inter-Cultural Relations," Proceedings of the 1992 People to People Conference: Selected Papers, Rochester Museum and Science Center, Research Records, no. 23 (1994), pp. 37–45.

16. Father J. Lalement, 1640, in C. M. Johnston, ed., *The Valley of the Six Nations: A Collection of Documents on the Indian Lands of the Grand River* (Toronto: Champlain Society, 1964), p. 12; R. C. Harris, *Historical Atlas of Canada*, vol. 1, plate 12.

17. W. C. Noble, "Thorold: An Early Historical Niagara Neutral Town," in *Villages in the Niagara Peninsula*, ed. J. Burtniak and W. B. Turner, Proceedings Second Annual Niagara Peninsula History Conference, Brock University (St. Catharines), 1980, pp. 59–60.

18. Noble, "Frenchmen in Neutralia."

19. W. G. Noble: "Historic Neutral Iroquois Settlement Patterns"; and "Tsouharissen's Chiefdom," pp. 131–46.

20. An early account is E. T. Williams, "Niagara County," in J. T. Horton et al., *History of Northwestern New York* (New York: Lewis Historical Publishing Company, 1947), 3:161–64. An overall appreciation is R. C. Harris, ed., *Historical Atlas of Canada*, vol. 1.

21. P. A. Porter, *Landmarks of the Niagara Frontier* (Niagara Falls, N.Y.: n.p., 1914), p. 9.

22. D. H. Kent, *Iroquois Indians II: Historical*

Report on the Niagara River and the Niagara River Strip to 1759 (reprint, New York: Garland, 1974), p. 20.

23. Louis Hennepin, *Nouvelle Decouverte*, Guillaume Broedet (Utrecht, Holland, 1697); translated in W. Barham, *Descriptions of Niagara: Selected from Various Travellers* (Gravesend, England: The Compiler, 1847), pp. 86–93. See F. Parkman, *La Salle and the Discovery of the Great West* (Toronto: New American Library, 1962), pp. 113–21.

24. F. Houghton, "Indian Village, Camp and Burial Sites on the Niagara Frontier," *Bulletin of the Buffalo Society of Natural Sciences* 9, no. 3 (1909): 372.

25. B. L. Dunnigan, *A History and Guide to Old Fort Niagara* (Youngstown, N.Y.: Old Fort Niagara Association, 1985), p. 3.

26. The succession of forts, with plans, is discussed in B. L. Dunnigan, *History and Development of Old Fort Niagara* (Youngstown, N.Y.: Old Fort Niagara Association, 1985).

27. Kent, *Iroquois Indians II*, pp. 32, 35.

28. H. J. Gagen, "Joncaire's Cabin—Magazin Royal," *Sentinel* 1 (Lewiston, N.Y.: Historical Association of Lewiston, 1974): 16–23 describes the excavation of this site.

29. F. H. Severance, "An Old Frontier of France," Buffalo Historical Society Publications, vol. 20 (1917), p. 273. The many histories of early days at the Frontier include W. P. Maloney, *The Niagara Frontier* (Albany, N.Y.: Boyd, 1923).

30. Kent, *Iroquois Indians II*, pp. 180–81.

31. F. H. Severance, "The Story of Joncaire: His Life and Times on the Niagara," Buffalo Historical Society Publications, vol. 9 (1906), pp. 81–219.

32. Kent, *Iroquois Indians II*, pp. 109–12.

33. B. L. Dunnigan, "Vauban in the Wilderness: The Siege of Fort Niagara, 1759," *Niagara Frontier* 21 (1974): 37–52.

34. F. H. Severance, "Studies of the Niagara Frontier," Buffalo Historical Society Publications, vol. 15 (1911), p. 324.

35. P. Pouchot, *Memoir upon the Late War in North America, between the French and the English, 1755–60*, published 1781; trans. and ed. F. B. Hough (Roxbury, Mass.: W. E. Woodward, 1856), 1:22–23; a new edition translated by M. Cardy and edited and annotated by B. Dunnigan was published by the Old Fort Niagara Association (Youngstown, N.Y., 1994). Details from pp. 62, 94, 386, 415–18, 430–36, 521.

36. Details from claims for compensation after the hostilities of 1759 are recorded in Daniel de Joncaire-Chabert, *Memoir for Daniel de Joncaire-Chabert*, and quoted in Severance, "The Story of Joncaire," pp. 151–58.

37. J. M. Coyne, "Explorations of the Great Lakes: 1669–1670," *Ontario Historical Society* 4 (1903): 81.

38. B. L. Dunnigan, *Siege—1759: The Campaign against Niagara* (Youngstown, N.Y.: Old Fort Niagara Association, 1986).

39. R. Macleod, *Cinderella Island* (Grand Island, N.Y.: Grand Island Chamber of Commerce, 1969).

40. Quoted in Porter, *Landmarks of the Niagara Frontier*, p. 10.

41. Deputy Surveyor-General Collins Re-

port, in *Third Report of the Bureau of Archives for the Province of Ontario* (Toronto: King's Printer, 1906), p. 355. See F. H. Severance, "The Achievements of Capt. John Montresor on the Niagara," Buffalo Historical Society Publications, vol. 5 (1902), pp. 1–19.

42. Collins Report., pp. 10, 37.

43. J. B. Brebner, *North Atlantic Triangle: The Interplay of Canada, The United States and Great Britain* (New York: Columbia University Press, 1945), p. 50.

44. H. Swigget, *War Out of Niagara: Walter Butler and the Tory Rangers* (1933; reprint, Port Washington, N.Y.: Ira J. Friedman, 1963).

45. *Sale of a Tract of Land by the Chiefs of the Chipeweighs and Mississagas Indians on the West Side of the Straits leading from Lake Erie to Lake Ontario to the Crown* (Niagara), 9 May 1781.

46. E. A. Cruickshank, *The Story of Butler's Rangers and the Settlement of Niagara* (Welland, Ont.: Lundy's Lane Historical Society, 1895; reprint, Niagara Falls, Ont.: n.p., 1975).

CHAPTER TWO

THE PIONEER FOUNDATIONS OF SETTLEMENT

When the former Indian lands became the property of the European invaders, the land was surveyed and divided into small units, a process first achieved on the Canadian Frontier. Substantial differences in emphasis emerged between the two sides of the Niagara River. By 1805 the American shore was still "a wilderness: but the British side is settled and cleared all the way to a depth of about 100 rods [550 yards; 503 meters (a rod is 5 meters [5.5 yards])] from the bank."[1]

THE NIAGARA RIVER BECOMES THE BOUNDARY

The provisional peace treaty between Great Britain and the United States, signed at Paris in 1782, defined the boundary of the United States of America as running through the middle of Lake Ontario, "until it strikes the Communication by Water between that Lake and Lake Erie; thence along the middle of the said Communication [the Niagara River] into Lake Erie."[2] Confirmed in the peace treaty of 1783, the concept of a "middle thread" had later to be clarified because of uncertainty over whether islands in the river belonged to Britain or the United States.[3] The decision of 1823 followed the deepest channel, and the boundary became a series of straight lines surveyed between fixed control points in the river. The Lower and Middle Rivers were about equally divided between the two banks except that most of the Whirlpool was awarded to Britain. The boundary at the Falls left Goat Island and the Three Sisters Islands in the United States, and the main Falls were given to Britain. Along the Upper River, all islands except Navy and Dufferin Islands were awarded to the United States. The future of Grand Island, its "ownership" claimed by Native groups, was uncertain until this demarcation.

From the British point of view, to use the Niagara River as a boundary between the new American Republic and British North America was an incredible misunderstanding of regional circumstances. Described as "a boundary devoid of geographical and historical meaning,"[4] people who knew the country were not involved in the negotiations. The terrain and the significance of regional location were either not known or not understood by the negotiators. Forts and trading posts, including Forts Niagara and Schlosser, the blockhouses, and the Niagara Portage that had not been captured were given to a foreign power, as was the British network of water and land routes to inland North America.[5]

The British, tired of war, considered that sugar, the West Indies, and the fisheries off Newfoundland were more important than the unknown continental interior. Since maintaining a chain of forts was costly, and whether fur was purchased through New York or Montreal was immaterial, the British leaders agreed to a boundary along the Niagara River.[6] This decision horrified the settlers and merchants at Fort Niagara, astounded the military, and alienated the colonial administration. The Peace Treaty of 1783 also utterly neglected the Iroquois to whom the British had pledged the lands bounded by the Ohio River. The treaty between Britain and the United States referred to neither the Natives as allies of Britain nor to their relations with the newly emerged American nation.

Whether the Natives were a free and independent nation as they claimed, or a subdued people overcome in war which was the American argument, it was "utterly incredible to them that the king could presume to grant to anyone land that was not his. . . . [In 1792 the Governor of Canada urged that] if, the area northwest of the Ohio between the Mississippi and the Lakes be secured exclusively to the Indians, and remain neutral ground in respect to Great Britain and the United States, peace between them and the Indians will be restored immediately, and established upon a solid foundation."[7] A Native state east of the Niagara River would "Secure our Posts, the trade, & the Tranquillity of the Country, whereas a boundary along the Niagara River would be a source of constant Contention & dispute."[8] As unilateral action by the British could not resolve this issue and as the United States did not withdraw, the boundary remained along the Niagara River. The Native groups had no realistic alternative except to comply with this demarcation and with later provisions for the surrender of their former territories.[9]

THE SURVIVING NATIVE HERITAGE

Inland from the Frontier the Iroquois, who had fought on the losing British side against the Americans during the Revolutionary War under the leadership of Captain Joseph Brant (Thayendanagea), a Mohawk war chief, were displaced from their traditional homelands in New York State. Crossing the Niagara boundary by proclamation of the Governor of Canada, Sir Frederick Haldimand, they were awarded 384,465 hectares (950,000 acres) on either side of the Grand River inland from Lake Erie to its upper waters. Here, with a settled population by 1785 of some 1,800 Native peoples, was built the Mohawk Village on a bluff above a bend in the Grand River near present-day Brantford.[10] This village soon contained the Council House, a mill, a school, a blacksmith, and over twenty Native log houses that had now displaced the historic longhouse for residential purposes. Centered on St. Paul's Church, the Protestant Royal Native Chapel of 1785, the oldest Protestant church in Ontario and the only Royal Native Chapel in the world, a residential school known as the Mohawk Institute was added to the village in 1830. Both buildings have survived to this day, as has Native loyalty to the British cause during the War of 1812, up to volunteer Native veterans fighting in Europe during the First and Second World Wars.

The Council House is now located in Ohsweken, the village near Brantford that has become the center of the reserve. The extent of Native territory has been attenuated to less than 5 percent of the original grant, as land was purchased for farming by White settlers and for urban development as at Dunnville and Brantford. Even so, the reserve carried a population of over ten thousand by the end of the twentieth century, and had some nine thousand other registered band members living off but entitled to return to the reserve. In 1924 the Canadian government established a band council over the traditional council of hereditary chiefs, with a chief and twelve councilors being elected every two years. Land claims against unfilled promises by the Canadian government are extensive, and given this uncertainty about the ownership of several lands within the extent of the original reserve, the Ontario Indian Commission in 1996 negotiated a unique agreement on economic development, land-use planning, and environmental issues. This agreement included the First Nations, eight municipalities, a conservation authority, and the two senior levels of government. As P. A. Monture, director of the Native Land Claims Office at Ohsweken, has stated, this "works well. However the real issue of the unresolved Six Nations Land Claims . . . continues to fester."[11] The situation remains unresolved, if not stonewalled, within the federal cabinet.

Chiefswood, built 1853–1856 for the Mohawk chief George Johnson and his English wife, became the childhood home of Pauline Johnson (Tekahionwake), the poetess of international renown, and is now a national historic site. At Kanata, Brantford, a longhouse in a palisaded setting has been recreated to represent a seventeenth-century Iroquoian village, and together with an Interpretive Centre provides cultural awareness for the Native way of life before and after European colonization. In the same vicinity the Woodland Cultural Centre houses a museum and a gallery and research center that reflect on Neutral-Iroquoian origins, cultural change through contact with European nations, and the onward process of acculturation to the present.

Closer to the boundary west of the now-divided Niagara River, the British purchased land extending from Four Mile Creek to Burlington Bay from the Natives in 1784. This treaty was confirmed in 1792, when the western boundary was redefined.[12] Herein lies the land basis for future settlement on the Canadian Niagara Frontier where, with the arrival of the European colonist, attitudes to life and land changed remarkably. The Native community ethic of respect for the land and its many attributes was replaced with the ownership of land by individuals, businesses, and governments. Land could now be bought and sold. Property rights, rules and regulations, laws, and enactments sought to control the use and development of land. A multitude of directions, bylaws, regulations, ordinances, restrictions, embargos, prohibitions, and guidelines were developed. Land now had a value. It became real estate, a commodity for sale that could be bought, sold, or bonded to another person for money.

To the Native, land was a combination of home, a storehouse to meet his daily needs, and a sacred place based on his beliefs. These communal rights changed to individual rights, with sales of increasing frequency as land was divided into ever smaller units for farm, home, commercial, business, and government purposes. As boundaries to properties were introduced, the landscape became framed by walls, hedges, and other markers in locations drawn on survey records to substantiate personal possession of former communal territory. A regular pattern of lots and concessions now divided the land. These smaller units were then subdivided successively, again and again, as new owners or occupants arrived on the scene. Farming, industry, private homes, or a new route of transportation might occupy the land. Even streams could be owned by individuals. Later but less frequently, the divided lots might be amalgamated to permit some new development, a costly and often controversial process as various ownerships and different attitudes might be involved. It was the start of a new era during which the old was steadily lost and merged into the new.

The portage around the Falls on the east side of the river was an important inheritance. This significant route must have existed around the Falls as part of a continental trade route for unknown centuries. The river and the Falls were indeed described and drawn on maps of the continent from Indian information by the early seventeenth century, before being seen by White men.[13] The Falls were described by Jacques Cartier after his expedition of 1535, and by Samuel de Champlain in 1608, but they were not described by sight until Louis Hennepin's account of 1678. Previous explorers and cartographers had used Native descriptions and drawings.

Trails through the forest followed the Welland River and Lyons Creek west of the Niagara River, the Tonawanda and Scajacquada Creeks, and the Buffalo River to the east. The "Iroquois Trail" along the shoreline of glacial Lake Iroquois has been described as the "major east-west route of eastern North American."[14] The complementary "Mohawk Trail" followed the crest of the Niagara Escarpment, descended to the Iroquois Trail, and crossed the Niagara River where it emerged from the gorge. Another trail followed the Onondaga Escarpment and crossed the Niagara River at Fort Erie.

These Native trails were used by European settlers and became convenient routes of entry, first as wagon roads and then as stagecoach routes. In St. Catharines, Ontario, a radial system of Indian trails provided the

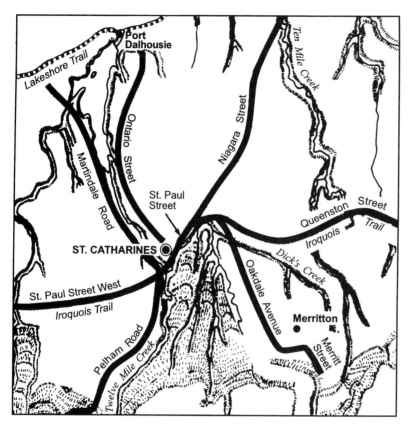

Fig. 2.1. The heritage of Indian trails provides the framework within which St. Catharines, Ontario, grew. These early routes of travel became the radial road pattern of the modern city. (Prepared by the Department of Geography, Brock University)

later grid surveys placed over the landscape.

The earliest settlers obtained land that had been worked by their Native predecessors, as well as raw forest, and took over existing practices, including raising corn as a valuable crop and tapping the sugar maple for its sweet sap. They learned to hunt and trap game, and to girdle trees to clear land. They adopted the toboggan, the canoe, the snowshoe, and field lacrosse as a game. They learned about edible plants and those with curative properties. Native legends were adopted, such as the "Maid of the Mist" saga where the Thunder God Hinum and his two sons supposedly lived in caves behind the Falls.[16] At an annual ceremony of appease-

foundation for the road system of the emerging city (fig. 2.1).[15] In the United States, Buffalo's Main Street (Highway 5) reflects the trail which followed the crest of the Onondaga Escarpment. The Portage Road in Niagara Falls, New York, succeeds the Indian portage around the Falls. The roads following natural features precede the ment a canoe laden with fruit and game was sent over this cataract. Embellished by Victorian sensibilities which added the provocation of a bare-breasted maiden to placate the gods, this story has become part of the legendary folklore of the Falls.

It is reasonably certain that temporary Native settlement sites underlie several later White settlements. Even though forsaken for a century or more before occupation by pioneer settlers, the sparser regenerated vegetation of these areas would have suggested to the pioneer a convenient location for settlement. The core areas of Niagara-on-the-Lake, Fort Erie, and St. Catharines west of the Niagara River, and Fort Niagara, Youngstown, Lewiston, and Buffalo to the east are locations where former Native sites may be presumed to have occupied the land.

The most familiar Native memories on the Niagara Frontier are its place-names.[17] The one most frequently used is Niagara, an Iroquoian name with early spellings including Ongiahra, Ongiara, Unghiara, and Oniagara, each being attempts to spell what was heard. The name often thought to mean "thunder of the waters" is more probably "neck," that is, the narrowing of Lake Erie into the strait of the Niagara River to Lake Ontario. Other names of Native derivation include of course Canada and Ontario, and

locally Chippawa, Mississauga, Onondaga, and Iroquois on the Canadian Frontier, and Tonawanda, Cheektowaga, and Scajaquada on the American Frontier. Together, they provide ever-present reminders of the deep and formative Native roots in the Niagara landscape. As this debt is substantial, it has indeed been argued that American society was uniquely shaped in its exploration, development, settlement, and cultivation by the Native presence.[18]

THE BRITISH TRANSFER TO THE WEST BANK

When it became clear that the boundary along the Niagara River would be permanent, the British transferred the portage and its defenses to the west bank. A chain reserve 20.1 meters (66 feet) in width was surveyed along the west side of the Niagara River. Queenston on the Canadian side became the most convenient site for a landing place and storehouse at the northern end of the new portage; Chippawa at the mouth of Chippawa Creek (Welland River) served the same function south of the Falls.[19] The new portage road which opened in 1789 provided an easier ascent of the Niagara Escarpment, and a continuous route on land from Niagara to Fort

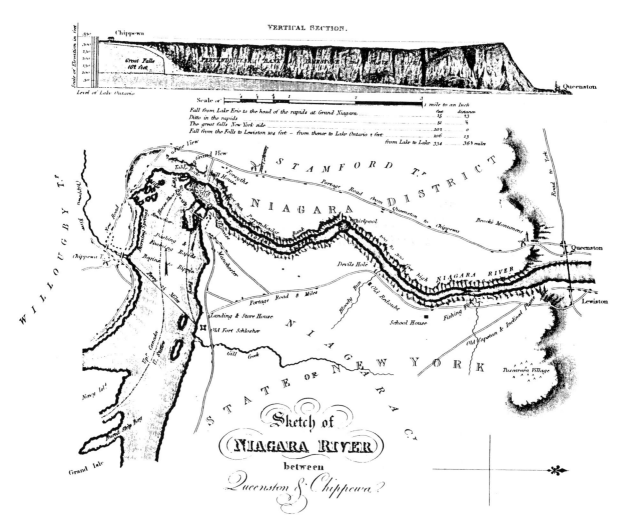

Fig. 2.2. The shorter, older Native, French, then British, and now American portage was replaced after 1783 by a later, longer portage on the Canadian Frontier. Both portages attracted forts and settlements, and both were later bypassed by the Welland and the Erie Canals. (From J. Bouchette, *The British Dominions in North America*, 1832)

After the transfer of British settlement to the west bank of the Niagara River, two forts commanded the river: Fort Erie (**top left**) controlled the southern entrance, and Fort Niagara (**bottom left**) the northern entrance. (John N. Jackson [both])

Erie (fig. 2.2). At the gorge, it turned inland from the curving and indented river frontage.[20] The portage encouraged trade, transport, and the growth of Newark (now Niagara-on-the-Lake), Queenston, Chippawa, and Fort Erie. In the meantime the older, east-bank portage, including Fort Niagara and its merchant establishments, dwindled as trade transferred to the new portage.

Fort Niagara and the blockhouses along the old portage were surrendered in 1796, and the defensive system then transferred to the new territories east of the river. Fort George, named after King George III of England, was constructed between 1796 and 1799 on the high ground above Navy Hall in present-day Niagara-on-the-Lake. Overlooking the Niagara River near its mouth, it housed the Indian Department and was the most important British post at the Frontier and the general command headquarters for Upper Canada.[21] Work in 1806 also began on a third and larger Fort Erie, a permanent structure with stone buildings located on higher ground than its predecessors. As Fort George was also strengthened, approximately doubling its size, when the United States declared war in 1812, the British defensive system was in place.

The new lands on the Canadian Frontier were settled by immigration from the United States, a large-scale, outward movement that included dispossessed people, disbanded troops, and those who had suffered retaliation after the peace treaty for their loyalty to the British Crown.[22] This enforced migration included English, Irish, and Scottish families; German-speaking Mennonites from Pennsylvania; French Huguenots; Dutch Calvinists; and Loyalist Natives of the Six Nations. Not always British in the cultural sense, they all distrusted the United States and owed allegiance to the Union Jack. Singly and as a group, they had been colonists with several generations of farming, trading, milling, and other experiences in the New World.

Many of the newcomers had lost homes, relatives, possessions, and land in the States.[23] They brought with them seeds, trees, and livestock. The garrisons along the Niagara River provided a local market for surplus products, and potash for the British textile industry guaranteed an immediate cash return as the forest cover was felled and burned to permit agriculture. Free from potential Indian attack, British defenses ensured that the Canadian Frontier was peaceful, permitting the rapid advance of agriculture and settlement from 1783 to 1812.[24]

Land was granted free to the Loyalist immigrants, the amount depending upon military rank or civil status, with more extensive tracts granted to officers and the upper echelons of society. A tight-knit group known as "The Family Compact" supplied the community with military, religious, social, economic, and political leadership.[25] Tenure was initially under the French seigneurial system but, as the British settlers objected strongly to this alien form of landholding, from 1791 grants were made with full rights to the owners.[26] When the Constitutional Act of that year created the Provinces of Upper and Lower Canada (Ontario and Quebec) out of the old Province of Quebec, the west bank of the Niagara River became part of Lincoln County in Upper Canada. English customs and laws now prevailed, and the French seigneurial system was relinquished.

The intention was to create a temporary government-sponsored farming community that would provide food for Fort Niagara. The settlers, it was expected, would return to their former homes in the United States. The Treaty of Paris in 1782 between Great Britain and the United States had recommended an amnesty for the Loyalists and the restoration of their properties but, as this policy was not pursued by the legislatures of the various states, the temporary settlement became permanent.

Some settlers brought their Black slaves with them.[27] An act of 1793 confirmed their status as property, but children born to a slave mother were freed at age twenty-five, and the further introduction of slaves was forbidden. This act created a considerable difference between the two sides at Niagara. After the turn of the century most Blacks on the Canadian Frontier were free. They could own land, farm, or work as tradesmen.

The Queenston-Lewiston ferry crossing of the Niagara River was probably the most important route of entry. Here, approached on both banks by the Iroquois trail, was easy access to both sides of the river, and the former Iroquois shoreline provided dry sites for settlement on both banks. When the Loyalists arrived, many crossed here. Their wagons could be caulked, and the animals might swim or be carried across by private ferries or in military boats. In 1793 regulations were formulated for the operation of ferries between Newark-Fort Niagara, Queenston-Lewiston, and Fort Erie-Black Rock.[28] These boats to freedom completely belied the idea of an isolated "peninsula"; they crossed the river to create a "land bridge" between the two Frontiers.

LINES ON THE LAND

Administrative decisions created regular patterns across the landscape as township sur-

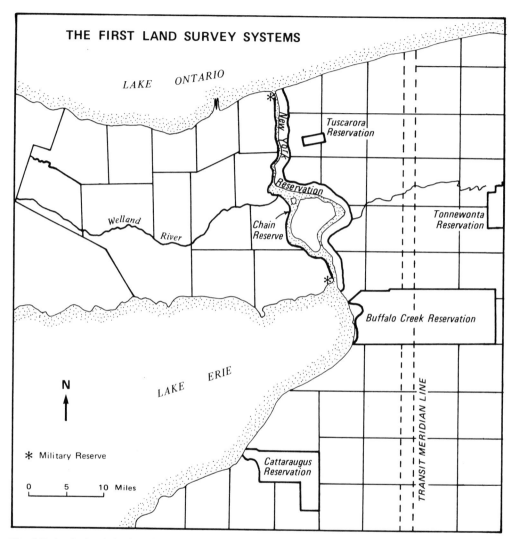

THE FIRST LAND SURVEY SYSTEMS

LAKE ONTARIO

Tuscarora Reservation

New York

Reservation

Welland River

Chain Reserve

Tonnewonta Reservation

Buffalo Creek Reservation

N

LAKE ERIE

TRANSIT MERIDIAN LINE

✳ Military Reserve

0   5   10 Miles

Cattaraugus Reservation

Fig. 2.3. As the land obtained from its former Native occupants was surveyed, the lines of roads and patterns of landownership were etched across the landscape. (Tonnewonta is now Tonawanda.) (Prepared by the Department of Geography, Brock University)

LINES ON THE LAND

NIAGARA REGION
FRONT AND REAR SYSTEM

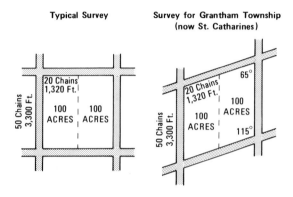

Fig. 2.4. Rigid but different patterns across the landscape were created by government surveys for incoming settlers on the Canadian Frontier, and by later private surveys undertaken for the Holland Land Company on the American Frontier. (Compiled by the Department of Geography, Brock University)

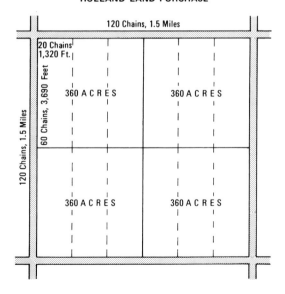

The standard road allowance is 1 chain, i.e., 66 feet.

veys were undertaken (fig. 2.3).[29] Divided into evenly spaced rectangular blocks and straight roads, they became administrative units for local government. On the Canadian Frontier, a "front line" of townships had been surveyed around Lake Ontario from Kingston to Niagara, and some along the Niagara River by 1786. By 1788 two areas were settled, south along the Niagara River to the Welland River, and west from Niagara across the Ontario Plain.[30]

The perimeter townships of the Canadian Frontier had a baseline on the Niagara River and either Lake Ontario or Lake Erie, and within the Niagara Peninsula a base followed the meandering Welland River (fig. 2.4). Townships were surveyed according to the "front and rear" system, using a surveyor's or Gunter's chain (20.1 meters, 66 feet long) and the acre (0.4 hectares) as standard measures.[31] Lots containing 100 acres (40.5 hectares) measured 20 by 50 chains with a road allowance of one chain in front of each lot and between every two lots.

These lots provided the pattern of ownership and the framework for land subdivision but, because of the cost of frequent road allowances, the front and rear system was used only in the Niagara Peninsula, which has a distinctive pattern compared with other settlements in Ontario or those which arose on the American Frontier.[32] This system of land allocation, designed to permit a large territory to be turned over to settlers easily and cheaply as farm lots, created a dispersed pattern of farming settlement. With the exception of Newark (Niagara-on-the-Lake) that was laid out as town, urban centers developed in response to local needs rather than as part of a planned process.

By 1812 an estimated 80 percent of the population of Upper Canada was American by birth or descent.[33] The boundary along the Niagara River had created a safe haven on British soil, but this peaceful incentive changed gradually as later settlers were attracted west by cheap land. By 1800 the price of land, its availability, and its quality had become more important than the political differences that existed between the two sides.[34] The Canadian Frontier also soon changed from a distinct area of settlement on the pioneer fringe to become but part of the vast pioneer movement west across continental North America.

NEWARK AND THE RIVER COMMUNITIES

The selection of an administrative seat for the Canadian settlements arose after the township surveys and the grants of land to incoming settlers. In 1790 meetings were held to select "the most eligible Plan for a Town and Public Buildings."[35] Crown lands outside Niagara Township near the harbor-government facilities at the mouth of the Niagara River were chosen as a result of a petition by the principal inhabitants and militia officers for lands near Navy Hall.[36] This request was changed to a more spacious site adjoining the military reserve.

The first surveys of the town, then Lenox, were taken in 1791. Subsequently this name was changed to Butlersburg after Colonel John Butler, deputy agent of Indian Affairs and former commander of Butler's Rangers. Occupants of the land were allowed to retain the lot on which their houses were located; the rest were drawn by lottery. The town was laid out, "one half acre [0.2 hectares] to each house, eight acres [3.2 hectares] at a distance and a large [common] for the use of the town."[37] Urban form was based on a regular gridiron road pattern, but the layout did not follow the cardinal directions because of the military reserve and the confined setting between the Niagara

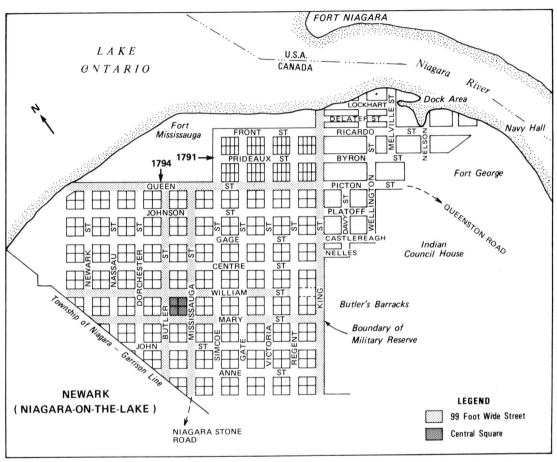

Fig. 2.5. A regular, small-scale layout was adopted for Newark (now Niagara-on-the-Lake), the first urban community to be established on the Canadian Frontier. (Compiled by the Department of Geography, Brock University)

River and Lake Ontario. Although intended in a central, internal location, commercial facilities located close to the garrison, the docks, and the trading center of Fort George.[38]

The town lots were eight half-acre (0.2 hectares) lots per block between Queen and Front Streets; the rest were four one-acre (0.4 hectares) lots per block (fig. 2.5). The town was framed by streets 99 feet (30.2 meters) wide, as were the approach roads to the proposed central square. The remaining streets had the traditional survey width of 66 feet (20.1 meters). The street names of King, Queen, Victoria, Regent, John, Anne, William, and Mary commemorated British monarchs.

Designated the capital of Upper Canada in 1791 and renamed Newark, Niagara became the official name after 1800. Later named Niagara-on-the-Lake, the town soon expanded as the major administrative and trading center of the Niagara District.[39] It contained the jail, the county court, and the registry offices. There were docks, a shipyard, and warehouses. A repaired Navy Hall served as Government House and the residence of the Lieutenant-Governor, John Graves Simcoe, who arrived in 1792. The town also enjoyed an active public life with its law courts, courthouse, Quarter Sessions, district, and town meetings. There were schools, churches, newspapers, stores, merchants, barracks, and a public library. The town, at first the only commercial center on the Canadian Frontier, served the whole of the Niagara Peninsula. A sawmill and a gristmill were soon built to the west on Four Mile Creek, the nearest point of power advantage.

Newark grew quickly, attracting merchants, soldiers, government officials, and professional services.[40] In 1794 the garrison was transferred from Fort Niagara across the Niagara River. Newark, the Mother Town of the Canadian Frontier, has been described as a "forward site," that is, a capital located not centrally but nearest to the principal foreign neighbor.[41] By 1796 there were about seventy houses, "built of wood; those next the lake are rather poor, but at the upper end of town there are several very excellent dwellings, inhabited by the principal officers of the government. . . . Few places in North America can boast of a more rapid rise."[42] Even the loss of capital status to York (now Toronto) in 1796 had little effect on the town's economic vitality, for here was the local center to which farmers brought their produce and where supplies were purchased. In 1801 merchants were granted permission to construct wharves and storehouses on the river next to Navy Hall. As settlement in Upper Canada increased, so too did the movement of goods along the portage.

Smaller centers emerged along the portage road next to its forts. Traders added storehouses and wooden houses at Waterloo (now Fort Erie) and Chippawa. Two corn mills and two sawmills operated south of Chippawa at the present location of Dufferin Islands. At Queenston a "tolerable inn, two or three good store-houses, some small houses, a block-house of stone . . . and barracks" were built. Here one merchant "owned a very fine house, a farm, a distillery, and a tanyard."[43] A visitor in 1799 noted four vessels unloading at the same time, sometimes sixty wagons being loaded in one day, and the portage provided "an increasing source of wealth to the farmers for many miles around."[44]

Queenston became a Port of Customs in 1801, and Chippawa obtained this status in 1808. By 1806 both villages had post offices, a wooden bridge had been constructed over the Welland River at Chippawa, a new stone fort was under construction at Fort Erie, and along Lake Erie the townships were rapidly gaining in population.[45] Tourism at the Falls was expanding through improved access. Various ladders took the more daring of travelers to the base of the gorge below the Horseshoe Falls, and from there to venture behind the sheet of falling water. Inland, Shipman's Corners (now St. Catharines) expanded as a local service center on Twelve Mile Creek;[46] a storehouse located there about 1790, followed by a church, a tavern, mills, a schoolhouse, and the discovery of salt.

Newspaper advertisements suggest that up to 15 percent of the forested land had been cleared by the turn of the century. The Canadian Frontier as a settled and expanding pioneer locality focused on Niagara, the portage centers, and the forts along the Niagara River. Villages were beginning to emerge inland on the fertile Ontario Plain as milling and local service centers. The transition from dense forest to pioneer clearings and then to an agricultural society of commercial importance had been rapid.

THE HOLLAND LAND COMPANY

With little expectation either that the Treaty of 1783 would be enforced or that the new American nation would survive, Fort Niagara continued to fly the British flag and the portage road was strengthened. This "holdover period" of British rule, with its occupancy of the eastern, now American, bank, continued for thirteen years before land on that side of the river could be purchased from the Iroquois.

The situation with regard to the release of Native land was slower and more complicated than on the Canadian Frontier. At the Treaty of Fort Stanwix (Rome) in 1784, with the exception of the Four Mile Strip that had been ceded to the Natives some twenty years previously, Native American ownership of all land west of Seneca Lake was acknowledged. Under pressure from the land-hungry colonists of the New England states, and through confusion in

British colonial charters over whether these Native lands belonged to New York or Massachusetts, in 1786 the right to purchase (the Preemption Rights) was granted to Massachusetts. It was also agreed that a One Mile Strip (fig. 1.4, p. 76) along the Niagara River should be reserved for the State of New York to provide for defense against possible aggression from British Canada to the west. This land, except Fort Niagara and the square of Lewiston at the foot of the portage, was not sold for private development until 1805.

Land speculators took over the right to buy and sell Native lands, and in 1792 much of western New York was sold to Dutch investors. Native rights were extinguished when the Seneca reluctantly sold their lands between the Genesee River and Lake Erie under the Big Tree Treaty of 1797. Some 1.3 million hectares (3.3 million acres) were then transferred to the Holland Land Company for $100,000, but leaving aside some land for reservations including the Cattaraugus, Buffalo Creek, Tonawanda, and Tuscarora Reservations (fig. 2.3) at the Frontier.

Joseph Ellicott, appointed Chief of Survey, became Resident Agent for the Holland Land Company.[47] From 1797 to 1821 he surveyed and then distributed the land, and located roads, mills, harbors, towns, and local trading centers.[48] These operations began in 1798 when a north-south transit meridian line, now Transit Road south from Lockport through Niagara and Erie Counties, was surveyed from Lake Ontario to the Pennsylvania boundary.[49] Also surveyed were the Native Reservations and the One Mile Strip along the Niagara River that were not included in the Holland Land purchase.

Townships 9.7 kilometers (6 miles) square were laid out (fig. 2.4). Equivalent to those being developed in Ohio, they were smaller than on the Canadian Frontier. As the Niagara River and the lakes were not used as baselines on the American Frontier, the townships bordering these physical features were either truncated as along the Niagara River or included additional segments along the shorelines of Lake Ontario and Lake Erie. These townships were then divided into sixteen sections, each 2.4 kilometers (1.5 miles) square, and then partitioned into twelve 48.6 hectares (120 acres). Variations were permitted where main roads, large streams, and lakes interrupted. The survey lots were larger by 8.1 hectares (20 acres), and the survey roads longer and straighter on the American than the Canadian Frontier, but in both instances a rigid, deterministic pattern had been placed over the land.

Land sales began in 1801 with the hope of selling extensive tracts, but in practice most lots were sold to individuals as farm lots. Cash was scarce, the settlers were poor, and payment could often be made over ten years with cattle, grain, or cords of wood, or through providing labor to open roads and construct buildings.[50] A "house," more often a crude shack or shelter, and a fenced clearing for the crops and animals had to be completed within a year. Mills, stores, and the services available in nearby Upper Canada encouraged settlement close to the Niagara River. Here the lots within townships were sold with few expenses other than surveying,[51] and cutting roads and improving the creeks for travel increased the value and sale of land.[52] As the area was inaccessible overland from the east, settlers often traveled by water to Niagara to reach their land, and some were attracted from settled areas in Upper Canada.

Batavia, east of Buffalo at the intersection of two major Native trails, became the commercial and administrative center for the Holland Land Company. Here a sawmill, a gristmill, and the first general store were constructed at the company's expense. As the area became populated, a subagency was established at Buffalo where help was provided to remove the sandbar that blocked the harbor entrance. Roads were constructed as an aid to settlement. The road from Batavia to Buffalo Creek opened in 1798. A branch route to the mouth of Tonawanda Creek provided a more direct link to the settled Canadian areas than the ferry at Black Rock. Another road connected Batavia to the head of navigation of the Lower Niagara River; long used as a drovers' road to move cattle to Fort Niagara and improved by the Holland Land Company in 1803, the Ridge Road (now NY 104) boosted the fortunes of the Landing at the foot of the old portage, became Main Street for the village of Lewiston, and encouraged settlement along its route.

Settlers were encouraged to locate at 16.1-kilometer (10-mile) intervals along these "roads," little more than widened Indian trails, to provide inns and a local base from which the new settlers might occupy and develop their land.[53] Local service centers developed at places later to be known as Clarence Hollow, Williams Mills (Williamsville), Tonawanda, and Amherst.[54] Sawmills, necessary to supply the pioneer with wood and boards for buildings, were constructed near the inns at Clarence and Williams Mills and at Bowmansville on Ellicott Creek. Gristmills followed later as the settlers harvested their crops. The inns and mills became local central points for meeting and, as further local services arrived, developed into villages.

A road constructed between Batavia and Buffalo Creek became Genesee Street (now

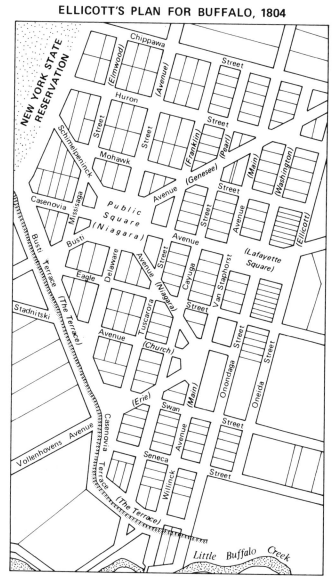

ELLICOTT'S PLAN FOR BUFFALO, 1804

Fig. 2.6. A graceful, Renaissance-style plan, prepared by Joseph Ellicott for the Holland Land Company, was centered on a grand square with eight radiating streets. (Prepared by the Department of Geography, Brock University)

NY 33).[55] Its terminus, named New Amsterdam by Ellicott, was generally called "Buffalo" by its residents, after the creek. Another road was built along the Niagara River to connect Fort Niagara to an intended fort at Black Rock, but plans for this fort were later abandoned. This road replaced the old portage road from Lewiston to the mouth of Cayuga Creek and, not completed for almost a decade, became Military Road across Niagara Falls.

BUFFALO, LEWISTON, AND BLACK ROCK

The Holland Land Company, separated from the Niagara River by the New York Reservation and from the shore of Lake Erie by the Buffalo Creek Reservation, had to obtain a landing place and harbor at the mouth of Little Buffalo Creek. Ellicott's plan

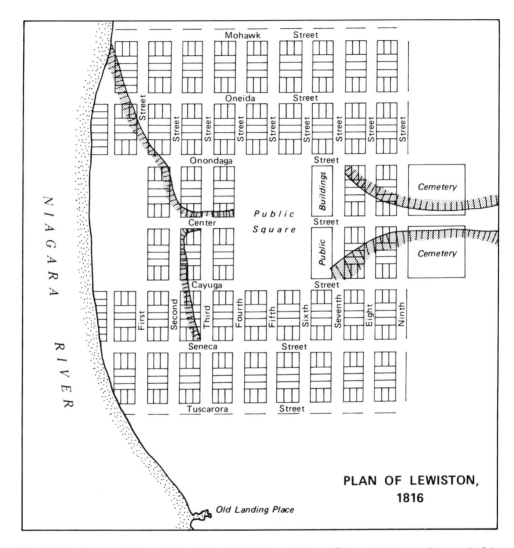

Fig. 2.7. Lewiston, at the head of navigation for the Lower Niagara River and at the northern end of the Niagara Portage, was planned with a main street along the Iroquois Shoreline and a public square at the center of the rectangular road layout. (Prepared by the Department of Geography, Brock University)

for the development of this site provided Buffalo with an elegant plan for the future, one that reflected Baroque Washington where his brother had helped to lay out Charles L'Enfant's design for the American capital.[56] The plan for Buffalo combined a radial pattern with gridiron roads (fig. 2.6). Centered on a grand square with eight radiating streets that has been described as one of "America's great classic squares,"[57] the bank above Lake Erie received a gracefully curving street, The Terrace, along its contours.

The principal streets, named after members of the Holland Land Company, were parts of the design. Willinck and Van Staphorst Avenues (Main Street) met at a spacious semicircular arc with radiating streets. Ellicott envisioned his mansion with vistas along the avenues, but this circle did not materialize and Main Street was straightened. The Ellicott Square Building, built in 1894, occupies this block. The historic Dutch street names have been changed, but the Indian names survive. Moving outward, a web of radiating diagonal and cross streets provided lots varying in size from 2 to 8.1 hectares (5 to 20 acres) on the periphery. The layout was confined in the northwest, where the New York State Reservation and the village of Black Rock provided limits.

A schoolhouse was organized in 1801, and then a post office. As the American flow of pioneer settlement moved west, growth in the new settlement was rapid. Buffalo became a designated center for the collection of customs in 1805, and the county seat when Niagara County was split from Genesee County in 1808. A courthouse and jail were constructed by the Holland Land Company. More than four hundred persons lived there by 1810 when Ellicott noted "A number of very well-built two-storey houses erected of Stone, Brick and Frame." The town soon had merchants, physicians, newspapers, and social activities.[58]

A second organized settlement, then known as "The Landing" at the northern end of the portage and at the western end of the Ridge Road, was named Lewiston in 1805 after Moran Lewis, the governor of New York State who had encouraged the promotion of this village. It lay opposite the established village of Queenston on the Canadian bank, and arose outside the boundaries of the Holland Land Purchase in the Mile Strip of the New York Reservation.

In 1798 the state legislature had instructed the Surveyor-General "to select, survey, and report on the location of a town on the Niagara [River] on land where the Indian titles had been extinguished."[59] Its plan contained an improved anchorage for riverboats and the ferry across the river, and a gradual rise to a central public square surrounded by rectangular blocks divided into lots (fig. 2.7). Reflecting the importance of the portage, a forwarding agency which built small vessels and organized trade to the Upper Lakes and a customs port of entry were added. The ferry to Queenston, the portage, the Ridge Road, and an anticipated canal link between the Upper and Lower Niagara Rivers promised growth. The Queenston-Lewiston crossing also became important for Canadian mail services when the Montreal-St. Lawrence outlet was frozen during the winters, and postal services to England were via the ice-free harbor at New York.

Black Rock, named after a bluff of black limestone rock projecting into the Niagara River, was laid out with a "long lot" grid that paralleled the river. A ferry service to Fort Erie perhaps existed by 1796. In 1805 the Porter-Barton partnership of Lewiston obtained a thirteen-year lease over the old portage and restarted the haulage business along the portage route between Lewiston and Black Rock. At Black Rock vessels carrying freight provided the first regular American line of transportation on the Great Lakes.[60] Because of the boundary, the American Frontier was developing its own routes that now competed with the Canadian portage.

Downstream at the Falls, when the One Mile Strip was sold, Augustus Porter purchased large tracts of land next to the river in 1806. Hydraulic potential, mills, and prospective industrial developments led to a settlement named Manchester after the English industrial city, now Niagara Falls, New York. Porter purchased Goat Island in 1816, established it as a tourist attraction, and laid the foundations for industry and tourism to develop along this frontage of the Upper River.

A FRONTIER OF HOSTILITY

Agricultural development typically began with a forest clearing and an isolated log house with few domestic possessions. Fences were then constructed and a garden planted. Within ten years, 12.1 to 16.2 hectares (30 to 40 acres) might be enclosed, with a larger and more comfortable house, a barn, more livestock, and a well. There would be neighbors and probably a schoolhouse nearby.[61] The isolation, dangers, and privations of pioneer Frontier life soon ended as a farming landscape with neighbors emerged.

By the beginning of the nineteenth century, stands of forest remained on the farms, and the unsettled localities would be either

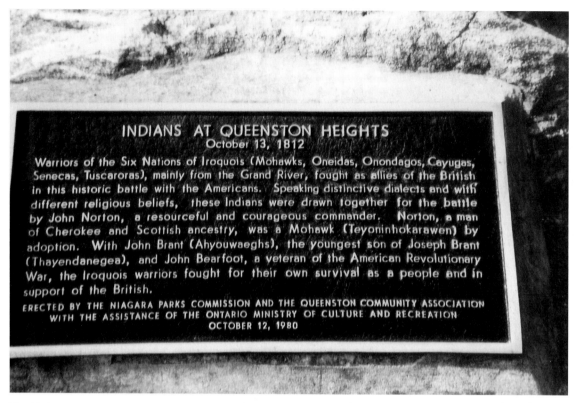

The Native population on the Canadian Frontier, denied recognition in the Peace Treaty of 1783 and relegated to inland reserves, remained staunch supporters of the British cause. Native units under English officers fought against American aggressors at the Battles of Queenston Heights and Beaverdams. (John N. Jackson)

those with the poorer, often heavier soils or land held by absentee landlords. The farms with their small surplus of wheat, fruit, and livestock supplied the nearby centers and the forts. The Canadian Frontier had a higher proportion of cleared land than the American Frontier and more intense farming because of its longer period of settlement.

These peaceful advances of agriculture, settlement, trade, and urban growth were brought to an abrupt halt in 1812 when American forces crossed the Niagara River to

Pioneer settlement advanced rapidly from a log house (**top**) to a fenced clearing with corn, potatoes, beans, and pumpkins (**middle**), to some ten years later when a mature farming landscape prevailed (**bottom**). (O. Turner, *Pioneer History of the Holland Purchase*, 1849)

invade Canadian territory.[62] Battles were fought at Queenston Heights, Beaverdams (near Thorold), Fort George, Fort Erie, Chippawa, Cook's Mill, and at Lundy's Lane in Niagara Falls.[63] Niagara-on-the-Lake and the villages of Queenston and St. David's were destroyed or severely damaged. American forces at certain periods of the war controlled both sides of the Niagara River. In retaliation for the American burning of Niagara in 1813, the British crossed the Niagara River and captured Fort Niagara. Lewiston, Manchester (Niagara Falls), Fort Schlosser, Black Rock, Buffalo, and the bridge over Tonawanda Creek were destroyed. Natives from the Six Nations Reservation on the Grand River, as allies of the British, fought at the battles of Queenston Heights, Beaverdams, and Chippawa, among others. At the Battle of Chippawa, Indian soldiers on both sides withdrew from the conflict when they learned that they faced their cousins from the opposite side of the Niagara River.

Between 1812 and 1814, cattle, food, and crops on the Canadian Frontier were carried off by foragers. Bridges, farms, and barns

Major-General Sir Isaac Brock, the Saviour of Upper Canada during the War of 1812, has been glorified by a monument on the heights of the Niagara Escarpment above the village of Queenston and by a memorial church in the village below. (John N. Jackson)

were burned. Farms were neglected as men enlisted for military duty. Supplies and equipment were commandeered for military use. Destruction and depopulation prevailed. An estimated three hundred buildings were destroyed on both sides. Casualties were high. Estimates vary, but the battle at Lundy's Lane in 1814 perhaps involved about 3,500 British and American troops; roughly 850 men from each side were killed, wounded, or missing compared with about 750 men in the hour-long battle of Chippawa Creek.[64]

Fort George and Fort Niagara were repaired and strengthened by the British after Niagara was burned, and Fort Mississauga (though not completed by the end of the war) was constructed to command the entrance to the Niagara River. In 1814, while the

British occupied the American Frontier, American troops captured Fort Erie, but their northward advance along the river was halted and the Canadian forts were not again attacked. British garrisons were substantial, with about 1,100 men in Fort George and 400 in Fort Mississauga in 1814.[65]

After the war ended, British negotiators sought to remove the Niagara River boundary, attempted to establish an Indian buffer state east of the river as a precaution against further attack, and argued that Fort Niagara should be returned to Britain.[66] These endeavors failed, the boundary was confirmed along the middle of the Niagara River, and both sides handed back territory and possessions taken during the war. The British thereby forfeited Fort Niagara and the east bank of the river for the second time.

The major battlefields on the Canadian Frontier soon became local points of interest that were developed as tourist attractions. At Lundy's Lane in 1836 a Presbyterian church was built with an outside gallery to view the field of conflict; an observation tower, the first of five, followed in 1845. A monument to Major-General Sir Isaac Brock, dedicated at Queenston Heights in 1824, became a popular place of pilgrimage.[67] Laura Secord, a heroine of the war, was commemorated by monuments and in literature.[68] On the Amer-ican Frontier, restored Fort Niagara became the key feature in the state park at the mouth of the Niagara River.

Tourism to the Falls, with its upper-class, leisured clientele, resumed. William Forsyth organized a coach service from Buffalo to Black Rock that crossed by ferry to Fort Erie, then followed the river to his hotel at the Falls; to the north the coach service served Niagara where vessels on Lake Ontario were met. On the American Frontier Augustus Porter bought Goat Island and the adjacent land described as "very valuable for water power." The channel between the island and the mainland became a millrace, but Goat Island was not developed. Saved as a natural haven, Porter built a toll bridge to it and charged visitors to view the natural setting and the cataract.

The War of 1812 created strong anti-American feelings on the Canadian side. Pro-British sentiments exalted the United Empire Loyalist for saving the Empire, emi-gration from the United States dwindled, and later immigrants now came mainly from the British Isles.[69] The Canadian Frontier was also now perceived as a place less desirable for settlement than the inland areas of Upper Canada. As Talbot (1824) reflected: "The peculiar advantages . . . of this District are almost counterbalanced by the circumstances of its proximity to the United States, which, in time of war, renders it no desirable residence for men of peace."[70]

These adverse attitudes caused the British government to construct the Rideau Canal inland between Lake Ontario and the Ottawa River. A canal joining Lakes Erie and Ontario, which would have avoided the costly overland transport of supplies and the need for separate lake fleets, received lower priority. When later constructed by the private Welland Canal Company, the canal lay inland from the boundary, had wooden rather than stone locks, and could not use the Lower Niagara River as the finest harbor on Lake Ontario because Fort Niagara in American hands on the opposite bank commanded the entrance to the river.

In 1827 a major British fortress was proposed on the Fonthill kame.[71] In 1865 a War Office map depicted "proposed works" at Fort Erie, Port Colborne, and Port Dalhousie to protect the entrances to the Welland Canal; a "Battery" opposite Black Rock and at the mouth of the Welland River; an "Entrenched Camp & Temporary Batteries" on Queenston Heights and at Fort Mississauga; and an "Entrenched Position" at Thorold.[72]

The boundary at Niagara had become one of mistrust, and only gradually were more friendly relationships reestablished. The War of 1812 not only disrupted the steady progress of agricultural development and settlement. It deferred or prevented some later Canadian developments, reinforced the boundary as a division in the minds of settlers and governments alike, and helps to explain some lingering Canadian distrust of American intentions and attitudes, while battlefield sites along the Canadian Niagara River Parkway continue to be developed as tourist attractions.

RECOVERY AND EXPANSION

The ferries across the Niagara River at Niagara-Youngstown, Queenston-Lewiston, and Fort Erie-Black Rock resumed their passage of people, animals, farm produce, and merchandise across the river. New crossings were added, below the Falls and between Fort Erie and Buffalo. The more important routes obtained new and larger ferries that were "mechanized" with horses working the paddle wheel as on a treadmill. Trade and movement between the two Frontiers assisted in overcoming the hostility of war, but tensions remained.

On the Canadian Frontier Niagara-on-the-Lake was rebuilt and enlarged after the war. Streets of the "New Survey" were extended southeast of King Street and named after soldiers prominent during the Napoleonic Wars (fig. 2.7).[73] The portage trade resumed, and the Portage Road was improved. The forts on Lake Ontario were served by steam vessels, and a stagecoach service to the capital at York (now Toronto) was added in 1816. Niagara again functioned as "the center of the wholesale trade for Western Canada."[74] Agriculture in the vicinity recovered.[75] Though in 1815 Fort Erie to the south lay "in ruins," a bridge was constructed over Chippawa Creek and new bridges over the other tributaries that entered the Niagara River. By 1815 two large naval vessels were under construction at Chippawa.[76] Queenston regained its status as a port of entry; the *Colonial Advocate* was published there for a short time, but rebuilding and recovery was slow because of the village's vulnerable position should American attacks be resumed.

The American Frontier expanded more rapidly. Trade along the old portage resumed.[77] Lewiston expanded both as a port and as the terminus of the Ridge Road. Wharves and warehouses were constructed at Fort Schlosser, and mills operated above the American Falls. Black Rock became an important shipbuilding and forwarding center and, with harbor and ferry services to Fort Erie, was expected to remain a major port at the western end of Lake Erie. Sailing vessels were constructed there, as was the first steamboat to sail on Lake Erie, the *Walk-in-the-Water* with side paddle wheels, in 1818.

Buffalo soon outgrew both Waterloo, the merchant center next to Old Fort Erie, and Niagara.[78] Over one hundred houses had been constructed in the city by 1815 and, when incorporated as a village in 1816, Buffalo contained more than one thousand inhabitants. The Bank of Niagara was established in 1816, and a courthouse built. The turnpike between Albany and Buffalo was completed in 1817. The village with its Eagle and other taverns became important as a stagecoach terminal. A theater faced the tavern, and an agricultural fair was organized in 1819. Buffalo grew rapidly into a commercial center of importance that housed a population of over two thousand by 1820.[79]

The population between Tonawanda and Cattaraugus Creeks expanded from six thousand to nearly eleven thousand between 1814 and 1820. In 1821 Niagara County was divided into two units separated by Tonawanda Creek. The northern county retained the historic name Niagara, and the southern with Buffalo still the county seat was named Erie County. Lewiston was designated the temporary seat for Niagara County, and the courts were held there until 1823. The four towns of Niagara County in 1816 had increased to ten by 1824, and in Erie County eleven towns were created within a decade of the War of 1812,[80] an administrative growth that reflects the expansion of settlement and population and the emergence of local political interests.

NOTES

1. T. Bigelow, *Journal of a Tour to Niagara Falls in the Year 1805* (Boston: John Wilson, 1876), p. 55.

2. *Report of the International Waterways Commission upon the International Boundary between the Dominion of Canada and the United States through the St. Lawrence River and Great Lakes* (Ottawa: Government Printing Bureau, 1916), pp. 9–10.

3. J. Delafield, 21 November 1821, in *The Unfortified Boundary*, ed. R. McElroy and T. Riggs (New York: Delafield Family Association, 1943), p. 50.

4. A. L. Burt, *The United States, Great Britain and North America* (New York: Russell and Russell, 1961), pp. 16–105.

5. D. Creighton, *The Empire of the St. Lawrence* (Toronto: Macmillan, 1970), p. 87; first published as *The Commercial Empire of the St. Lawrence, 1760–1850* (Toronto: Macmillan, 1937).

6. R. S. Allen, "A History of Fort George, Upper Canada," in *Canadian Historical Sites: Occasional Papers in Archaeology and History*, no. 11 (Ottawa: National and Historic Parks Branch, Department of Indian Affairs and Northern Development, 1974), p. 63.

7. R. S. Allen, "The British Indian Department and the Frontier in North America, 1755–1830," *Canadian Historical Sites: Occasional Papers in Archaeology and History*, no. 14 (Ottawa: National Historic Parks and Sites Branch, Parks Canada, 1975), pp. 43–44.

8. Quoted in ibid., p. 42.

9. E. A. Cruickshank, *The Story of Butler's Rangers and the Settlement of Niagara* (Welland: Lundy's Lane Historical Society, 1893; reprint, Niagara Falls, Ont., 1975).

10. G. Beaver, *A View from an Indian Reserve: Historical Perspective and a Personal View from an Indian Reserve*, Six Nations (Ohsweken) (Brantford: Brant Historical Society, Brant Historical Publications, 1993); E. Cork, *The Worst of the Bargain* (San Jacinto, Calif.: Foundation for Social Research, 1962); and B. Hill et al., *Six Nations Reserve* (Markham, Ont.: Fitzhenry & Whiteside, 1987).

11. Six Nations Council, *Six Nations of the Grand River: Outstanding Financial and Land Issues* (Ohsweken, Ont.: Land Claims Office, 2000).

12. *Indian Treaties and Surrenders: From 1680 to 1890* (Ottawa: King's Printer, 1905), 1:5.

13. M. Trudel, *Atlas de la Novelle France* (Quebec: Les Presses de l'Université Laval, 1968).

14. A. F. Burghardt, "The Origin and Devel-

opment of the Road Network of the Niagara Peninsula," *Annals of the Association of American Geographers* 59 (1969): 423; and for the portage, T. Vinal, *Niagara Portage: From Past to Present* (Buffalo, N.Y.: Henry Stewart, 1955).

15. J. N. Jackson, *St. Catharines, Ontario: Its Early Years* (Belleville, Ont.: Mika, 1976), pp. 47–53.

16. L. R. Grol, *Tales from the Niagara Peninsula and Lelawaha: A Legend of the Maid of the Mist* (Fonthill: Fonthill Studio, 1975). For Indian stories, myths, and pictographs, see the series of Iroquois Reprints, *Iroqrafts* (Ohsweken, Ont.), including Tehanetorens, *Tales of the Iroquois*, vols. 1–2 (1992); E. A. Smith, *Myths of the Iroquois* (1994); and J. J. Cornplanter, *Legends of the Longhouse* (1992).

17. F. Houghton, "Indian Village, Camp and Burial Sites on the Niagara Frontier," *Bulletin of the Buffalo Society of Natural Sciences* 9, no. 3 (1909): 367–74. See J. Tydjord, *Indian Place Names: Their Origin, Evolution and Meanings* (Norman: University of Oklahoma Press, 1968); W. B. Hamilton, *The Macmillan Book of Canadian Place Names* (Toronto: Macmillan of Canada, 1978); T. H. McKaig, "Place Names of Western New York," *Niagara Frontier* 1 (1953): 62–63; and J. N. Jackson, *Names at Niagara* (St. Catharines: Vanwell Publishing, 1989).

18. Jennings, *Invasion of America*, pp. 173–74.

19. Deputy Surveyor–General Collin's Report, 6 December 1788, in *Third Report of the Bureau of Archives for the Province of Ontario* (Toronto: King's Printer, 1960), p. 355. A chain, a surveyor's measuring instrument, becomes the standard width for roads.

20. "Tender" by Robert Hamilton et al., in E. Green, *The Niagara Portage Road*, Ontario Historical Society: Papers and Records 23 (1926): 266.

21. R. S. Allen, "A History of Fort George, Upper Canada," in *Canadian Historic Sites: Occasional Papers in Archaeology and History*, no. 11 (Ottawa: National and Historic Parks Branch, Department of Indian Affairs and Northern Development, 1974).

22. W. H. Breithhaupt, "First Settlements of Pennsylvania Mennonites in Upper Canada," *Ontario Historical Society: Papers and Records* 23 (1926): 8–10; M. Dunham, *The Trail of the Conestoga* (Toronto: McClelland and Stewart, 1927); R. J. Foley, *Niagara Story*, vol. 1 (Niagara Falls, Ont.: Haunted Press, 1994); W. Kirby, *Annals of Niagara* (Toronto: Macmillan, 1927), p. 86; W. Koene, *Loyal She Remains: A Pictorial History of Ontario*, (Toronto: United Empire Loyalists Association of Ontario, 1984); C. E. Reaman, *The Trail of the Black Walnut* (Toronto: McClelland and Stewart, 1957); J. J. Talman, "The United Empire Loyalists," in *Profiles of a Province* (Toronto: Ontario Historical Society, 1967), pp. 34–42; and J. T. Waugh, *The United Empire Loyalists: With Particular Reference to the Niagara Frontier*, University of Buffalo Studies, Monographs in History, vol. 4, no. 3 (1925).

23. R. S. Allen, "The British Indian Department and the Frontier in North America, 1755–1830," in *Canadian Historical Sites: Occa-*

sional Papers in Archaeology and History, no. 14 (Ottawa: National Historic Parks and Sites Branch, Parks Canada, 1975), pp. 63–64; and C. M. Johnston, ed., *The Valley of the Six Nations: A Collection of Documents on the Indian Lands of the Grand River* (Toronto: Champlain Society, 1964); and "United Empire Loyalists: Enquiry into the Losses and Services in Consequence of Their Loyalty," *Second Report of the Bureau of Archives for the Province of Ontario* (Toronto: King's Printer, 1905), pp. 190–91, 982.

24. E. A. Talbot, *Five Years' Residence in the Canadas* (London: Longman, Hunt and Rees, 1824), 1:159. See also G. Reaman, *A History of Agriculture in Ontario*, vols. 1–2 (Toronto: Saunders, 1970); E. C. Guillet, *Pioneer Days in Upper Canada* (Toronto: University of Toronto Press, 1964); and G. P. de T. Glazebrook, *Life in Ontario: A Social History* (Toronto: University of Toronto Press, 1968). See also R. L. Jones, *History of Agriculture in Ontario, 1613–1880* (Toronto: University of Toronto Press, 1946), pp. 18–19.

25. H. V. Nelles, "Loyalism and Local Power," *Ontario History* 58 (1966): 99–100.

26. Land Board Nassau, 29 October 1789, *Third Report of the Bureau of Archives*, pp. 295–96.

27. D. G. Hill, *The Freedom-Seekers: Blacks in Early Canada* (Agincourt, Ont.: Book Society of Canada, 1981), pp. 16–17, 46–48, 114–18.

28. Q. Innis, ed., *Mrs. Simcoe's Diary* (Toronto: Macmillan, 1965), p. 81; and letter from Robert Hamilton to John Askin, 20 October 1799, in E. A. Cruikshank, "Some Letters of Robert Nichol," *Ontario Historical Society, Papers and Records* 20 (1923): 47; and *Correspondence of Lieut-Governor John Graves Simcoe* (Toronto: Ontario Historical Society, 1923–1931), 4:352.

29. L. F. Gates, *Land Policies of Upper Canada* (Toronto: University of Toronto Press, 1968); and G. C. Patterson, "Land Settlement in Upper Canada, 1783–1843," *Sixteenth Report of the Department of Archives for the Province of Ontario* (Toronto: King's Printer, 1921). See J. L. Ladell, *They Left Their Mark: Surveyors and Their Role in the Settlement of Ontario* (Toronto: Dundurn Press, 1993).

30. J. N. Jackson, *St. Catharines, Ontario: Its Early Years* (Belleville, Ont.: Mika, 1976), pp. 61–122.

31. W. F. Weaver, *Crown Surveys in Ontario* (Toronto: Ontario Department of Lands and Forests, 1968), p. 16.

32. R. L. Gentilcore, "Lines on the Land: Crown Surveys and Settlement in Upper Canada," *Ontario History* 61 (1969): 57.

33. M. L. Hansen, *The Mingling of the Canadian and American People*, vol. 1: *Historical* (New Haven, Conn.: Yale University Press, 1940), p. 90.

34. F. Landon, *Western Ontario and the American Frontier* (Toronto: Ryerson, 1941), p. 19; and Hansen, *The Mingling of the Canadian and American People*.

35. Land Board, Nassau, 21 June 1790, in *Third Report of the Bureau of Archives*, p. 299.

36. Ibid., 25 August 1790, p. 300.

37. A. Campbell, "Reminiscences of Niagara," *Niagara Historical Society*, Publications, no.

11 (1914): 40. Early days are discussed in F. V. Whitfield, "The Initial Settling of Niagara-on-the-Lake, 1778–1784," *Ontario History* 83, no. 1 (1991): 3–22. See J. Ormsby, "Building a Town: Plans, Surveys, and the Early Years of Niagara-on-the-Lake," in *The Capital Years: Niagara-on-the-Lake, 1792–1796*, ed. R. Merritt, N. Butler, and M. Power (Toronto: Dundurn Press, 1991), pp. 15–45.

38. P. Stokes, *Old Niagara-on-the-Lake* (Toronto: University of Toronto Press, 1971), p. 8.

39. Cruikshank, *The Correspondence of Lieutenant Governor John Graves Simcoe*; and E. A. Cruikshank, ed., "Records of Niagara," *Niagara Historical Society Publications*, nos. 38–44 (1927–1939).

40. D. Fleming, *A History of the Town of Niagara-on-the-Lake (1791–1970)* (Ottawa: National Historic Sites Services, Parks Canada, 1971).

41. V. Cornish, *The Great Capitals: A Historical Geography* (London: Methuen, 1923), pp. vii–ix.

42. I. Weld, *Travels through the States of North America and the Province of Upper Canada* (London: Stockdale, 1799), pp. 296–97. For details of buildings see F. B. LeDoux, *Sketches of Niagara* (St. Catharines: Peninsula Press, 1955); and J. L. Field, *Niagara-on-the-Lake Guidebook* (Niagara Falls, Ont.: Renown Printing, 1984).

43. La Rochefoucault-Liancourt, "Travels in Canada, 1795," in *Thirteenth Report of the Bureau of Archives*, pp. 23–25.

44. J. C. Ogden, *A Tour through Upper and Lower Canada* (Litchfield, 1799), p. 100.

45. G. Heriot, *Travels through the Canadas* (London: Phillips, 1807), pp. 150–56, 166, 174–75; Heriot was Deputy Postmaster-General of British North America.

46. Jackson, *St. Catharines, Ontario*, pp. 123–34; and J. N. Jackson and S. M. Wilson, *St. Catharines: Canada's Canal City* (St. Catharines: The Standard, 1992), pp. 15–35.

47. P. D. Evans, *The Holland Land Company*, Publications, vol. 28 (Buffalo, N.Y.: Buffalo Historical Society, 1924), pp. 215–328. For original documents see R. W. Bingham, *Holland Land Company's Papers: Reports of Joseph Ellicott*, Publications, vols. 32–33 (Buffalo, N.Y.: Buffalo Historical Society). Prime sources include O. Turner, *Pioneer History of the Holland Purchase* (Buffalo, N.Y.: Jewett, Thomas, 1849); R. W. Bingham, *The Cradle of the Queen City*, Publications, vol. 31 (Buffalo, N.Y.: Buffalo Historical Society, 1931); and W. Chazanoff, *Joseph Ellicott and the Holland Land Company* (Syracuse, N.Y: n.p., 1970). See also J. L. Babcock, *Joseph Ellicott: The Founder of Buffalo* (Batavia, N.Y.: Batavia Times, 1934); and W. K. Wyckoff, *Joseph Ellicott and the Western New York Frontier* (Ph.D. diss., Syracuse University, 1982). See also R. Horsman, *Expansion and American Indian Policy, 1783–1812* (East Lansing: Michigan State University Press, 1967); F. Houghton, "History of the Buffalo Creek Reservation," Publications, vol. 24 (Buffalo, N.Y.: Buffalo Historical Society, 1920), pp. 3–181; C. F. Milliken, "The Holland Purchase," in *History of the Genesee Country*, ed. L. R. Doty (Chicago: S. J. Clarke, 1925), 1:389–96; A. C. Parker, "The White Man

Takes Possession," in Doty, *History of the Genesee County*, 1:268; and R. W. Silsby, "The Holland Land Company in Western New York," *Adventures in Western New York History*, vol. 8 (Buffalo, N.Y.: Buffalo and Erie County Historical Society, 1961).

48. D. W. Meinig, "Geography of Expansion, 1785–1855," in *Geography of New York State*, ed. J. H. Thompson (Syracuse, N.Y.: Syracuse University Press, 1966), p. 151.

49. O. Lindberg, "Transit Road," *Niagara Frontier* 11 (1964): 86–88.

50. Evans, *The Holland Land Company*, pp. 201–203. The process of clearing the land and creating a farm is examined in C. Johnson, *Centennial History of Erie County* (Buffalo, N.Y.: Mathews and Warren, 1876).

51. Evans, *The Holland Land Company*, pp. 223–24.

52. "Report of Joseph Ellicott for the Year 1801," in *Holland Land Company's Papers*, vol. 1, p. 171.

53. Ibid., p. 145.

54. Ibid., pp. 142–43. See W. Chazanoff, "Politics, Roads and Taxes in the Holland Purchase," *Niagara Frontier* 5 (1958–1959): 57–65, 410.

55. J. Ellicott, "Report and Account of the Survey of the Genesee," *Holland Land Company's Papers*, vol. 1, pp. 104–106.

56. "Joseph Ellicott to Theophile Cazenove," 25 September 1798, in Babcock, *Joseph Ellicott*, p. 44.

57. A. Heckscher, *Open Spaces: The Life of American Cities* (New York: Harper and Row, 1977), p. 143.

58. "Report of Joseph Ellicott for the Year 1810," *Holland Land Company's Papers*, vol. 1, p. 48.

59. H. Kimball, *Lewiston Sesquicentennial 1822–1972* (Lewiston, N.Y.: Sesquicentennial Committee, 1972), p. 20; and M. D. Robson, *Under the Mountain* (Buffalo, N.Y.: Henry Stewart, 1958), pp. 63–64.

60. J. B. Mansfield, *History of the Great Lakes*, vol. 1 (Chicago: J. H. Beers, 1899); reprinted as *The Saga of the Great Lakes* (Toronto: Coles, 1980), p. 123.

61. Turner, *Pioneer History of the Holland Purchase*, pp. 562–66.

62. With conflicting Canadian and American interpretations, many publications refer to this war. P. Berton, *The Invasion of Canada 1812–1813* (Toronto: McClelland and Stewart, 1980) and *Flames Across the Border* (Toronto: McClelland and Stewart, 1981); and E. A. Cruikshank, *The Documentary History of the Campaign on the Niagara Frontier in 1814, Parts I and II*, 9 vols. (Niagara Falls, Ont.: Lundy's Lane Historical Society, 1896–1908). A documentary collection is F. C. Drake and W. B. Turner, *The War of 1812 in the Niagara Peninsula* (St. Catharines: History Department, Brock University, 1981). American interpretations include W. Dorsheimer, "Buffalo during the War of 1812," Publications, vol. 1 (Buffalo, N.Y.: Buffalo Historical Society, 1879), pp. 185–211; "Papers Relating to the War of 1812 on the Niagara Frontier," Publications, vol. 5 (Buf-

falo, N.Y.: Buffalo Historical Society, 1902), pp. 21–111; L. Babcock, *The War of 1812 on the Niagara Frontier* (Buffalo, N.Y.: Buffalo Historical Society, 1927); R. A. Bowler, *War Along the Niagara Frontier: Essays on the War of 1812 and Its Legacy* (Youngstown, N.Y.: Old Fort Niagara Association, 1997). The Battle of Beaverdams involved over 465 Natives, many from the Grand River reservation, and several chiefs and warriors were killed; D. K. Dewar, *The Battle of Beaverdams: The Story of Thorold's Battle in the War of 1812* (Thorold: Slabtown Press, 1996), p. 50; and P. Katcher, *The American War: 1812–1814* (New York: Hippocrene Books, 1974).

63. W. B. Turner, *Field Trip Guide: The War of 1812 Battlefield Sites*, Eighth Annual Niagara Peninsula History Conference, Brock University, St. Catharines, 1986. See also E. Cruikshank, *The Battle of Lundy's Lane, 25th July, 1914: A Historical Study*, 3d ed. (Welland: The Tribune, 1893); C. K. Duquemin, *The Driver's Guide to the Niagara Battlefield in the War of 1812* (St. Catharines: Norman Enterprises, 1994); R. J. Foley, *The War of 1812: Niagara Story*, vol. 2 (Niagara Falls, Ont.: Haunted Press, 1994); E. Graves, *Where Right and Glory Meet: The Battle of Lundy's Lane, 1814* (Toronto: Robin Brass, 1977); and W. B. Turner, *The War of 1812: The War That Both Sides Won* (Toronto: Dundurn Press, 1990). A chronological military history of the Niagara Frontier up to the Fenian invasion of Canada in 1866 is R. Higgins, *The Niagara Frontier: Its Place in U.S. and Canadian History* (Kitchener, Ont.: Upney Editions, 1996).

64. Kirby, *Annals of Niagara*, p. 228. See also E. A. Cruikshank, "Post-War Discontent at Niagara in 1818," *Ontario Historical Society, Papers and Records* 29 (1933): 14–15; A. E. Coombs, *History of the Niagara Peninsula* (Toronto: Historical Publishers Association, 1930), p. 40.

65. Allen, "A History of Fort George," p. 81.

66. J. Burt, *The United States, Great Britain and British North America* (New York: Russell and Russell, 1961), pp. 351–63.

67. R. K. T. Symons, "The Brock Monument and a Visitor Book, 1829 and 1830," *Ontario Historical Society, Paper and Records* 29 (1933): 72. See D. J. Goodspeed, *The Good Soldier: The Story of Isaac Brock* (Toronto: Macmillan of Canada, 1964).

68. Laura Secord in 1813 walked some 30 kilometers (20 miles) from Queenston to DeCew Falls to warn a British outpost of an intended American attack. Jingoistic poems recall this arduous walk; see S. A. Curzon, "Laura Secord, the Heroine of 1812," in *Women Pioneers*, ed. A. Wagner (Toronto: Canadian Theatre Review Publications, 1932).

69. A. Short, "The Economic Effect of the War of 1812 on Upper Canada," in Morris Zaslow, *The Defended Border: Upper Canada and the War of 1812* (Toronto: Macmillan, 1964), p. 301.

70. Talbot, *Five Years' Residence in the Canadas*, p. 169. As Talbot owned extensive land on the north shore of Lake Erie, this perspective could be biased; he might have had a vested interest in denigrating the Niagara Frontier.

71. A. H. Bonnycastle, *Sketch of the Isthmus or*

Belt of Niagara Showing the Situation of the New Fortress (Quebec: Engineer's Office, 1827).

72. R. H. Stotherd et al., *Niagara Frontier*, Plan 2 (Southampton, England: Topographic Department of the War Office, 1865); reproduced in part by the Association of Canadian Map Libraries, Facsimile 21.

73. Fleming, *A History of the Town of Niagara-on-the-Lake*, p. 40.

74. Kirby, *Annals of Niagara*, p. 261.

75. See R. Gourlay, *Statistical Account of Upper Canada*, 2 vols. (London: Simpkin and Marshall, 1822); Cruikshank, "Post-War Discontent at Niagara," pp. 14–45; and R. L. Gentilcore, "The Niagara District of Robert Gourlay," *Ontario History* 54 (1962): 228–36.

76. W. Barlow and D. O. Powell, "A Physician's Journey through Western New York and Upper Canada in 1815," *Niagara Frontier* 25 (1978): 89–90. The physician was Malthus A. Ward.

77. McElroy and Riggs, *The Unfortified Boundary*, pp. 164–66.

78. Ibid., pp. 165–66.

79. J. T. Horton, "Old Erie—The Growth of an American Community," in J. T. Horton et al., *History of Northwestern New York* (New York: Lewis Historical Publishing, 1947), 1:56.

80. Doty, *History of Genesee County*, 2:1152, 1414–16; and L. L. Pechaman, *Niagara County and Its Towns* (Lockport, N.Y.: Niagara County Historical Society, 1958).

CHAPTER THREE

TWO CANALS TRANSFORM THE PIONEER LANDSCAPE

During the 1820s, two canals drastically remodeled the landscape with its advancing tide of settlement and industrial advance in towns and villages on both sides at the Frontier. The Welland Canal transferred the emphasis of Canadian activity inland from the Niagara River to a line of settlement that developed where waterpower was available between Port Dalhousie and Port Colborne. The Erie Canal fostered the primacy of Buffalo and created Lockport and Tonawanda as manufacturing towns. Cultural distinctiveness was introduced as immigration from abroad added to the changing patterns of landscape on both Frontiers.

THE ERIE CANAL

The Louisiana Purchase of 1803 required a cheap mode of transportation to ship crops and raw materials from the West to the Atlantic, the traditional route via the Mississippi River to New Orleans being too expensive. The growing settlements of the Holland Land Company greatly increased this demand for an Atlantic seaboard outlet.[1] The American Frontier was isolated from the expanding concentration of settlement in the Hudson Valley. The overland journey was long and tedious, and costs were high for the export of agricultural products and the import of supplies.

Among the prior alternatives at the Frontier, an early possibility was to route the

Table 3A
The Welland and Erie Canals: Changing Dimensions through Time

Date	Event	Depth of Channel in Feet — Welland Canal	Erie Canal	Size of Locks in Feet — Welland Canal Length	Width	Erie Canal Length	Width	Approximate Cargo of Vessels in Tons — Welland Canal	Erie Canal
1817	Start of Erie Canal Works at Rome								
1824	Start of Welland Canal Works at Allanburgh								
1824	Completion of the First Erie Canal		4			90	15		75
1828	Completion of the Oswego Canal from Syracuse to Lake Ontario								
1829	Opening of the First Welland Canal (Lake Ontario to the Niagara River)	8		110	22			165	
1833	Completion of the First Welland Canal (Lake Ontario to Lake Erie)								
1845	Completion of the Second Welland Canal	10		150	26.5			750	
1862	Completion of the Enlarged Erie Canal		7			110	18		240
1887	Completion of the Third Welland Canal	14		270	45			2700	
1918	Completion of the New York State Barge Canal		14			300	43.5		3600
1932	Completion of the Fourth Welland Canal	25		859	80			25,000	
1959	Fourth Welland Canal deepened to accord with the standards of the St. Lawrence Seaway	27.0						29,500	
1973	Welland Canal Bypass at Welland opened	30.0							

(Prepared by the Department of Geography, Brock University)

intended canal from the Upper River around the Falls into the Lower River at Lewiston, and another was to use Eighteen Mile Creek at Lockport to avoid the Falls. Either would have drastically changed the character of the Frontier, and both were discarded as American trade might then be diverted via Lake Ontario to the British port of Montreal. Authorized in 1817, construction of the later approved route for the Erie Canal began that year in Rome, and sections opened successively as canal construction moved west (fig.

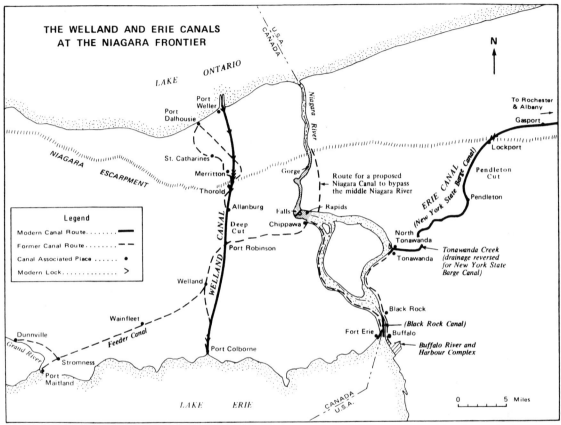

Fig. 3.1. The Erie Canal (1825) and then the Welland Canal (1829) transformed the pioneer landscapes on both sides at the Niagara River. Both canals were highly successful commercially, and both introduced new lines of settlement along their respective routes. (Prepared by the Department of Geography, Brock University)

3.1).[2] At Lockport the route was then changed from the western to the eastern spillway of former Lake Tonawanda. Here a double set of five stone locks were constructed, one for upbound and one for downbound vessels. The lift of 19.8 meters (65 feet), hewn from the solid rock, brought the canal down to the 152.4-meter (500-foot) level at the base of the

Niagara Escarpment, which was followed east to Rochester. The gates opened directly into the next lock, whereas all other locks on the canal were single structures. South of Lockport, with depth influencing the location of the port or ports at the Lake Erie entrance to the Niagara River, over one thousand men excavated the vertical-sided Pendleton Cut, over 8.2 meters (27 feet) wide and 9.1 meters (30 feet) deep through hard dolomitic limestone of the Niagara Escarpment; a towpath was then carved into its side.

In the west where the canal followed the lower Tonawanda Creek, a dam raised the height of the river by 1.5 meters (5 feet), the flow of the creek was reversed to supply water to the canal, and a lock cut through the dam allowed boats to pass into the harbor on the Niagara River. South from Tonawanda the canal, constructed along the bank next to the Niagara River, had a slight northward slope of 2.5 centimeters per 1.6 kilometers (one inch per mile). It was also deeper and wider than the standard canal dimensions, which allowed the canal to serve as both a water conduit and to carry barge traffic. A towpath separated the canal from the Niagara River.

A major port was anticipated at the western end of the canal where canal barges would link with shipping on Lake Erie. Three sites were considered. The village of Black Rock, then the chief lake port in Western New York, had been declared a port of entry in 1811, and with its shipyard and warehouses provided a safe natural harbor at the mouth of Scajaquada Creek, protected from westerly winds by Bird and Squaw Islands. The problem of upstream navigation to Lake Erie against the powerful current in the Niagara River could be offset by constructing a dam across the channel between the mainland and Squaw Island, and an embankment from Squaw Island to Lake Erie, which would both raise the level of water in that section to that of Lake Erie and provide space for a large harbor.

The second possibility, Buffalo, had been an official port of entry since 1805. Here the water on Lake Erie was 1.2 meters (4 feet) higher than at Black Rock, a height that would save on costly excavation to and at the Pendleton Cut, but required an extra length of canal. Winter ice, lake storms, and a sandbar across the mouth of the Buffalo River were potential problems, but the Holland Land Company had provided lands for the development of the canal under the condition that the Buffalo River be used as the harbor on Lake Erie. To improve this harbor, the Buffalo River was dredged, a channel was cut through the sandbar, and a pier was built to prevent further silting, projects that were

It could have been otherwise. Had no boundary intervened, a canal route as part of the Erie Canal system might have interlinked the Upper Niagara River past the Falls on the American bank to cross the Niagara Escarpment and then join the Lower Niagara River close to the square at Lewiston. (Smithsonian Institution, Washington, D.C.)

completed under the incisive leadership of Samuel Wilkeson.[3]

A third possibility, to use the Niagara River, would have required substantial deepening of the cut at Pendleton, and the problem presented by upstream access to Lake Erie against the current had still to be overcome. To resolve these difficulties the Canal Commissioners decided to have three western harbors: at Black Rock, Buffalo, and the Niagara River.[4] The canal would extend along the bank of the Niagara River to Buffalo as the terminal and as the source of its water supply, but provision would also be made for boats to be locked into the Niagara River at both Tonawanda and Black Rock. This solution spread the potential for economic development along the shoreline of the Niagara River, but Buffalo soon became the dominant center because of its situation at the eastern end of Lake Erie and the height factor relative to the canal crossing the escarpment at Pendleton-Lockport.

Canal construction had reached Lockport by 1823, and the last section of canal opened between Buffalo and Lockport in 1825. The Erie Canal was then 584.2 kilometers (363 miles) long, 1.2 meters (4 feet) deep, 8.5 meters (28 feet) wide at the bottom, and slightly over 12.2 meters (40 feet) wide at the top. Boats of 27.2-tonne (30-ton) capacity were towed by horse or mule from a towpath beside the canal. Eighty-three stone locks with wooden gates ascended 174.7 meters (573 feet). Buffalo and Lake Erie were connected with Albany at 0.3 meters (1 foot) above sea level, and the route then used the navigable Hudson River to New York City. The traditional Canadian route from the interior to Montreal and the St. Lawrence was bypassed by the Erie Canal as the new, vital funnel of communication opened between inland North America and the Atlantic Ocean for passengers, freight, and mail. Known as "Clinton's Ditch" or the "Grand Canal," the canal and its slow-moving barge traffic were crossed by numerous low bridges that carried roads and connected farmers' fields.

The Erie Canal was an immediate success. Transportation costs fell dramatically, and travel time between Buffalo and New York City was reduced from twenty to six days. "Lumber, staves, ashes, grain, and vegetables, previously unmarketable except by way of the St. Lawrence, were now profitably transported to the markets of the Atlantic Seaboard. . . . Farms bordering the route doubled and quadrupled in value; undeveloped areas of either side blossomed, . . . and towns and villages sprang up along the whole line of the canal."[5] More passengers and freight were carried every year, and boom port towns were created. Known as "the Mother of Cities," new and expanded towns created along its route included Lockport, Pendleton, the Tonawandas, Black Rock, and Buffalo on the American Frontier.

The canal system expanded rapidly from a single trunk line to a pattern with short links as feeder canals were added. Although an American canal bypassing the Falls to Lake Ontario had previously been rejected, the growing commercial strength of New York City now made a route via Lake Ontario feasible. In 1828 after the Oswego Canal opened between the Erie Canal at Syracuse and Lake Ontario, trade passing through the Welland Canal could be diverted via this canal to the eastern section of the Erie Canal for Albany and the east coast.

In 1835 the New York legislature authorized enlargement of the Erie Canal so that boats of 217.7 tonnes (240 tons) could be accommodated. Work began in 1836 to increase the depth to 2.1 meters (7 feet), the surface width to 21.3 meters (70 feet), to raise bridges to 3.4 meters (11 feet), and to provide double locks of greater size, 33.5 by 5.5 meters (110 feet by 18 feet),[6] which reduced the length of the canal and the number of locks. A double set of five locks was completed at Lockport in 1847, but the full reconstruction of the Erie Canal was not completed until 1862 (Table 3A). There were many problems and delays, and also severe and growing competition from the advancing railway network.

THE WELLAND CANAL

The Canadian Frontier also required access to the Eastern Seaboard. As Aitken (1954) has stated: "The Erie Canal, finally completed in 1825, succeeded brilliantly in achieving what military force [the War of 1812] had failed to achieve: the destruction of Montreal's commercial empire around the lower lakes. No longer was western New York tributary to Montreal. . . . No longer did the steadily expanding exports of the Midwest have to find their way over the Niagara portage. . . . Montreal's commercial supremacy . . . was at an end."[7]

An independent canal would retain British links with Montreal.[8] This project of meeting the challenge posed by the Erie Canal began fortuitously when William Hamilton Merritt, who owned a mill on Twelve Mile Creek in St. Catharines, had insufficient water in summer to drive his machinery. In 1818 he proposed that water be diverted north from the Welland River over intervening low moraines to supply his mill.[9]

The Feeder Canal, cut across the Wainfleet Marsh from Welland to Dunnville in 1829, drained the neighboring land and promoted agricultural development. (John N. Jackson [both])

The Welland Canal Company was incorporated in 1824, work then started, but plans had to be changed considerably during the course of construction.[10]

Intended was a tunnel through the moraines south of the Niagara Escarpment, but the outcome was a substantial trench known as the "Deep Cut," some 3 kilometers (2 miles) long and 21.3 meters (70 feet) deep between Allanburg and Port Robinson. The difficulty of excavating through heavy clay and quicksand, and the collapse of the banks also caused the Welland Canal Company to change its intended source of water supply from the Welland River to the Grand River. This new route required a dam across the Grand River at Dunnville, 8 kilometers (5 miles) upstream from Lake Erie; a Feeder Canal across Wainfleet Marsh for 43.5 kilometers (27 miles) to supply the canal level at Port Robinson; and an aqueduct to carry this Feeder Canal across the Welland River at the center of present-day Welland. These developments, like the Pendleton Cut and the locks at Lockport on the Erie Canal, were amazing feats of engineering for the period. The name Welland Canal survives from this period, even though the canal never tapped the Welland River as was the original intention.

As the channel through the moraines was now in a cutting rather than a tunnel, larger vessels could pass through the Deep Cut. This meant that the idea of an incline railway across the escarpment at DeCew Falls was abandoned, and an alternative canal route chosen from various options was to follow Dick's Creek east from St. Catharines. A series of locks was constructed across both the gently rising Ontario Plain and the more abrupt slopes of the Niagara Escarpment. Through this change of plan, Thorold and Merritton became canal towns with an abundant supply of water for industrial purposes; previously, urban-industrial development might have been expected at DeCew Falls and along Twelve Mile Creek. The analogy of change in the location of the locks at Lockport might be noted.

The First Welland Canal opened in 1829.[11] It was deeper, wider, with larger locks, and had a greater cargo capacity for its vessels than the Erie Canal (Table 3A). After an entry lock on Lake Ontario at Port Dalhousie, the canal followed the valley of Twelve Mile Creek south to St. Catharines, then used Dick's Creek with twelve locks, intervening ponds, and a canal cut to the base of the Niagara Escarpment. This slope was then climbed by a channel with seventeen locks parallel to the brow of the escarpment, with passing basins between the locks and water supply reservoirs feeding these basins.

Four locks then took the channel through the Deep Cut to Port Robinson. Here, the main route was downstream along the Welland River to Chippawa where a canal cut (fig. 3.2) enabled vessels to turn into the Niagara River and then be towed upstream to Fort Erie or Buffalo. This towpath later became the route for the Niagara River Parkway.

The wooden locks had a length of 33.5 meters (110 feet) between the gates and a width of 6.7 meters (22 feet). The depth of water over the sills was 2.4 meters (8 feet), but a vessel drawing 1.2 meters (4 feet) could cross the aqueduct at Welland and then transit the Feeder Canal to the Grand River at Dunnville. It must be stressed that the canal did not connect with the Lower Niagara River, the greatest potential harbor on Lake Ontario, even though engineering plans had established this possibility. Also, because the Welland Canal was for sailing vessels whereas the Erie Canal was for barges with low superstructures, bridges crossed the Welland Canal with less frequency and only where main roads existed. They were also swing bridges to enable the passage of tall-masted vessels, thereby creating significant differences in canalscape along the two canal systems.

As the southern length of the First Welland Canal via the Welland and Niagara Rivers to Chippawa and Fort Erie was slow and circuitous for navigation between Lake Ontario and Lake Erie, a more direct alignment was required. This became the Feeder Canal between Port Robinson and Welland, and then a new channel from south of Welland direct to Lake Erie was constructed (fig. 3.1). Opened in 1833, the new southern entrance to the canal at Port Colborne had the advantages of a longer navigation season than the entrance into the Erie Canal at Buffalo and avoided the ice that clogged the Niagara River and eastern Lake Erie in spring. The improved First Welland Canal now had three southern points of entry: from the Niagara River at Chippawa via the Lower Welland River; from Port Colborne, the main line of the canal for Lake Erie commerce; and from the Grand River at Dunnville, which tapped the extensive hinterland of that river.

The line of the improved First Welland Canal soon became inadequate. The private Welland Canal Company had more limited financial resources than the Erie Canal as a state enterprise. The decaying wooden locks and slumping banks delayed ships. In 1836 the canal was closed for half the season. Reconstruction and upgrading were required and in 1841, when the new Province of Canada was formed, the canal was placed under the direction of its Board of Works and redesigned.

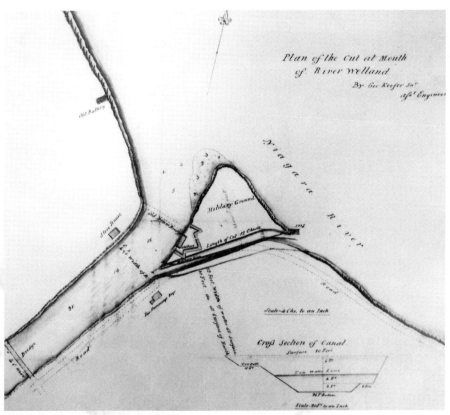

Plan of the Cut at Mouth
of River Welland

By Geo Keefer Junr
Asst Engineer

Cross Section of Canal
Surface 70 Feet

Scale 70 F. to an Inch

Fig. 3.2. To prevent vessels from being swept over the Falls when rounding the headland between the Welland and the Niagara Rivers, a canal was cut across the former military land at Fort Chippawa. The mouth of the Welland River was later closed, and the direction of flow in the canal cut reversed for the Lower Welland River to serve as a conduit to the Queenston Power Plant. This scene has become Kingsbridge Park managed by the Niagara Parks Commission, with historical plaques describing the varied history of this significant site. (*Plan of the Cut at Mouth of River Welland*, 1829, by Geo. Keefer Jr., assistant engineer [Welland Canal Company], in the National Archives [Ottawa], Cartographic Archives and Architectural Drawings Division, NMC 5236.)

The Second Welland Canal, completed in 1845, had cut twenty-seven stone locks with a depth of 2.7 meters (9 feet). This depth permitted the transit of vessels with a cargo capacity of 680.4 tonnes (750 tons). The enlarged channel between Lake Erie and Lake Ontario followed virtually the same route.

During the construction period at the southern end, the Feeder Canal to Dunnville and a new canal cut between Stromness and Port Maitland on Lake Erie were used. While the channel of the First Canal between Welland and Port Colborne was excavated, the northern alignment of the First

The route, locks, and the water system of the Second Welland Canal crossed the Niagara Escarpment at Merritton by a gradual ascent parallel to the contours, and in turn attracted lockkeepers' cottages that are among the first provision of public housing in Canada. (John N. Jackson)

Canal was straightened in several places, and across the Niagara Escarpment a new set of locks was constructed to the west of the earlier channel, which was then abandoned and filled. A dam across Twelve Mile Creek at Port Dalhousie created Martindale Pond, which became the Upper Harbour separated from the Lower Harbour next to Lake Ontario by a lock. At the southern end of the canal, Port Colborne was introduced to the urban landscape. The improved Welland Canal could now handle vessels three times larger than on the improved Erie system (Table 3A).

Traffic through the original and improved Welland Canal increased rapidly through the 1830s.[12] Tolls established in 1829 were at first low and experimental, as the canal had to compete with both the Erie Canal and the Niagara Portage. Rates raised at the end of 1835 indicated the canal's success. Tolls favored the movement of flour rather than wheat, thus providing an economic incentive to mill wheat before it passed through the canal, a fact that helps to explain the ubiquitous development of flour mills in the canalside communities.

THE TWO CANAL SYSTEMS

The Welland Canal made possible the downward movement of wheat, but access to Montreal was restricted as the St. Lawrence system was not yet canalized, and much of the trade transferred to the American Erie Canal at Oswego. In the opposite direction, Canadian timber from the Ottawa Valley was exported upstream through the Welland Canal to the American south shore of Lake Erie, where settlement and economic growth were rapid. In 1831 the Welland Canal carried 30,000 barrels of flour and 210,000 bushels of wheat, against 11,000 barrels of flour and 65,000 bushels of wheat carried across the portage.

By the early 1830s the Niagara Frontier had four possible water outlets to the Atlantic. The two American routes were via the Erie Canal to New York City; or via Lake Ontario, the Oswego Canal, to the eastern end of the Erie Canal, also to New York City. The main Canadian route was via Lake Ontario, the St. Lawrence River, and the Lachine Canal to Montreal. As this traffic was restricted at the Lachine section, which carried only 1.5 meters (5 feet) of water over the sills, the regular commercial and military route, completed in 1832, was via the Rideau Canal from Kingston to Ottawa, then used the Ottawa River to Montreal. The Canadian routes could not compete with the Erie Canal. Lake Ontario had become a bottleneck on the passage to the Atlantic. Moreover, New York City offered year-round port facilities against an ice-bound winter harbor at Montreal, and also had a shorter and cheaper Atlantic passage to Liverpool. Canada now suffered from its more northerly latitude, and the St. Lawrence canals were not improved as an integrated system until 1848.[13]

Wheat from Ohio passed through the Welland Canal via Oswego to New York. Of the 256,000 bushels of wheat that passed through the canal in 1834, only 7 percent came from Canadian ports on Lake Erie. The remainder, from American ports, was consigned primarily to New York City. Traffic at Oswego was primarily "wheat down and salt up," and new vessels were constructed on the American side of Lake Erie to serve this traffic. The Welland Canal had become subsidiary to the Erie Canal and the American trade system. Contrary to initial expectations, it now did more to swell the Oswego Canal than to supply Montreal, thereby placing both sides of the Niagara Frontier within the commercial hinterland of New York City.

Coal, first carried through the Welland Canal in 1834, provided an important new trade. Used extensively for domestic heating and gradually replacing waterpower in industry, it was American coal that made the industrial revolution possible in Southern Ontario. The first movement came from Ohio via Lake Erie. Trade on the Welland Canal also included goods shipped between communities within the Niagara Peninsula. In 1835 St. Catharines shipped barrels of beer to Dunnville and Port Colborne, and barrels of salt to Dunnville, Thorold, Port Robinson, and Chippawa; Port Robinson shipped barrels of beer, flour, whiskey, apples, and pork to Dunnville. The canal's outward trade also included bushels of potatoes, and castings that were sent to Dunnville and Port Colborne. Port Dalhousie dispatched staves to St. Catharines, and the port received goods

from Toronto, Prescott, Hamilton, Niagara, Kingston, and Brockville.

The canal greatly stimulated the development of the countryside in its vicinity. The Wainfleet Marsh was drained, which enabled 12,141 hectares (30,000 acres) of land to be cultivated. As areas along the Upper Welland River and the Grand River Valley were cleared and changed to farmland, a strong barge trade in timber and agricultural products resulted, mostly destined for Buffalo, or to the Tonawandas for the Erie Canal. The Canadian Frontier was beginning to operate on a wider regional stage, with the Erie Canal and American influence playing an important role in this expanding affluence.

The Welland Canal, like the Erie Canal, greatly reduced the costs of transportation. In 1832: "The price of conveying a barrel of flour from Fort Erie to Queenston, twenty-eight miles [45 kilometers] around the falls of Niagara, was formerly 2s.3d. It is now conveyed from Cleveland to Prescott through Lake Erie, the Welland Canal, Lake Ontario and seventy miles [112.7 kilometers] down the River St. Lawrence, in all 500 miles [804.7 kilometers] for 2s.2d."[14]

DEVELOPMENT ALONG
THE ERIE CANAL

Both canals promoted employment through their construction works, then again through the impetus of the new infrastructure that arose; the new opportunities to import and export; the vessels that had to be constructed, repaired, replaced, and manned; the services and facilities required by the vessels, their crews, and the tow animals; the ports, harbors, and wharves that developed; the availability of a new source of waterpower that could be harnessed at the locks and wherever water was diverted from the canal, and the new manufacturing activities that arose along the line of both canals. This growth was cumulative. Service activities begat new activities as the population expanded, and manufacturing industries required further resources and materials as their productive output increased. It was a Frontier of expansion as the two canals added their considerable momentum to the existing situation.

On the Erie Canal at its western end, Buffalo quickly drew ahead of all competitors, and wharves and warehouses were added to the Canadian canal. Buffalo became the funnel, the toll gate, and the terminal at the eastern end of the Upper Great Lakes navigation system, and the hinge between lake and canal traffic. As goods were transshipped between canal barges and lake vessels, Cooley's (1894) dictum was fully exemplified: "Population and wealth tend to collect wherever there is a break in transportation." At Buffalo, the commercial activities centered on the harbor, where Little Buffalo Creek had been enlarged with lateral cuts, slips, and basins to provide most of the lower town with access to water.[15]

Named "The Queen City of the Lakes" and chartered as a city in 1832, Buffalo had some two thousand houses by 1835, and a population of over eighteen thousand by 1840. The Buffalo Creek Indian Reservation was absorbed in 1843, and the village of Black Rock in 1853. A continuous urban complex then extended along the Upper Niagara River and the eastern end of Lake Erie. Its active commercial nodes were the docks and wharves. "Canallers, dock-hands, sailors, steamboat runners, immigrants, travellers rich and poor, confidence men, ship captains, merchants and merchants' clerks mingled in a noisy and colorful crowd" at what had become the largest inland port in North America.[16] Dubbed "The Barbary Coast of the East" with awesome vice and crime, Buffalo nevertheless expanded considerably during the heyday of the canal era.

By 1847 eastbound exports from Buffalo

and Black Rock by the Erie Canal were 645,000 tonnes (over 700,000 tons), and imports were almost 140,000 tonnes (154,000 tons).[17] Six thousand men were employed in lake commerce, and almost 250,000 passengers arrived and departed during the season, with regular departures to Erie, Cleveland, Toledo, Detroit, Chicago, and other ports on the Upper Great Lakes. In 1840 over four thousand vessels entered and cleared Buffalo; by 1855 the number had doubled. Vast quantities of wood were imported from nearby areas on the Canadian Frontier, including the valleys of the Grand and Welland Rivers then being cleared for settlement, and in New York State from the Holland Land Purchase. Wood powered the increasing number of steam vessels; a steamship sailing from Buffalo to Chicago required over six hundred cords of wood, that is the harvest from some 4 hectares (10 acres) of timber, to power its journey. The city expanded year by year as ever-increasing streams of commerce and immigrants from Europe flowed through its facilities. Many of the barge and steamship lines were owned by Buffalonians, and Buffalo's Wells-Fargo Express coach schedules were tied in with the steamer services.

A wide-ranging retail, wholesale, economic, and cultural infrastructure grew to serve this commercial growth. Banks, including a branch of the Bank of the United States, and a marine insurance company were established.[18] The foundations of the Buffalo Exchange were laid in 1836, and the University of Buffalo was chartered in 1846. Waterpower at "The Hydraulics," about 4 kilometers (2.5 miles) east of the canal terminal, and along the canal encouraged small-scale manufacturing. Local industry soon included flour and textile mills; stockyards for cattle, sheep, and pigs, and leather production; glassmaking; iron and brass foundries; engine and machine shops; the processing of timber into lumber products including furniture and shipbuilding; a full range of agricultural products; and the manufacture of farm implements. The vibrant community published three daily newspapers by the 1830s. A writer who arrived in 1836 expected to find a small place with wooden buildings; instead he "found Main Street to be entirely of brick and the Stores really splendid. Fine brick buildings were springing up in all directions. At the foot of Main Street there were 17 Brick Stores nearly finished."[19] Housing ranged from shacks to opulent mansions.

In the 1830s and 1840s wheat and other grains were grown east of Buffalo in the Genesee River area, but this production transferred to the west and increased many times in volume. Laborers carried sacks of wheat on their backs up a series of ladders in the ships to wharf level, a tedious but labor-intensive and costly system that made much use of an Irish labor force. Then in 1842 Joseph Dart, a Buffalo merchant, used steam-driven, bucket conveyors to raise grain from the ships' holds to storage bins at the top of the elevator;[20] the grain was then gravity fed through the various milling processes. This invention introduced monumental industrial architecture to the American Frontier. The grain industry with severe price fluctuations, extreme and intermittent unemployment, and winter closure through ice at the eastern end of Lake Erie also provided an uncertain basis for trading activities.

Buffalo's harbor was improved steadily and continuously. Seawalls and piers were necessary for protection from easterly driven waves off Lake Erie. A series of small canals connected to Buffalo Creek, which was dredged and widened to accommodate larger vessels and renamed Buffalo River. The Erie Canal basin, where canal barges and lake vessels converged, received new docking space, and as all waste of every type was dumped in the nearest body of water, the Erie Canal, the Buffalo River, and the Niagara River each received effluent. Cholera as part of a national epidemic struck in 1832, and again in 1834,

bringing almost all waterborne commerce to a halt, but was a factor in the midcentury establishment of Buffalo General Hospital.

Early settlers in Buffalo arrived from New England and elsewhere, mostly via the Erie Canal. By 1850 the proportion of Yankees had diminished as some six thousand Irish Catholic immigrants settled below the Terrace near the canal waterfront where they worked as unskilled laborers.[21] The German population of skilled workers, both Catholic and Lutheran, located east of Main Street, had risen to about 6,800. In 1847 the Catholic diocese of Western New York was created over an area that had been essentially Protestant. By 1848 Polish Jews had also organized their first synagogue,[22] and a separate Black public school was established during the same year.[23] Buffalo, with a population of about forty-two thousand by 1850, had become an ethnically diverse city with the rich who managed various activities and the laboring classes from various European countries. As the various linguistic, ethnic, and religious groups often distrusted one another and brought with them the cultures and prejudices of their European homelands, rival residential areas dominated the city outside its centers of commercial activity.

Black Rock, its rivalry with Buffalo over by 1829, remained a distinct community. The harbor, the Erie Canal, and waterpower at the lock and dam had attracted flour and sawmills, an iron foundry, and a steam-engine manufactory by 1836. Commercial activity clustered around the ferry to Canada. The Upper Village contained a window-glass manufactory, five taverns, as many stores, and about 350 dwellings.[24]

In the Tonawandas, the dam across Tonawanda Creek caused flooding, but yielded waterpower. By 1836 sawmills, taverns, and about forty dwellings foreshadowed the area's future as the greatest lumber-milling center in the United States before the end of the century.[25] To the south, where the Erie Canal was inset along the bank of the Niagara River, the farming landscape prevailed with a marked difference in the patterns and size of landownership between the former One Mile Strip and the Holland Land Company Survey inland from the Niagara River (fig. 3.3).

In 1825 Mordecai Manuel Noah acquired some 809.4 hectares (2,000 acres) of land on Grand Island, directly opposite the entrance to the Erie Canal at Tonawanda. His intention was to found "a city of refuge for the Jews"[26] to be named Ararat, but this attempt failed. In 1833 the East Boston Company of Massachusetts purchased some 6,475.2 hectares (16,000 acres) of land to harvest the high-quality white oak much in demand for shipbuilding.

The company established a sawmill at Whitehaven, and between 1833 and 1840 ship frames manufactured in the Tonawandas were shipped along the Erie Canal to the company's shipyard in Boston to be used in building clippers, the wooden sailing vessels that dominated the marine trade of the era. Whitehaven, with its sawmill, a store, church, and school, was abandoned after the forest was exhausted and the company ceased operations, but the foundations had been laid for the development of the Tonawandas as a lumber center, this time based on white pine from the forests of Ontario and the Midwestern states of the United States.

At Lockport, an instant canal community that began in 1821, over 1,200 laborers worked under the supervision of state engineers and surveyors to construct the canal locks. A steady stream of settlers then moved into the area; merchants, doctors, and lawyers followed. The center became the county seat of Niagara County in 1823, and in 1824 the legislature for Niagara County designated the place as a town. Here was the current marvel of vessels "sailing up hill"; all had to be manned, supplied, and repaired. By 1836 eight mills used the waterpower developed along Eighteen Mile Creek. Nearby Cambria and Royalton had been settled earlier, but Lockport had the advantage of centrality

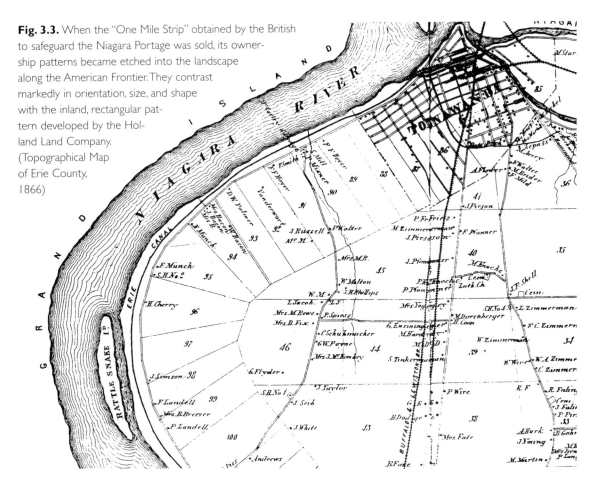

Fig. 3.3. When the "One Mile Strip" obtained by the British to safeguard the Niagara Portage was sold, its ownership patterns became etched into the landscape along the American Frontier. They contrast markedly in orientation, size, and shape with the inland, rectangular pattern developed by the Holland Land Company. (Topographical Map of Erie County, 1866)

within the county and the strong expectation of growth because of the canal and water-power from the locks.

Lockport's population had grown to 8,861 by 1850. The town that developed above and below the Niagara Escarpment was centered on the famous Wide Bridge that crossed the canal. With water from the canal harnessed in raceways to serve factories, Lockport soon became the key industrial center of Niagara County and the largest American city after Buffalo on the American Frontier. Eighteen

The Erie Canal crossed the Niagara Escarpment at Lockport, where the locks constructed in a glacial overflow channel of former Lake Tonawanda provided waterpower, introduced mill developments, and, together with services for canal traffic, added a new canal-oriented community to the American Frontier. (Bartlett Print, 1890, John H. Jackson Collection)

Mile Creek, used as a tailrace into which spent water from below the water wheel flows, had attracted eight mills by 1836. By 1850 Lockport's industries included extensive flour mills, lumber factories, a cotton mill, and several mercantile establishments associated with the Erie Canal.[27] The many stone and brick build-ings built in this period reflected the economic and commercial importance of the town and the wealth of the inhabitants.

Nearby Pendleton blossomed temporarily during canal construction along an earlier portage between Lockport and Tonawanda Creek. As the city laid out by a canal surveyor never materialized, by 1836 the small village contained only a post office, two stores, two taverns, and twenty dwellings.

THE WELLAND CANAL INITIATES URBAN COMMUNITIES

The excitement of urban growth also followed the Welland Canal.[28] This progress began with the arrival of construction workers, including the transfer of Irish workers who had helped to build the Erie Canal. The first centers of employment, at the sites of major construction works, included: the aqueduct at Welland; the dam at Dunnville; the lock sites across the Niagara Escarpment where shanty dwellings initiated those communities later to be named Merritton and Thorold; and the villages of Allanburg and Port Robinson at both ends of the Deep Cut.

Ports soon followed the canal. Port Dalhousie tied the northern entrance of the canal to Lake Ontario and the St. Lawrence outlet; Port Colborne did likewise for Lake Erie and the Upper Lakes; and Port Robinson connected the canal with the Lower Welland River en route to the Erie Canal at Tonawanda and Buffalo. The names associated with these ports reflect the social prestige of the ruling upper class and its financial support for the canal venture. Port Dalhousie is named after the governor-general of Canada from 1819 to 1828, Port Colborne after the lieutenant-governor of Upper Canada from 1819 to 1836, Port Robinson recognizes the chief justice of Upper Canada in 1829, and Allanburg refers to the president of the Bank of Upper Canada. Port Colborne also recognized royalty of the period in its street names.

Port Dalhousie and Port Colborne as lake terminals contrasted with each other as harbors, the former located on the natural outlet of Twelve Mile Creek behind a protective sandbar, and the latter a man-made construction excavated along the canal inland from the shoreline. Both ports expanded substantially when the Second Canal was constructed. At Port Dalhousie, a weir constructed across the broad channel and floodplain of Twelve Mile Creek created an Upper and a Lower Harbour, connected by a lock and providing a new source of waterpower. At Port Colborne, where the original lock at the entrance to the canal was relocated nearly 0.8 kilometers (0.5 miles) inland, a wider basin was created on both sides of the channel to accommodate vessels. The commercial center grew around this basin on both sides; at Port Dalhousie the width of the Lower Harbour restricted growth to the western side.

The natural mouth of Twelve Mile Creek at Port Dalhousie became the harbor for the northern entrance of the Welland Canal. The Second Canal added a weir across the canal valley, creating an Upper and a Lower Harbour, and a new opportunity for water-power. (This aerial photograph © A19358-15 © 1965/09/26 Her Majesty the Queen in Right of Canada, reproduced from the collection of the National Air Photo Library [Ottawa] [top], and John Burtniak [left])

Port Dalhousie grew as an independent entity. St. Catharines, its nearest neighbor upstream, was likewise an independent center. These two urban units did not amalgamate until late in the twentieth century, whereas Port Colborne soon annexed its near neighbor and the earlier community of Humberstone. Location on different lakes also contributed to divergent commercial histories. Port Dalhousie had exports to the Canadian ports along the north shore of Lake Ontario, to the St. Lawrence outlet, and to Oswego for the Erie Canal; by contrast, Port Colborne lay under the direct influence of Buffalo, and its shipping activities served American ports south of Lake Erie.

Although not receiving the port prefix, other places along the Welland Canal functioned in this category. Chippawa at the southern end of the Niagara Portage was revived as a canal-river port on the Upper Niagara River. At Welland port facilities arose where the canal aqueduct crossed the Welland River. The higher level carried sailing vessels from Lake Ontario and Lake Erie and barges via the Feeder Canal from the Grand River, and the lower level carried barges with timber and agricultural produce from the Upper Welland River.

All ports developed facilities that served the canal. Here cargo was loaded, discharged, stored, or transferred to other vessels or wagons. Taxes and tolls might be imposed. Close to the wharves were forwarding agents and customs offices, and next to the canal arose shipbuilding and ship-repair facilities, chandlers, storage sheds, and often local processing or manufacturing activities. These service, industrial, and commercial enterprises, though fewer and less important than along the Erie Canal, nevertheless provided the basis for economic growth in the communities that developed along the canal.

Very important as a foundation for this growth, the Welland Canal also brought waterpower, the prime element for industrial location during this period. At Dunnville the dam across the Grand River, the diversion of water into the Feeder Canal, and the height of the channel above the river provided opportunities for mill development. At Welland the height difference between the canal on its aqueduct and the river below provided an abundance of opportunities for mill development. At Thorold-Merritton the sequence of closely spaced locks across the edge of the Niagara Escarpment provided many opportunities for the diversion of water into millraces and ponds. A millrace known as the Hydraulic Raceway extended this power resource to St. Catharines, where the fall from the top of the bank to the canal of about

Welland Canal Locks and Aqueduct at Welland, Ont.

Welland grew at the upper level, where the Feeder Canal from Dunnville and the aqueducts of the First, Second, Third, and Fourth Canals crossed the Welland River. With waterpower available at each of the four corners of the aqueduct, mills supplied with water from the canal developed along the Welland River. Barge traffic along the Feeder Canal from the Grand River and the Welland River provided timber, agricultural products, and gypsum to the growing settlement. (John Burtniak)

24.4 meters (80 feet) permitted a series of parallel millraces along the canal bank; the town then developed on flat land above the canal bank.

By 1831 "there are twelve saw mills in operation on and contiguous to the line of Canal—six grist mills are built and in course of building, besides various other machinery."[29] Next year, described as the "public advantages arising from the canal," there were: "At Dunnville Grand River dam (a place which before the construction of the canal was a

The man-made, excavated southern entrance to the Welland Canal at Port Colborne became dominated by a grain elevator where laden vessels transferred cargo to the Welland (later Grand Trunk) railway (**top right**). The commercial streets that emerged on both sides of the harbor were connected by a swing bridge (**bottom right**). (John Burtniak [both])

St. Catharines changed from a small rural center to an industrial town because of the First Welland Canal. A series of millraces fed from the canal line the hillside below the town center to provide the power for industrial development. (*Canadian Illustrated News*, 1871)

waste, or not inhabited), ... three lumber mills, one flour, fulling and carding mills, three merchant's shops, three store houses and some thirty or forty dwelling houses; and the lands in the neighbourhood, formerly valueless, are now selling at from $4 to $8 per acre. A small village, with a grist and saw mill, is springing up at Marshville [Wainfleet]. Another is laid out [Stromness] and will form a prominent point at the junction. ... Thorold is rapidly increasing. The largest grist mill in the province; four lumber mills, and a large village, are erected, where it was quite a wilderness when the canal was commenced."[30]

Port Robinson and Allanburg, depicted as "small villages," developed at both ends of the Deep Cut. Each had grist and lumber mills with raceways, ponds, and mill wheels powered from the canal. To the west, large areas of marshland at Port Colborne and in the surrounding townships had been drained and "rendered valuable" as a result of the canal's operation.

By 1836 St. Catharines, with a population of about seven hundred but growing rapidly with new houses, stores, and mills, was described as "in the first rank of improving places in the Provinces."[31] The Hydraulic Raceway, in conjunction with the trade and waterpower available along the canal, had promoted immediate transition from a local, rural service center to a prosperous industrial town. By 1846, with a population of about 3,500, it was "a place of much trade, which arises partly from its contiguity to the Welland Canal and partly from its extensive water-power, an immense quantity of wheat being annually converted into flour."[32] The town had stagecoach services, a shipyard and dry dock, the Welland Canal offices, and a fire company. As a growing regional center it housed central functions such as a grammar school, a post office, barracks, a newspaper, and many service activities. A town center had developed at the west end of the main street, a former Native trail. The banks, the legal and assurance offices, the majority of shops, and the principal hotels and inns had been attracted to this street, and subsidiary developments to contiguous areas.

As the dozen or so centers that had arisen along the canal together contained some seven thousand people, the Frontier's regional pattern of settlement had been changed remarkably by the First and Second Welland Canals. Flour milling had moved to the area between Port Dalhousie and Thorold, and by 1840 one-third of the mills in the Niagara Peninsula had been attracted to canal sites.[33] Woollen mills, formerly scat-tered, were attracted to St. Catharines, Merritton, and Thorold. Shipbuilding, previously centered at Niagara, had also moved to the canal towns. The emphasis of settlement along the Niagara River prior to 1820 had changed to hubs along the canal by the 1840s. St. Catharines, in the lead of these new developments, had a population of almost 4,500 by 1851. Even so, this town was only half the size of Lockport, its locational counterpart where the Erie Canal crossed the Niagara Escarpment. Despite growth, the Canadian Frontier was eclipsed by more vigorous growth on the American Frontier, where Buffalo, the preeminent city, dominated a service distribution or hinterland area that included the southern and eastern sections of the Canadian Frontier. Urban growth had reduced the meaning of the international boundary.

THE RIVER COMMUNITIES

Bypassed by the two canals, the centers along the Niagara River each declined. The Welland Canal and its communities now took precedence for population, industry, and trade over the portage, and the canal carried a far greater quantity and range of goods than the portage. Thus when new county seats were created, these were inland at Welland in 1856 and at St. Catharines in 1862. As in Niagara County on the American Frontier where Lockport became the county seat in 1821, the urban focus had moved inland away from the Niagara River to the new canal communities.

Despite this transfer of regional emphasis, Niagara in 1836 could still be described as a "scene of great bustle and gaiety. [The town had] three churches, several taverns, large wharves, a spacious dry dock and harbor, and some handsome edifices."[34] The Niagara Harbour and Dock Company, formed in 1830, occupied the riverfront north of Navy Hall.[35] The town reached a peak population of about four thousand in 1840 but, after the dock company failed in 1848, Niagara survived as only a local service center.

Queenston also declined. The portage closed down, but the docks remained in use for lake steamers bringing tourists to Queenston Heights and the Falls.[36] By contrast, Chippawa experienced a brief boom from 1829 to 1833 as the southern port of entry to the Welland Canal, and then survived as the port at the head of navigation on the Upper Niagara River with steamer services from Buffalo as a location en route to the Falls. By 1836 there were thirty new buildings, stores, grist and sawmills, a post office, two churches, and a population of about four hundred.[37]

On the American portage, by 1836 Lewiston was a post-office village and a port of entry. Located at the head of navigation on the Lower Niagara River, the village contained a customs house, two churches, an academy, a grist mill, four taverns, and about seventy dwellings.[38] It exported lumber, received daily steamboats from Lake Ontario, and supported a regular ferry service across the Niagara River to Queenston.

Youngstown, about half the size of Lewiston and also a post-office village and port, had three taverns, two stores, about thirty-five dwellings, and a ferry across the Niagara River to Niagara.[39] Lake vessels constructed during the 1830s used oak timbers from nearby forests, and grain was a significant export. Neither Youngstown nor Lewiston grew substantially after the opening of the Erie Canal; like Niagara and Queenston, both centers had been bypassed by major shifts in the waterborne transportation network. Also, many of the mill settlements on the smaller streams were now unable to compete with the greater waterpower resource available on the two canals. St. Johns and Effingham in the Short Hills south of St. Catharines became almost ghost communities,[40] and on the American Frontier the villages that lacked access to the Erie Canal likewise remained either small or disappeared.

CULTURAL DIFFERENTIATION

By the mid-1840s the Frontier had a total population of about one hundred thousand. Nearly forty thousand people occupied Canada's Niagara District (then the Counties of Lincoln, Welland, and Haldimand), about the same number in the smaller area of American Erie County and slightly more in Niagara County. The essential background was farmed, agricultural land. The principal crops were wheat, oats, barley, corn, and a variety of vegetables. Farmers raised beef and dairy cattle and some sheep. Turner (1849) stated about the Tonawanda Plain that "perhaps the productions of the soil in no country on earth yield a greater variety and at the same time so great an abundance . . . as this territory."[41] There were also complaints that many of the farms were becoming "worn-out" from the practice of "taking too much wheat off the ground, and putting too little manure on it."[42]

The Frontier's rich soil had attracted several distinct cultural groups.[43] A strict Lutheran sect named The Community of True Inspiration, founded in Germany in 1714, persecuted as a religious minority and arriving in America in 1842, purchased land in West Seneca in Erie County where the town of Ebenezer was founded. Four self-sufficient residential communities of up to five hundred people organized on communal lines occupied some 3,237.6 hectares (8,000 acres) of land. Canadian offshoots, now known as Ebenezer Societies, located near the mouth of Black Creek and at Kenneberg, now Canboro, further inland.[44] These colonies on both Frontiers sold their land in the late 1850s when their desire for isolation was threatened by railways and encroachment from Buffalo, and moved to the relative isolation of Amana, Iowa.

German farmers settled on the American Frontier at Bergholtz, Martinsville (named after Martin Luther), Johnsburg, and Walmore in Wheatfield Township. At Bergholtz, a German village in Wheatfield Township, 1,052.2 hectares (2,600 acres) were purchased in 1843 to establish a Lutheran colony. The village square survives, as do some half-timbered homes, Lutheran churches, and German road names. Wolcottsville, settled from Bergholtz, was once known as Prussia, and East Hamburgh, now Orchard Park, was founded as a Quaker community in 1805.[45]

Comparable immigration to Willoughby and Bertie Townships on the Canadian Frontier included German-speaking settlers from Alsace, who arrived in the Niagara Peninsula during the 1830s and 1840s via New York City and the Erie Canal.[46] Snyder, known locally as New Germany, and the area's

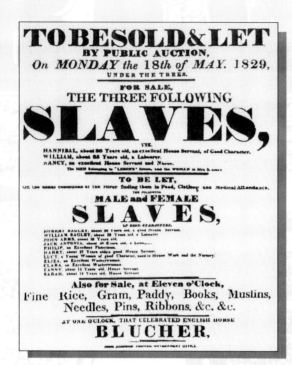

TO BE SOLD & LET
BY PUBLIC AUCTION,
On *MONDAY* the 18th of *MAY*, 1829,
UNDER THE TREES.
FOR SALE,
THE THREE FOLLOWING

SLAVES,

VIZ.
HANNIBAL, about 30 Years old, an excellent House Servant, of Good Character.
WILLIAM, about 35 Years old, a Labourer.
NANCY, an excellent House Servant and Nurse.
The MEN belonging to "LEBEN'S" Estate, and the WOMAN to Mrs. B——.

TO BE LET,
On the usual conditions of the Hirer finding them in Food, Clothing and Medical Attendance,
THE FOLLOWING
MALE and FEMALE

SLAVES,

BY GOOD STANDINGS.
ROBERT BAGLEY, about 20 Years old, a good House Servant.
WILLIAM BAGLEY, about 18 Years old, a Labourer.
JOHN ARMS, about 18 Years old.
JACK ANTONIA, about 40 Years old, a Labourer.
PHILIP, an Excellent Fisherman.
HARRY, about 27 Years old, a good House Servant.
LUCY, a Young Woman of good Character, used to House Work and the Nursery.
ELIZA, an Excellent Washerwoman.
CLARA, an Excellent Washerwoman.
FANNY, about 14 Years old, House Servant.
SARAH, about 14 Years old, House Servant.

Also for Sale, at Eleven o'Clock,
Fine Rice, Gram, Paddy, Books, Muslins,
Needles, Pins, Ribbons, &c. &c.

AT ONE O'CLOCK, THAT CELEBRATED ENGLISH HORSE
BLUCHER,

In 1793, with the Upper Canada Abolition Act, the Canadian Frontier became the first British territory to legislate against slavery. Harriet Tubman of St. Catharines is reputed to have made nineteen trips and to have brought out three hundred or more slaves from the South; not one was recaptured, and some descendants continue to live in St. Catharines and Niagara Falls, Ontario. (Norval Johnson Heritage Library, Niagara Falls, Ontario [both])

REWARD
HARRIET TUBMAN
$40,000
DEAD OR ALIVE

Lutheran churches are a result of that influx and earlier German immigrations by adherents to the Mennonite and Tunker faiths.[47] This Mennonite influx is remembered through naming rural roads in Willoughby Township after families such as Beam and Bossert, while Weinbrenner, Winger, and Sherk are Tunker names, and the later German-Alsatian names include Dentenbeck, Morningstar, Miller, Nye, Ort, Weaver, and Willick.[48] Here is a vivid reminder of landscape as biography.[49]

The boundary line in the Niagara River separated different attitudes toward the Black population. Upper Canada in 1793 was the first British possession to renounce slavery. Blacks in the United States were not emancipated until the 1860s. In New York State, slavery was abolished in the mid-1820s and voting extended to Black males with property. The first Black church was established in 1831 in Buffalo; the Michigan Avenue Baptist Church was organized in 1836 and completed in 1847. The Black community numbered about seven hundred, but as the Fugitive Slave Law of 1850 required that escaped Blacks could still be returned to their Southern slaveholders, a route to safety and freedom was provided by emigration to Canada. Parts of Western New York and Buffalo became stations on the "Underground Railroad." Abolitionist sentiment was strong in the county with its evangelical Protestant settlers, Clarence became an important stop on the way to freedom, and slaves converged on the Buffalo area from Ohio and Pennsylvania either along the shore of Lake Erie or through the southern tier of counties. Escapees could then cross the Upper Niagara River, referred to as "The Crossing," to Fort Erie for asylum.[50] Bertie Hall (built in 1813) became a presumed safe house for fugitive slaves, and "Little Africa" developed as an all-Black community for escaped slaves that included Josiah Henson.

The joys of freedom have been interpreted by Josiah Henson in his classic narrative of 1846. "When I got on the Canada side [at Waterloo, now Fort Erie] . . . my first impulse was to throw myself on the ground, and giving way to the riotous exultation of my feelings, to execute sundry antics which excited the astonishment of those who were looking on."[51] He rolled in the sand, and hugged and kissed his wife and child in the great excitement of being free.

On the Canadian Frontier at Niagara-on-the-Lake, a community of up to two hundred people referred to as the "colored village" developed in the area of Mary and William Streets.[52] Blacks escaping as fugitives from the United States, and free as soon as they crossed the Niagara River, owned and rented properties and operated businesses. Black congregations arose in the town and nearby, as at Lawrenceville (now Virgil). A "Negro Burial Ground" survives where a Baptist church was erected in 1829.[53] Schooling was provided in the local Common School. As stated in 1854 by the editor of the Black newspaper, "The Coloured Citizens are prosperous. Nearly every family possessing a homestead. There is no prejudice. Lots can be had on reasonable terms and tradesmen, laborers, etc. are on active demand."[54] Another settlement, a small village called "Little Africa," developed near Fort Erie.[55]

Drummondville, now part of Niagara Falls, had a Black district known as "Polly-town," where some people worked locally in the service trade as hotel waiters and tour guides, including trips to Behind the Falls at Table Rock. Here in 1836 was founded the Nathaniel Dell B.M.E. Church to serve the Black population, and many prominent Blacks are buried in the Drummond Hill Cemetery.

In St. Catharines, where Black settlement concentrated in the North Street and Welland Avenue areas, a procession of 1838 "contained near 100 gentlemen and about fifty ladies of colour."[56] The shipyards of Louis Shickluna on the Welland Canal employed Black carpenters; they also worked on building construction, in the town's spa industries, as hotel waiters, and on the vessels that crossed Lake Ontario from Niagara. By 1856 a segregated "colored school" with about 250 Black children is recorded. The community was served by Zion Baptist and British Methodist Episcopal churches.[57]

Richard Pierpoint (c.1746–c.1838), born in Africa and then sold as a slave, served in Butler's Rangers and the War of 1812. As a Black Loyalist, he received two land grants, then as a popular citizen gave his name to Dick's Creek, which became part of the First Welland Canal. Anthony Burns (1834–1862), born a slave in Virginia, became pastor of the Zion Baptist Church; buried in Victoria Lawn Cemetery, a historical plaque honors his dedication and courage. The most famous of the three, Harriet Tubman (c. 1820–1913) used St. Catharines as the base from which she launched several rescue missions in the United States; called "The Black Moses," she reputedly made nineteen trips on the Underground Railroad and brought out three hundred or more "passengers," with not one being recaptured.[58] After 1833, when an act of the imperial parliament ended slavery throughout the British Empire, Emancipation Day ceremonies and parades in St. Catharines became among the largest in the province of Ontario, and culminated in big picnics in Lakeside Park at Port Dalhousie from the late 1920s to about 1950.

NOTES

1. R. W. Bingham, ed., *Holland Land Company's Papers: Reports of Joseph Ellicott*, Publications, vol. 33 (Buffalo, N.Y.: Buffalo Historical Society, 1941), pp. 49–50.

2. A major source is N. E. Whitford, *History of the Canal System of the State of New York*, 2 vols. (Albany, N.Y.: State Legislative Printer, 1906). See also R. K. Andrist, *The Erie Canal* (New York: American Heritage Publishing, 1964); E. Brunger and L. Wyld, *The Grand Canal New York's First Thruway*, Adventures in New York History, vol. 12 (Buffalo, N.Y.: Buffalo and Erie County Historical Society, 1964); H. W. Hill, *Historical Review of Waterways and Canal Construction in New York State*, Publications, vol. 12 (Buffalo, N.Y.: Buffalo Historical Society, 1908); J. W. Percy, *The Erie Canal: From Lockport to Buffalo* (Kenmore, N.Y.: Partner's Press, 1979); and R. Shaw, *Erie Water West: A History of the Erie Canal, 1792–1854* (Lexington: University of Kentucky Press, 1966).

3. J. C. Lord, *Samuel Wilkeson*, Publications, vol. 4 (Buffalo, N.Y.: Buffalo Historical Society, 1896), pp. 71–85; A. Bigelow, *The Harbor Maker of Buffalo*, Publications, vol. 4 (Buffalo, N.Y.: Buffalo Historical Society, 1896), pp. 85–91; "Historical Writings of Judge Samuel Wilkeson," *Publications of the Buffalo Historical Society* 5 (1902): 185–212; T. W. Symons and J. C. Quintus, "Buffalo Harbour: Its Construction and Improvement During the Nineteenth Century," *Publications of the Buffalo Historical Society* 5 (1902): 239–85.

4. "Annual Report of the Erie Canal Commissioners, 1824," in Shaw, *Erie Water West*, pp. 157–58.

5. W. R. Willoughby, "The Impact of the Erie Canal," *Niagara Frontier* 3 (1956–1957): 39. See also J. Walden, "The Influence of the Erie Canal upon the Population along Its Course" (Ph.D. diss., University of Wisconsin, 1900).

6. Whitford, *History of the Canal System of the State of New York*.

7. H. G. J. Aitken, *The Welland Canal Company: A Study in Canadian Enterprise* (Cambridge, Mass.: Harvard University Press, 1954), pp. 20–21. For context, see C. Andreae, *Lines of Country: An Atlas of Railway and Waterway History in Canada* (Erin, Ont.: Boston Mills Press, 1997).

8. J. Strachan, *A Visit to the Province of Upper Canada* (Aberdeen: D. Chalmers, 1820), p. 106.

9. J. P. Merrit, *Biography of the Hon. W. H. Merritt, M.P.* (St. Catharines, Ont.: H. S. Leavenworth, 1875), pp. 42–43. See J. Williams, *Merritt: A Canadian Before His Time* (St. Catharines, Ont.: Stonehouse Publications, 1985).

10. J. N. Jackson, *St. Catharines, Ontario: Its Early Years* (Belleville, Ont.: Mika, 1976), pp. 168–206; and J. Burtniak and W. B. Turner, eds., *The Welland Canals*, Proceedings of the First Annual Niagara Peninsula History Conference, Brock University (St. Catharines, Ont., 1979).

11. J. P. Heisler, *The Canals of Canada*, Occasional Papers in Archaeology and History, no. 8 (Ottawa: National Historic Sites Service, Department of Indian Affairs and Northern Development, 1973). See also R. J. Foley, *The Welland Canal, Niagara Story*, vol. 3 (Niagara Falls, Ont.: Haunted Press, 1995); and R. M. Styran and R. R. Taylor, with J. N. Jackson, *The Welland Canal: The Growth of Mr. Merrit's Ditch* (Erin, Ont.: Boston Mills Press, 1988), and its successor volume, R. M. Styron and R. R. Taylor, *Mr. Merrit's Ditch: A Welland Canals Album* (Erin, Ont.: Boston Mills Press, 1992).

12. Statistical data from the Annual Reports of the Welland Canal Company, in Aitken, *The Welland Canal Company*, pp. 139–48, and included in *Appendix to the Journal of the House of Assembly of Upper Canada Session 1836–1837*, vol. 2 (Toronto: Queen's Printer, 1836).

13. Completion dates are Beauharnois Canal, 1845; the Cornwall Canal, 1843: the Williamsburg Canals, 1848; and the Lachine Canal, 1848.

14. "Report of the Board of Directors of the Welland Canal Company for the Year 1832," *Appendix to the Journal of the House of Assembly*, p. 496.

15. M. A. Rapp, "Port of Buffalo, 1825–1850," *Niagara Frontier* 6 (1960): 21–31. See also W. Laux, *The Village of Buffalo: 1800–1832*, Adventures in Western New York History, vol. 3 (Buffalo, N.Y.: Buffalo and Erie County Historical Society, 1960), p. 18; and J. Fowler, *Journal of a Tour in the State of New York* (London: Whittaker, Treacher and Arnott, 1831).

16. J. T. Horton, "Old Erie—The Growth of an American Community," in J. T. Horton et al., *History of Northeastern New York* (New York: Lewis Historical Publishing, 1947), 1:72. See also O. B. Augspurger, "Buffalo's Earlier Crossroads: Samuel Wilkenson and the Seaway, Skyway and Thruway," *Niagara Frontier* 4 (1957–1958): 36; and S. M. Welch, *Recollections of Buffalo During the Decade from 1830 to 1840* (Buffalo, N.Y.: Peter Paul, 1891).

17. For the rates and frequency of canal and lake traffic, see J. B. Mansfield, *History of the Great Lakes*, vol. 1 (Chicago: J. H. Beers, 1899), reprinted as *The Saga of the Great Lakes* (Toronto: Coles, 1980), pp. 176–82, 200.

18. Horton, "Old Erie," pp. 68–172; see R. W. Bingham, *The Cradle of the Queen City*, Publications, vol. 31 (Buffalo, N.Y.: Buffalo Historical Society, 1931); R. Holder, *The Beginnings of Buffalo Industry*, Adventures in Western New York History, vol. 5 (Buffalo, N.Y.: Buffalo and Erie County Historical Society, 1960); F. H. Severance, *The Picture Book of Earlier Buffalo*, Publications, vol. 16 (Buffalo, N.Y.: Buffalo Historical Society, 1912); and H. P. Smith, *History of the City of Buffalo and Erie County* (Syracuse, N.Y.: D. Mason, 1864). A recent summary is M. Goldman, *High Hopes: The Rise and Decline of Buffalo, New York* (Albany: State University of New York Press, 1983).

19. D. Fulton, ed., *New York to Niagara, 1836: The Journal of Thomas S. Woodcock* (New York: New York Public Library, 1938), p. 14; see also J. G. Buckingham, *America, Historical, Statistic, and Descriptive*, vol. 3 (London: Fisher and Son, 1841).

20. J. Dart, *The Grain Elevators of Buffalo*, Publications, vol. 1 (Buffalo, N.Y.: Buffalo Historical Society, 1879), pp. 391–401; and Goldman, *High Hopes*, p. 57.

21. Goldman, *High Hopes*, pp. 72–123.

22. M. Plesure, "The Jews of Buffalo," *Niagara Frontier* 3 (1955–1956): 30.

23. S. Gredel, *People of Our City and County*, Adventures in Western New York History, vol. 13 (Buffalo, N.Y.: Buffalo and Erie Historical Society, 1971).

24. T. F. Gordon, *Gazetteer of the State of New York* (Philadelphia: T. K. and P. G. Collins, 1836), p. 440. See also W. L. Mackenzie, *Sketches of Canada and the United States* (London: Effingham Wilson, 1833).

25. J. W. Percy, *Tonawanda: The Way It Was—A History of the Town of Tonawanda from 1805–1903* (Kenmore, N.Y.: Partners' Press, 1979); and F. S. Parkhurst, *History of the Town of Tonawanda, Erie County, New York, 1905–1930* (Kenmore, N.Y.: The Author, 1930).

26. L. F. Allen, *Founding the City of Ararat on Grand Island—By Mordecai M. Noah*, Publications, vol. 1 (Buffalo, N.Y.: Buffalo Historical Society, 1879), pp. 305–28.

27. Gordon, *Gazetteer of the State of New York*, p. 558. See A. Muller, *Looking Back So That We May Move Ahead*, Lockport Canal Sesquicentennial (Lockport, N.Y.: Gooding, 1975); and Lockport Area Chamber of Commerce, *Lockport—To The Canal and Beyond: A History of Lockport's Settlement and Growth* (Lockport, N.Y.: Chamber of Commerce, 1980) (typescript).

28. A major statement is J. N. Jackson, *The Welland Canals and Their Communities: Engineering, Industrial, and Urban Transformation* (Toronto: Toronto University Press, 1997).

29. Report of the Board of Directors of the Welland Canal Company for the Year 1831, ibid., p. 488.

30. Report of the Board of Directors of the Welland Canal Company for the Year 1832, ibid., pp. 495–96.

31. T. Rolph, *A Brief Account . . . Together with a Statistical Account of Upper Canada* (Dundas, Ont.: G. Heyworth Hackstaff, 1836), pp. 192–93.

32. W. H. Smith, *Smith's Canadian Gazetteer* (Toronto: H. & W. Rowsell, 1846), pp. 177–78.

33. J. W. Watson, "The Changing Industrial Pattern of the Niagara Peninsula," *Ontario Historical Society, Papers and Records* 37 (1945): 51.

34. Rolph, *A Brief Account*, pp. 192–93.

35. A. I. G. Gilkison, *Early Ship Building at Niagara*, Publications, no. 18 (Niagara Historical Society, 1900), pp. 29–31.

36. Rolph, *A Brief Account*, p. 203; and A. E. Huggins, *Queenston* (St. Catharines, Ont.: Niagara Regional Library System, 1973).

37. Ibid., p. 203.

38. Gordon, *Gazetteer of the State of New York*, p. 558; L. W. Hawes, *Lewiston: Past, Present and Future* (Lewiston, N.Y., 1887); and H. Kimball, *Lewiston Sesquicentennial, 1822–1972* (Lewiston, N.Y.: Sesquicentennial Committee, 1971).

39. Gordon, *Gazetteer of the State of New York*, pp. 558–59; E. L. and V. M. Howard, "The His-

tory of Youngstown," in J. T. Blixt, *Youngstown, 1854–1954* (Youngstown, N.Y.: Youngstown Centennial Committee, 1954).

40. C. Duquemin, "St. Johns, Short Hills: From Bloom to Doom," in *Villages in the Niagara Peninsula*, ed. J. Burtniak and W. B. Turner, Proceedings Second Annual Niagara Peninsula History Conference, Brock University (St. Catharines, Ont., 1980), p. 33.

41. O. Turner, *Pioneer History of the Holland Purchase of Western New York* (Buffalo, N.Y.: Jewett, Thomas, 1849), p. 573.

42. Smith, *Smith's Canadian Gazetteer*, p. 125.

43. A. E. Coombs, *History of the Niagara Peninsula and the New Welland Canal* (Toronto: Historical Publishers Association, 1930), pp. 164–67.

44. F. J. Lankes, *The Ebenezer Society* (1960 typescript; West Seneca, N.Y.: West Seneca Historical Society, 1963).

45. J. N. Printy, *Orchard Park before We Remember* (Orchard Park, N.Y.: Orchard Park Historical Society, 1980).

46. J. E. Ruch, "The German-French of Willoughby Township: Mid-Nineteenth Century Alsatian Immigration to Welland County," *Families* 17 (1978): 25–39; and R. S. Ort, *Willoughby and the Ort Family* (private printing, Kenmore, N.Y., 1969).

47. F. H. Epp, *Mennonites in Canada, 1786–1920* (Toronto: Macmillan, 1974), pp. 57–75; and L. U. Burkholder, *A Brief History of the Mennonites in Ontario* (Markham, Ont.: Mennonite Conference of Ontario, 1935), p. 31.

48. The exact religious affiliation of each name is blurred through intermarriage and the merging of different groups.

49. M. S. Samuels, "The Biography of Landscape: Cause and Capability," in *The Interpretation of Ordinary Landscapes: Geographical Essays*, ed. D. W. Meinig (New York: Oxford University Press, 1979), pp. 51–88.

50. H. Graf, "The Underground Railroad in Erie County," *Niagara Frontier* 1 (1953): 69–71. See also L. Bramble, *Black Fugitive Slaves in Early Canada* (St. Catharines, Ont.: Vanwell, 1987); and W. R. Riddell, "The Slave in Upper Canada," *Journal of Negro History* 4, no. 4 (1919): 372–411.

51. *The Life of Josiah Henson* (1849; reprint, Dresden,Ont.: Uncle Tom's Cabin Museum, 1965). This book provided the inspiration for the famous work of fiction by Harriet Beecher Stove, *Uncle Tom's Cabin*. Henson purchased 200 acres of land in Kent County near the present town of Dresden in 1841, and lived in that area until his death in 1883. His home, known popularly as "Uncle Tom's Cabin," is now a museum.

52. N. Butler, "Starting Anew: The Black Community of Early Niagara," in M. Power and N. Butler, *Slavery and Freedom in Niagara* (Niagara-on-the-Lake, Ont.: Niagara Historical Society, 1993).

53. F. B. LeDoux, *Sketches of Niagara* (St. Catharines, Ont.: Peninsula Press, 1955), pp. 8–9, 41.

54. M. A. Shadd, *Provincial Freeman*, 26 August 1854, quoted in Butler, "Starting Anew," p. 65.

55. D. G. Hill, *The Freedom-Seekers: Blacks in Early Canada* (Agincourt, Ont.: Book Society of Canada, 1981), pp. 5, 52, 94–95, 105, 123–25, 166–67; and D. G. Hill, "Early Black Settlement in the Niagara Peninsula," in *Immigration and Settlement in the Niagara Peninsula*, ed. J. Burtniak and P. C. Dirks, Proceedings Third Annual Niagara Peninsula History Conference, Brock University (St. Catharines, Ont., 1981).

56. *St. Catharines Journal*, 2 August 1838.

57. Junius (Seymour Phelps), *St. Catharines Journal*, 1856, reprinted as *St. Catharines A to Z* (St. Catharines, Ont.: St. Catharines and Lincoln Historical Society, 1967). Blacks as part of the community are discussed in J. N. Jackson and S. M. Wilson, *St. Catharines: Canada's Canal City* (St. Catharines, Ont.: The Standard, 1992), pp. 19–21, 45, 78, 181–82, 188.

58. H. Graf, "The Underground Railroad in Erie County," *Niagara Frontier* 1 (1953): 69–71; R. Sadlier, *Harriet Tubman and the Underground Railroad: Her Life in the United States and Canada* (Toronto: Umbrella Press, 1997); and O. A. Thomas, *Niagara's Freedom Trail: A Guide to African-Canadian History in the Niagara Peninsula* (Thorold, Ont.: Niagara Economic and Tourist Corporation, 1996), for locations to visit when following the Niagara Peninsula/Black History Freedom Trail. For personal accounts of escape to freedom that mention the Niagara Frontier, see B. Drew, *The Refugee; or, The Narratives of Fugitive Slaves in Canada Related by Themselves* (Boston: J. P. Jewett, 1856), and for the meaning of being a slave see J. Lester, *To Be a Slave* (New York: Scholastic, 1968).

CHAPTER FOUR

THE RAILWAY ERA OF DEVELOPMENT

The advancing rail network from the 1830s onward introduced new landscapes to both Frontiers as stations, yards, bridges, and lines of track were built (fig. 4.1).[1] More intense on the American than the Canadian Frontier, when the two banks of the river were connected by bridges, new permanent linkages were created, and extensive urbanization followed on both Frontiers inland from these nodal locations. It was a buoyant era of radical change that transformed and added to the pioneer and canal landscapes that had been created.

THE EXPANDING RAILWAY NETWORK

The first rail lines served areas as adjuncts to the canal system. They competed with stagecoaches, and were conceived primarily as passenger carriers to provide access to tourism at the Falls. The Buffalo and Black Rock street railway was in operation by 1834, and in 1836 the Lockport and Niagara Falls carried passengers from the Erie Canal at Lockport along the edge of the Niagara Gorge to Niagara Falls. In the same year the Buffalo and Niagara Falls opened to connect the expanding city with the nearby tourist mecca.

On the Canadian Frontier the horse-drawn Erie and Ontario railway opened in 1839 between Queenston and Chippawa in

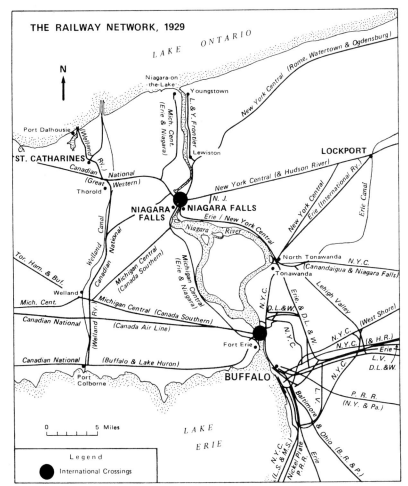

Fig. 4.1. Railways developed after the mid-1830s and again after the mid-1860s to interconnect all major places on both sides of the Frontier, and to link Canadian and American territory across the Niagara River. Although the system was linear, significant hubs were created where bridges crossed the Niagara River, and where railways converged at Buffalo, Lockport, Niagara Falls, and Tonawanda on the American Frontier, and at Welland to a lesser extent on the Canadian Frontier. (Prepared by the Department of Geography, Brock University)

Welland Canal, the horses had difficulty in hauling heavy loads up the Niagara Escarpment, and the limited seasonal tourist trade did not justify the costs.

As short rail segments connected the towns along the Erie Canal corridor, by 1842 Buffalo was linked to Albany by a series of lengths operated by different companies, complicated by different gauges.[2] This was only seventeen years after the completion of the Erie Canal to Buffalo, and was

an attempt to serve the portage communities bypassed by the Welland Canal. This railway, with steamer connections at Queenston for Toronto, expected to attract tourist traffic to the Falls, but it failed to compete with the achieved when the Buffalo and Attica was completed to Batavia. The routes paralleled the Erie Canal and reinforced this corridor to the Hudson River. The Atlantic seaboard could be reached either by rail via Albany to Boston or by steamship from Albany along the Hudson River to New York, with year-round operation, speed, and cost providing the railway with a considerable advantage over transportation by water.

The Lockport and Niagara Falls lines were extended to Rochester parallel to the Erie Canal in 1852, and added a direct route from Lockport through Tonawanda to Buffalo in 1853. Buffalo's position as a transportation hub was further strengthened by the construction of a direct route to Rochester via Batavia in 1851. Although the Canandaigua and Niagara Falls line bypassed Buffalo in 1853 en route to the Tonawandas and Niagara Falls, the major western terminal for the rail system in New York State was undoubtedly Buffalo.

Rail lines southeast, particularly the Erie to the "Southern Tier" of settlement, reinforced this nodality, as did the westward extension of the Buffalo and State Line along the shore of Lake Erie to Erie, Pennsylvania, and Cleveland, Ohio, in 1853. Complicated by different ownership and gauges, a crude trunk line had now been completed from the eastern seaboard to Chicago and the expanding West.

In 1854 several companies with lines between New York City and Buffalo consolidated into the New York Central and Hudson River, the predecessor of the New York Central that competed with the Erie for through traffic and local trade in western New York, and with Buffalo being in the central position on both of these major lines.

Later than these American developments, in the 1850s the Canadian Frontier obtained four rail lines. The Great Western opened from Windsor to Niagara Falls in 1853; this route crossed the Ontario Plain from Hamilton, ascended the Niagara Escarpment east of St. Catharines, and, after 1855, crossed the gorge of the Niagara River by the railway Suspension Bridge. Using Canadian terrain to connect Detroit and Niagara, the purpose was to divert western rail traffic from the longer haul on American territory south of Lake Erie.

Buffalo interests financed a second east-west route, also with the aim of capturing the western grain trade for American markets. The Buffalo and Lake Huron opened from Waterloo (near Old Fort Erie) to Goderich on Lake Huron in 1854. The Niagara River was crossed by ferry at Buffalo, and then the route ran parallel to Lake Erie until it turned north via the valley of the Grand River to Lake Huron.

Revitalized as a steam railway, the Erie and Ontario was extended north from Niagara Falls to Lake Ontario in the early 1850s. It climbed the Niagara Escarpment via a circuitous but easy gradient, using the buried St. David's Gorge to link Niagara and Niagara Falls. Extended south to Fort Erie, it reached Buffalo by ferry, to provide that city with an outlet on Lake Ontario and a link to Niagara Falls, Ontario, for tourist traffic.

The Port Dalhousie and Thorold railway was incorporated in 1853 to provide a link from the Great Western at Merritton to Port Dalhousie, where a station and freight sheds were built east of the harbor facing the commercial core on the west bank. An extension to Port Colborne was obtained in 1856. Renamed the Welland railway, it opened in 1859 to interconnect Lake Erie with Lake Ontario, and provided an auxiliary system of transportation in conjunction with the Welland Canal. Ships laden with wheat, too deep in draft to pass through the canal, were unloaded at Port Colborne. The wheat was then carried overland between the two lakes by the Welland railway; the lightened ships then passed through the canal, to be reloaded at Port Dalhousie.[3]

The American Civil War interrupted rail developments, but after 1865 new rail lines broadened Buffalo's hinterland by tapping coal and timber resources south of the city. Coal, the major power resource of the period, was used domestically in industry and to power locomotives and steamers, and as an export to Canada. The Buffalo, New York and Philadelphia was completed through Arcade and Olean to Pennsylvania by 1873, and with the Buffalo, Corry and Pittsburgh from Dunkirk along Lake Erie in 1882 became part of the Pennsylvania system. The Buffalo and Jamestown entered Buffalo in 1875, the Delaware, Lackawanna and Western paralleled the Erie to Buffalo from Binghamton to provide an alternative source of coal in 1882, and the Buffalo, Rochester and Pittsburgh with its extensive ownerships of coalfields entered the city from the south in 1887.

The Rome, Watertown and Ogdenburg ("Hojack" locally), completed along Lake Ontario to Lewiston in 1876, was extended to Niagara Falls in 1881. The New York, Chicago and St. Louis (Nickel Plate Road) paralleled the New York Central to Cleveland, the largely redundant West Shore line opened in 1884 between Buffalo and New York, the Lehigh Valley as a major coal-hauling line reached Buffalo's waterfront in 1892, and the Buffalo and Susquehanna from Wellsville opened in 1906.

Except for Grand Island, all places on the American Frontier by the 1900s were served by or within a few miles of a railway during this expanding period of coal-based, industrial expansion. The regional landscape became interlaced with an excessive provision of competitive lines of track, with Buffalo at the hub of this complicated network, its rivalries, and rate wars. The two systems that served Buffalo in 1875 had increased to six by 1900. With some 1126.5 kilometers (700 miles) of track in the city, the ownership of over 1,618.8 hectares (4,000 acres) of land, and with car, wheel, and locomotive shops, a major new industry with substantial employment and great urbanizing potential had been established. The urban environment became divided into a large number of small units by this trackage. These isolated areas often became neighborhoods associated with a particular ethnic group.

In Canada two east-west lines were added to compete with the western trade across Southern Ontario between Buffalo and Detroit. The Canada Southern, opened in 1873 west from Fort Erie, used the International Bridge before the Niagara Cantilever Bridge over the gorge opened in 1883. A double track laid from Welland to Niagara Falls served this bridge and the associated Montrose Yards at Chippawa. American-controlled, the railway, operated by the Michigan Central from 1894, was absorbed by the New York Central in 1929. The Canada Air Line opened in competition in 1873. Part of the Great Western system, it again linked the Niagara and Detroit Frontiers, but avoided the double crossing of the Niagara Escarpment at Hamilton and St. Catharines.

In 1884 the Toronto, Hamilton and Buffalo, owned by the New York Central and Canadian Pacific, was incorporated to build a line from Toronto via Hamilton to the International Bridge. It crossed the Niagara Peninsula from northwest to southeast, and promoted growth at Welland where it crossed the Welland Canal and linked with other rail systems.

Two short tourist routes extended the holiday trade from Buffalo to summer resorts along the Canadian north shore of Lake Erie: the Ontario Southern or "Peg-Leg Railway" operated from 1896 to 1898 between Ridgeway and Crystal Beach; and the Fort Erie, Snake Hill and Pacific followed the shoreline of Lake Erie between Fort Erie and the amusement park at Erie Beach. This narrow-gauge steam railway, known locally as the "Peanut Special" or the "Sandfly Express," lasted from 1885 until about 1910, when a pier was built at Erie Beach for cross-lake steamer traffic from Buffalo.

LINKS ACROSS THE BOUNDARY

Described as "the most important traffic gateways between the two countries on the Great Lakes Frontier,"[4] and with each acclaimed an engineering marvel, three railway bridges were built over the Niagara River in the second half of the nineteenth century.[5] As traffic increased and trains became heavier, these structures were each improved or replaced. The bridges required international agreement and charters from both nations, and different names were given for the same bridge; one example is that at Niagara Falls the charter from the Canadian government was to the Niagara Falls Suspension Bridge Company, while the State of New York licensed the Niagara Falls International Bridge Company.

The first contract to cross the Niagara River was awarded to Charles Ellet, who completed a fragile wooden suspension hanging from four massive towers. This bridge, for pedestrians only, opened across the gorge north of the Falls in 1848. It was a great event. The river had been spanned for the first time. Previously ferries crossed at Fort Erie-Buffalo, at the Falls across the pool below the Horseshoe Falls, and between Queenston-Lewiston north of the Whirlpool. The bridge provided a magnificent but precarious viewing platform of the gorge for pedestrians, and was an immediate tourist success, but Ellet was unable to complete a railway bridge and had to resign his commission with the bridge authorities.

The successor railway bridge, the Niagara Suspension Bridge with John A. Roebling as its engineer,[6] was completed in 1855. Roebling, who had invented a stronger, lighter, and more durable wire rope than the hemp rope then in use, took over the contract in 1850. Using Ellet's span as a service bridge, he completed a two-level structure 250.2 meters (821 feet) long that carried a single railway track. Leased to the Great Western, two different gauges used three rails on the upper deck, and an enclosed roadway below carried pedestrian, coach, and horse traffic. This wooden bridge, suspended from stone towers at either end by four cables with thousands of internal wires, was anchored firmly into the limestone bedrock that formed the sides of the gorge by a series of cables, trusses, and girders. The structure was rigid; it would neither sway nor twist in the wind, nor undulate with passing traffic. The bridge, a novel engineering venture, was built to last—and did.

The inspiring view was onto the gorge and the river, not the Falls as was anticipated by many tourists and publicized extensively by prints, souvenir books, and postcards. The

Ferries with rail access, later carrying automobiles, crossed the entrance of the Niagara River to interconnect Fort Erie with Buffalo. (John Burtniak [both])

bridge, an immediate success, nurtured communities and hotels for visitors at each entrance. Within a few months of opening, the bridge carried nineteen trains a day during the summer season. This bridge was replaced in situ by iron and steel trusses after twenty-six years of service, and the masonry towers were supplanted by iron within four years. Renamed the Niagara Steel Arch Bridge and now carrying a double railway on the upper deck, the new structure was built out from the walls of the gorge into its predecessor in 1897, and then modernized in 1919.

The Clifton Suspension Bridge, designed by Samuel Keefer, opened in 1869 about 0.2 kilometers (0.125 miles) below the American Falls. This wooden structure provided a long, spectacular crossing for pedestrians and carriages and, because of proximity to the Falls, was a bridge for tourists. The first ropes to start construction were carried across the winter ice bridge; for the Ellet structure a kite-flying competition had landed the first rope from west to east across the river. The Clifton Suspension Bridge, constructed with a timber deck, had timber towers at both ends to support the cables. Only 3 meters (10 feet) wide, the bridge allowed one-way carriage traffic only, which caused lengthy delays at both ends until widened in 1888. When destroyed by a storm in 1889, the bridge was replaced with a new structure of iron hung from steel cables, in turn outdated when the horsecar was replaced by the heavier electric streetcar. The Upper Steel Arch Bridge, built 1897–1898, then carried double track for the interurban streetcar service between the two Frontiers.

The second railway bridge to cross the Niagara River, the International Bridge across the southern entrance to the river between Fort Erie and Black Rock, was built by the Grand Trunk after taking control of the Buffalo and Lake Huron. Its charter was approved by the two governments in 1857. Construction now involved placing the supporting piers in the deep, fast-flowing Niagara River, a task undertaken by Sir Casimir S. Gzowski.[7] Four spans of 60 meters (197 feet), and three of 86.6 meters (284 feet) crossed the main river channel to Squaw Island, where two further arching spans carried the bridge across the Erie Canal. The single-track bridge opened in 1873, to replace the Fort Erie-Black Rock Ferry and the Grand Trunk Ferry from near Old Fort Erie to near Fort Porter on the American Frontier. The iron superstructure of the International Bridge was changed to steel in 1901, and in 1910–1911 the approach on the American side became a double-track swing bridge over the Black Rock Channel.

The two-level Suspension Bridge across the gorge (**above**) and the International Bridge across the neck of the Niagara River (**below**) were the first bridges to carry railway traffic across the river and connect Canada and the United States at the Niagara Frontier. Both bridges generated freight yards, industrial developments, service activities, and urban growth on the two banks of the river. (John Burtniak [both])

The third railway bridge, the Niagara Cantilever Bridge, was constructed across the gorge at Niagara Falls in 1883. Located next to and immediately south of the railway Suspension Bridge, and designed by Charles C. Schneider for the Canada Southern-Michigan Central railways, it was the world's longest double-track truss span. The river below the Falls was now the world's preeminent building site for bridges. The awesome natural landscape had been overcome by engineers, and the two countries now had direct overland links which provided many new opportunities for personal, trade, and business interchange. Strengthened in 1900 and replaced in 1925 by the Michigan Central bridge immediately north of the original structure, the Niagara Cantilever Bridge remains as one of the most acclaimed engineering structures to cross the river.

Even though the design was published in the *Encyclopaedia Britannica*, no railway bridge has ever crossed the Niagara River between Queenston and Lewiston, a route that would have avoided the steep slopes of the Niagara Escarpment and provided the shortest route between New York, Toronto, and urban Southern Ontario. Another failed attempt is the incorporation of the Niagara Grand Island Bridge Company in 1874 to construct a bridge from Grand Island to near

Black Creek on the Canadian shore. Also, the idea of a tunnel under the Niagara River between Fort Erie and Buffalo, discussed in Buffalo in 1880, was abandoned.

The rail crossings across the gorge and at the entrance to the Niagara River have exerted a very considerable impact on the Frontier's landscape. Ports of entry, freight yards, passenger and freight stations, repair and maintenance facilities, and homes for rail employees were added to both sides of each bridge. The lines, the yards, and the stations each attracted volumes of industry to their vicinity and, until the arrival of truck transport, the railway promoted and served all manufacturing plants. Railroad tracks also presented severe barriers to movement within the towns and attracted low-income housing to their vicinity, and trains added clouds of smoke pollution to the environment.

At the Suspension Bridge below the Falls, Niagara Falls became a port of entry named Port Stamford on the Canadian Frontier. Its business district attracted hotels for an increasing number of tourists, and the Great Western yards to the north added to this growth. The industrial-tourist center, first called Elgin, became the town of Clifton, and then the town of Niagara Falls in 1881. Similarly, the village of Bellevue arose downstream from the American Falls. Incorporated in 1854 as Niagara City, it later became Suspension Bridge, the legal port of entry to Canada. In 1892 it joined with the industrial center of Niagara Falls to the south to form the incorporated City of Niagara Falls. The International Railway Bridge played equally significant roles for urban evolution at Fort Erie and at Black Rock, where stations, yards, miles of track, and all their accoutrements again engulfed the landscape on both sides of the river.

The rail bridges were located at the narrowest points of the river. Earlier ferries and their communities at Chippawa-Fort Schlosser, Queenston-Lewiston, Fort Erie-Black Rock, and Niagara-Youngstown lost their transportation advantages and, lacking a rail crossing, declined in importance. Further, as bridges were not constructed over the Lower Niagara River except for a short-lived crossing by the Suspension Bridge between Queenston and Lewiston, the new population and industrial distributions associated with the railways favored southern rather than northern locations at the Frontier. They included Fort Erie-Buffalo, the two cities of Niagara Falls, and Welland, where the Welland Canal was crossed by all east-west railway routes.

The different parts of the Niagara Frontier were now being welded together by the iron horse. Ties of economic interdependence arose as agriculture, manufacturing, quarrying, trade,

and business activities expanded, and as both Frontiers were together partners in an expanding North American industrial heartland. This interaction necessitated a process of standardization described as the Americanization of Canada. For railways, the Canadian system was made compatible with the American. "The engines, the ordinary passenger cars, the sleepers, the dining cars, and the freight cars, are all exactly like those used on American lines. . . . The standard gauge is used throughout the continent and the rolling stock of American and Canadian roads is mutually interchangeable. So is the personnel."[8]

The railway encouraged Buffalo to grow as the regional trading and market center for both the Canadian and the American Frontiers (fig. 4.2). Organizations such as the Buffalo Freight Committee and the Buffalo Westbound Passenger Committee had representatives from the Canadian railways, as did the labor groups concerned with working conditions. Canadian railways lapped into the United States, and American routes penetrated Canada. Also, as telegraph lines followed every railway, this new form of intercommunication again closely linked the two sides at the Frontier.

The great majority of trains passing through the Canadian Frontier were to or from Buffalo. No local Canadian center could

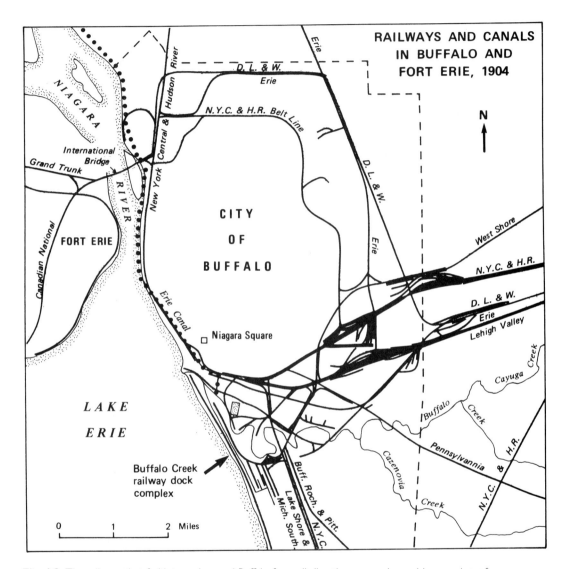

Fig. 4.2. The railways that fed into and served Buffalo from all directions caused a rapid expansion of industry, population, and service activities. (Prepared by the Department of Geography, Brock University)

match the range of goods and services that were available there. The country and small-town storekeepers could telegraph their orders to this city for immediate delivery by rail, and shopping excursions and theater trips to Buffalo became commonplace. The Canadian Frontier, while developing and expanding its own centers under railway auspices, did so under the commercial dominance of Buffalo. The railway bridges across the Niagara River were powerful artifacts of social and economic integration between the two Frontiers after the mid-1850s.

THE EXPANSION OF BUFFALO

Railroads fostered rapid expansion in Buffalo (fig. 4.2). The city doubled in population size from 62,000 in 1850 to 120,000 in 1870, then tripled to over 352,000 by 1900 when ranked the eighth largest city in the United States. Railways had appeared at Buffalo's waterfront by the late 1840s and, from 1855 when the New York Central built a large depot on Buffalo Creek, they began to take traffic from the Erie Canal. The lines of track brought in raw material from all directions, attracted manufacturing industries which supplemented the existing harbor enterprises,[9] and encouraged some movement of industry

away from former waterfront locations. Distance and accessibility had been transformed, Buffalo in 1899 being but three hours by rail from Toronto, six from Detroit, nine from Pittsburgh and New York, and thirteen hours from Chicago and Philadelphia.[10]

Within the city, the Buffalo Creek railroad and others provided switching facilities to move freight to the main lines, between the railroads, and between the railroads and the lake and canal terminals. They linked mills, warehouses, and industrial plants. In 1883, to reduce congestion, the New York Central opened 24.1 kilometers (15 miles) of inner belt line railroad around the city, that attracted additional industries and housing. New residential areas located beyond the loop, and passenger stations made regular commuting to downtown Buffalo possible. In 1888 two passenger trains an hour circulated the track each way, and the forty-five-minute journey had twenty stops. Substantial outward suburban growth of the city was underway.

Previously the Erie had built a belt line to the east and north of Buffalo, and in 1882 the Delaware, Lackawanna and Western built an additional belt line almost parallel to the Erie railway. The Lehigh Valley branches to Lackawanna and Niagara Falls formed a more distant loop. In the central business district, the railway stations served as focal points for streetcar lines and attracted hotels, stores, and warehouses.[11] The heavily used New York Central's Exchange Street Station, a major center of activity and a focal point within the city, was enlarged five times between 1855 and 1907.

By 1910 some fourteen trunk lines had terminals at Buffalo or passed through the city. In addition, steamship lines on the Upper Great Lakes had their terminals and offices at Buffalo. Waterborne freight exceeded 4.5 million tonnes (5 million tons) annually. The waterfront, its piers, and a series of inner and outer breakwaters extended for 32.2 kilometers (20 miles); its 16.1 kilometers (10 miles) of wharves were densely served by railways (fig. 4.3).

Buffalo's diverse economy received manufactured goods from the east and raw materials from the west and south.[12] The city became one of the principal grain and flour markets in the world, as grain flowed in from the west. With over forty elevators by 1874, two hundred million bushels of grain and ten million barrels of flour were handled by the early twentieth century. Stockyards in East Buffalo sold over 10 million live animals each year. The horse market was the largest in North America. Lumberyards, handling large quantities of timber annually, lined the shore of Lake Erie and the Niagara River. The

movement by rail of anthracite increased fivefold between 1872 and 1884. The Delaware, Lackawanna and Western provided direct access to the anthracite fields of eastern Pennsylvania. The company's huge coal dock remained on the city's waterfront until the 1950s. The bituminous tonnage from southwestern Pennsylvania went from 58,967 tonnes (65,000 tons) in 1882 to 1.7 million tonnes (1.9 million tons) in 1884.[13]

Coal via rail, combined with newly discovered Minnesota iron ore brought in by ship, made possible the major steelmaking complex at Lackawanna, then the largest in the world, and the first outward movement from the American heartland of steel production to a new location on the Great Lakes. Four hundred hectares (1,000 acres) of marshy lakeshore land were purchased, construction began in 1901, and full production was reached by 1906.[14] This enterprise initiated the City of Lackawanna in 1909. Two company villages were built, each with about five hundred attached brick houses for the workforce which had grown to six thousand by 1907. A major new North American iron and steelmaking center had arisen at the Frontier. The site had direct rail connections to the Pennsylvania coalfields, used Onondaga limestone imported from the Canadian shore of Lake Erie on large ore boats, and accessed

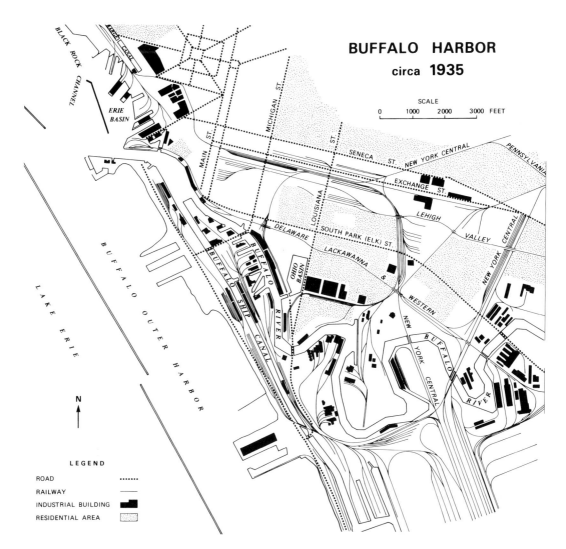

Fig. 4.3. The place of greatest activity in Buffalo was the waterfront where canal barges, lake shipping, and railways merged to promote warehousing, manufacturing industry, and the expansion of service activities. (Prepared by the Department of Geography, Brock University)

The Lackawanna Steelworks dominated the eastern end of Lake Erie south of Buffalo. (John N. Jackson)

low-cost hydroelectric power from the new generating plants at the Falls. The town had as its major feature Our Lady of Victory Basilica, located inland from Lake Erie on high ground, and with its great dome. Here were also an orphanage and a hospital.[15]

The iron industry in Buffalo had started in 1846 with the Buffalo Iron and Nail Works.

With four manufacturers, and including the production of large castings for locomotives, in 1862 they associated as the Union Iron Works to build a rolling mill, which in 1890 became the Buffalo Furnace Company. The output of iron, then steel, was prodigious. The Union Bridge Company was the largest fabricator of bridges anywhere in the world, the car shops of the New York Central in East Buffalo were one of the largest employees, and iron was used in increasing quantities for agricultural machinery, railroad cars, and road-building equipment. Union Dry Dock on the Buffalo River built and repaired many different types of vessels.

The railroads and the iron industry were closely related. The railways (and boats) brought in the raw materials that were required for iron and then steel production, and the railroad enterprises required first iron, then steel, for their bridges and lines of track. Railway rolling stock and equipment suppliers located in Buffalo, and railway shops concentrated in South Buffalo and east of the stations. The New York Central, the largest railway company, had facilities east of downtown, and founded the village of Depew for its shops.

Many other industries were attracted because of the range and availability of materials by rail and water. Buffalo became a meatpacking center, which stimulated tanneries, fertilizer industries, the manufacture of soap, and harness factories. Hardwood from northern Pennsylvania was used in making furniture and boxes and in the wagon and carriage trades. Linseed oil extracted from western flaxseed gave rise to the manufacture of varnish, turpentine, oil, meal, and

paint. From grain came flour milling, cereal and animal feed products, breweries, and the glucose (obtained from cornstarch) that industries use as a sweetener. Brick, glass, stone and lime works, lithographing establishments, patent medicine, chemical works, and petroleum refineries were added to the industrial economy.

The townscape incorporated a remarkable number of large industrial buildings. Over one thousand manufacturing establishments existed by 1884, and over four hundred industrial buildings were added from 1890 to 1905. Many of the buildings were described as "among the largest in existence,"[16] and residential villages "of comfortable homes" for the working classes were built near these industries.[17] The Larkin factories by 1909 covered over 20.2 hectares (50 acres) of floor space. In business since 1875, they were the largest manufacturers of soap and toilet preparations in the world and produced many home needs, including food specialties, paints, varnishes, polishes, notions, and other sundries. Their products were sold at half price through a battery of local agents to nearby consumers, thus saving on the expenses and profits of wholesalers and retailers.

AN AMBIVALENT CITY

Seasonal unemployment occurred when Lake Erie and the Erie Canal closed during the winter months. Employment also fluctuated according to the demand for labor, and declined for jobs associated with the Erie Canal. Harsh cyclical unemployment existed, as in 1907 when the railroads and steel industries suffered severe depression. Violent strikes erupted to improve working conditions on the waterfront and in industry. Smoke from coal-powered industry, lake vessels, and locomotives indicated progress and prosperity. It also spelled pollution and, as the shore of Lake Erie and the frontage of the Niagara and Buffalo Rivers were taken over by industry, the rivers and waterways became open dumps for industrial waste.

In a period now perceived as "the shame of the cities,"[18] Buffalo encountered severe social problems in its low-income areas. In 1871 "it was sown with saloons. Along the waterfront were solid rows of dives of the worst order. . . . Cutting affrays were a daily affair. There were streets where the police walked at mid-day and only in pairs. . . . And the Erie County jail received more convicts than any jail in the state."[19] In 1880 when the federal census tabulated brothels, Buffalo had 104, and Canal Street between the Erie Canal and Lake Erie obtained a most unsavory reputation (fig. 4.4).

Factory hands and railroad labor recently arrived from southern and eastern Europe were housed in substandard buildings in polluted surroundings near the tangle of rail lines. The large-scale immigration of non-English-speaking people to work in the growing industries created ethnic neighborhoods, such as those near the waterfront where Italians displaced Irish and where Polish immigrants settled near the rail lines on Buffalo's East Side. The Lackawanna mill brought in more cheap immigrant labor. Tied together by language and religion, these unskilled workers clustered in the vicinity of the mill near churches which tried to alleviate their culture shock, exploitation, and poverty.[20] New arrivals often had rural backgrounds with little or no prior experience of urban-industrial conditions. Misery, poverty, and the degradation in neighborhoods lacking open space and public services became part of the depressed urban landscape. Social welfare was badly needed, and many charitable and philanthropic institutions were founded. It was a city of both conspicuous wealth and conspicuous poverty, a challenge to both industrialists and reformers. This remedial work was exemplified by Father Nelson H. Baker who built Our Lady of Victory Home in

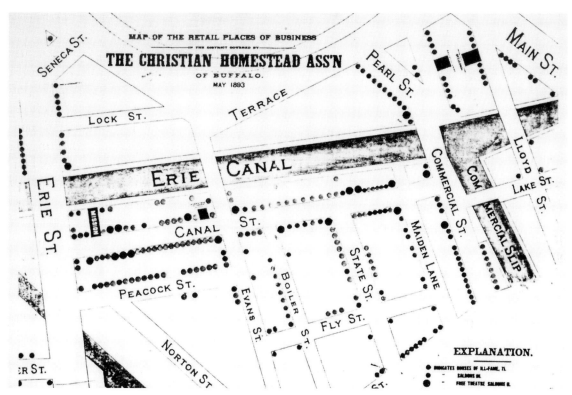

Fig. 4.4. Houses of ill-fame and saloons bespatter and defame the notorious Canal District of Buffalo. (U.S. Federal Census, 1880)

Lackawanna for destitute Catholic boys; a hospital was later added to this church-educational complex.

Away from its squalid slums, Buffalo was a city of wealth, pride, and ability. When parks were being considered, the civic leaders turned to Frederick Law Olmsted, the noted landscape architect who, imbued with the ideas of English landscape design, had designed Central Park in New York City with Calbert Vaux.[21] Invited to visit Buffalo in 1868, Olmsted designed the 141.6-hectare (350-acre) space known as the Park, now Delaware Park. Featuring a lake fed by Scajaquada Creek, a boathouse, a casino, and pleasant meadows, it became a popular attraction by the 1880s, augmented the foundation plan of Joseph Ellicott, and "was the first park and parkway system for an American city."[22]

Then distant from the city, Delaware Park was protected by Forest Lawn Cemetery to the south, the low-density private suburb of Parkside to the east and north, and the Buffalo State Hospital to the west. Olmsted also designed the grounds of this psychiatric hospital and planned the layout of the Parkside community. As Delaware Avenue was extended north to the park, it attracted upper-income residences, and when this avenue passed through the park, it crossed over the parkway by a stone bridge to provide an early example of traffic separation by function. Olmsted also designed a park system for the booming city. This system included large parks, such as the Parade, and Front, interconnected by tree-lined boulevards and spacious landscaped circles (fig. 4.5).

Olmsted suggested other parks and the expansion of green space along the waterfront and watercourses. His belief that urban areas should be structured around open space to provide a more humane and natural urban dimension created much of benefit to Buffalo. Although frustrated by the prior industrial, commercial, and transportation uses along Lake Erie, the Niagara River, and the Erie Canal frontages, Olmsted contributed to park space at the Falls, and was among those who helped to create the State Reservation in 1885.

INDUSTRIAL EXPANSION IN THE SMALLER URBAN CENTERS

Expansion based on railways, canals, and industry was not confined to Buffalo. At Lockport, in the 1850s an underground raceway tunnel, 690.4 meters (2,430 feet) in length fed water from the upper level of the Erie Canal to supply the lower or Genesee level. This in turn was used for power, and with rail access attracted industrial development that included sawmills and factories which produced sewing machines, pumps, and hydraulic machinery.[23] The population of Lockport had grown to twenty thousand by 1890. In the City of Tonawanda new streets and a public square were laid out about 1850 after the arrival of the Buffalo and Niagara Falls railroad (fig. 4.6).

Augmented by the railroads and by canal improvements, the City of North Tonawanda became known as "The Lumber City." Described in 1907 as the largest wholesale lumber market in the world, planing mills manufacturing pine shingles and wood laths in great quantities lined the 9.7 kilometers (6 miles) of dock facilities along the harbor, Tonawanda Island, and the Niagara River.[24] These activities peaked in 1890, when over 214 million meters (700 million feet) of timber were handled; one account then

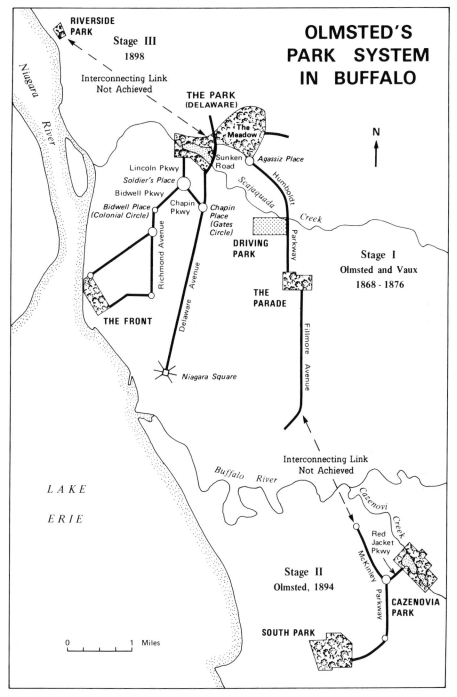

Fig. 4.5. Frederick Law Olmsted, high in the record of late-nineteenth-century planning for parks and thoroughfares, embellished the urban scene at Buffalo and enlarged upon the design foundations established by Joseph Ellicott. (Prepared by the Department of Geography, Brock University)

OLMSTED'S PARK SYSTEM IN BUFFALO

RIVERSIDE PARK

Stage III
1898

Interconnecting Link Not Achieved

THE PARK (DELAWARE)

The Meadow

N

Niagara River

Sunken Road

Agassiz Place

Lincoln Pkwy

Soldier's Place

Bidwell Pkwy

Chapin Pkwy

Bidwell Place (Colonial Circle)

Chapin Place (Gates Circle)

Scajaquada

Creek

Humboldt Parkway

DRIVING PARK

Stage I
Olmsted and Vaux
1868 - 1876

Richmond Avenue

Delaware Avenue

THE PARADE

THE FRONT

Niagara Square

Fillmore Avenue

Buffalo River

Interconnecting Link Not Achieved

Cazenovi Creek

Red Jacket Pkwy

McKinley Parkway

CAZENOVIA PARK

Stage II
Olmsted, 1894

LAKE ERIE

SOUTH PARK

0   1 Miles

Frederick Law Olmsted, his park system, its setting for buildings, and its focal points for urban design have helped considerably to raise the status of Buffalo to a great North American city. (John N. Jackson)

described no fewer than fifty-seven lake vessels unloading lumber in the harbor.[25] Some of this wood in the hands of skilled local woodcarvers produced organs, musical instruments, and carved horses for merry-go-rounds.

Niagara Falls, New York, where the New York Central, Lehigh Valley, and Erie had terminals, also began to emerge as a manufacturing center,[26] the value of its factory products being $8.5 million in 1900 when Buffalo was assessed at $105.6 million. Early industries included flour mills, pulp and paper mills, copper shops, and a brewery. Two major focal points existed by 1890: the village at the Falls with a population of 5,330, and the railroad village at the Suspension Bridge with 3,915 people. When the City of Niagara Falls incorporated in 1892, it boasted two downtown stations and one at the Suspension Bridge. The railway was also a mixed blessing; it brought in tourists, but tracks and yards divided the urban environment and debased scenic quality along the gorge.

Across the river, Canadian centers also expanded with the development

Fig. 4.6. Railways converged on Tonawanda and North Tonawanda, where they crossed the Erie Canal. By contrast Grand Island, which received neither a connecting bridge nor a railway, remained undeveloped. (Surveys and Mapping Branch, Ottawa, 1:63.360 Sheet, 30L/15, 1907)

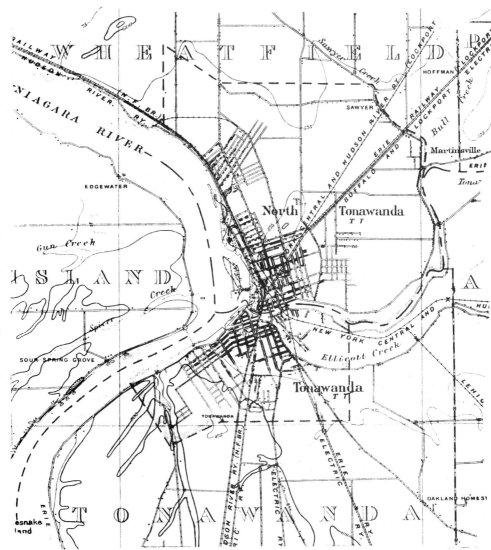

of rail transport. West of the Suspension Bridge, the railhead villages of Elgin and Clifton amalgamated in 1856 to form the Town of Clifton.[27] Renamed the Town of Niagara Falls in 1881 and then the City of Niagara Falls in 1903, the population of 5,702 in 1901 clustered around the international rail bridges, associated rail facilities, and the services which they attracted, including hotels.

In 1854 Waterloo, the settlement near Fort Erie, contained local stores, churches, and a blacksmith shop.[28] With the arrival of the Buffalo and Lake Huron, the population increased to about nine hundred. Both centers formed the Village of Fort Erie in 1857. When the focus of activity moved north to the International Bridge, a new settlement known sequentially as Victoria, Bridgeburg, and then International Bridge evolved (fig. 4.7). Freight yards, coal docks, a roundhouse, shops, customs and immigration buildings, and stations were soon added. The town center developed east-west along a main street parallel to the tracks, and the freight yards and the lines of track created severe barriers to crosstown movement. Industries and warehouses followed the railways, and poor-quality housing located on inferior sites next to the tracks.[29]

At Niagara-on-the-Lake a railcar works briefly serviced the Erie and Niagara, but the economic fortunes of the town were not improved. Welland received a series of rail facilities, and transportation advantages increased when the Third Welland Canal opened in 1887. With the motto "Where Rails and Water Meet," Welland provided industry the choice between canal or rail for sites and shipment. As the town expanded from its core across the canal, tracks, industry, and the waterway broke the new urban developments into distinct areas.

Although St. Catharines was the principal center of the Niagara Peninsula by 1851, its railways produced only modest increments to urban growth. The town had a semicircle of railways to the south after the late 1850s, but the main-line Great Western station to the west and the station of the Welland railway to the east lay outside the central area. Neither railway served either the urban core or the canal industries next to the city center. Furthermore, the Great Western station was separated by distance and the deep valley of Twelve Mile Creek from the urban community. The main line between Niagara Falls and Hamilton-Toronto had bypassed St. Catharines, and the station that served the city became little more than an incidental stop. The town council tried to reroute the Great Western through the town, but to no avail, and not until 1888 did the locally sup-

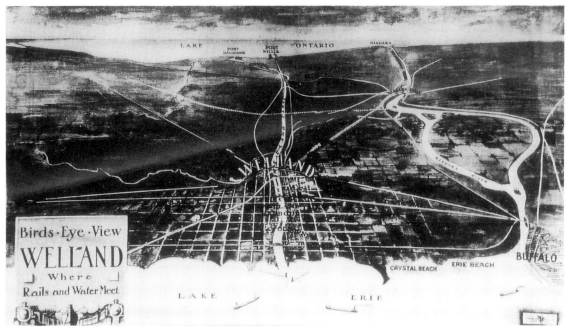

Birds·Eye·View
WELLAND
Where
Rails and Water Meet

At Welland, east-west railways to and from Frontier bridges crossed the north-south Welland Canal to provide industrial sites with rail and/or canal access, leading to the urban motto "Where Rails and Water Meet." (John Burtniak)

ported St. Catharines and Niagara Central railway penetrate the town center.

Instead of at St. Catharines, industrial growth took place at Merritton, where 200.3 hectares (500 acres) of land were purchased to take advantage of a unique situation: the convergence of waterpower from the locks, the Hydraulic Raceway, and the Welland Canal; the crossing of the Great Western and the Welland railway lines with their competitive rates; and access via the Welland railway to all east-west lines in the Niagara Peninsula. A cotton mill, a cement plant, the first sulphite paper mill in Canada, and a hammer works were attracted.[30]

St. Catharines declined relatively against more vigorous growth and the rise of manufacturing at Hamilton, Toronto, and other centers in south-central Ontario.[31] Toronto became the focus for a series of radiating lines, and greatly expanded its hinterland. Hamilton grew industrially for similar reasons, but to a

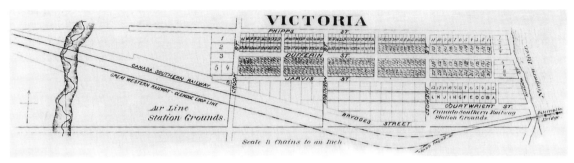

Fig. 4.7. Victoria, later Bridgeburg and now part of the town of Fort Erie, grew as the Canadian railhead settlement parallel to the lines of track at the western end of the International Bridge over the Niagara River. (H. R. Page, *Illustrated Historical Atlas of the Counties of Lincoln and Welland, Ont.,* 1876)

lesser degree. As the industrial impetus moved inland to the "Golden Horseshoe" around the western end of Lake Ontario, the advancing rail network placed the Canadian Frontier on the edge of Ontario's expanding urbanization. By contrast, the American Frontier was a prime location for rail-fostered industrial growth and urban development.

Port Colborne (fig. 4.8) and Port Dalhousie, as harbors and as ports of entry to the Welland Canal, were strengthened by rail improvements. Both were terminals on the Welland railway, and Port Colborne a railway junction where the Buffalo and Goderich branch of the Grand Trunk crossed the Welland Canal. Both ports had sawmills and flour mills, and by the 1880s a population of one thousand to fifteen hundred.[32] The large elevator at Port Colborne could transfer six thousand bushels of grain per hour from lake vessels to railcars. Both centers were incorporated as villages; both had residential and commercial developments on the west bank of the canal, with railways and associated industrial activities on the east bank.

AGRICULTURE AND THE RURAL LANDSCAPE

As railways opened extensive western areas in North America for wheat production and refrigerated railcars made possible new markets to farmers, land at the Frontier could be used for different crops. Previously, fresh produce could travel but a short distance and remain fresh; now delivery to Ottawa, Montreal, and New York City was possible within

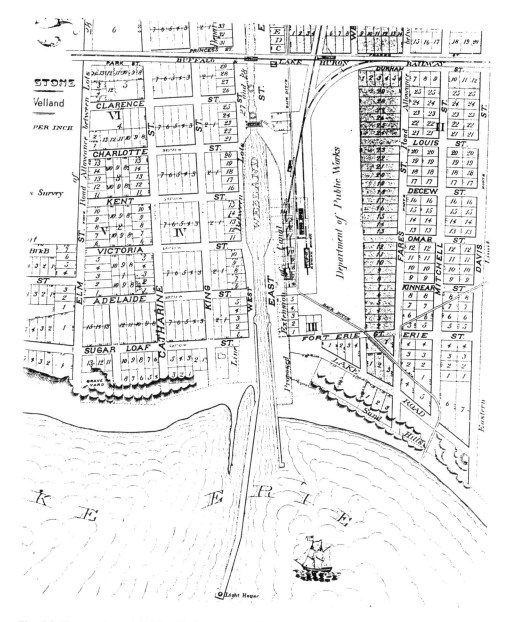

Fig. 4.8. The north-south Welland Railway at Port Colborne helped lake vessels transfer grain to Port Dalhousie on Lake Ontario. The harbor inland from the sand dunes was artificial. East Street was later removed to accommodate the Third Welland Canal. The bridge crossing at the head of the harbor, moved north to Clarence Street when the harbor was widened and extended, became the pivot of commercial growth. (H. R. Page, *Illustrated Historical Atlas of the Counties of Lincoln and Welland, Ont.,* 1876)

a day. Ice companies sprang up, packing ice cut from ponds in sawdust, then selling it to distant customers. In Niagara Township on the Canadian Frontier, little fruit was sold commercially before 1860; twenty years later fruit-growing predominated,[33] peach orchards with two thousand trees were common, and about 350,000 bushels were harvested annually from some 125,000 trees.

St. Catharines became a center for shipping fruit, exporting by rail and water an aggregate total of some 5.9 million kilograms (13 million pounds) by 1900.[34] Fruit and vegetable canning expanded from one cannery in 1891 to six by the turn of the century. All had direct rail access. By 1901 advances in the storing and shipping of perishable products enabled the railways to export fruit with efficiency and speed from centers across the Fruit Belt. Fruit graded by shippers and loaded in cars by 6 P.M. could be sent by rail to all centers in Ontario and western Quebec, arriving early the next morning.

Grapes for wine-making were planted extensively in the St. David's area in 1857. The Ontario Vine Growers Associated, a collective of farmers from the Niagara Peninsula, received its charter in the 1860s. By 1890 about 2,023.5 hectares (5,000 acres) of grapes were in production. Wineries with rail access were established in St. Catharines and Niagara Falls by the 1870s. By 1913 Lincoln County had over 5,908.6 hectares (14,600 acres) under fruit production that included peaches, grapes, apples, and minor crops of plums, pears, and berries.

Agriculture on the American Frontier was likewise affected by rail transport and the new possibilities of refrigeration. By the 1840s Erie County was producing corn, wheat, oats, and livestock, and Hamburg, New York, was famous for its cheese. After the railway linked the area to national markets, fruit growing was encouraged in Niagara County below the Niagara Escarpment. In the Town of Porter a large-scale planting of apples and pears took place during the 1870s and the 1880s.[35] Peaches also became profitable, followed about 1900 by prunes, quinces, and cherries. Grain elevators developed next to the rail tracks in Ransomville in the late 1800s, followed by a poultry business after 1887. Market gardening in the fringe areas became important as a new activity to serve the expanding population in the city of Buffalo.

Niagara County, with 1.4 million apple trees by 1900, became famous for the quality and quantity of apples that were produced and barreled. Fruit-storage warehouses lined the Rome, Watertown and Ogdensburg (Hojack) in Ransomville, Wilson, and Burt.

At St. Catharines, the railway with refrigerated cars helped to establish the Niagara Fruit Belt and made possible the distribution of ripe fruit over extensive distances. (John Burtniak)

Youngstown and Olcott exported fruit by boat. The Youngstown Cold Storage Company shipped 30,000 bushels of apples and 3,500 bushels of peaches from the area in 1870.[36] An evaporator for drying apples was constructed in 1880, cider and vinegar were made, and barrels manufactured for the fruit industry. Commercial grape growing, introduced to Niagara County in 1872, specialized in production of the indigenous hybrid Niagara Grape, which was grown extensively until the turn of the century when the entire crop was destroyed by a pest.

Buffalo's markets exerted an impact on

Railways and their stations, now mostly nostalgic memories, have been provided with a new lease on life as here at the Fort Erie Historical Railroad Museum. (John N. Jackson [both])

agriculture that extended across the boundary to the Canadian Frontier. Consumer demand and improved transportation overrode the political boundary. As noted for Welland County in 1886, "Buffalo creates a ready market for cattle, poultry, and the products of the dairy and garden."[37] Fish from the Niagara River and Lake Erie were exported to this large consumer market, as were horses from the Fonthill area, sand from the dunes next to Lake Erie, limestone from the Onondaga Escarpment, and fruit from the now-established fruit belt.

RAILWAYS IN DECLINE

Rail passenger traffic declined through the advancing use of automobiles, long-distance buses, and aircraft. Freight traffic was lost with the coming of the interconnected highway system, and as trucks of increasing size displaced trains for all but bulk goods and some through traffic. This story of drastic change is epitomized by the construction in 1929 of a new Central Terminal on Buffalo's East Side that contained a seventeen-story office tower, complete express facilities, extensive yard and service facilities, landscaped approaches to the station, and a capacity of two hundred passenger trains a day. But this spectacular terminal never lived up to its promise. The Great Depression precipitated a decline in all forms of travel. The terminal worked to full capacity only during the Second World War. Then, outlasting the downtown stations, it was abandoned in 1973 and remains an empty and silent reminder of the glory that was the New York Central and of railroading in Buffalo.

Rail closures included the Buffalo and Susquehanna, which was declared surplus by 1916; the line from Swormsville to Tonawanda, which closed in 1939; and by the mid-1950s lines of track had disappeared from several routes. In 1960 the Erie and the Delaware, Lackawanna, and Western merged as the New York Central and the Pennsylvania amalgamated as the Penn Central, which caused the further abandonment of lines, stations, and facilities. The creation of Conrail in 1973 by the United States government eliminated most of what remained of the Lehigh Valley and the Erie and Lackawanna belt lines. In Niagara Falls, New York, during the 1950s the principal routes in the center of the city were relocated to the east and connected to the New York Central between Lockport and the Suspension Bridge.[38]

Despite attempts at revival and improved rail efficiency through the change in motive power from coal and steam to diesel-electric,[39]

Drastic change in railway circumstances since the 1950s is reflected on both Frontiers. **Above right:** The main Canadian National line through St. Catharines was in use by 1999 for infrequent passenger and regular freight traffic, but the side track that served industry (left) was derelict, and the industrial area (right) centered on the station no longer had rail access. **Below right:** Strong evidence of former rail-water interlinkages is provided by the Buffalo terminal of the Lackawanna railroad, now but a ghost of the past. (John N. Jackson [both])

the downtown stations, lines of track, railyards, and many bridges were eliminated. They became sites for sections of the Robert Moses Parkway and for many new buildings such as the Niagara Falls Public Library. Even the gigantic and relatively new Bison yard of the Erie-Lackawanna railway, itself the product of a merger, was torn up and then turned over to the City of Buffalo which promoted its large space as a future industrial park.

On the Canadian Frontier the line of the former Erie and Ontario between Fort Erie and Niagara-on-the-Lake was the first to be abandoned, and sections of the north-south Welland railway no longer exist. The surviving modernized network includes lines that approach the International Railway Bridge at Fort Erie and those converging on the two railway bridges at Niagara Falls. Tracks such as sections of the Erie and Ontario route close to the Lower Niagara River and the Fort Erie-Port Colborne length of the former Buffalo and Lake Huron have become trails. The Toronto, Hamilton and Buffalo line has become part of Canadian Pacific. The Canadian National's former Buffalo and Lake Huron line through Fort Erie was in part taken over to lay a pipeline, and sections are to become a hiking trail linking the Niagara River Parkway with the Welland Canal Parkway.

On the American Frontier contraction and consolidation brought the Delaware and Hudson and Canadian Pacific to Niagara, together with considerable traffic interchange between American lines and Canadian National for freight movements. "Piggyback" services have expanded, with flatcars carrying loaded trucks to combine rail and truck transport, and three-level railcars to carry automobiles and their parts. Railyards as in East Buffalo have been upgraded, and advanced computer systems developed to route railcars. By 1997 passenger traffic had been reduced to ten weekly Amtrak trains to Washington, eight to New York, and seven to both Chicago and Toronto.

Though much changed, the railways continue to serve manufacturing industries with freight haulage on both Frontiers. They remain important points of interchange between the two Frontiers and their hinterlands, and may now compete successfully with highway, canal, and air modes of transportation for certain commodities on particular routes. On the Canadian Frontier new rail facilities were provided when the Welland Canal Bypass was constructed around Welland, and track has been rerouted in Port Colborne to serve a milling company. On the American Frontier in the 1980s a line carrying coal was introduced to Somerset from Lockport.

Automobile and truck transport have clearly triumphed. The decline of railways has left behind a relict landscape where lines of track, embankments, cuttings, stations, yards, sidings, and industry formerly existed. Rail operations have been scaled down, local and redundant lines are gone, many yards are deserted and weedy, most stations have disappeared, and several lengths of track have been redeveloped as highways, used for building sites and open space, or utilized as rights-of-way for pipelines, transmission wires, or walking trails.

By the late 1990s the trend to amalgamation and consolidation was for a smaller number of large continental railway corporations. Montreal-based Canadian National (CN) acquired the Illinois Central, and announced a potential merger with the Fort Worth, Texas–based Burlington Northern Santa Fe, which would have created North America's largest railroad. As this union was effectively stopped by the American Surface Transportation Board, the planned amalgamation was canceled. In the meantime, Calgary-based Canadian Pacific (CP) forged an alliance with Union Pacific, the largest American railway corporation, to provide a "seamless service" that would link with trans-Atlantic container services at the Atlantic ports, especially New York. This would benefit lines across the Niagara Peninsula and their links across the Niagara River, whereas the competing CN links would tend to be south through the Detroit Tunnel to New Orleans.

After the CN/Burlington Northern Santa Fe merger was canceled, the rival CN/CP railways announced a three-year agreement to share their lines of tracks, an implication being that CP would use CN tracks across Southern Ontario to the St. Clair Tunnel at Sarnia, Ontario. At the Niagara Frontier if one, or even two, of the three railway bridges across the Niagara River is declared redundant, former railway tracks might be used to accommodate expanding highway traffic volumes, but the bridge(s) that remain continue to provide a vital means of freight movement and intercommunication between the two countries.

The transportation situation has changed drastically since the long period during the nineteenth and twentieth century when the railways had the greatest popularity, power, and economic success. By the year 2000 the map shown in figure 4.1, which depicts the climax railway network by 1929, had become history as strong external political, economic, and corporate forces were reshaping the Frontier's landscape. The boundary had become of little importance in this international decision-making process.

NOTES

1. Terminology changes as the boundary is crossed. As "railway" is Canadian and British usage, and "railroad" American, "rail" will be used as an adjective in this text. Canadian sources include J. N. Jackson and J. Burtniak, *Railways in the Niagara Peninsula: Their Development, Progress and Community Significance* (Belleville, Ont.: Mika, 1978); and C. A. Andreae, *A Historical Railway Atlas of Southwestern Ontario* (London, Ont: n.p., 1972), and *Lines of Country: An Atlas of Railway and Waterway History in Canada* (Erin, Ont.: Boston Mills Press, 1997). For American developments see H. H. Pierce, *Railroads of New York* (Cambridge, Mass.: Harvard University Press, 1983); D. W. Meinig, "Geography of Expansion, 1785–1855" and "Elaboration and Change, 1850's–1960's," in *Geography of New York State*, ed. J. H. Thompson (Syracuse, N.Y.: Syracuse University Press, 1966), pp. 162–65, 172–77. An international statement is W. J. Wilgus, *The Railway Interrelations of the United States and Canada* (New Haven, Conn.: Yale University Press, 1937).

2. *Gauge* is the distance between rails. *Standard gauge* is the distance between each pair of rails. *Broad gauge* is generally 1.8 meters (6 feet), as on the Erie and the first Canadian lines.

3. T. C. Keefer, *The Philosophy of Railways* (1849; reprint, Toronto: University of Toronto Press, 1972). See L. Murphy, *Thomas Keefer* (Don Mills, Ont.: Fitzhenry and Whiteside, 1977).

4. Wilgus, *The Railway Interrelations of the United States and Canada*, p. 18.

5. J. Carnochan, *Bridges over the Niagara River*, Niagara Historical Society, Publication no. 36 (1924), pp. 26–37; C. J. Christensen et al., *History of Engineering in Niagara* (St. Catharines, Ont.: Niagara Peninsula Branch, Engineering Institute of Canada, 1977), pp. 25–37; and R. Greenhill, *Spanning Niagara: The International Bridges 1848–1962* (Niagara Falls, N.Y.: Niagara University, 1984).

6. B. Steinman, *The Builders of the Bridge: The Story of John Roebling and His Son* (New York: Arno, 1950), p. 157. Suspension bridges as new feats of engineering enabled major physical obstacles to be overcome, and thereby permitted greater distances to be overcome. Precedents included the Fribourg Bridge of 1834 in Switzerland, which had been viewed by a son of William Hamilton Merritt, entrepreneur of the Welland Canal and a promoter of the bridge across the Niagara Gorge; and the Menai Strait Bridge between Anglesey and the Welsh mainland. As the bridge across the Niagara Gorge lay on the direct route between Boston and New York to Detroit and Chicago, considerable profit was expected from both the increase in the year-round freight-carrying trade and the expanding summer passenger traffic to and through Niagara Falls.

7. C. S. Gzowski, *Description of the International Bridge* (Toronto: Cobb, Clark, 1873).

8. S. E. Moffet, *The Americanization of Canada* (Toronto: University of Toronto Press, 1972), pp. 57–58.

9. J. T. Horton, "Old Erie—The Growth of an American Community," in J. T. Horton et al.,

History of Northwestern New York (New York: Lewis Historical Publishing, 1947), 1:224; and M. Goldman, *High Hopes: The Rise and Decline of Buffalo, New York* (Albany: State University of New York Press, 1983), pp. 124–43.

10. *Hand-Book to the Pan-American Exposition: Buffalo and Niagara Falls* (Chicago: Rand, McNally, 1899), p. 88.

11. R. L. Squire, *Erie County Railroads: 1936–1972*, Adventures in Western New York History, vol. 20 (Buffalo, N.Y.: Buffalo and Erie County Historical Society, 1973), pp. 13–14; and *The Railroads That Serve Buffalo* (1927; reprint, Buffalo, N.Y.: Buffalo Chapter, National Railway Historical Society, 1982).

12. Horton, "Old Erie," pp. 317–58; W. S. Dunn, ed., *History of Erie County, 1870–1970* (Buffalo, N.Y.: Buffalo and Erie County Historical Society, 1972), pp. 21–36; and W. Thurstone, *A Sketch of the Commerce, Industries and Resources of Buffalo* (Buffalo, N.Y.: Buffalo Merchants' Exchange, 1883). Annual review, *Trade and Commerce of Buffalo* (Buffalo, N.Y.: Buffalo Board of Trade, n.d.) provides considerable factual detail. A photographic appreciation is M. H. Hubbell, *The Industrial Empire of Niagara Pictorially Portrayed* (Buffalo, N.Y.: Buffalo Trust Publishing Company, 1918–1919).

13. Horton, "Old Erie," p. 219.

14. T. E. Leary and E. C. Sholes, *From Fire to Rust: Business, Technology and Work at the Lackawanna Steel Plant, 1899–1983* (Buffalo, N.Y.: Buffalo and Erie County Historical Society, 1987).

15. This complex is associated with the leadership and charitable work of Father Nelson H. Baker (1842–1936).

16. For the character of this growing city, see *Paul's Dictionary of Buffalo, Niagara Falls, Tonawanda and Vicinity* (Buffalo, N.Y.: Peter Paul, 1846); and *Thomas' Buffalo Directory for 1866* (Buffalo, N.Y.: C. F. S. Thomas, 1866). Studies include R. Holder, *The Beginnings of Buffalo Industry*, Adventures in Western New York History, vol. 5 (Buffalo, N.Y.: Buffalo and Erie County Historical Society, 1960); W. Thurstone, *A Sketch of the Commerce, Industries and Resources of Buffalo* (Buffalo, N.Y.: Buffalo Merchants' Exchange, 1883); *Buffalo To-Day: Domestic and Industrial* (Buffalo, N.Y.: Chamber of Commerce, 1905–1906); and Buffalo Evening News, *A History of the City of Buffalo* (Buffalo, N.Y.: Buffalo Evening News, 1908). Growth during the First World War is covered by D. J. Sweeney, *History of Buffalo and Erie County 1914–1919* (Buffalo, N.Y.: Committee of One Hundred Under Authority of the City of Buffalo, 1920); and the port in F. R. Harris, *Report on the Port of Buffalo* (New York: F. R. Harris, 1955).

17. *Thomas' Buffalo Directory for 1866*, p. 10. H. W. Hill, ed., *Municipality of Buffalo, New York: A History, 1920–1923*, 4 vols. (New York: Lewis Historical Publishing, 1923).

18. B. McKelvey, *The Urbanization of America, 1860–1915* (New Brunswick, N.J.: Rutgers University Press, 1963), pp. 86–98; and Goldman, *High Hopes*, pp. 157–74. A massive literature has accumulated on the evils of the industrial city, but

see J. L. Hammond and B. Hammond, *The Rise of Modern Industry* (London: Methuen, 1925) (a British study); C. N. Glaab and A. T. Brown, *A History of Urban America* (New York: Macmillan, 1967); L. Mumford, *The City in History: Its Origins, Its Transformation, and Its Prospects* (New York: Harcourt, Brace & World, 1961); L. Mumford, *Technics and Civilization* (New York: Harcourt, Brace & World, 1962); and A. F. Weber, *The Growth of Cities in the Nineteenth Century* (1899; reprint, Ithaca, N.Y.: Cornell University Press, 1963).

19. G. Cleveland, quoted in Goldman, *High Hopes*, p. 166.

20. F. J. Walter, "Organizing Social Welfare, 1865–1901," *Niagara Frontier* 7 (1960): 105–12; and O. Lindberg, *Buffalo in the Gilded Age, 1870–1900*, Adventures in Western New York History, vol. 24 (Buffalo, N.Y.: Buffalo and Erie County Historical Society, 1977).

21. L. W. Roper, *A Biography of Frederick Law Olmsted* (Baltimore, Md.: John Hopkins University Press, 1973); J. G. Fabos, G. T. Milde, and V. M. Weinmayr, *Frederick Law Olmsted, Sr.: Founder of Landscape Architecture in America* (Amherst: University of Massachusetts Press, 1968); and C. Beveridge, "Buffalo's Park and Parkway System," in *Buffalo Architecture: A Guide*, ed. R. Banham et al. (Cambridge, Mass.: M.I.T. Press, 1981), pp. 15–23. A local group is the Buffalo Friends of Olmsted Parks.

22. S. H. Olsen, *The Distinctive Charms of Niagara Scenery: Frederick Law Olmsted and the Niagara Reservation* (Niagara Falls, N.Y.: Buscaglia-Castellani Art Gallery, 1985), p. 9.

23. C. A. Kaiser, *The Streets of Lockport* (Lockport, N.Y.: Niagara County Historical Society, 1949); I. O. Lacey, *Dusty Lockport Pages* (Lockport, N.Y.: Niagara County Historical Society, 1952); and H. M. Nicholls, *The Twilight Years of My Native Town* (Lockport, N.Y.: Niagara County Historical Society, 1956).

24. J. W. Percy, *Tonawanda, The Way It Was* (Kenmore, N.Y.: Partner's Press, 1979); and F. S. Parkhurst, *History of the Town of Tonawanda* (Kenmore, N.Y.: F. S. Parkhurst, 1930).

25. C. P. Lenz, quoted in E. W. Treen, "The Niagara Frontier and Lumber," *Niagara Frontier* 16 (1969): 29.

26. H. B. Mizer, *Niagara Falls: A Topical History, 1892–1932* (Lockport, N.Y.: Niagara County Historical Society, 1981); and T. Holder, *A Complete Record of Niagara Falls and Vicinity* (Niagara Falls, N.Y.: the author, 1882), and *The Times, A History of the City of Buffalo and Niagara Falls* (Buffalo, N.Y.: The Times, 1896).

27. G. A. Seibel, *Niagara Falls, Canada: A History of the City and the World Famous Beauty Spot* (Niagara Falls, Ont.: Kiwanis Club of Stamford, 1967), p. 41.

28. M. A. Raymond, "From 1857 On," in *Times Review, Fort Erie Centennial, 1857–1957* (Fort Erie, Ont.: n.p., 1957), pp. 8, 45; and E. W. Johnson, "Bridgeburg Store," ibid., p. 10.

29. Jackson and Burtniak, *Railways in the Niagara Peninsula*, provide detail for the Canadian Frontier.

30. A. E. Coombs, *History of the Niagara*

Peninsula and the New Welland Canal (Toronto: Historical Publishers Association, 1930), p. 104.

31. *St. Catharines Journal*, 4 October 1855; see *Lovell's Business and Professional Directory of the Province of Ontario for 1882* (Montreal, Que.: John Lovell, 1882).

32. J. Spelt, *Urban Development in South-Central Ontario* (1955; reprint, Toronto: McClelland and Stewart, 1972).

33. A. J. Rennie, *Niagara Township: Centennial History* (Virgil, Ont.: Township of Niagara, 1967), p. 94.

34. St. Catharines Board of Trade, *Annual Report for the Year 1900* (St. Catharines, Ont.: Board of Trade, 1901), p. 9.

35. J. W. Davis, chairman, Town of Porter Committee for Updating Local History, *The Town of Porter 1776–1976: A Bicentennial History* (Porter, N.Y.: Historical Society of the Town of Porter, 1976), pp. 14–16. Other studies of urban growth on the American Frontier include J. W. Percy, *Growing Pains: Kenmore-Tonawanda Comes of Age: Classic Stories from Kenmore and the Town of Tonawanda during the Twentieth Century* (Kenmore, N.Y.: Partner's Press, 1986); G. S. Sipprell, *Town of Hamburg, Sesquicentennial, 1812–1962, Reflections Through the Years* (Hamburg, N.Y.: Town of Hamburg, 1962); L. M. Smith, *Pictorial and Historical Review East Aurora and Vicinity* (Holland, N.Y.: History Recording Association, 1940); and S. M. Young, *A History of the Town of Amherst, New York* (Amherst, N.Y.: The Town Board, 1965).

36. V. M. Howard and E. L. Howard, "The History of Youngstown," in J. T. Blixt, *Youngstown 1854–1954 Centennial* (Youngstown, N.Y.: n.p., 1954), p. 15.

37. *A Historical and Descriptive Sketch of the County of Welland* (Welland, Ont.: Sawle and Snartt, 1886), p. 39.

38. L. Segoe and J. B. Sullivan, *Report to the City Council on Railroad Grade Crossing Elimination* (Niagara Falls, N.Y.: Niagara Falls Planning Board, 1944).

39. One example: the last steam locomotive passed through St. Catharines on the Canadian National (former Great Western) line in 1959. On the American Frontier the last steam locomotive to enter the Lackawanna terminal was in 1955.

CHAPTER FIVE

HYDROELECTRICITY, INDUSTRIAL EXPANSION, AND THE STREETCAR

The power base on both Frontiers of millstreams and then the use of coal was augmented considerably when hydroelectricity was generated in the late nineteenth century at the Falls, first on the American and then on the Canadian side. This generation of power later transferred to the Queenston-Lewiston areas at the edge of the Niagara Escarpment. An earlier source had diverted water from the Third Welland Canal to a generating station at Decew Falls south of St. Catharines. These developments all added canals, generating stations, reservoirs, tunnels, and the radiating poles and wires of the distribution network to the landscape.[1] Industrial growth using this new power source was greater on the American Frontier where the resultant industrial complex extended south from Niagara Falls to Buffalo; on the Canadian Frontier the contrary policy of dispersing power to the towns of Southern Ontario was followed. As urban and interurban streetcar networks each evolved from hydroelectricity, and as industrial expansion using this new resource was encouraged, the urban fabric on both Frontiers expanded and became more closely interwoven as a regional urban unit.

POWER DEVELOPMENTS ON THE AMERICAN FRONTIER

As early as 1842 it was established that the Falls, in principle, could satisfy the then power demands of the entire world.[2] Here was an inexhaustible supply of energy running to waste. In 1847 Augustus Porter, the owner of Goat Island, proposed a hydraulic canal from Port Day above the rapids to a basin north of the American Falls from which water could feed into millraces to power a series of mills.[3] A canal 10.7 meters (35 feet) wide across the village of Niagara Falls was completed in 1861 (fig. 5.1). Blasting and construction were harmful for tourism and inhibited access to the Falls. The development of this power resource was delayed by the American Civil War, and then by industrialists who feared that the force of falling water would be too powerful for their machinery. By 1875 only one grist mill, Charles Gaskill's flour mill, had been completed.

The hydraulic company was purchased in 1877 by a consortium under Jacob F. Schoellkopf, a German immigrant from Buffalo.[4] He formed the Niagara Falls Hydraulic Power and Manufacturing Company, and built a six-story flour mill and two pulp mills. The earlier Gaskill mill also expanded. These water-powered mills with deep-sunk wheelpits occupied the Lower Milling District, which clustered around the canal basin along the rim of the gorge. Earlier industrial buildings had occupied sites on the rapids next to Goat Island, but their power capacity was limited. Though most mills used less, a drop of some 30.5 meters (100 feet) was available at the Falls. To use this surplus, a flume along the face of the gorge to catch the tailwater was suggested, and land secured at its base. In 1889 the Quigley pulp mill was added to the site. Fed from a tailrace leaving the wheelpit by a penstock has been described as "the acme of hydromechanical power developments . . . [at] the falls."[5]

Three small, crude electric generators installed in the earlier Quigley mill had by 1881 developed 1,800 horsepower for use in the mill, a silver-plating works, and a machine shop. The village used this early electric power to light streets and to pump its water supply. The power was also carried across the Niagara River to light Niagara Falls, Ontario.

The new era of hydroelectric power involved two companies and two locations. At the upper location the Gaskill company was succeeded by the Niagara Falls Power Company. Here the direct use of water to drive machinery was abandoned when Edward Dean Adams proposed to generate power at a large central station and then transmit the electricity to where it could be used. His plan called for an intake canal upstream from Goat Island, a powerhouse at the side of the canal with a wheelpit 54 meters (178 feet) deep,

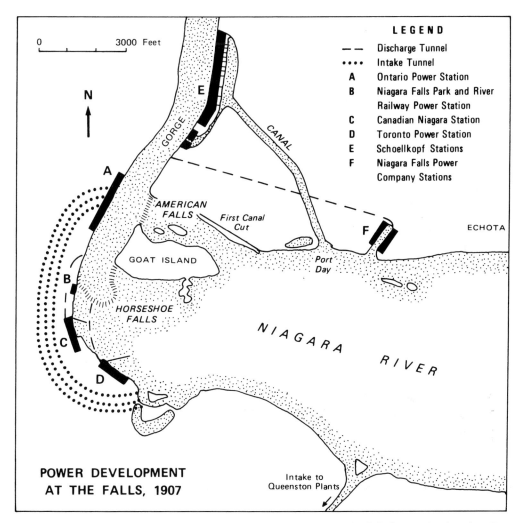

Fig. 5.1. The Niagara River was harnessed for hydroelectric power at the Falls, first on the American Frontier and then on the Canadian Frontier. The American Frontier used this power resource locally. The Canadian Frontier exported the power to serve the growing towns of Southern Ontario, leading to contrary industrial landscapes at the Falls. (Prepared by the Department of Geography, Brock University)

Hydroelectric power, diverting water from the Niagara River, started on the American Frontier in two locations: upstream at the Edward Dean Adams No. 1 plant which began operations in 1895 (**right**), and then at the Schoellkopf plant close to the American Falls, shown after its dramatic destruction in 1956 (**below**). (John Burtniak [both])

and then the use of an underground tailrace to discharge water to an outlet below the Falls. To implement this visionary plan, not knowing how the power would be distributed, a new technology of generators, turbines, motors, transformers, and power transmission had each to be invented. Nikola Tesla's polyphase alternating current (AC) was used,[6] and in 1895 the first current was sent over a distance less than 1 kilometer (0.6 miles) to the Pittsburgh Reduction Company and the Carborundum Company.[7]

These few sentences do not express the daunting series of problems that had to be overcome. As recorded by Carr (1992), when this generating station opened:[8] "it marked the climax of one of the most exhaustive industrial and design projects ever attempted and at the same time heralded the era of modern electric utility operations. This generating station is widely recognized as one of the most historically significant industrial sites in the world, since it incorporated a critical culmination of many technical developments and involved so many of the leading scientists, engineers and financiers of the day."[9]

A second power plant in an almost identical design was completed in 1904 on the opposite side of the intake canal. These two plants, Adams No. 1 and Adams No. 2, operated until 1961 when the Robert Moses plant at Lewiston provided power. The site then became a sewage treatment plant, using the original tailrace tunnel to the foot of the cliff to discharge effluent into the river below the American Falls. Recognizing its intrinsic historic and engineering importance, the front doorway was moved to Goat Island and there became the Power Arch. Remaining on the site is the original transformer building, and part of the inlet canal with its stone retaining wall.

The construction of these two plants by the Niagara Falls Power Company attracted some thirteen hundred Italian, Polish, and Black workers to overcrowded housing in the nearby Tunnel District. They blasted away day and night. The powerhouses, designed by Stanford White, the prominent American architect of the day, were substantial structures of local Queenston limestone. The power company also built Echota, again designed by White, a model industrial village where the then unusual use of electricity in homes for heating, lighting, and cooking was pioneered. The village had paved streets, water supply, sewage disposal, local community facilities, and rental housing for power station employees. Called "Alphabet Town" after its lettered streets, it remains a distinctive part of Niagara Falls, New York.

Schoellkopf's Niagara Falls Hydraulic Power and Manufacturing Company north of the American Falls was simultaneously involved in the development of electric power. In 1895 the old hydraulic canal was enlarged and Power Station No. 2 constructed at the base of the gorge. The first electricity was delivered in 1896, the station completed in 1901, and, after enlarging the canal to obtain more water, Plant No. 3 followed in 1904.[10] Power was sold to the Aluminum Company of America (ALCOA, formerly the Pittsburgh Reduction Company) and to the Cliff Electrical Distributing Company, a Schoellkopf subsidiary. This energy was used mostly within about 366 meters (400 yards) of the plant in electrometallurgical and electrochemical manufacturing, and to manufacture paper. To blend with the natural scenery, the office building and a wall of rubble masonry were built down the face of the gorge to hide the penstocks (the pipes carrying water to the turbines).

Electricity, the technology to transport this power, and the invention of the electric furnace transformed Niagara Falls from a tourist resort to "Power Center of the World" and "Electrochemical Center of North America." Long-distance transmission over 30 kilometers (20 miles) to Buffalo came in 1896. Two-phase alternating current (AC) was converted into three-phase for high-tension transmission, then reconverted to serve Buffalo's direct current (DC) system. Cheaper, cleaner, and easier to use and control than coal-based steam power, electricity greatly assisted the local expansion of industry.

As demand increased, many other schemes were considered,[11] including a dam across the gorge and the creation of a lake to generate electricity. The now infamous Love Canal was projected from LaSalle on the Upper Niagara River to the edge of the Niagara Escarpment east of Lewiston, with Model City planned in 1893 on the Ontario Plain below. The canal was excavated for some 914.4 meters (3,000 feet) before the project was abandoned. Power canals from the Upper Niagara River to the lower gorge at Lockport were also proposed. Another innovative idea was to use a bridge, later the Peace Bridge, across the entrance to the Niagara River to obtain power; wheels suspended below the bridge would be turned by the powerful current to generate electricity.

POWER DEVELOPMENTS ON THE CANADIAN FRONTIER

Electric power in the Niagara Peninsula was first generated at the locks of the abandoned Second Welland Canal. In 1886 the St.

Catharines Electric Light and Power Company constructed a small plant at Lock 5 to produce direct current, and electric street lighting replaced gas lamps on certain city streets. Power was also generated for use by small industries at Lock 3, and in Merritton a waterwheel generating 30 horsepower lit streets and several homes.[12]

More significantly, the Cataract Power Company of Hamilton organized in 1896 to develop power at DeCew Falls on the Niagara Escarpment south of St. Catharines.[13] For a short time this plant became the cradle of the Canadian hydroelectric industry. The diversion of 2.8m³/sec (100 cfs) of water from the Third Welland Canal was into a 7-kilometer (4.5-mile) cut from Allanburg to a series of interconnected lakes at DeCew. Penstocks down the edge of the escarpment served the generating station and used an enlarged Twelve Mile Creek to Lake Ontario as its tailrace. The head of 81 meters (265 feet) was higher than at the Falls, greater than at the Adams No. 1 Plant, and the concept similar to the intended but failed American Love Canal. The first power was transmitted at 22,500 volts to Hamilton in 1898 along the Grand Trunk (former Great Western) railway over a distance of 56 kilometers (35 miles), a greater distance than from Niagara Falls to Buffalo, an engineering feat of the day, and one of the first long-distance, high-voltage transmission lines in the world.

The water lease was upgraded in 1902; the power canal, reservoirs, and powerhouse enlarged; and additional penstocks constructed. The initial capacity of 1,700 horsepower had increased to 50,000 horsepower by 1911, and the small village of Power Glen was constructed on the bank of Twelve Mile Creek for company employees. Directors of the enterprise (J. M. Gibson, John Patterson, and John Moodie) are commemorated in the names of the reservoirs constructed on the brow of the escarpment.

At Niagara Falls, water was first diverted in 1893 to a small power station upstream from the Horseshoe Falls to supply the Niagara Falls Park and River Railway, which operated between Chippawa and Queenston along the river. A head of 18 meters (60 feet) at the wheelpit (where water drawn from the river through large pipes was carried to below-ground turbines) generated about 3,000 horsepower for the railway, park lighting, and local industry.[14] A steam booster station at Queenston helped trains ascend the escarpment.

In 1892 the Canadian Niagara Power Company, a subsidiary of the American Edward Adams Niagara Falls Power Company, was granted a monopoly franchise to

The DeCew Power Station at St. Catharines drew water from the Third Welland Canal at Allanburg to reservoirs at the edge of the Niagara Escarpment. Penstocks down this slope supplied the generating station, and Twelve Mile Creek became the tailrace. (John N. Jackson)

develop power in Queen Victoria Park a few hundred yards upstream from the Falls and to export electricity across the river. This agreement was replaced in 1899 by a lease of water rights to develop 110,000 horsepower. The eleven generating units installed by 1904 used a 43-meter (141-foot) head of water. The Canadian Niagara (William B. Rankine) plant built at the side of the river obliterated Cedar Island. A submerged gathering weir diverted water from the river to the station's intake, and an outlet tunnel discharged the

The neoclassical design of the Toronto Power Company Generating Station next to the rapids south of the Falls (**top**) and the unobtrusive location (to Canadian eyes) of the Ontario Power Company Generating Station in the gorge below the Horseshoe Falls (**left**) introduced powerful new architectural forms to the Niagara Frontier. (John Burtniak [both])

tailrace into the river below Table Rock House at the Falls. Heavy cables connected the power plant across the river to the two powerhouses of the Niagara Falls Power Company, an arrangement that allowed power from any plant to be distributed to the other bank. In fact, the first cables to Buffalo followed the shorter Canadian riverbank, and most of the power generated was transmitted across the river to American companies.

The third and largest generating station on the Canadian side, again American owned, was the Buffalo-based Ontario Power Company plant which had been incorporated in 1887. Water from above the Falls at Dufferin Islands was piped underground to the top of the cliff below the Falls, then dropped 55 meters (100 feet) to a plant in the gorge just below the Horseshoe Falls. The 34,000 horsepower produced by 1905 was transmitted inland to Welland and across the river to customers in Lockport, Buffalo, and Syracuse. To offset the problem of winter ice forced up from the river, the generating station was designed with walls 2.7 meters (9 feet) thick and high windows. Even so, ice occasionally smashed the windows and filled the power hall. The solution—a floating, timber ice boom across the entrance to the river at Fort Erie-Buffalo to hold back the lake ice—was installed in 1964.

Provoked by American ownership and use of a Canadian resource, and then angered by a severe shortage of coal through strikes in the coal mines of Pennsylvania, in 1905 the Electrical Development Company (later Toronto Power Company) used Canadian capital and Canadian industrial management to reclaim land near Dufferin Islands and to build a handsome, colonnaded, neoclassical building in Italian Renaissance style. A short intake from the river dropped water 57 meters (187 feet) under its floor to provide power to its turbines. A tunnel returned this water to the river behind the veil of water at the Horseshoe Falls.

POLICY DIFFERENCES IN THE DISTRIBUTION OF POWER

Policies for the distribution of electricity varied considerably between the two Frontiers.[15] Ontario, lacking coal, had not been able to compete industrially with the access of Western New York to nearby coalfields. As coal had to be imported from either Alberta or Pennsylvania, to Canadians the "white coal" of hydroelectric power provided the hope of a more robust industrial future.[16] How best to use this new resource was hotly debated,[17] the outcome being a campaign for cheap public power, and in 1906 the establishment of the Hydro-Electric Power Commission of the Province of Ontario (later Ontario Hydro) to transmit power from Niagara Falls to the municipalities of Southern Ontario.[18] Adam Beck, then mayor of London, led this movement for "the people's power," with distribution in the hands of the province and a provincial commission regulating the private companies. A worry was that Toronto would obtain all the Canadian power; the smaller towns, now often industrialized, wanted their share.

The commission contracted with the Ontario Power Company at the Falls for power. It had the support of thirty-four municipalities and, when the first transmission line was completed across the Niagara Peninsula, electricity from the Falls lit the streets of Berlin (now Kitchener) in 1910. As demand grew, the commission built its own generating stations. At the Falls the American-owned Ontario Power Company, purchased in 1917, expanded in 1918. The Toronto Power Company fought against public power, but the Niagara plant was acquired in 1927, and the Hamilton Cataract Power, Light and Traction Company (formerly Cataract Power) at Decew was acquired in 1930. By 1920 the commission supplied fourteen local systems and over 275 municipalities with some 340,000 horsepower

from the Falls. Power at the Canadian Frontier, considered a public rather than a local resource, was exported inland to the urban communities of Southern Ontario.

A contrasting situation is that competing private power companies dominated the American Frontier.[19] The Schoellkopf interests acquired the Niagara River Hydraulic Tunnel, Power and Sewer Company in 1918. Under the name of the Niagara Falls Power Company, it became part of the Buffalo, Niagara, and Eastern Power Company in 1925, and then in 1929 of the even larger Niagara-Hudson Power Company, a precursor of the Niagara-Mohawk Power Company. The New York State Power Authority was not established until 1931, and power on the American Frontier is still distributed through private power companies. State law requires electricity to be distributed to various localities, and the Niagara Frontier has retained relatively low-cost power from its local resource to provide an industrial advantage.

The two sides of the Niagara River now differed in ownership, control, and policy for the distribution of power. A government-controlled public utility served distant municipal interests in Ontario, whereas private enterprise supplied a greater amount of power for local consumption in New York State. It was the same river and the same resource, but again a divergence in landscape between the Canadian and the American Frontiers at Niagara. The resulting contrasts are vividly evident in the landscape. As Mavor (1925) stated: "for more than fifty years every observant tourist ... has been impressed by the vigorous industrial development on the American side and the complete absence of any such development on the Canadian side of the Falls."[20] Canadian industrial development in association with the power resource, dispersed widely across Southern Ontario, also proceeded more slowly.[21]

HYDROELECTRICITY AND AMENITY IN CONFLICT

As more hydroelectric plants were built, rock outcrops close to the Falls were exposed. For every 141.6 m³/sec (5,000 cfs [cubic feet per second]) withdrawn from the river, the American Falls lost about 1.3 centimeters (0.5 inches) of depth, and the Horseshoe Falls about 5.7 centimeters (2.25 inches).[22] It soon became evident that the diversion of water for power conflicted with the Falls as a scenic resource, a problem compounded by the possibility of further upstream diversions from the Upper Great Lakes.[23] The controversial question was, should the Niagara River continue to be used to expand industrial opportunities or should the world-famous scenery be conserved?[24]

H. G. Wells in his 1908 novel, *The War in the Air*, refers to the "silly great cataract. There ain't no sense in it, fallin' and fallin'." The International Waterways Commission of 1906, taking the opposite view, recognized the international value of the scenery, recommended limits on the diversion of water from the Niagara River, and suggested regulations for the equitable distribution of power capacity between the two countries while preserving the spectacle at the Falls. Also in 1906 the American federal government passed the Burton Act (named after Theodore Burton of Ohio, chairman of the House Committee on Rivers and Harbors) for the control and regulation of the river's waters; diversions could not exceed 243.5 m³/sec (15,600 cfs). The 1910 Boundary Waters Treaty between Great Britain and the United States allocated water from the river above the Falls for power generation at the rates of 1019.4 m³/sec (36,000 cfs) to Ontario, and 566.3 m³/sec (20,000 cfs) to New York, the apparent Canadian advantage reflecting American-owned plants and their export of electricity to the United States. The Falls had been saved, but industries based on diversions of water from the river kept operating.

In 1918, to obtain the highest return from the flow available for power, on the American Frontier the less efficient Adams stations were shut down, and the Schoellkopf plants in the gorge used for the generation of power. The canal to the lower powerhouses was deepened to utilize the full volume of treaty water, and a new generating station was constructed in the gorge. Capacity was doubled to 615,000 horsepower by these plants, which remained the only operating generating facilities on the American side until 1956.

More radical was the thought of transferring power generation from the Falls to the edge of the Niagara Escarpment (fig. 5.2). If water were diverted from above the rapids to the brow of the Niagara Escarpment, a possible fall of about 89.6 meters (294 feet) existed at Queenston Heights.[25] The corresponding height at the Falls was 54.9 meters (180 feet). The treaty allowance, equivalent to 408,000 horsepower at the Falls, would produce nearer to 1 million horsepower if diverted to Queenston Heights. Spurred by increased demands for power by the munitions and other industries during the First World War, and by power blackouts, this project was approved by the Ontario Legislature in 1917. The first unit of the Queenston-Chippawa Development Project, now the Sir Adam Beck-Niagara Generating Station No. 1

(named after the commission's first chairman), came into service in 1921.[26]

Further radical changes were introduced to the landscape. Eight thousand laborers worked on the project. The Lower Welland River was deepened and reversed to draw water from the Niagara River. A deep cut, nearly 13.7 kilometers (8.5 miles) long, excavated to serve the forebay at Queenston placed the city of Niagara Falls on an island, and necessitated thirteen road and rail bridges across this cut. The powerhouse was placed next to the river at the bottom of the gorge. Penstocks dropped the head of water through some 91.4 meters (300 feet) to nine turbines by 1925, then increased to ten in 1930. Material excavated from the project created new hills of spoil on the flat landscape west and north of Niagara Falls. The generating plant, now duplicated by later plants on the American side of the river, was the largest hydroelectric plant in the world, and Ontario Hydro the largest power company.

Power resources other than hydroelectricity were also developed at the Frontier. Natural gas, pumped in the 1880s from under Welland County and Lake Erie on the Canadian Frontier, and from under Erie County on the American Frontier, contributed a landscape of pipes, compressor stations, and pumps, some of which are still seen in the

THE LANDSCAPE OF POWER BY THE 1960s

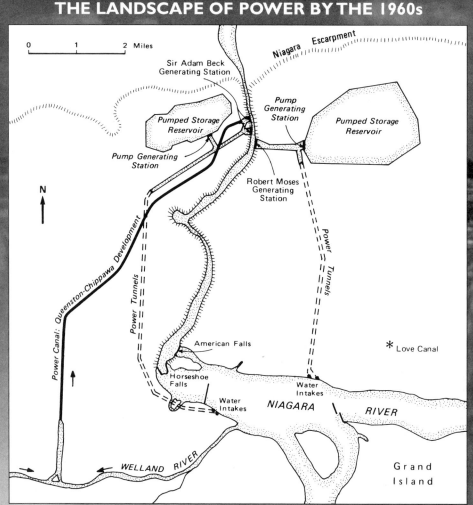

Fig. 5.2. The generation of hydroelectric power transferred from its birthplace at the Falls to the Queenston-Lewiston area on the heights at the edge of the Niagara Escarpment. Here the massive new works of power tunnels, power reservoirs, and generating stations transformed the landscape into the largest power complex in the world. (Prepared by the Department of Geography, Brock University)

Why should all that water flow uselessly to the sea when it might be diverted for the generation of power to the advantage of us all? (John N. Jackson)

area.[27] And the power demands from the First World War led to the building in 1916 of the coal-fired Charles R. Huntley Steam Generating Station in Tonawanda, north of Buffalo. Named after the president of the Buffalo General Electric Company, this plant used cooling water from the Niagara River. It was expanded in 1917, and again in 1926. As international treaties now restricted diversions from the river for hydroelectric power, the Huntley generating station helped to reinforce the Tonawanda-Buffalo area as the locus for heavy industry. Coal was brought in from Pennsylvania either by rail or by ship through ports on Lake Erie to the Black Rock Canal.

THE AMERICAN INDUSTRIAL BELT

Hydroelectricity made possible the large-scale production of three widely used commercial products: aluminum, calcium carbide, and carborundum.[28] Aluminum could now be obtained from bauxite ore through an electrolytic process, calcium carbide had been invented and could be used to man-

Gas from under Lake Erie and Welland County, Ontario, provided heating for homes and industrial power for a glass industry at Port Colborne. Exports of gas from the Canadian Frontier to Buffalo assisted its industrial advance. (John N. Jackson [right], and M. H. Hubbell, *The Industrial Empire of Niagara*, 1918–1919 [left])

ufacture acetylene gas, and carborundum had been discovered as an industrial abrasive to replace expensive diamond dust. Each required a series of heroic inventions equivalent in importance to those required for hydroelectric power and its distribution.

With the development of these electrometallurgical and electrochemical industries, Niagara Falls within a decade was transformed into an industrial giant. The value of factory products increased thirteen times from $8.5 million in 1900, to $108 million by 1925. The 1892 population of about ten thousand had increased fourfold by 1915. An extensive array of manufacturing soon ranged from shredded wheat to corsets, paper, flour, and silverplate.[29] By 1915 almost all the world's aluminum was produced in Niagara Falls; ALCOA, supplied by both power companies, was the largest user of hydroelectric power in the world. More abrasive materials were produced than in any other city, and Niagara Falls became the chemical manufacturing center of North America.[30] It was indeed suggested that Buffalo would soon become a suburb of Niagara Falls, the reverse of the suggestion that electricity would be transported to Buffalo as the major customer! Industrial production peaked in 1929 when Niagara Falls was the leading world manufacturer of products that included abrasives, carbon, chlorine, and ferro-alloys. Lockport was overtaken as the principal industrial center of Niagara County. The area near the Falls was overrun by industrial establishments; upstream, where the Niagara Power Company owned about 3 kilometers (2 miles) of river frontage, the land was developed for heavy manufacturing activities, and both air and water pollution became severe problems.

The new industries used electricity as a promotional device, but tourism was now secondary to industry on the American Frontier.[31] Power production could be viewed at both power plants, and the upper and lower promenades of the Schoellkopf Station had flowers and shrubbery along their length and decorative lighting at night. Spirella Corsets provided free demonstrations in their modern factory,[32] the Niagara Wall Paper Company demonstrated how logs were converted to wallpaper, and the Niagara Chocolate Company wedded manufacturing with tourism to the advantage of both.

The Shredded Wheat Company (previously the Natural Food Company, and later Nabisco) located its model factory in a residential neighborhood away from the smoke and dust of the factories and railways,[33] and extolled the link between the production of whole wheat, a natural product, and a site where nature provided such a powerful background. The factory, part of the City Beautiful Movement and a showplace described as a "palace of light," contrasted sharply with the typical unhygienic industrial building of the period. "The inner plant was completely air conditioned and its temperature was thermostatically controlled. . . . It was a 'temple of cleanliness', and provided, in the company's dining room, proper food for . . . [the] employees."[34] There were tubs and shower baths, the "invention" of the coffee break, and nursing care available to the employees.

Electricity was also used to promote tourism. Illumination of the Falls and the Whirlpool Rapids extended their viewing hours. Nightly "Illumination Specials" ran along the Great Gorge trolley route from 1901: "See the beautiful illumination of the famous Whirlpool Rapids from the waters' edge. View in comfort the colorful electrical display of one billion three hundred million candlepower on the American and Horseshoe Falls."[35] A Festival of Lights, started in 1925, attracted thousands until closed during the Depression in the 1930s.

The industrial belt based on power from Niagara extended east to Lockport and south along the river through the Tonawandas to Buffalo and Lackawanna.[36] In Buffalo, hydroelectricity was used for lighting, to run trolley cars, and in manufacturing. Homes changed from the use of flickering gaslights to lighting by the new wonder of electricity, and streetlights helped to change night into day.

Manufacturing flourished in Buffalo even more than at Niagara Falls. Chemical, iron, and steel production grew as the value of manufactured products increased from $106 million in 1900 to $325 million in 1913. Power made possible entirely new industrial processes.[37] For example, by developing and patenting new procedures for dyestuffs, the Schoellkopf, Hartford and Hanna Company (later National Aniline and Chemical, then Allied Chemical) produced half the American output by 1917. With supplies from abroad cut off by the First World War, J. P. Devine Company produced chemicals, colors, and dye for American manufacturers.

The American Frontier became increasingly the domain for major national companies: Acheson Graphite, Alox Chemical, Anaconda, Auto-Lite Battery, Carborundum, Hooker Electro-Chemical, Niacet Chemical, and Union Carbide in Niagara Falls; Buffalo Electric Chemical, Dunlop Tire and Rubber, and DuPont Rayon in Tonawanda; and Cataract Chemical, National Aniline and Chemical, and Lucidol in Buffalo.[38] Together with the giant Lackawanna (Bethlehem) Steel works south of Buffalo, an integrated manufacturing economy had arisen, with hydroelectricity rapidly replacing coal as the major supply of energy for industrial uses.

This industrial advance had a reverse side. Coal was dirty, its fumes poisoned the air; electricity, supposedly clean, was the savior. Clean waters produced this novel form of power, but the new industrial chemistry of alkalis, bleaches, caustic soda, chlorine, and sodium unexpectedly sullied the environment. Sometimes dormant or hidden in spoil dumps, or spilling into the Niagara River, or hidden and blown away in the air, a new era of chemical pollution increased rapidly to bedevil the former high quality of the natural environment.

CANADIAN INDUSTRIAL GROWTH

Industrial progress was slower and less concentrated on the Canadian Frontier. Even so, the towns expanded considerably. Between 1901 and 1921 the population of Niagara Falls grew from 4,244 to 14,764, Welland from 1,863 to 8,654, and St. Catharines from 9,946 to 19,881. Often American subsidiaries, Canadian plants in Niagara Falls by the 1920s included the abrasive companies of Canadian Carborundum, Lionite Abrasives, and the Norton Company; Oneida Silverware;

Nabisco Shredded Wheat; Bissel Carpet Sweeper; Ohio Brass; Niagara Wire Weaving; and Burgess Batteries.[39]

The attraction of the Ontario Paper Company to Thorold in 1911 was through an option on power available from the Falls through the American-owned Ontario Power Company.[40] At Welland, electricity in 1907 cost thirteen dollars per horsepower, against twenty dollars in Hamilton and twenty-five dollars in Buffalo. In 1905 Plymouth Cordage of Plymouth, Massachusetts, producing rope and binder twine, located next to the Welland Canal in Welland; power was again supplied by the Ontario Power Company.[41] Steelworks and textile mills using Niagara's power also concentrated south of the town near rail facilities and the Welland Canal. Factories and employee homes, including a planned village by Plymouth Cordage for its workers, intermixed here. In Dain City (Welland Junction) where the Grand Trunk railway crossed the canal, Dain Manufacturing Company (later John Deere) produced farm machinery. Algoma Steel produced pig iron next to the Welland Canal in Port Colborne after 1913, and International Nickel located there in 1918.

New power resources fostered the growth of manufacturing industries in St. Catharines during the early 1900s.[42] Auto parts were produced at McKinnon Industries, large industrial equipment at Foster Wheeler, English Electric made heavy electrical equipment, and bicycles were manufactured by the Welland Vale Manufacturing Company. By 1921 large industries such as Anthes-Imperial manufactured electrical motors and transformers; Columbus McKinnon, chains and hoists; Yale and Towne, locks, hoists, and trolleys; and Canadian Warren Pink, tools, marine hardware, and forgings. In the meantime, many of the mills and small plants located on the now abandoned Second Welland Canal went out of existence, outmoded by the new power technology, and with production often in old buildings using antiquated machinery.

THE URBAN AND INTERURBAN STREETCAR NETWORKS

By the mid-1800s, rudimentary local transit systems served the more important centers of the Niagara Frontier. The earliest vehicles were horse-drawn, generally with steel wheels on tracks that helped to overcome the problems of movement on muddy streets, but horsecars were also slow, unable to cope with steep grades, and the horses could be troublesome and costly with dirty droppings. In 1874 St. Catharines had horsecars along its main street, and services soon extended to Merritton and Thorold. Another line served Niagara Falls and Stamford Township. Buffalo had horsecar routes along Main Street by 1835, and from the docks to Cold Spring by 1847.[43] By 1860 tracks had been built from Main Street to Fort Porter and Black Rock. Other routes were added along Batavia (now Broadway) and Genesee Streets, to the principal streets of the East Side, and very extensively through the West Side and north to Delaware Park. Nearly all the built-up area of the city was served. In Niagara Falls, New York, horse-drawn service extended along Main Street during the 1880s.

Hydroelectricity changed the landscape. One of the first applications of electricity to streetcars in North America was in 1887 on the St. Catharines, Merritton and Thorold Street Railway.[44] Powered from a plant in Merritton on the Second Welland Canal, this early effort used double overhead wires and chain-driven front wheels. Well patronized, routes were extended from St. Catharines to Thorold, the city limits on Ontario Street, and east to Victoria Lawn Cemetery. Reduced evening fares encouraged rides between St. Catharines and Thorold, and small parks were built at the terminals. Lakeside Park at Port Dalhousie became a popular pleasure beach, and the manufacture of

Plymouth Cordage at Welland, an American company in the van of Canadian industrial achievement with a social conscience, provided spacious company houses with gardens and tree-lined streets for their workers. (John Burtniak [above] and John N. Jackson [left])

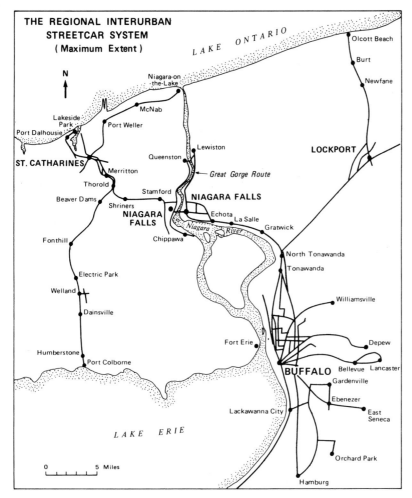

THE REGIONAL INTERURBAN STREETCAR SYSTEM (Maximum Extent)

Fig. 5.3. Hydroelectricity encouraged the development of interurban and intraurban streetcar networks on both Frontiers. These networks interconnected across the Niagara boundary at Queenston-Lewiston and between the two cities of Niagara Falls. A Great Gorge Route of high scenic quality followed both sides of the turbulent river, to provide an exciting tourist trip along the crest of the gorge in Canada, and along its base in the United States. (Prepared by the Department of Geography, Brock University)

streetcars by a St. Catharines company supplied local and national markets.

This streetcar system became part of the Niagara, St. Catharines and Toronto (NS&T)

in 1902. This interurban network, modernized and extended between 1922 and 1928, linked most urban centers on the Canadian Frontier (fig. 5.3). An anomaly, although announced in 1902, is that no route was ever achieved west from St. Catharines. Because of the physical problem of overcoming the deeply incised valleys of Twelve and Fifteen Mile Creeks, Vineland, Beamsville, and Grimsby connected west via the Hamilton,

When the streetcar first arrived at the Frontier, the iron rails were laid in muddy streets as at Welland (**top right**), but then later embedded into paved surfaces as at Niagara Falls (**bottom right**). Two- and three-story brick or brick and stone commercial buildings lined both Main Streets. (John Burtniak [both])

Grimsby and Beamsville Electric railway. Opened in 1908,[45] farmers in the western part of the Niagara Fruit Belt brought produce to the market and canning factories in Hamilton. As the cars also brought shoppers and work people to Hamilton, as well as high-school children to school there, these people and their activities became divorced from their county town in St. Catharines and the Canadian Frontier, an issue that later became important when regional government was under consideration.

By contrast the eastern section of the NS&T streetcar system linked across the river into the American system at Niagara Falls. The eastern section of the Niagara Peninsula thereby had easier access to American centers than to nearby towns in Ontario. Expansion in Buffalo as the more accessible and larger retailing-entertainment center was assisted because of this hinterland extent over Canadian territory. The Canadian-American link across the Niagara River was strengthened over first the railway and then the streetcar eras of development.

On the American Frontier, streetcar lines first connected the villages at the Falls along Main Street in 1892. Lines were extended to LaSalle; within the city along Ontario, Hyde Park, Highland, Pine, and Nineteenth Streets; and the Riverview line ran north to Devil's Hole. Of great tourist potential was that, when the Niagara Falls Park and River Railway was purchased by the International Railway of Buffalo, a grand international tour of magnificent scenic interest had been created. Beginning in 1898, track along the top of the gorge on the Canadian side connected via the Queenston-Lewiston Suspension Bridge and the Upper Steel Arch Bridge at the Falls with the track along the bottom of the gorge on the American side.[46] This circular route had magnificent views of the gorge and the foaming river from both banks; the round trip took about two hours, and stopovers could be made. Closed in the 1930s because of rockfalls, landslides, and the sale of water rights to permit the construction of power stations in the gorge, over thirteen million passengers were carried on this popular excursion during the line's forty-four-year history.

In Buffalo, all streetcars were powered by locally generated direct current by 1894 and, after the arrival of electricity from Niagara, lines were extended to outlying areas by several companies which merged into the International Railway in 1902.[47] This company ran local lines in Buffalo, Lockport, both cities at the Falls, the Great Gorge Route, and suburban lines to Hamburg, Lancaster, and the Tonawandas. Lines extended as land was subdivided for housing. The Delaware Avenue

The Niagara River was crossed by streetcar on the Great Gorge Route at the Queenston-Lewiston Suspension Bridge (**above**), and at the Upper Steel Arch Bridge between the two cities of Niagara Falls (**left**). (John Burtniak [both])

The scenic Great Gorge trip provided a grand link between tourism and the natural scenery. It followed the crest of the Niagara Gorge on the Canadian Frontier and ran next to the foaming river on the American Frontier.
(John Burtniak [both])

line went to Elmlawn Cemetery, and Buffalonians took weekend and seasonal rides to beach and amusement facilities at Olcott on Lake Ontario. Interurban access by streetcar to Pennsylvania and Ohio came via the Buffalo and Lake Erie to Dunkirk and Erie by 1906; the Buffalo terminal was located in Lafayette Square. The Buffalo, Rochester and Lockport used the International Railway east through the Tonawandas to Lockport and then to Rochester and beyond, but links to Albany were not achieved.

To offset the slow running speeds on street rights-of-way, in 1918 the International Railway opened a fast double-track line from Buffalo to Niagara Falls. Bridging roads and railways in the Tonawandas, this interurban link followed an elevated route for 5.6 kilometers (3.5 miles); known locally as the "Chinese Wall," it severely limited development. The route, starting at the Lackawanna depot on Buffalo's Main Street, ran in that street to the Erie Belt Line, followed that line to Tonawanda, then diverged to follow a route along Division Street in North Tonawanda, to make its way via River Road to downtown Niagara Falls. With a fifteen-minute schedule in summer and thirty minutes in winter, the cars, designed to travel at 96.6 kilometers (60 miles) per hour, were slowed by street traffic at both ends.

ELECTRICITY ASSISTS URBAN EXPANSION

The electric railways helped to extend the trading area of the larger cities, which in turn enlarged their central service functions and drew the smaller centers into their influence. Buffalo in particular was strengthened by new outlying neighborhoods on streetcar lines. Department stores, banks, offices, and hotels sought central locations, while structural steel and elevators permitted "skyscrapers" which changed drastically the scale and visual character of downtown.[48] By 1929 Buffalo had twenty-six buildings over ten stories in height. Each displaced smaller-scale commercial and residential uses.[49] The city had a Canadian catchment area but, as competition with Rochester was strong for the trade of Western New York, the newspapers of both cities ran competing columns of village news and advertisements to attract this patronage.[50]

At the Falls, both sides competed for the tourist dollar. Rail access was now supplemented by streetcar lines from nearby towns, and excursions were encouraged through the ease of using the International Railway. St. Catharines, the largest town on the Canadian Frontier, gained in importance as a regional service center when its radiating lines were extended; in 1900 the Board of Trade noted that the NS&T brought in hundreds of new regional customers to its retail establishments,[51] but this growth excluded the area served by Hamilton to the east of the city.

The streetcar contributed to the closer interweaving of urban communities, making it easier to shop, travel to work, or take an excursion. The cities grew along their streetcar lines, and, as these routes were extended, new real-estate locations became available. Kenmore on the American Frontier provides an instructive example.[52] In 1883 land was purchased and lots made available next to the outer, belt line railway, a development opportunity grasped by L. P. A. Eberhardt, an entrepreneur who had just subdivided a farm in Tonawanda. At first served by horse-drawn omnibus to the belt line station, after 1894 the village was served along Elmwood, Delaware, and Kenmore Avenues by electric railway. Streetcar suburbs in Amherst, Cheektowaga, Hamburg, Orchard Park, Tonawanda, and West Seneca replaced farmland and expanded greatly between 1890 and 1920 (fig. 5.4).[53]

The streetcar also permitted the wider dispersal of factories. Industrial locations no longer were dependent on coal and the railway and, as workers could now travel by streetcar, plants could locate beyond the city limits where land values and taxation were lower and municipal controls either less restrictive or nonexistent. On the Canadian Frontier, a new General Motors plant located on the outskirts of the town on Ontario Street, and the industrial growth of Welland to the south provides many further examples. On the American Frontier, visits by streetcar to the Lackawanna steel plant under construction south of Buffalo were in vogue by 1902, and the International Railway brought workers to riverside factories in the Town of Tonawanda north of the Buffalo city limits.

Streetcar terminals became hubs of activity. They were meeting places as well as transportation centers within the urban environments. In St. Catharines the retail, entertainment, and service establishments of downtown expanded along St. Paul Street. In Buffalo streetcar lines converged on Shelton Square and the Lower Terrace. Downtown expanded, as did specialized retailing and the new concept of the department store as showcase establishments. Administration, finance, entertainment, and warehousing functions also grew.[54]

The department store greatly enhanced retailing activity in Buffalo. As the steam railway and then the streetcar had greatly extended the city's hinterland in all directions, a day's excursion to Buffalo and the new emporia became possible. There was also the increasing wealth of society, a larger and more leisured middle class with money to spend, and the draw of women to the many establishments where goods and services were available. The partnership of Adam and Meldrum became Adam, Meldrum and Anderson in 1892, and the Sweeney Company, Hengerer, and Flint and Kent each established strong, successful businesses over the later years of the nineteenth century.

Streetscape changed. Commercial premises were attracted to streetcar stops and terminals. Higher land values along the streetcar lines encouraged higher retailing and residential densities, streets were now more frequently paved, and rails for the electric streetcar were incorporated in the surface of existing roadways. Poles and overhead wires along streetcar routes, telegraph wires along rail tracks, and tiers of power lines radiating from generating stations became new features of the urban townscape.

In 1901 the grand showcase for all the new developments achieved through electricity, the extravaganza of the Pan-American Exposition, opened in Buffalo. Here was the stage where the long-distance transmission of power from the Niagara River could be displayed for the world to view. Planned over the previous five years, the exposition ran for six months and attracted some eight million visitors who marveled at the wonders of the modern world.[55] Centered on a 124.7-meter (409-foot-) high electric tower crowned with a winged Goddess of Light, the temples, palaces, fountains, and promenades were all aglow at night. Shows, parades, elaborate exhibitions, entertainment, a simulated trip to the moon, a Venetian Grand Canal, and an African village—all praised the glories of electric power.

POWER PRODUCTION MOVES TO THE NIAGARA ESCARPMENT

Power distribution expanded rapidly from a few radiating lines to a grid that served large areas of Ontario and New York State, and soon evolved into a grid of high-voltage transmission lines across northeastern North America. This extensive catchment area from the Falls was demonstrated dramatically in 1965, when a power failure in the Canadian Sir Adam Beck plant shut off electricity from Toronto to New York City, plunging thirty million people into darkness. Ironically, powered by the coal-fired Huntley plant, the lights remained on in Buffalo.

In 1950 the Boundary Waters Treaty between Canada and the United States was replaced by new legislation to ensure visual quality at the Falls. The earlier agreement had specified the maximum flow that could be diverted from the Niagara River for power. The new treaty specified that the minimum flow necessary to preserve the scenic grandeur at the Falls (2831 m³/sec, or 100,000 cfs) would pass over the Falls from 8 A.M. to 10 P.M. from April to mid-September, and from 8 A.M. to 8 P.M. during the fall.[56] A flow of 1416 m³/sec (50,000 cfs) was guaranteed at other times. The remaining flow available for the production of power was higher at night and outside the tourist season. This volume was divided almost equally between the two countries.

A few days later, Ontario Hydro initiated its more advanced project. A new and larger Sir Adam Beck Generating Station No. 2 opened at Queenston Heights in 1954 (fig. 5.2).[57] An intake system was constructed on the bank of the Niagara River north of Chippawa. Two tunnels 8.4 kilometers (5.5 miles) long, blasted under the city of Niagara Falls, Ontario, discharged into an open canal 3.6 kilometers (2.25 miles) long. An open cut extended to the forebay, where penstocks served the new power station at the base of the gorge, upstream from the older plant. A raised artificial reservoir with a canal and pumping station was built close to the edge of the Niagara Escarpment to store water for peak demand periods. As the pumping station also acted as a generator, in effect two generating stations had been constructed.

On the American Frontier, lengthy debate took place over whether private industry, the state, or the federal government should construct a similar large-scale project.[58] The issue became immediate and serious when in 1956 the Schoellkopf Power Station at the Falls, the largest in the Niagara-Mohawk power system, was destroyed suddenly. The accumulated force of water seeping from old power canals and tailraces into unlined rock strata burst through the cliff into the Niagara River, carrying with it most of the power station in a flood of water and rockslides. As the United States had now lost its major source of domestic power supply from the river, the conflict between socialism or private enterprise over how to develop the Lewiston site was quickly resolved in favor of the New York State Power Authority with distribution by private power companies.

In 1958 construction began on the American Robert Moses power plant at the lower end of the gorge. Control structures regulated intake from the river below Grand Island. Huge tunnels then carried the water under the City of Niagara Falls to a point above the gorge, where the rock debris was used to

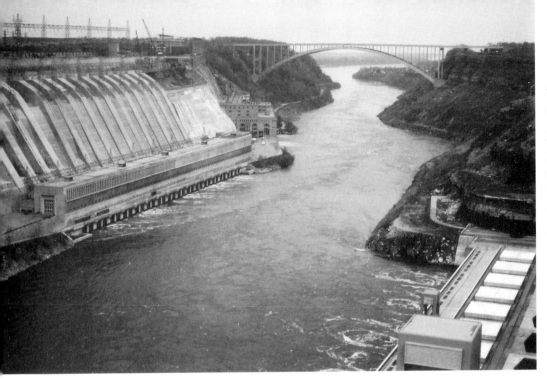

The generation of hydroelectric power transferred from the Falls to the edge of the Niagara Escarpment, where the Canadian Sir Adam Beck (**above left**), and the American Robert Moses (**below left**) power complexes faced each other across the gorge of the Niagara River. An effusion of hydro lines and poles then radiated out over both Frontiers to serve an extensive hinterland in each nation. (John N. Jackson [both])

build a reservoir for a pump generating station on land taken under dubious legal argument from the Tuscarora Indian Reservation. The land was not a reservation; it had not been acquired by treaty but by gift purchase, and was therefore not government land held in trust for the Native American, but owned by the Tuscarora.[59]

Named after its builder, Robert Moses (1888–1981), this comparable plant in the gorge faced the Canadian Sir Adam Beck complex. Water dropped 93 meters (305 feet) to feed thirteen turbines with a capacity of 1,950,000 kilowatts. The first power was produced in 1961.[60] Plans for additional generation north of the main reservoir on the site of the former Stauffer Chemical plant were announced in 1984. Robert Moses was also responsible for achieving a new extent of parkland along the rim of the gorge from Grand Island past Goat Island and Lewiston to Fort Niagara, its purpose being to restore a natural atmosphere to this length of the American Frontier that had been despoiled by industry, power lines, and railways.

Displays at both power plants were added as tourist attractions. On the Canadian Frontier these included a museum, a model of the project, and guided visits to the generating hall, exhibits that were discontinued in the 1970s. A floral clock taken over by the Niagara Parks Commission has survived as an annual display, but the reservoir banks of bare rock have been neither landscaped nor developed as community open space. On the American Frontier the displays, exhibits, and viewing area have remained, but less is now open to the public than the planned three-level Power Vista with its diorama of the plant in operation, complete with running water. Both plants barred public access along the base of the gorge, and the reservoirs deleted sections of Ontario's historic Portage Road and New York's Military Road. The American reservoir also eliminated the still-surviving possibility of an American bypass canal between the Upper and the Lower Niagara Rivers.

Niagara prospered initially from expanded hydroelectric production.[61] But as power grids advanced across the landscape, the Frontier's comparative advantage for industry was reduced to specific operations that required large quantities of electricity at favorable bulk rates. Again with differences in approach between the two sides, New York State negotiated for lower-cost electricity to local industries. On the Canadian Frontier these advantages were lost in 1996 when Ontario Hydro equalized rates throughout the province. Many companies then either curtailed their Frontier operations or relocated, including the abrasive and some chemical industries, which displaced labor and contributed to industrial decline.

As power production moved north to the Niagara Escarpment, the older power plants at the Falls became redundant. Although often controversial in location and design when built, they survive on the Canadian Frontier as important visual monuments that have been integrated into the park landscape by the Niagara Parks Commission. The Canadian Niagara and Ontario Power plants remain as operating units, but Toronto Power was retired from service in 1974. On the American Frontier, the remnants of the Schoellkopf power complex are marked by ruins along the side of the gorge; the industrial plants have been replaced by public open space and the Schoellkopf Geological Museum. The hydraulic canal has been filled in, and only one building of the Adams Station survived into the 1990s.

In 1979 New York State's energy plan suggested a reduction in the flow of water over the Falls.[62] Power produced from the additional water diverted to downstream power plants would have lessened the state's dependence on imported oil, but such a plan would have required Canadian approval and amending international legislation. These possibilities started thought in both countries about the relationship between power production and the quality of the environment at the Falls. One experiment suggested that the daylight flow of water over the Falls could be reduced to 1699 m^3/sec (60,000 cfs) without reducing their dramatic effect.[63]

In 1989 Ontario Hydro, because of the poor performance in its nuclear plants, the closure of reactors, and the high costs of burning fossil fuels such as coal, proposed a new generating station, Sir Adam Beck No. 3, on the Niagara River.[64] In 1998 the construction of a 10.5-kilometer (6.5-mile) tunnel for the diversion of water from the Grass Island Pool upstream from the Falls to a new generating station next to the Sir Adam Beck complex was approved. This project would provide for a more efficient use of the river's flow of water, without detracting from the scenic character and grandeur of the river scene. Expected to be in operation by 2002, power production at the Sir Adam Beck plants would be increased by 12 percent. The proposal takes advantage of the water surplus to minimum requirements available to Canada under international treaty. Indicative of the importance of the Beck plants to Ontario's economy, its turbines produced 10 percent of the energy supplied to Ontario in 1997.

A further hydroelectric development has been the construction of a small generating station in Lock 1 of the abandoned Third Canal at Port Dalhousie in St. Catharines, taking advantage of the fall in water level across the weir between Martindale Pond and Lake Ontario for this new purpose.[65] Other lock sites, such as Welland Vale in St. Catharines or on the Erie Canal at Lockport, might also be used for the local purpose of supplementary power generation.

NOTES

1. An overall statement is J. Carr, "Hydro-Electric Power Development in the Niagara Peninsula," in *Industry in the Niagara Peninsula*, ed. J. N. Jackson and J. Burtniak, *Proceedings Eleventh Annual Niagara Peninsula History Conference* (St. Catharines, Ont.: Brock University, 1992).

2. D. E. R. Blackwell and Z. Allen, *American Journal of Science* 46 (1843): 67–73, quoted in K. J. Tinkler, "Déjà vu," in *Niagara's Changing Landscapes*, ed. H. J. Gayler (Ottawa: Carleton University Pres, 1994), p. 85.

3. A. Porter, "To Capitalists and Manufacturers" (Niagara Falls, 1847), in E. D. Adams, *Niagara Power: History of the Niagara Falls Power Company, 1886–1918* (Niagara Falls, N.Y.: Niagara Falls Power Company, 1927), 1:337. Other American sources include C. D. Kepner: "Niagara's Water Power," *Niagara Frontier* 15 (1968): 97–105; vol. 16 (1969): 33–41, 75–80; and vol. 17 (1970):

69–79; J. and R. Aiken, *Power, The Gift of Niagara*, Adventures in Western New York History, vol. 10 (Buffalo, N.Y.: Buffalo and Erie County Historical Society, 1962), p. 2; *Niagara Falls—The Great Manufacturing Village of the West: Being a Statement of the Operations of the Niagara Falls Hydraulic Company* (Boston: Dutton and Wentworth, 1853), pp. 4–7; and C. Spieler and T. Hewit, *Niagara Power: From Joncaire to Moses* (Lewiston, N.Y.: Niagara Power, 1959), p. 7.

4. Jacob F. Schoellkopf (1819–1899), A German immigrant to Buffalo in 1844, became a leading businessman building houses, stores, mills, tanneries, and highways. His name is recalled by the Schoellkopf Geological Museum, Niagara Falls, New York.

5. Kepner, "Niagara's Water Power," vol. 17, p. 77.

6. Nikola Tesla (1856–1943), an immigrant from Yugoslavia, is discussed in V. Popovic, *Nikola Tesla: Life and Work of a Genius* (Belgrade, Yugoslavia: Yugoslav Society for the Promotion of Scientific Knowledge, 1976); and T. L. Richardson, *Introducing Nikola Tesla Through Some of His Achievements* (Vancouver: Tesla Research Headquarters, 1960).

7. The first plant at Buffalo Avenue and Nineteenth Street was followed by a second on the bank north of the Falls. It started operations in 1896, a third nearby in 1897, and became the Aluminum Company of America in 1914. See C. C. Carr, *ALCOA—An American Enterprise* (New York: Rinehart, 1952).

8. Kepner, "Niagara's Water Power," vol. 17, p. 77.

9. Carr, "Hydro-Electric Power Development in the Niagara Peninsula," p. 21.

10. S. D. Greene, "Distribution of the Electrical Energy from Niagara Falls," in *The Harnessing of Niagara*, ed. Louis Cassier, 5th ed. (London, England, 1899). For electrical details see American Institute of Electrical Engineers, *The Niagara Falls Electrical Handbook* (Niagara Falls, N.Y.: The Institute, 1904); and D. E. Nye, *Electrifying America: Social Meanings of a New Technology* (Cambridge, Mass.: MIT Press, 1990).

11. *Industrial Niagara Falls* (Niagara Falls, N.Y.: Gazette Press, 1902); and E. T. Williams, *Niagara: Queen of Wonders* (Boston: Chapple Publishing Company, 1916).

12. St. Catharines Board of Trade, *Annual Report of the St. Catharines Board of Trade* (St. Catharines, Ont., 1901), p. 13. See L. G. Denis and A. V. White, *Water-Powers of Canada* (Ottawa: Commission of Conservation, 1911).

13. Data from the Lorna Robson Collection, Morningstar Mill, DeCew Falls, St. Catharines. See also J. R. Patterson, "Power Glen: Where Hamilton Gets Her Electricity," *Canadian Epworth Era* 7 (1905): 166–67.

14. Canadian power achievements are summarized in Ontario Hydro, *Power from Niagara* (Toronto, 1970). See Appendix J, "Power Development at Niagara Falls," in *The Preservation of Niagara Falls: Final Report of the Special International Niagara Board* (Ottawa, 1930), p. 391; M.

Fram, *Niagara: A Selective Guide to Industrial Archaeology in the Niagara Peninsula* (Toronto: Ontario Society for Industrial Archaeology, 1984), pp. 64–81; and N. Freeman, "Turn-of-the-Century State Intervention: Creating the Hydro-Electric Power Commission of Ontario, 1906," *Ontario History* 84, no. 3 (1992): 171–94.

15. J. T. Miller, *Foreign Trade in Gas and Electricity in North America: A Legal and Historical Study* (New York: Praeger, 1970), pp. 11–15; and for the cost of power, E. T. Williams, *Tabloid Information about Industrial Niagara Falls* (City of Niagara Falls, N.Y.: Industrial Agent, 1915), p. 8.

16. T. C. Keefer, "Canadian Water Power and Its Electrical Product in Relation to the Undeveloped Resources of the Dominion," *Royal Society of Canada, Proceedings and Transactions* 5 (1899): 3–40. Keefer was born in Thorold and educated in St. Catharines, see L. Murphy, *Thomas Keefer* (Don Mills, Ont.: Fitzhenry and Whiteside, 1977).

17. H. V. Nelles, *The Politics of Development: Forests, Mines and Hydro-Electric Power in Ontario, 1849–1941* (Toronto: Macmillan, 1974), p. 216.

18. M. Denison, *The People's Power: The History of Ontario Hydro* (Toronto: McClelland and Stewart, 1960), p. 18. See also W. R. Plewman, *Adam Beck and the Ontario Hydro* (Toronto: Ryerson, 1946); and Hydro-Electric Power Commission of Ontario, *Hydro-Electric Power in the Niagara District* (Toronto, 1921).

19. For the rivalry between federal, state, and private power factions, see D. L. Nass, *Public Policy and Public Works: Niagara Falls Redevelop-*

ment as a Case Study, Essays in Public Works History, no. 7 (Chicago: Public Works Historical Society, 1979).

20. J. Mavor, *Niagara in Politics: A Critical Account of the Ontario Hydro-Electric Commission* (New York: E. P. Dutton, 1925), p. 17.

21. A restored drilling rig and a history of natural gas in this area are presented in the Canadian Drilling Rig Museum, Rainham Centre, Haldimand County, Ontario.

22. J. L. Romer, *Some Facts Concerning the Use of the Water of the Niagara River* (Buffalo, N.Y.: Niagara Falls Hydraulic Power and Manufacturing Company, 1906). For amenity at the Falls, see J. T. Gardner, *Special Report of New York State Survey on the Preservation of the Scenery of Niagara Falls* (Albany, N.Y.: C. Van Benthuysen, 1880).

23. A. B. Hulbert, *History of the Niagara River* (1908; reprint, Harrison, N.Y.: Harrison Hill Books, 1978), p. 116.

24. Contrary statements include Lord Kelvin, 1897, in *Industrial Niagara Falls*, p. 7; and J. H. McFarland, President of the American Civic Association, "A Brief Summary of the Niagara Campaign," *Chautauquan* 47 (Niagara Preservation Issue) (1907): 279–86.

25. A. Beck, Chairman, Hydro-Electric Power Commission of Ontario, *First Report Niagara District* (Toronto, 1906). See P. Watson, *The Great Gorge Route* (Niagara Falls, Ont.: P. Watson Associates, 1997).

26. Hydro-Electric Power Commission of Ontario, *Power Development on the Niagara River: Power Plants of the Hydro-Electric Power Commission of Ontario* (Toronto, 1925 and 1930); A. V. White, *The Niagara Power Shortage* (Ottawa: Commission on Water and Water Power, Commission on Conservation, 1918); and Sir Adam Beck, *The Hydro-Electric Power Commission: Its Origins, Administrations and Achievements* (Toronto: Hydro-Electric Power Commission of Ontario, 1924).

27. D. A. Clute, "History of Natural Gas in Ontario," *Welland County Historical Society, Papers and Records* 2 (1925): 94–104; H. L. Learn, "Natural Gas Development," *Times Review: Fort Erie Centennial, 1859–1957* (Fort Erie, Ont., 1957), pp. 55–56; and E. S. Howard, *The Story of Natural Gas in the Niagara Peninsula* (St. Catharines, Ont.: Provincial Gas, 1965).

28. Williams, *Tabloid Information about Industrial Niagara Falls*, p. 93.

29. Ibid., pp. 100–101. See also *Niagara Falls: The Greatest Electric and Power City of the World* (Niagara Falls, N.Y.: Niagara Falls Chamber of Commerce, 1899).

30. The Carborundum Company of Niagara Falls, N.Y., *The Romance of Carborundum* (Buffalo, N.Y.: Bensler Press, 1932); F. J. Tone, President of the Carborundum Company, Niagara Falls, N.Y., *Abrasives in the Service of Industry* (Niagara Falls, N.Y.: Carborundum Company, 1940); F. J. Tone, *Norton Folks Contribute to Industry* (Worcester, Mass.: Norton Company, 1944). See also M. M. Trescott, *The Rise of the American Electrochemicals Industry, 1880–1910* (Westport, Conn.: Greenwood Press, 1981).

31. See Editorial, *Cataract-Journal* (Niagara Falls, New York), 15 December 1900; and *Power and Progress Exposition*, Niagara Falls Power Company and the Niagara, Lockport & Ontario Power Company (Niagara Falls, N.Y.), 1925.

32. J. Edbauer, *New Guide and Key to Niagara Falls* (Niagara Falls, N.Y., 1920), p. 45. Spirella also opened prestige buildings in Letchworth Garden City, England; Malmo, Sweden; and Copenhagen, Denmark. A plant in Niagara Falls, Ontario, operated from 1908 to 1959.

33. Williams, *Tabloid Information about Industrial Niagara Falls*, p. 104.

34. H. B. Mizer, *Niagara Falls: A Topical History, 1892–1932* (Niagara Falls, N.Y.: Niagara County Historical Society, 1981), p. 99. See Shredded Wheat Company, *The Wonders of Niagara: Scenic and Industrial* (Niagara Falls, N.Y.: Shredded Wheat Company, 1914). The company is evaluated as a model factory in B. Meakin, *Model Factories and Villages: Ideal Conditions of Labour and Housing* (1905; reprint, New York: Garland Publishing, 1985).

35. Mizer, *Niagara Falls*, p. 94.

36. T. E. Leary and E. C. Sholes, *From Fire to Rust* (Buffalo, N.Y.: Buffalo and Erie County Historical Society, 1987).

37. S. Dunn, ed., *History of Erie County, 1870–1970* (Buffalo, N.Y.: Buffalo and Erie County Historical Society, 1972), p. 33.

38. J. T. Horton, "Old Erie—The Growth of an American Community," in J. T. Horton et al., *History of Northwestern New York* (New York: Lewis, 1947), 1:414.

39. J. A. Montgomery, "Industry," in George Seibel, Project Coordinator, *Niagara Falls, Canada: A History of the City and the World Famous Beauty Spot—An Anthology* (Niagara Falls, Ont.: Kiwanis Club of Stamford, 1967), pp. 80–88; J. C. Morden, *Historic Niagara Falls* (Niagara Falls, Ont.: Lundy's Lane Historical Society, 1932); and *Niagara Falls: The Power City* (Niagara Falls, Ont.: Chamber of Commerce, 1925). In 1907 the two cities of Niagara Falls compared their respective cities and industries in special issues of their newspapers, with the same compiler and the same format: C. M. Nichols, *Special Issue of the Niagara Falls Record*, Niagara Falls, Ont., published by Niagara Falls Printing & Advertising Co., 1907; and C. M. Nichols and F. D. Hyde, *Special Issue of the Niagara Falls News*, Niagara Falls, New York, published by Power City Publishing Company, 1907.

40. C. Wiegman, *Trees to News* (Toronto: McClelland and Stewart, 1953), pp. 11–12.

41. Welland data in J. N. Jackson, *A Planning Appraisal of the Welland Urban Community: Trends-Transition-Potential, for Disposal of Lands Surplus to Canal Requirements* (Ottawa: Department of Public Works, 1974), pp. 27–35; and F. A. Sayle, *Welland Workers Make History* (Welland, Ont.: F. A. Sayle, 1963), p. 47.

42. E. Tweed, "The Evolution of St. Catharines, Ontario" (master's thesis, McMaster University, Hamilton, Ont., 1960), pp. 92, 96.

43. W. McCausland, "Fares, Please," *Niagara Frontier* 3 (1957): 93–95. The varied terminology

for "streetcar" includes "interurban," "tram," "trolley," "trolley car," and "tramcar."

44. J. M. Mills, *History of the Niagara, St. Catharines and Toronto Railway* (Toronto: Upper Canada Railway Society and the Ontario Electrical Railway Historical Association, 1967); and J. F. Due, *The Intercity Electric Railway Industry in Canada* (Toronto: University of Toronto Press, 1966).

45. W. E. Blaine, *Ride through the Garden of Canada: A Short History of the Hamilton, Grimsby and Beamsville Electric Railway Company, 1894–1931* (Grimsby, Ont., 1967). Lines radiated out from Hamilton to Dundas; across the beach strip to Burlington and eventually to Oakville; to Ancaster and then to Brantford; and to Grimsby and Beamsville. These lines provided passenger and freight services and placed the areas served within the trading catchment area of Hamilton, which became the eastern regional rival to St. Catharines.

46. W. R. Gordon, *Ninety Years of Buffalo Railway, 1860–1950* (Rochester, N.Y.:, 1970), p. 249; and G. W. Hilton and J. F. Due, *The Electric Interurban Railways in America* (Stanford, Calif.: Stanford University Press, 1960); and P. Watson, *The Great Gorge Route* (Niagara Falls, Ont.: P. Watson and Associates, 1997).

47. R. H. Lloyd, *Trolley Days in the Tonawandas* (Tonawanda, N.Y.: Historical Society of the Tonawandas, 1969).

48. M. Goldman, *High Hopes: The Rise and Decline of Buffalo, New* York (Albany: State University of New York, 1983), p. 188.

49. Skyscrapers are discussed in *American City*, September 1929, p. 1930; October 1929, p. 130; October 1929, p. 163; and November 1929, p. 95.

50. B. McKelvey, *Rochester: The Quest for Quality, 1890–1925* (Cambridge, Mass.: Harvard University Press, 1956), 3:254–55.

51. St. Catharines Board of Trade, *Annual Report of the St. Catharines Board of Trade for the Year 1900* (St. Catharines, Ont., 1901), pp. 6–7.

52. J. W. Percy: *Tonawanda, The Way It Was* (Kenmore, N.Y.: Partners' Press, 1979), p. 95; and *Pioneer Suburb: A Comprehensive History of Kenmore, New York, 1899–1974* (Kenmore, N.Y.: Partners' Press, 1974).

53. P. Beaudet: "The Growth of Buffalo's Suburban Zone," *Niagara Frontier* 18 (1971): 50; and "The Concepts of Suburb, Balanced Suburb, and Satellite Applied to the Buffalo, N.Y. Area" (Ph.D. diss., Clark University, 1968).

54. Horton, "Old Erie," 1:297.

55. Interpretations of the extravaganza, with descriptions of Buffalo, Niagara Falls, and their vicinity, include R. H. Barry, *The Grandeur of the Exhibition* (Buffalo, N.Y.: Robert Allan Reid, 1909); and I. V. James, *The Pan-American Exposition*, Adventures in Western New York History, vol. 6 (Buffalo, N.Y.: Buffalo and Erie County Historical Society, 1961); *A Souvenir of Buffalo, New York, Niagara Falls and the Great Pan American Exposition of 1901* (Grand Rapids, Mich.: J. Boyne, 1901); R. H. Barry, *The Grandeurs of the Exposition* (Buffalo, N.Y.: Robert Allan Reid, 1901); A. M. Fox, *Symbol and*

Show: The Pan American Exposition of 1901 (Buffalo, N.Y.: Mayer Entreprises, 1987); and *The Rand-McNally Hand-Book to the Pan-American Exposition* (Chicago: Rand-McNally, 1899). A novel, L. Belfer, *City of Light* (New York: Dial Press, 1999), uses Buffalo, power development at the Falls, and the Pan-American Exposition as background to the culture and conflicts of the period.

56. For treaty details, see American Falls International Board, *Preservation and Enhancement of the American Falls at Niagara*, Final Report to the International Joint Commission, Appendix A (Ottawa and Washington, 1974), pp. A2–A12.

57. Ontario Hydro, *Power from Niagara* (Toronto: Ontario Hydro, 1970), p. 26; and J. Carr, "Hydro-Electric Power Development in the Niagara Peninsula."

58. An issue was tax payment, the Power Authority having the legal status of a nontaxable agency; D. A. Nass, *Public Policy and Public Works: Niagara Falls Redevelopment as a Case Study*, Essays in Public Works History, no. 7 (Chicago: Public Works Historical Society, 1979), pp. 26–35.

59. G. J. Pederson, "The Supreme Court Decision in the Tuscarora Case," *Niagara Frontier* 7 (1960): 48–52; and T. F. Farrell, "Memorandum to Chairman Moses," *Paralleling the Welland Canal and Effects on the Niagara Power Project* (Niagara Falls, N.Y.: Power Authority of the State of New York, 1958), p. 6.

60. Power Authority of the State of New York, *Niagara Power Project—Data* (Buffalo, N.Y.: Power Authority of the State of New York, [1964]).

61. *Niagara Falls of Today, Anno Domini, 1907, Special Issue of the Niagara Falls News* (Niagara Falls, N.Y.: Power City Publishing Company, 1907).

62. "Hydro Plan Wants Flow Cut at Falls," *St. Catharines Standard*, 13 August 1979.

63. American Falls International Board, *Preservation and Enhancement of the American Falls at Niagara*; and B. F. Friesen and J. C. Day, "Hydroelectric Power and Scenic Provisions of the 1950 Niagara Treaty," *Water Resources Bulletin* 13 (1977): 1181.

64. Ontario Hydro, *Niagara River Hydroelectric Development Project: New Generating Station Proposed for Niagara River* (Toronto: Ontario Hydro, 1989).

65. St. Catharines Hydro-Electric Commission, *Port Dalhousie Generating Station: Environmental Study Report* (Niagara Falls, Ont.: Acres International, 1988).

CHAPTER SIX

THE MOTOR VEHICLE DOMINATES

As the automobile and truck steadily became dominant as the primary modes of transportation in the early twentieth century, a new highway network was constructed to meet the demands of these more flexible, high-speed forms of travel. Existing roads were improved and an entirely new system added that included scenic parkways, multilane highways, and bridges over the Niagara River and the two canals. As the motor vehicle vigorously and profoundly redefined the landscape on both sides at the Niagara Frontier, the focus of activity changed from closely defined urban areas to the extensive dispersal of population, industry, services, and housing.

NEW HIGHWAYS AND URBAN STREETS

Roads paved with concrete or asphalt to provide a smooth surface were introduced in the mid-1880s to meet the demands of cycling. At St. Catharines bicycles were produced at the Welland Vale Works on Twelve Mile Creek before the turn of the century, and Buffalo became "the Greatest Wheel City in the World."[1] Apart from the paving of roads, the marketing and financial arrangements for the purchase of bicycles assisted the nascent automobile industry, which copied certain innovative manufacturing and sales techniques. The annual unveiling of new models, insurance against theft, collision damage, and payment by installment all preceded the automobile.

Bicycles were manufactured at the Frontier by the turn of the nineteenth century in both St. Catharines and Buffalo. (*Welland Vale Bicycle Catalogue*, St. Catharines, 1898)

The production of motor vehicles began in the late nineteenth century, when innovators produced steam, electric, and gasoline engines, and the automobile began to find a place in personal and goods transportation. The first motorcars were patented in the 1880s, and within ten years they were produced in every industrialized nation as playthings for the rich, often as an innovation by the same craftsmen who made horse-drawn carriages. Mass production soon made wide-spread ownership possible. In 1908 Henry Ford launched his Model T, and over the next twenty years, fifteen million vehicles rolled off his continuous assembly line at Detroit, Michigan. By the late 1920s about two hundred thousand passenger cars and thirty-two thousand trucks were registered in the counties on both sides of the Frontier. The use of the automobile, slowed by the Depression and then halted briefly by the Second World War, emerged as the dominant form of transportation and exerted a major and increasing impact on the urban landscape for the rest of the twentieth century.

Family cars were used as recreational vehicles for local trips. On the Canadian Frontier the Niagara River Parkway was created to provide access for tourists to view the natural scenery of the river. First known as "The Boulevard," this road, taking advantage of the Chain Reserve that had been retained for Crown purposes since the 1780s, was envisioned in 1904 as a "well-built boulevard, properly ornamented with shade trees, constructed and maintained over the whole distance" from Fort Erie to Niagara.[2] The section along the river from Bridgeburg (now Fort Erie) to Queen Victoria Park at the Falls was completed by 1915, then extended as far as Niagara-on-the-Lake by 1931. Designed as a well-maintained scenic road, commercial traffic was forbidden and local service use discouraged. A major point of access was by ferry across the Niagara River at Fort Erie, until the Peace Bridge opened in 1927, and the streetcar bridges at Niagara and Queenston-Lewiston were also used.

Inland from the river on the Canadian Frontier, major highway improvements were made to the Niagara Stone Road from Niagara-on-the-Lake to St. Catharines, Queenston Road to St. Catharines, Lundy's Lane from Niagara Falls to Allanburg, and Old Garrison Road from Fort Erie to Port Colborne (fig. 6.1).[3] These and other east-west roads had to cross both the Third Canal and also the Fourth Welland Canal then under construction. Fourteen highway bridges were built across the channel of the Fourth Canal between 1927 to 1931. These included nine vertical-lift and four rolling-lift structures; all carried pedestrian sidewalks. The vertical-lift bridges rose to 36.6 meters (120 feet) above the water level to enable ships with their masts to pass below. With priority awarded to marine traffic and as highway traffic increased, these bridges as focal points on the highway network became frustrating points of delay, and on the major routes they were later replaced by high-rise bridges or tunnels.

On the American Frontier, paved roads were developed from Youngstown to Olcott and Lockport, and along the river from Niagara Falls through the Tonawandas to Buffalo. Niagara Falls Boulevard, Sheridan Drive, and River Road provided paved access to the Falls. River Road carried streetcars, had seventeen grade crossings, and was

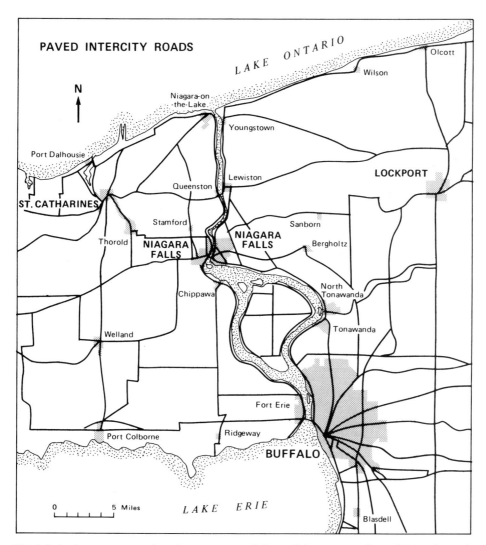

Fig. 6.1. As the motor age gathered momentum and changed the patterns of travel, the main roads were paved with asphalt or concrete, graded, and provided with bridges, which together introduced a new system of highway movement by the 1930s on both Frontiers. (Prepared by the Department of Geography, Brock University)

As roads were paved inland from the boundary, all east-west routes on the Canadian Frontier had to cross the Third Welland Canal, where swing bridges, like the one here at Humberstone (now Port Colborne), were constructed. Note the attraction of stores to this new focal point in the landscape. On the Fourth Welland Canal then under construction, this channel was crossed by lift bridges. (John Burtniak)

blocked frequently by long lines of freight cars; by 1930 these routes were so heavily traveled that the trip to the Falls could take two hours of bumper-to-bumper traffic on a Sunday afternoon.

A public highway system emerged on both sides of the Frontier as dirt roads, dusty in summer and muddy after rain, were widened, graded, and provided with bridges over streams and with hard smooth surfaces to meet the special requirements of that new-fangled device—the motorcar. This changing

The Niagara River Parkway, an outstanding commitment to high-quality landscape design, follows the river frontage on the Canadian Frontier. (John N. Jackson)

landscape detail is illustrated by Delaware Avenue in suburban Kenmore and Tonawanda, New York.[4] In 1894 the avenue had been paved with vitrified brick and featured an electric streetcar track; by 1929 the brick pavement, the streetcars, and the numerous bicycles which traveled over it were all but gone. Kenmore was proud of being the only village in the United States with all its streets paved. In 1920 at Tonawanda, the annual highway budget jumped from $250 to $26,000 to handle an extension of the lighting system, railway switches, water and gas lines, sewers, telephone and power lines, docks for the ferries to Grand Island, bridges over the Erie Canal, and new streets.

To meet demands from an increasing number of vehicles, the now smooth surfaces were marked to separate opposing streams of traffic, and parking, speed limits, and traffic lights were added. Guidelines were provided.

The automobile created new highway landscapes. **Left:** A gas station with adjacent fruit stand. **Below:** A store with tourist cabins. (John Burtniak [both])

Local street systems had to be consistent with national and international standards for safety and were controlled within towns and cities by zoning rules, ordinances, and traffic regulations according to the administrative classification of each street.[5] As a result, the street scene tends to be similar on both Frontiers. The common requirements of the automobile created a trend toward uniformity in streetscapes and townscapes across North America.

The shortage of parking space became acute in those inner-city environments that predate the 1920s, and perhaps a third of all land in developed urban areas is now devoted to streets, roads, parking, and access. As auto-oriented suburbs extended out from the older core, main road frontages became desirable commercial sites and urban development inched steadily outward. "No Parking" areas were introduced, and the roadside shopping center originated when shops were set back from the road with space for parking along the forefront of the buildings. Retail strips spread out along Lundy's Lane (Highway 20) west from Niagara Falls; Garrison Road (Highway 3) in Fort Erie; and Ontario Street, Hartzel Road, and Fourth Avenue in St. Catharines. The northern entrance to Welland on Highway 58, much of Highway 3 through Port Colborne, and Highway 20 east of Fonthill exhibit similar characteristics.

The streetcar, on fixed routes and the forerunner of public transit, gradually disappeared in the wake of improving automobile and more flexible bus transportation between cities and from the city out into its growing suburbs. On the Canadian Frontier, Niagara-on-the-Lake lost its line in 1931, the St. Catharines to Niagara Falls line closed in 1947, and service to Port Dalhousie was ended in 1950. The line from Thorold to Port Colborne survived until 1959.[6] As the NS&T network on the Canadian Frontier became a subsidiary of the Canadian National railway system, some spur lines survived to provide freight services, but these "survivor routes" were eliminated by the 1990s.

On the American Frontier, sections of the Great Gorge Route became a hiking trail, the last streetcar ran in Niagara Falls in 1937, and when the high-speed line to Buffalo was abandoned in the same year, its elevated stretch was removed and parts were later replaced by an expressway. Local streetcar lines were replaced by generally less frequent and smaller buses, a process that began in the 1920s though the streetcar survived in Buffalo until 1950.[7]

The other major casualty on both Frontiers was the decline of the railway after the Second World War, for freight and passenger movements, with the automobile and truck dominating for all short- and long-distance traffic, and the airplane for long-distance, intercity travel. The motor age was dominant by the end of the Second World War and has continued to expand as the major contributor to urban form and character at the Frontier and across the Western world, and indeed to urbanization everywhere.

AIR TRANSPORT ARRIVES

With the fledgling development of air flight and travel, flying clubs sprang up at airstrips in various outlying areas at the Frontier.[8] By the late 1920s the municipal Buffalo Airport (renamed the Greater Buffalo International Airport after 1959, and part of the Niagara Frontier Transportation Authority from 1967) was established in Cheektowaga on a relatively high, flat area northeast of the city. Airmail schedules, started by Colonial Western Airways (later American Airlines), connected Buffalo with other North American cities after 1927. Los Angeles was then twenty hours away by air.[9]

Airports also developed east of St. Catharines (now the Niagara District Airport) and at Niagara Falls, New York. Both, used for military purposes during the Second World War, now serve private interests. Niagara Falls International Airport in New York retains its

military function, but demand has not been sustained for commercial flights, and recent private ventures have been short-lived. A flight ramp in what is now LaSalle Park in Buffalo provided a daily seaplane service to Toronto. The urban environment has changed continuously over time, and remnants from earlier times remain in the current landscape.

With the rise of regular scheduled passenger services after the Second World War, Buffalo was connected to North American cities previously accessible only by rail and, with modern jet aircraft, Buffalo International Airport linked with all major air hubs of North America. Greatly expanded, with a second terminal that opened in 1997, the airport became a commercial hub in the metropolitan landscape, attracting car rental agencies, hotels, restaurants, and new high-technology industries to its vicinity. An active air service is maintained between Buffalo and Toronto's Lester Pearson International Airport, which serves as the major center for international and especially European flights on both sides of the Niagara River. Depending on destination, cost, and convenience, citizens now cross the boundary to use the most suitable airport for their needs. Interconnecting flights, multilane highways, and scheduled ground transportation services make both airports fully accessible to both Frontiers.

MULTILANE HIGHWAYS

As highway traffic multiplied, travel was slowed at the numerous junctions in towns and cities. In the 1930s the concept of a limited-access, separated highway system began to emerge, inspired by the German Autobahn and the Italian Autostrade. Both words mean a superhighway designed solely for vehicles. Following these precedents, the Queen Elizabeth Way (QEW) from Toronto to Niagara Falls, Ontario, was opened in 1939 at St. Catharines by King George VI and Queen Elizabeth.[10]

The limited-access multilane highway (fig. 6.2) was a glorious new idea. People drove miles out of their way to see the highway's carefully landscaped median, which carried the longest continuous lighting system in the world. The quality of the QEW remains evident in the design of a Viking galley, nautical reliefs, and the ornate lamp standards on the Henley Bridge over Twelve Mile Creek in St. Catharines, and the original landscaping in Ontario may still be observed within the cloverleaf crossing where the highway is crossed by the Niagara Stone Road in Niagara Falls.

The QEW, extended to Fort Erie as a gravel road in 1941 and completed as a paved four-lane highway to the Peace Bridge in 1956, was upgraded during the 1970s into a fully controlled, limited-access highway. Service roads and new intersections were constructed and traffic circles removed to promote a faster flow of traffic. The highway displaced the former Queenston-Grimsby route (Highway 8, now Regional Road 81) as the major highway of the Niagara Peninsula, and fostered the urbanized spread of the Golden Horseshoe around the head of Lake Ontario from Hamilton and Toronto toward the Niagara River. Improvements have continued; the QEW between Hamilton and St. Catharines became a six-lane highway during the late 1990s.

New York State passed a Thruway bill in 1943, promoting a new road system for the Buffalo area, but construction had to await the end of the Second World War.[11] The Governor Thomas E. Dewey section, the "main line" of the system, was completed through New York State via Albany to the edge of Buffalo in 1954. The Thruway, toll-free where it passes through Buffalo's suburban eastern townships, bounds the city to the east and southeast, and connects to Cleveland and Chicago south of Lake Erie as part of the I-90. This heavily traveled through passenger and truck traffic route bypassed the central area of Buffalo and replaced the traditional east-west movements by canal, lake traffic, and rail.

Fig. 6.2. Multilane highways designed solely for vehicles began with the QEW on the Canadian Frontier. A network of these superhighways soon provided the capability of high-speed movement between and within the centers at the Frontier; a new pattern of mobility that transformed urban spatial relationships, and encouraged the outward movement of all types of activity from the established towns to the suburbs and beyond. (Prepared by the Department of Geography, Brock University)

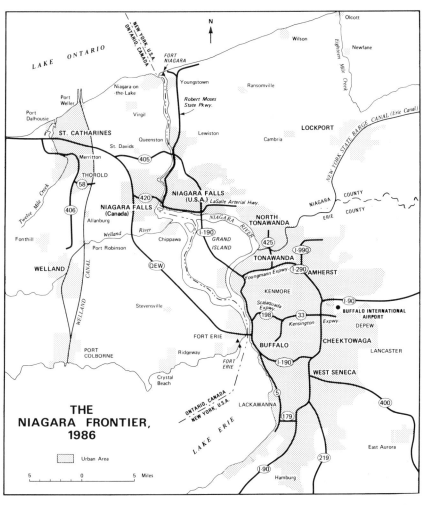

THE NIAGARA FRONTIER, 1986

Truck terminals, hotels, and many other highway-oriented services sprouted at the junctions along this route.

A series of multilane ring and radial roads soon penetrated the city of Buffalo. Spurs from the Thruway extended to East Aurora (NY 400) and Orchard Park (US 219). The Niagara Section of the Thruway (I-190), completed in the late 1950s, connected with the Canadian Frontier via Niagara Falls, New York, and the Queenston-Lewiston Bridge. The section from downtown to the Peace

Top right: The original Queen Elizabeth Way carried a lighting strip along the median, and cloverleaf interchanges connected with the established system of roads. (Archives of Ontario, RE 14-162-5-166).

Below right: Where the QEW was carried over Twelve Mile Creek (that is the former Second Welland Canal), the bridge was designed to look like a Viking ship in recognition of the point of crossing of two major transportation modes. (J. N. Jackson)

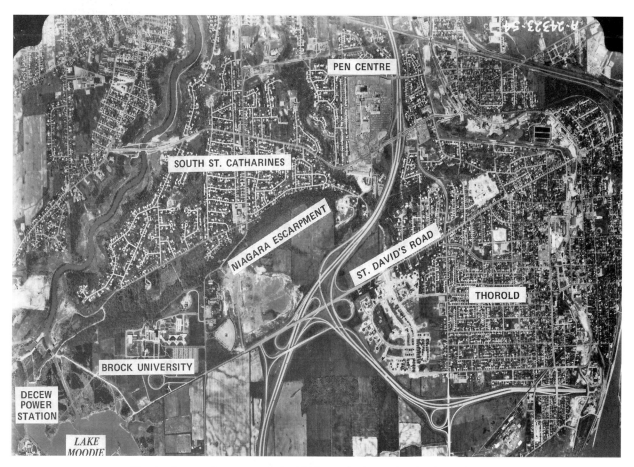

The dominance of streets, roads, and highways in the modern landscape is indicated by this scene from the Canadian Frontier where Highway 406 crosses the Niagara Escarpment. The centerpiece, a massive highway junction, uses more land than either the campus of Brock University or the regional Pen Center. This highway markedly divides land use activities in the urban environment, and provides a defining edge to urban development. Note how the old compact residential areas of Thorold with its regular layout contrasts with the post-1960s suburbs of South St. Catharines in terms of density, age, and the curving road layout. (This aerial photograph A24323-54 © 1976/04/30 Her Majesty the Queen in Right of Canada, reproduced from the collection of the National Air Photo Library, Ottawa, with permission of Natural Resources Canada)

Bridge, built in the 1940s, followed the bed of the abandoned Erie Canal. The Youngmann Expressway (I-290) linked the Niagara Section of the Thruway across Buffalo's northern suburbs, and provided the direct route from the Queenston-Lewiston Bridge for Canadian traffic traveling to Buffalo International Airport and to the north and east of the city.

The Scajaquada-Humboldt-Kensington Expressway complex (NY 198-NY 33) provided an inner ring within Buffalo, and a radial to Buffalo International Airport and to the eastern suburbs. The Humboldt-Scajaquada link degraded Delaware Park, designed by Frederick Law Olmsted, and the principal park in the city. Expressway segments in the cities of Tonawanda and North Tonawanda, and the LaSalle Expressway east of Niagara Falls, intended as a route between Niagara Falls and Buffalo, were never completed because of opposition from residents of the suburbs along the planned path.

Highway building continued with the extension of the I-990 from the Youngmann Highway toward Lockport, and on the Canadian Frontier with Highway 406 advancing south from St. Catharines to Welland during the 1980s, and Highways 405 and 420 linking from the QEW to the Queenston-Lewiston and the Rainbow Bridges across the Niagara River.[12] A point to be noted is that the concentration of highways in conjunction with the Niagara River, the Welland Canal, and Ontario Hydro's power canals has resulted "in an unusually large number of bridges being required throughout the area. Several of these were at the leading edge of technology."[13] Not bottlenecks, they help to assist materially with the through movement of vehicles within and across the Frontier environment.

A difference between the highway landscapes at the boundary is that Canadian tolls on the Garden City Skyway of the QEW in St. Catharines over the Welland Canal have been removed, whereas they remain in place on the bridges across the Niagara River to Grand Island, and along the New York State Thruway to the east and west of Buffalo. The multilane, limited-access highways at the Niagara Frontier are "funnels" that serve as major traffic arteries. They link the Frontier to places beyond and fulfill the peninsula's long-term strategic role as a land bridge. The historical and trading significance of these highways and their political significance for Canadian-American relationships are illustrated by the fact that the QEW and the New York Thruway together connected Toronto and New York City to provide an international interlinkage before Toronto-Montreal, Toronto-Ottawa, and New York-Montreal were similarly connected.

Like other multilane highways at the Frontier, the QEW at St. Catharines created a transportation swathe across the urban landscape with space-consuming junctions and service roads. Commercial centers were drawn to this highway, which confined residential development and divided the urban environment. (Ontario Department of Highways)

As previously with the railways, the new highways divided the areas through which they passed. They added noise, pollution, and vibration. St. Catharines is separated into northern and southern sections by the QEW, and the I-190 separated Buffalo from its waterfront. In Niagara Falls the Robert Moses "Parkway" passed through the heart of the Niagara State Reservation Park next to Goat Island and blocked scenic views and access.

Abandoned canal or railway routes have sometimes been taken over for highways; more often, new routes were purchased across land in or close to urban areas, including farmland. The highways were separated from their surroundings by chain barriers and, unlike the previous pattern or roadways, no access to adjacent land was provided. Cloverleaf or diamond crossings at spaced intervals connected the new highways with the preexisting pattern of roads, and vast land-consuming junctions interconnected the freeways. The highway destinations were interurban, and the routes carried heavy volumes of truck traffic, mingled with tourist and local traffic, including commuters. The highways helped considerably to extend the outward growth of cities on both sides of the Frontier and made them more accessible and more interdependent, including across the international border.

A possible new highway development on the Canadian Frontier, a Mid-Peninsula Transportation Corridor, is supported by the Regional Municipality of Niagara in order to transfer pressures for development away from the congested QEW and the Niagara Fruit Belt, and to encourage development in the southern part of the Niagara Frontier. This route would link directly from the Niagara River to the Highway 401/402 Windsor-Sarnia Corridor, and carry east-west flowing truck traffic between the Niagara and Detroit Frontiers. On the American Frontier, the extension of Highway 219 south could link Buffalo to Miami and Florida. As it may be expected to promote trade and travel, it may be anticipated that its completion will add to the pressure for improved highway crossings over the Niagara River, either at the Peace Bridge or from Grand Island to the QEW.

New roads and especially the multilane highway systems on both sides of the Frontier are major consumers of land. Some of the best agricultural land at the Niagara Frontier has been taken permanently out of production to permit numbered highways to cross the landscape. Further losses occurred as these highways generated shopping plazas, industrial and service complexes, housing developments, parks, and golf courses. The QEW to Fort Erie, Highway 406 through St. Catharines, and Highway 420 to the Queenston-Lewiston Bridge have also eaten up agricultural land. The loss of land from agriculture was also high when US 190 crossed Grand Island, and along the Aurora Expressway (Highway 400) southeast from Buffalo.

The new paved highways also changed rural-urban relationships, more so than even the railways, for they made it possible for farm families to more easily go to the nearest urban center for shopping; entertainment; and legal, medical, and financial concerns. Through improved access coupled with the outward movement of urban services, the rural areas were drawn increasingly into the urban web. Retailing activities, including mail-order purchases, could now supply rural needs more cheaply, easily, and at a lower price than before. The rural-urban dichotomy was ending as highways advanced. Both Frontiers became urban regions. Their rural areas now depended on services in their nearby urban centers.

NEW BRIDGES CROSS THE NIAGARA RIVER

Automobile traffic between the two sides of the Niagara River at first used existing bridges and car ferries. The two-level Whirlpool Rapids Bridge at the Falls carried early highway traffic, and autos could be accommodated on the streetcar crossings between Queenston and Lewiston and the two cities at Niagara Falls. Car ferries crossed between Fort Erie and Buffalo until 1949.

The Peace Bridge, designed by Edward P. Lupfer of Buffalo and constructed by the independent Buffalo and Fort Erie Public Bridge Company, opened in 1927 between Fort Erie and Buffalo, to forge a major highway link between the two nations. First proposed in 1902 but not then built, and with both a tunnel and a causeway considered, the new bridge carried a roadway 5.5 meters (18 feet) wide. This width was at first thought to be more than adequate, but the heavy traffic generated soon required a heavier road base and a greater width of 7.3 meters (24 feet).[14] In 1972, the four narrow traffic lanes were reduced to three, with the center lane redesigned to accommodate a reversible flow.

The opening of the Peace Bridge to traffic in 1927 was several years before the development of the multilane highway system, and decades before the QEW and the Niagara Section (I-190) of the New York Thruway (I-90) that are now attached to the bridge. The bridge structure includes five steel arch spans that cross the Niagara River, and a further span on the American side that carries the bridge some 33 meters (100 feet) over the Black Rock ship canal. This asymmetrical structure displaced earlier ferries. It brought Canadian customers to downtown Buffalo, encouraged American companies to locate across the river, brought an increased number of American visitors to the Falls, promoted the Niagara River Parkway as a major tourist route, provided improved access for Buffalonians to their cottages and recreational areas along the Canadian beaches of Lake Erie, and more closely linked the two nations through an expanding trade flow.

The Peace Bridge is associated closely

with Mather Park and Arch, a Depression-era gateway work project named after Alonzo Mather, a wealthy Chicago industrialist. This opened in 1940 and involved the construction of a seawall along the edge of the Niagara River, and the draining, filling, reclamation, and seeding of the area inland from the wall. These works permitted the extension of the Niagara Parkway over landscaped grounds to Old Fort Erie.

Brokerage companies to handle the logistics of moving freight across an international boundary and to act as agents for importers and exporters on both sides of the boundary have concentrated at both ends of the bridge, but mostly on the Canadian side where two adjacent streets in Fort Erie provide a distinct land-use cluster specializing in shipping documentation and customs clearance for international truck traffic. Customs and immigration offices for truck inspection, trucking companies, and their terminals have also located at both ends of the bridge, as have duty-free shops at both the Canadian and the American plazas.

To the north, the Rainbow Bridge at Niagara Falls was built in 1940–1941 as a replacement structure for the Upper Steel Arch Bridge, which collapsed after its base structure was torn away by ice in 1938.[15] The piers of the bridge, now embedded in the walls of the gorge some 15.2 meters (50 feet) back from the river's edge and the same distance above the surface of the water, were designed to be beyond the reach of any anticipated winter ice. The Rainbow Bridge, downstream from both the former bridge and the American Falls, commands magnificent views of the river scene, and as a tourist viewing platform may be without parallel in the world.

With a span of 289.6 meters (950 feet), the bridge provides highway access from the QEW via Highway 420 to the American Frontier at Niagara Falls, New York. A two-level bridge-road system has been designed; the upper level crosses the Niagara River Parkway, and at the lower level are the Oakes Garden Theatre, the Rainbow Carillon Tower with concerts on its set of tuned bells, and tourist-commercial outlets and facilities. This complex contrasts with the less happy circumstances on the American Frontier, where traffic flows directly onto the streets of downtown Niagara Falls with many junctions; through, local, and cross traffic; and urban renewal including hotels, a shopping center, a stadium, and museums to improve a decayed urban scene. Opened in 1998, the first phase of an enlarged U.S. Customs and Immigration Rainbow Bridge Processing Center featured an 182.9-meter (600-foot) glass arc on top of three stone buildings.

Downstream, the Whirlpool Rapids Bridge carries a railway track on the upper level and a highway below. With the smallest capacity and difficulties of access at both ends, this bridge is the least used of the four highway crossings. In late 1998 it became an experimental CanPass-Dedicated Commuter Lane program in which Revenue Canada and Customs and Immigration cooperated to simplify border crossings. Later applied at the Peace Bridge, customs and immigration clearance are provided in advance for approved applicants to enter Canada, this being the outcome of computer technology and a Canadian-United States accord to promote trade, tourism, and travel between the two countries.

To the north the most recent highway bridge to cross the Niagara River, the Queenston-Lewiston Bridge, opened in 1962 to replace the earlier Suspension Bridge that had from 1899 to 1962 connected the villages of Queenston and Lewiston across the Niagara River. The bridge site was changed from the head of the Lower Niagara River to upstream across the gorge at the top of the Niagara Escarpment. With a span of 304.8 meters (1,000 feet), this bridge became the longest fixed-end, steel arch bridge in the world.

Superlatives are not without merit when the bridges across the Niagara River are under discussion.[16] As with the earlier power stations, all bridges are important en-

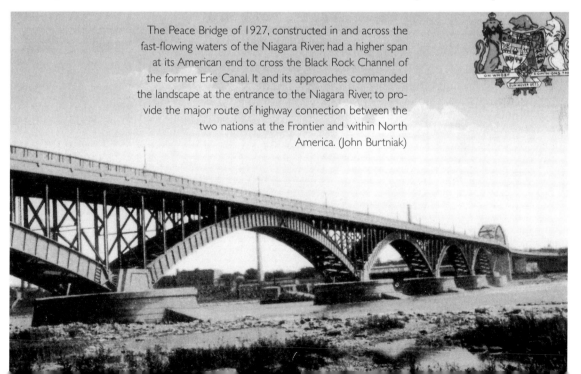

The Peace Bridge of 1927, constructed in and across the fast-flowing waters of the Niagara River, had a higher span at its American end to cross the Black Rock Channel of the former Erie Canal. It and its approaches commanded the landscape at the entrance to the Niagara River, to provide the major route of highway connection between the two nations at the Frontier and within North America. (John Burtniak)

gineering design achievements and noted visual landmarks when traveling along the river. Each also enjoys a spectacular river setting, and all have rich panoramic views for pedestrians from their decks. National flags flown at their centers add further character and the reminder that each bridge marks the end of one nation and the start of the other.

Skyways, soaring over the adjacent landscape, also reflect the dominance of the automobile and the incisive impact of engineering decisions on the landscape. Built after the Second World War, these bridges include the Garden City Skyway in St. Catharines, which carries the QEW over the Fourth Welland Canal. Opened in 1963, this structure is 2.5 kilometers (1.5 miles) long and 37.5 meters (123 feet) high. On the American Frontier south of central Buffalo, the now-demolished Father Baker Bridge was built high to clear the Union Ship Canal, and the high double bridges that connect Grand Island to the mainland carry the Niagara Section of the New York State Thruway (I-190) to serve local, long-distance, and international traffic.

As highway traffic flows have increased, the international bridges across the Niagara River have became bottlenecks that impede or slow down the flow of traffic. There can be long lines of stalled traffic, especially during the daily rush hour, at holiday weekends, when customs and immigration staff are reduced by government cuts, or when insufficient booths are open for truck inspection. For transport trucks there are the additional problems of expanding commercial traffic; an antiquated, paper-based processing system; and not all companies take advantage of the advanced preprocessing procedures. Behind the administrative and congestion issues lies the fact that the European Union has eliminated border posts which inhibit the free movement of goods, services, and people between nations; the argument is that Canada and the United States should achieve the same under their Free Trade Agreements.

At the Peace Bridge, alternatives for improvement considered by its authority in the mid-1990s were to widen the existing structure and/or to construct a second bridge either north or south of the existing span, with variations between concrete and steel in the use of materials. The design announced in mid-1998 was for a second bridge south of the current structure. This would be a four-lane span similar in appearance to the present bridge. The aim was for completion by 2002, the seventy-fifth anniversary of the present structure. The new bridge would carry a 3-meter- (10-foot-) wide bicycle lane for pedestrians and bicycle riders, provide space for anticipated increase in traffic flows, and, upon completion, the deck of the original bridge would be replaced to bring two bridges into operation with twice the present capacity. Construction would be paid for through truck and auto tolls, include a percentage of duty-free sales on both sides of the bridge, and be financed through bonds backed by these revenues.

Controversy arose when the American side with competing engineering companies lobbied for a single-span replacement design, a "signature bridge" of high aesthetic appeal to beautify Buffalo's waterfront rather than the twinning proposal. A court injunction issued to prevent the proposed twinning has mired the twinning proposal in the American courts, to provide an unfortunate and regrettable example of supposed binational collaboration.

What is needed is a design for an increasing free flow of people and goods over the border crossings, which is more complicated than rival engineering-aesthetic considerations at the Peace Bridge. It should reflect how best to use the Frontier's infrastructure of highway and railway bridges, as highway traffic increases and the diminished railway traffic is reorganized. A causeway could be constructed across the mouth of the Niagara River which, as along the Zuider Zee and the Dutch coast, might carry multilane highways,

and also be used to control water levels in Lake Erie and to generate electricity; a tunnel might be constructed between the two nations under the entrance to the Niagara River; and a new bridge could be constructed from the QEW across the western branch of the Niagara River to Grand Island, where it would connect via the I-190 to the New York Thruway and its eastern end perhaps to a Mid-Peninsula Transportation Corridor across the Niagara Peninsula.

There is also the factor of possible conversions to highway or joint rail-highway use of one or more of the three current railway bridges that cross the Niagara River, and then to use parts of the now underutilized freight yards on one or both sides of the Niagara River as a hub with customs and other transportation service activities. One such project involves the Niagara Falls Bridge Commission, a different public agency in competition with the Peace Bridge Authority, which has proposed the addition of express lanes for trucks across the top of this bridge, and then the use of existing CN rights-of-way to connect the Whirlpool Bridge to Highway 405 south of Niagara Falls.

If the St. Lawrence Seaway can be achieved as a major project between the two nations, then a similar comprehensive engineering-economic analysis of the various possibilities as one unified, international venture might reasonably be undertaken for travel and movement between the two nations across the Niagara River. We should no longer have to rely on idiosyncratic decisions by powerful interest groups. The total environment at the Niagara Frontier has to be viewed as a whole, more so than the study of its individual parts.

THE HIGHWAY BRIDGES AS INTERNATIONAL GATEWAYS

The value of transborder surface freight flows by all surface modes across the Niagara Frontier has steadily increased over the later years of the twentieth century but, when comparisons are made with the value of freight crossing the Detroit Frontier, then Detroit has obtained higher values than at Niagara. Although freight traffic along the QEW has remained high with increasing volumes, flows along the Highway 401 corridor to Windsor-Detroit and along Highway 402 to Sarnia-Port Huron have increased at a greater rate.[17] Freight rail traffic has diminished but remains as an important part of the total equation, promoting mergers between the Canadian and American rail companies.

The highest volume of automobile cross-ings have been at the Detroit Frontier. At the Windsor-Detroit Tunnel 4.2 million autos entered the United States in 1995, followed by Windsor's Ambassador Bridge with 3.6 million autos; then came the Peace Bridge with 3 million autos. For commercial flows the Ambassador Bridge carried more than 1 million commercial vehicles into the United States; the second- and third-largest entry points were the Blue Water Bridge and then the Peace Bridge with some 600,000 commercial vehicle entries into the United States.[18]

The four bridges on the Niagara Frontier in 1995 carried 18.4 percent of Canadian exports to the United States, a figure that had increased by an average annual growth rate of 5.8 percent over the period from 1988 to 1995. By contrast trade across the Detroit River (including the Windsor-Detroit Tunnel and the Ambassador, Blue Water, and International Bridges) was 42 percent of the Canadian exports in 1995, a figure that had increased by 8.3 percent during the period from 1988 to 1995.[19]

This data indicates that the Detroit River crossings, and the associated Highway 401 and 402 traffic corridors between Toronto and Windsor/Sarnia, had become more important than the traffic corridor along the QEW to the Niagara Frontier. Both corridors, however, were of considerable national importance, together carrying some 60.4 percent of Canadian exports. In a commercial vehicle survey of 1995, the QEW carried a daily cargo value of $245 million Canadian and a daily truck volume of 8,450 vehicles, against the comparable value of $290 million and 7,300 trucks on Highway 401 to Windsor-Detroit, and $150 million and 3,700 trucks to the Sarnia-Port Huron crossing.[20] In partial explanation of these flows, and the transition from the Peace Bridge as the most important international crossing, are the respective catchment areas of the Detroit and Niagara bridges in the United States and the impact of close manufacturing links between the two nations. For example, the North American auto industry includes automotive components, assembled vehicles, and a connected assembly line with just-in-time deliveries in the Detroit-Michigan area.

For traffic-flow data across the highway bridges at the Niagara Frontier, whether for truck or automobile traffic, the Peace Bridge clearly dominates. Truck traffic increased from 0.7 million vehicles in 1984, then almost doubled to 1.3 million vehicles by 1997.[21] Truck traffic flows over the Queenston-Lewiston Bridge reflect the same trend of a steady annual increase, from 0.5 million vehicles in 1984 to 0.8 million vehicles by 1997. Automobile traffic increased from 11.8 million vehicles in 1984 to 15 million a decade later, and to 15.6 million vehicles by 1997. The Peace Bridge again dominated with 6.3 million annual auto vehicles in 1997. The Queenston-Lewiston Bridge followed with 4.2 million autos, and then came the Rainbow Bridge; and the Whirlpool Bridge carried the lowest volumes of auto traffic.

Ironically, at the same time that traffic capacity across the bridges was being improved by more efficient inspection procedures, infrastructure developments to improve traffic flow, with increasing trade and travel flows in both directions, and with proposals to widen the Peace Bridge stalled in American courts, the American side was adding restrictions on traffic flows into that nation through the application of Section 110 of the Illegal Immigration and Immigrant Responsibility Act. In 1997 American immigration officials were provided with sweeping new powers to restrict immigration; transborder crime, drugs, terrorists, illegal immigration, and smugglers were now perceived as a threat. Although the American-Mexican border provided the greater problem, the Canadian-American border was treated the same. Further, with traffic delays at the Niagara bridges being primarily a problem of increased delays through lengthier inspections and longer interrogations rather than

Skyways dominate the urban landscape where the QEW crosses the Welland Canal in St. Catharines (**top**) and at the waterfront in Buffalo (**bottom**). (John N. Jackson [top], and Gregory P. Stein [bottom])

the passing number of vehicles, the threat of new surveillance raised the specter of extensive delays, a problem for private individuals, for just-in-time commercial deliveries between the two nations, and for all movement across the line of divide between the two nations. In late 1998 the solution to these different standards, a top item on the Canadian agenda of bilateral relations for more than two years, was for the application of the new American law to be delayed for thirty months.[22]

URBAN EXPANSION AND CHANGE

As the vast new system of highways with their attendant bridges was introduced to the landscape on both sides of the Niagara boundary, immense and still-continuing changes were originated everywhere. The central business districts lost their earlier advantages as terminals on the railway and streetcar networks. As people moved out to the suburbs, these residents were followed by shopping centers, office complexes, and industry, with all activities requiring larger sites to accommodate the buildings, their surrounding open spaces, and the required building lots. The greater mobility of car and truck transport permitted travel and movement of all types to expand

The high-level Garden City Skyway carries the QEW over the Fourth Welland Canal in St. Catharines where it supercedes the previous double-leaf, rolling-lift bridge that was completed in 1928. The canal and then the roadworks for the high-level bridge virtually destroyed the village of Homer. (John N. Jackson)

greatly. A "postindustrial city" was being born at the Niagara Frontier, and this in turn required changes to the long-established administrative units of town and township as suburbs advanced into rural areas. It also aroused public concern that agricultural land uses could not compete with urban land values as urbanization extended outward from the city over adjacent agricultural and rural areas.

As the automobile proliferated, industrialists looked for open sites on the edge of towns where land was cheaper, taxes lower, and municipal controls less stringent. The buildings were now typically one story with surrounding space for outdoor storage and car parking. To provide this space for vehicles, houses were often designed parallel to the road, rather than in depth from the road. Employees had no longer to live close to their place of work; they could commute to work by car. A pervading openness, strings of suburbs, and many individual buildings were being added to the fringes of towns by the widespread dispersal of homes, workplaces, and every other conceivable land-use activity. A wide, lower-density, automobile-dominated peripheral dimension was being added to the existing city. This belt lay outside the inner city. The new pattern was also defined by links with other parts of the peripheral zone, for example, between suburban residential areas and diverse clusters of other external activities such as shopping, educational, health, and employment centers; office parks; outer industrial districts; and the local airport. Many people had no longer to visit the inner and traditional city. Life could be carried on in the suburb and urban fringes.

The journeys between these outer activities had not necessarily to be into or through the inner central areas as previously. Movement could follow a circumferential transportation artery. On the Canadian Frontier the QEW bypassed the centers of St. Catharines and Niagara Falls, and on the American Frontier the New York State Thruway (I-90) was located some 8 kilometers (5 miles) from downtown Buffalo. Journeys were now relatively easy, and the periphery along external transportation arteries attracted real-estate development to unbuilt land. The inner city with higher taxes, more congestion, and aging structures, but also with greater historical-architectural-renewal character, was avoided. Commuting, formerly unidirectional into the city center in the morning and out in the late afternoon, became more complex as numerous cross-town journeys were added. Two cities—the inner and the outer—with different sets of characteristics were in the process of creation.

The new mobility led to the development of "country parks" with automobile access. The Canadian park system along the Niagara River was steadily expanded from lake to lake. In the 1920s the Erie County Parks Commission organized parks and recreation space on rural land beyond the extent of the city's developed urban areas. These purchases included a large acreage in the vicinity of Ellicott Creek, Como Lake, Chestnut Ridge, and Emery Park at distances up to 35 kilometers (22 miles) from Buffalo.[23] At Niagara Falls, visitors forsook the railways and arrived by motor cars to stay in "motels," literally a hotel for motorists. Campgrounds, cabins, and motels clustered along the approaching highways. Overnight facilities, formerly grouped near the railway stations and close to the Falls, transferred after the 1930s to linear extensions along such highways as Ferry Street-Lundy's Lane on the Canadian Frontier and Pine Avenue-Niagara Falls Boulevard on the American Frontier.

Automobiles and trucks had to be sold and maintained. Blacksmith shops, livery stables, and feed barns were replaced by garages for servicing vehicles and by gas stations. Junkyards of rusting vehicles were added to the urban fringe, and used-car lots vied for attention with new vehicles in glass-plated showrooms.[24] Advertisements competed for the driver's attention along the major highways and in strip-commercial areas. Conflicts arose between vehicle and pedestrian flows, and turning vehicles and pedestrian movements at intersections. The demands for more parking space reduced green areas of front, back, and side yards to bare ground, and large homes near downtown were converted to commercial uses as their occupants moved to the suburbs. Every town faced these changes, restricted during the Depression years of the 1930s but resuming with vigor after the Second World War in the 1950s and 1960s.

To cope with an increasing number of vehicles, one-way streets were introduced in St. Catharines, Buffalo, and Niagara Falls, New York, a process which often disrupted the previous character of residential streets. Commercial premises at right angles to the street were replaced by buildings parallel to the street with parking space at the front, side, or rear. Commercial strips at the edge of towns competed with established businesses in the central areas. A whole new urban form was arising, as people at the Frontier, as elsewhere in North America, Europe, and the urbanized world, preferred the convenience of their own vehicles for transportation. Subsidized mass transit (bus services) became necessary for the poor, the young, the elderly, the infirm, and the incapacitated who were unable to have their own means of transportation.

As most local municipalities believed in the virtues of expansion and local boards were reluctant to restrict growth, neither the location nor the quality of the development received much public attention.[25] When the Beacon and Sun Oil Companies requested permits at Tonawanda for the construction of oil tanks holding millions of gallons of fuel, the attitude was that these companies would make the town "an oil center and one of the most important on the Niagara Frontier. . . . The acres covered with modern buildings . . . form a skyline

Grand Island lost its previous degree of isolation when a single, then a dual set of bridges provided multilane highway access and encouraged development across and around the perimeter of the island. (John N. Jackson)

with the Niagara River and Canadian Frontier as a back-ground that is impressive."[26]

With an emphasis throughout the Frontier on growth, a few attempts were made to control the enlarging city. A New York State Conference on Regional and City Planning, held in Buffalo in 1924, spurred the organization of the Niagara Frontier Planning Association.

With limited powers, a series of reports from 1926 to 1946 aroused more interest and discussion than action, but it became accepted that a wider regional awareness was necessary and that the form of the city should and could be influenced by positive government actions.

When suburbs extended from the urban core, main road frontages became desirable commercial sites, a type of development often critized for its unattractive appearance and as a hindrance to the free movement of through traffic.[27] In Ontario, retail strips extended along Lundy's Lane (Highway 20) west from Niagara Falls, Garrison Road (Highway 3) in Fort Erie, and Ontario Street and Hartzel Road in St. Catharines. The northern entrance to Welland on Highway 58, much of Highway 3 through Port Colborne, and Highway 20 east of Fonthill exhibited similar characteristics. Comparable shopping malls, fast-food outlets, motels, and gas stations lined Pine Avenue-Niagara Falls Boulevard (US 62) from Niagara Falls to Buffalo. Retail commercial strips followed most highways that radiated from central Buffalo, as well as Transit Road from the Thruway exit to Lockport.

Shopping centers, ranging from neighborhood strip plazas to huge regional shopping malls, emerged on the urban fringe during the late 1950s and early 1960s. These malls, set within paved parking space, were usually next to arterial streets, and the largest regional centers located near the junction of major routes. On the Canadian Frontier the first enclosed mall was the Fairview Mall in the northern suburbs of St. Catharines. The Seaway Mall in Welland and Niagara Square in Niagara Falls on the QEW followed. The Pen Centre in south St. Catharines had replaced the downtown area of that city as the prime retail locality by the 1970s, and by the late 1990s the cost of renting retailing space in the large malls was some three times or more over that which prevailed for downtown retail space in that city. Despite active but incomplete urban renewal schemes in the historic downtown cores, the trend is for retailing in the principal downtown areas to decline.

On the American Frontier the craze for auto-dominated shopping plazas began in 1939 with Amherst's University Plaza and greatly proliferated as leading downtown stores opened branches in suburban shopping centers. Among many others, the Eastern Hills-Transit Town Plaza-Clarence Mall complex served Buffalo's eastern suburbs. Located on Main Street (NY 5) where there was little but a crossroads before the 1960s, it equaled the retail sales of downtown Buffalo by the 1970s. Likewise, Summit Park Mall in suburban Wheatfield attracted retail business from the central areas of Niagara

Falls and the Tonawandas. The two-story Walden Galleria Mall, with over 220 stores that opened in 1988 in the Town of Cheektowaga next to the I-90, advertised to attract customers from as far away as Rochester and Toronto.

A major blow to the former supremacy of downtown occurred when branches of the major, long-established downtown emporia opened in suburban locations. Here they were closer to their now suburban customers, who no longer had to face the inconvenience of travel to the inner city with its parking difficulties, traffic congestion, and railway crossings at grade along the major access routes. This outward process started in 1947 with the move of Adam, Meldrum and Anderson, a leading downtown store, to Amherst's University Plaza. Other former

Strip-development took place along major highways on both Frontiers. Depicted are a commercial strip in St. Catharines, Ontario (**above**), and a commercial motel strip in Niagara Falls, Ontario. (John N. Jackson [both])

downtown stores were attracted to out-of-town major plazas, and retailers who did not transfer their businesses from downtown failed.

The retail groups that moved out from the inner city gradually removed much of the vital commercial life from the established downtown centers. The historic urban cores survived, but precariously, during this period of change and became shadows of their former prosperity. As people and services moved to the suburbs, fewer journeys were made to the traditional central business district for shopping, entertainment, and work. The automobile thus encouraged the decline of the established central areas, which faced severe economic uncertainty as population and trade moved outward. Another difference was that the earlier stores in the inner and older parts of the city, often owned by local family businesses, were replaced by national or regional chain-store names. Localism was lost as greater uniformity in management styles, store types, and merchandise arose across the dispersed trading scene of both nations.

Another change was that after the 1950s, legislation gave local municipalities, through their engineering, traffic, planning, and highway committees, the authority to direct the character of urban change in many aspects of their environments. There arose a proliferation of official plans that established intended land uses and guidelines for future development. Land could be purchased to eradicate slums, an opportunity pursued especially in Buffalo. Urban renewal projects in many town centers encouraged pedestrianization and redevelopment schemes to remove obsolete or objectionable development. The municipalities now had the responsibility to ensure that development proposals conformed with the guidelines laid down in the development plan for that area. The city was now to be shaped by an intricate mass of administrative and technical rules, regulations, and controls to curb or to promote different aspects of the environment.

New patterns and standards were introduced. Streets in the new residential areas should curve. Their junctions should be T-shaped rather than be crossroads, for reasons of safety. Residential areas should be designed as neighborhood units, provided with small parks and playground space, and through traffic should be discouraged from cutting through the neighborhood. Local shopping centers should be located to provide the residents with convenience facilities. There should be a centrally located primary school if warranted.

Varying densities permitted different housing types and dwelling units per acre to meet the perceived different needs and requirements of single-family, two-family, townhouse, and apartment developments. Detached homes had wider lot dimensions

Location is immaterial. As the automobile advanced, wires, poles, signs, advertising signs, lane markings, paved highways, one-way streets, traffic signals, road junctions, and parking space added their unsightly clutter to the urban environment. (John N. Jackson)

than semidetached homes, and these dimensions were narrower for townhouses, though each might have the same depth. It was often urged that a reasonable diversity of housing types would lead to a better-balanced community plan with social integration between different groups. Parking standards for different types of land use, setbacks for buildings, spacing between buildings, and sight lines at junctions became formalized.

This standardized approach varied much in detail, but all municipal plans have divided the town into various land-use zones, with sections on transportation; the different categories of land use; and parking requirements for the health, safety, and convenience of the public. As the motor vehicle presented comparable problems (and opportunities) everywhere, the architectural, legal, highway, traffic, engineering, and planning professions used, interpreted, rejected, or applied the actions that have taken place elsewhere in the world. The result is a sameness and a conformity that has been described as "placeless geography," defined as "a sort of dehydrated landscape mix which provides alternative guidelines for lighting, ways of trimming street trees, the design of street signs, house layouts, street classification criteria, parking lots, athletic fields, shopping center configurations, neighbourhood units, transition zoning, bridge design, and several hundred other elements of landscape."[28] The fundamental distinction that had arisen at both Frontiers was between the old and the new in every town. The dividing line might be placed at 1916, the First World War, but the sheer and increasing dominance of the motor vehicle over all aspects of the modern environment by the start of the twenty-first century must continually be stressed.

NOTES

1. R. Squire, *Manufacturers of Wheels and Motors*, Adventures in Western New York History, vol. 5 (Buffalo, N.Y.: Buffalo and Erie County Historical Society, 1969), pp. 1–5.

2. R. L. Way, *Ontario's Niagara Parks: A History*, rev. ed. (Fort Erie, Ont.: Review Company, 1960), p. 76. See also J. Wilson, Superintendent, 28 July 1895, in *Tenth Annual Report of the Commissioners for the Queen Victoria Niagara Falls Park, 1895* (Toronto, 1896), pp. 30–46.

3. Rand, McNally and Co., *Rand McNally Auto Road Atlas of the United States* (Chicago, 1926), pp. 16–17.

4. F. S. Parkhurst, *History of the Town of Tonawanda, Erie County, New York, 1805–1930* (Tonawanda, N.Y.: Parkhurst, 1930), p. 51.

5. F. A. Schwilgin, *Town Planning Guidelines* (Ottawa: Department of Public Works, 1974), pp. 85–97; J. R. McKeever, *The Community Builders Handbook* (Washington, D.C.: Urban Land Institute, 1968); and J. DeChiara and L. Koppelman, *Planning Design Criteria* (New York: Van Nostrand Reinhold, 1969).

6. A. W. Panko, "The Niagara, St. Catharines and Toronto Railway: Its Inter-Urban Operations," *Proceedings Ninth Annual Niagara Peninsula History Conference* (St. Catharines, Ont.: Brock University, 1987).

7. R. C. Brown and B. Watson, *Buffalo: Lake City in Niagara Land* (Buffalo, N.Y.: Windsor Publications, 1981), pp. 151–52.

8. J. Williams, *Wings over Niagara: Aviation in the Niagara District, 1911–1944* (St. Catharines, Ont.: Niagara Aviation Pioneers, 1985). For Buffalo Airport see A. D. Palmer, ed., *Buffalo Airport 1926–1976* (Buffalo, N.Y.: Niagara Frontier Transportation Authority, 1976).

9. "In Aeronautics" and "Progress of Air Mail," *The Niagara Area*, special edition of the *Buffalo Journal of Commerce*, 1930, pp. 33–37.

10. *The Queen Elizabeth Way: Ontario's First Super-Highway* (Toronto: Ontario Ministry of Transportation and Communication, 1975), p. 1; R. M. Stamp, *QEW: Canada's First Superhighway* (Erin, Ont.: Boston Mills Press, 1987); and R. M. Stamp, "The Queen Elizabeth Way: American Gateway to Canada," *Proceedings Ninth Annual Niagara Peninsula History Conference* (St. Catharines, Ont.: Brock University, 1987).

11. City Planning Department, *Report on the New York State Thruway and Arterial Routes in the Buffalo Area* (Buffalo, N.Y.: City of Buffalo, 1953).

12. Copious documentation for highways, existing and proposed, exists in engineering, planning, highway, and consultants' offices at provincial/state, regional/county, and municipal levels in both countries. Only a few of these reports find their way into library and museum archives.

13. J. Menzies and E. M. Taylor, "Urban Geology of St. Catharines-Niagara Falls," in *Urban Geology of Canadian Cities*, ed. P. F. Tarrow and O. L. White, Special Papers 42 (St. John's, Nfld.: Geological Association of Canada, 1998), pp. 287–321.

14. A. W. Spear, *The Peace Bridge 1927–1977 and Reflections of the Past* (Buffalo, N.Y.: Buffalo and Fort Erie Bridge Authority, 1977); and G. A. Seibel, *Ontario's Niagara Parks: 100 Years: A History* (Niagara Falls, Ont.: Niagara Parks Commission, 1985), pp. 249, 251, 153. See also, "The Bridge that Peace Built," *U. S. News & World Report*, 3 August 1956; and R. M. Stamp, *Bridging the Border: The Structures of Canadian-American Relations* (Toronto: Dundurn Press, 1992), pp. 80–93.

15. G. A. Seibel and O. M. Seibel, *Bridges Over the Niagara Gorge: Rainbow Bridge, 50 Years, 1941–1991: A History* (Niagara Falls, Ont.: Niagara Falls Bridge Commission, 1991). The bridges at the Whirlpool Rapids, Queenston-Lewiston, and at the Falls are also covered.

16. *Spanning Niagara: The International Bridges 1848–1962* (Niagara Falls, N.Y.: Niagara University, 1984); this 1984 exhibition was displayed in the Buscaglia-Castellani Art Gallery of Niagara University (Niagara Falls, N.Y.); National Museum of American History, Smithsonian Institution (Washington, D.C.), 1985; and Rodman Hall Arts Centre (St. Catharines, Ont.), 1985.

17. Bureau of Transportation Statistics, U.S. Department of Transportation, *Trans-Border Surface Freight Flows at the Niagara and Detroit Frontiers, 1994–1997*. This data includes transshipment where the final destination was other than Canada or the United States from 1994 to 1996.

18. I. J. Rubin, Eastern Border Transportation Coalition, *Trade and Traffic Across the Eastern*

US-Canada Borders: An Assessment Prepared for the Eastern Border Transportation Coalition and Member Agencies (Youngstown, N.Y.: Eastern Border Transportation Coalition, 1997).

19. Ibid., pp. 27–32. These statistics in computer form have been obtained from various provincial highway and engineering sources on the Canadian Frontier.

20. R. Tardiff and G. F. R. Consulting, *Province of Ontario 1995 Commercial Vehicle Survey: Station Summary Report*, Strategic Priorities and Assessment Office, Transportation Systems Planning Office (Downsview, Ont.: Ministry of Transportation, 1997). See also, *Niagara Frontier International Gateway, Traffic Volumes 1984–1997*, PB EBTC, vol. 2., US-Canada Bridge and Tunnel Operator's Association; and IMC Consulting Group, *International Bridges Travel Survey: Final Report*, prepared for International Travel Survey Steering Committee, 1991.

21. A. Phillips, "Trouble on the Border," *Macleans* 3, no. 31, 3 August 1998, pp. 30–34.

22. The Canadian ambassador to the United States lobbied members of Congress and worked with business groups to oppose this legislation. Within Congress regional differences prevailed, with support from the south to deter illegal immigration from Mexico, and with the congressman representing the Buffalo area being opposed because of the potential adverse impact for businesses and residents of Western New York. The law that came into operation on 1 October 1998 was then deferred by the U.S. Immigration and Naturalization Service as it had neither the money, the staff, nor the technology to enforce the new requirements. The Canadian expectation (hope) is that the temporary freeze will become permanent, and that trade between the two nations will not be jeopardized.

23. Erie County Park Commission, *County Parks: Erie County Park System* (Erie County, N.Y., 1926).

24. The literature is abundant. For an overall account, see J. A. Jakle, *The American Small Town: Twentieth-Century Place Images* (Hamden, Conn.: Archon Books, 1984), pp. 119–66; M. Clawson, *Suburban Land Conversion in the United States: An Economic and Governmental Process* (Baltimore, Md.: Johns Hopkins Press, 1971); and C. Tunnard and B. Pushkarev, *Man-Made America: Chaos or Control?* (New Haven, Conn.: Yale University Press, 1963).

25. Buffalo Chamber of Commerce, "Area Homes Push Outward to the Breathing Zones," *The Niagara Area*, pp. 57–59; and D. Bain, "The Suburban Wilderness: Metropolitanization in New York, 1900–1950," *South Atlantic Urban Studies* 1 (1977): 229–52.

26. Parkhurst, *History of the Town of Tonawanda*, pp. 94–108.

27. An example is G. Clay, *Close-up: How to Read the American City* (New York: Praeger, 1973), p. 85: "The Dirty Old Man of the urban scene is the highway strip. . . . In short, the strip is the urban/suburban scapegoat."

28. Canadian attitudes are presented in F. A.

Schwilgin, *Town Planning Guidelines* (Ottawa: Department of Public Works, 1974); and American thought in R. McKeever, ed., *The Community Builder's Handbook* (Washington, D.C.: Urban Land Institute, 1968). See also the journals of the respective professional societies. For an international literature, see F. Gibberd, *Town Design* (London: Architectural Press, 1953); J. De Chiara and L. Koppelman, *Planning Design Criteria* (New York: Van Nostrand Reinhold, 1969); K. Lynch, *Site Planning* (Cambridge, Mass.: MIT Press, 1962); I. L. McHarg, *Design with Nature* (Garden City, N.Y.: Doubleday, 1971); and A. Whittick, ed., *Encyclopedia of Urban Planning* (New York: McGraw-Hill, 1974). For the distinction between "authentic geography, a geography of places which are felt and understood for what they are," and "placeless geography" in which different localities both look and feel alike, see E. Relph, *Place and Placelessness* (London: Pion, 1976), pp. 117–18. For a discussion of the relationships between urban forms and transportation see P. O. Muller, "Transportation and Urban Form: Stage in the Spatial Evolution of the American Metropolis," in *The Geography of Urban Transportation*, ed. S. Hanson (New York: Guilford Press, 1995), pp. 26–52.

CHAPTER SEVEN

THE LATER CANAL DEVELOPMENTS

The Erie and Welland Canals as pioneer projects diverged considerably in status and importance with the arrival of railways. The Erie Canal, formerly the more dominant enterprise but now unable to compete with the new railway dominance, sank almost to oblivion. The Welland Canal working with the Welland railway continued to advance in status and character as a major marine transportation artery. The Third Canal of 1887 was replaced by the Fourth Canal of 1932, which in turn became an integral part of the St. Lawrence Seaway in 1954. These changes promoted growth in the larger urban centers along the Welland Canal, whereas Buffalo steadily lost its advantageous through marine trade.

By the late twentieth century both canal systems had abandoned routes, and some former active lengths had become recreational waterways with a focus on urban renewal and redevelopment along the banks. With the advancing tide of tourism and tourist developments, the transition was from commercial waterways of exceptional importance to some belated recognition that their surviving engineering and urban features had become historical assets of more than local importance. Vessels can now only be viewed along the Welland Canal, but the older canals on both banks have still to receive the full recognition that is their due.

THE ERIE CANAL DECLINES

In 1857 a channel dug from the Erie Canal at Tonawanda permitted vessels to reach Niagara Falls, New York, downstream along the Niagara River for the first time,[1] and new wharves and breakwaters were constructed in Buffalo during the 1860s. Even so, the Erie Canal could not retain its traffic against strong competition from the railways. The canal, frozen for a third of the year, carried slow-moving traffic, faced lower rail rates, and was weakened further when the railroads purchased and controlled the steamship companies. The movement of flour on the canal diminished by more than 75 percent between 1864 and 1869 and, by the latter year, more grain was carried east by rail than by the canal. Tolls were abolished in 1882 and, in an effort to compete with the rails, funding for the canal was provided through general taxation.[2] Despite a temporary improvement, traffic on the canal continued to decline.

The New York State Barge Canal was

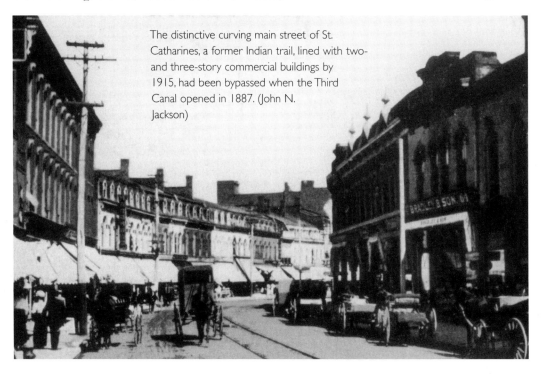

The distinctive curving main street of St. Catharines, a former Indian trail, lined with two- and three-story commercial buildings by 1915, had been bypassed when the Third Canal opened in 1887. (John N. Jackson)

authorized in 1903, and a wider and deeper channel completed in 1918 to a depth of 4.3 meters (14 feet) (fig. 3.1, Table IIIA). Its barges, now towed by tug or self-propelled, had a capacity of 3,265 tonnes (3,600 tons). The dam across Tonawanda Creek was removed, returning this creek to its original level, and the canal to the east was straightened by cuts across its meandering route, leaving midstream islands.[3]

At Lockport, two large locks replaced the flight of five locks, a widening that removed buildings from the town center.[4] The Pendleton Cut was deepened and widened. A new canal terminal and a line of breakwaters were built at Buffalo. The Black Rock Channel and Harbor were deepened, a lock was provided between Black Rock Harbor and the Niagara River, and the Tonawanda-Buffalo section of the Erie Canal abandoned. Depths reached 8.2 meters (27 feet) in the harbor at Buffalo, 6.4 meters (21 feet) through the Black

At Lockport, although commercial trade along the Erie Canal has declined drastically, the visual and amenity potential of the locks and the canal as the centerpiece for the community and for public open space, recreation, and pleasure boating remains high. (John N. Jackson [both])

(**Above**) The first lock of the Third Canal in Port Dalhousie. (**Right**) The last-surviving freight-carrying canaller en route to the break-up yard, a demolition yard for the salvage of its materials and equipment. (John N. Jackson [both])

The Third Welland Canal is carried over a tunnel on the Great Western railway at Merritton (**left**). (**Right**) This canal crosses the Ontario Plain northeast of St. Catharines. (John Burtniak [both])

Rock Canal and along the navigation channel in the Niagara River, and 3.7 meters (12 feet) in the canal east from Tonawanda.

Despite these improvements and the occasional use of the canal for local waterborne deliveries, its once prolific barge traffic has gradually disappeared. As the once highly successful Erie Canal has diminished greatly in importance, its many former industrial-urban associations have become residual features in the landscape. The riverside route along the bank of the Niagara River was either filled in or allowed to deteriorate, used for public open-space recreational purposes, and part of the canal in the 1950s provided the right-of-way for the Niagara Section (I-190) of the New York State Thruway. Another highway used a canal length in Tonawanda. To the east the canal has remained as a feature in the landscape. Used increasingly for pleasure boats, its historical significance and its future have been recognized as a linear park across the state where open space, tourism, canal cruises, and the historic preservation of old buildings and structures have become important themes.

THE THIRD WELLAND CANAL

When in 1870 a Canadian Royal Commission assessed the best means of providing access to the Atlantic seaboard, the St. Lawrence-Welland Canal route received full endorsement. The commission recommended a uniform depth of 3.7 meters (12 feet) for the canal, which was increased to 4.3 meters (14 feet) in 1875 and achieved when the Third Canal opened in 1887 (fig. 3.1, p. 127).[5] Built across open land northeast of St. Catharines with passing basins between the locks, the canal followed a new channel across the Ontario Plain southeast from Port Dalhousie; bypassed the established canal centers of St. Catharines, Merritton, and Thorold; and then used a new cut south to Allanburg.[6] The route across the Erie Plain, an enlarged version of the Second Canal, included a new aqueduct across the Welland River in the center of Welland, a guard lock at Lake Erie, new bridges, and improved harbors at both entrances to the canal. Widening the southern length required the removal of buildings and streets next to the canal in Port Colborne. The canal for the first time in its history now received a reliable supply of water from Lake Erie, rather than via the Feeder Canal from the fluctuating levels of the Grand River.

After much debate, waterpower privileges were not allowed where the Third Canal crossed the Niagara Escarpment. Now of diminishing importance with the change from steam power to hydroelectricity, these rights were retained along the Second Canal, where sections north from Thorold and between Port Dalhousie and St. Catharines remained open for navigation. The industries associated with the Second Canal continued to operate. By 1886 the largest industrial plants were the cotton and the pulp and paper mills in Merritton and two metal manufacturing establishments in St. Catharines.[7] Some 750 persons were employed in the three plants in Merritton and 450 in the two plants in St. Catharines. Forty-three industrial establishments lined the canal, the capital invested was nearly $2.7 million, and some 2,600 persons were employed in their manufacturing activities.

The year 1887, when the Third Canal opened, was in many ways a turning point in the canal's history. With fewer locks, a shorter route, and a faster passage with larger vessels, the cargo capacity of vessels had increased from 680.4 to 2449.4 tonnes (750 to 2,700 tons). The freight carried increased steadily, especially after the early 1900s and into the First World War. By 1890 the average tonnage of vessels had more than doubled over a twenty-

The Third Welland Canal and its water supply reservoirs across the Niagara Escarpment east of Thorold. Note that the supply system changes from one side of the canal to the other and, unlike the First and Second Canals, mills and millraces no longer follow the canal. (John N. Jackson)

year period, steamers and not sailing vessels now carried most of the cargo, and less than half the number of vessels now moved the same volume of freight. The smaller number of American vessels tended to be larger than their Canadian counterparts; they also carried a larger proportion of the canal's traffic. A major canal disadvantage was that, as only the smaller-sized vessels could pass through the downstream locks between Prescott and Montreal, Montreal-bound grain was transferred to either the railway network or to small freighters at either Port Colborne or Prescott.

By 1888 the canal system between Lake Superior and tidewater had fifty-three locks, half on the enlarged Third Welland Canal. The freight carried on the Welland averaged almost 798,322.8 tonnes (880,000 tons) over the period from 1886 to 1888. Wheat and corn were the prime commodities, and then coal and forest products. Over 907,185 tonnes (1 million tons) were carried in most years from 1889 to 1898. By 1909 the freight carried had doubled, and in 1913 and 1914 it was over 2.7 million tonnes (3.9 million tons) with about half that amount being mine products. There were also some 326,536.6 tonnes (360,000 tons) of both manufactures and forest products. As this increasing trade was carried through the canal, its vessels had to be manufactured, manned, repaired, and serviced, which were significant factors for the regional economy and the canal communities on the Canadian Frontier. The canal had graduated from primarily a local waterway to an essential component of both the new Canadian nation (Confederation was in 1867) and the developing Great Lakes urban system.

By 1930, the last year when the Third Canal was in commission, 5.5 million tonnes (6.1 million tons) of freight was carried. As Leggett (1979) has stated: "The system of 14-foot St. Lawrence Canals . . . [had] served Canada well, and the United States of America, until the coming of the Seaway [in 1959]. The system was itself a minor Seaway and several steamship companies had ocean-going vessels built to dimensions that would just enable them to use the 14-foot locks. At the end of this service, no less than 14 overseas shipping companies were using the St. Lawrence [and Welland] Canals in regular sailings into the Great Lakes; 120 vessels were involved. . . . For inland trade a fleet of almost 200 '14-footers' was gradually built up . . . vessels generally 253 feet [77.1 meters] and capable of carrying 2,800 tons [3,086.4

tonnes] of iron ore or 106,000 bushels [2,219.36 cubic inches in the British Imperial System] of grain."[8]

The Third Canal became increasingly obsolete as a result of changes in the size and design of vessels, and also through the increasing volume of grain that had to be discharged into elevators for onward routing to Montreal. There was also the expanding trade in iron ore from the Mesabi Range north of Duluth, Minnesota, on Lake Superior. As a consequence the new canal had to be enlarged to accommodate the ever-increasing size of vessels and the expanding volumes of marine trade. These factors required the construction of a Fourth Welland Canal across the Canadian Frontier and for navigation to be extended from Montreal to the head of the Upper Great Lakes, developments that were undertaken in 1932 and in 1959 when the Fourth Canal and then the St. Lawrence Seaway opened.

Meantime, as the Third Canal became a remnant feature in the landscape, the 132-year reign of Port Dalhousie as the northern port of entry to the canal system came to an end. The village lost its shipyard and the through movement of vessels. Then, as marinas were steadily added and renewal of the commercial frontage took place, the transition was made to a distinctive suburban-tourist locality within the wider embrace of St. Catharines. In 1990 Lock 1 of the Third Canal became the site of a small hydroelectric power station operated by the St. Catharines Hydro-Electric Commission using the fall of water through the lock for this new purpose. Martindale Pond was retained and used as the site for the Henley Rowing Regatta. East of Martindale Pond, Lock 2 became a feature in the park setting of Martindale Park.

The length of the Third Canal southeast across the Ontario Plain was either filled in or, when above the level of the surrounding country, the channel was bulldozed to ground level. The narrow highway swing bridges were removed and their sites became part of the improved road system extending out from the growing city of St. Catharines. The isolation of the low-income Facer Street area that had arisen beyond the Third Canal ended and, with the canal as a barrier removed, the city expanded northeast after the Second World War. Urban land uses, including a park, a golf course, housing, and light industry, were gradually attracted to the abandoned canal lands and are recognized in the modern landscape by roads constructed along the canal perimeter that do not conform with the pioneer survey grid that had been laid across Grantham Township.

Along the abandoned length across the Niagara Escarpment, the flow of water was retained to supply the northern length of the Fourth Canal. The weirs and storage reservoirs have been removed, and free-flowing water now cascades down through the gateless former locks, like a river of small waterfalls. The site, of great historic importance and of substantial marine and engineering interest, has been proposed for different types of development including hotels, landscaped open space, campgrounds, golf courses, and the provision of an outlook tower to view the modern Fourth Canal at the flight locks. National or provincial parks have also been proposed, but no action has followed and the site remains unused as abandoned open space.

South of the escarpment, the Third Canal has virtually disappeared from the landscape. An exception is north of Welland, where spoil dumps from canal excavations after decades of consolidation were by the 1990s receiving residential developments. At Port Colborne an abandoned arm of the Third Canal is used for activities that include the break-up of vessels and winter ice fishing, and a length south through the town is used as the water supply system from Lake Erie to the Fourth Canal. At the head of the harbor, the locks of the Second, Third, and Fourth Canals provide a setting for urban renewal that takes advantage of the canal and the surviving commercial buildings from earlier eras that line the harbor.

THE FOURTH WELLAND CANAL

The construction of the Fourth Canal, at first referred to as the Welland Ship Canal, was first delayed by the First World War and then by the Queenston Power Project with prior demands on the scarce resources of labor, equipment, and materials. The new Fourth Canal, opened officially for navigation in 1932, also proceeded through numerous stages. The first of the new large-scale construction works in 1908 included a government grain elevator, and large breakwaters at Port Colborne. The harbor was deepened, its approach dredged to 7 meters (23 feet), and the elevator increased in capacity in 1912–1913.

In 1913 the valley of Ten Mile Creek east of St. Catharines was selected as the new northern length for the Fourth Canal (fig. 3.1). The canal rose across the Ontario Plain through three locks to the foot of the Niagara Escarpment, then climbed this steep slope by a spectacular twin series of three Flight Locks (Locks 4, 5, and 6) with a total lift of 42.5 meters (139.5 feet). Lock 7 then carried the canal to the summit level at Thorold, and Lock 8, a guard lock at Port Colborne, protected the canal from fluctuating water levels in Lake Erie.[9] At Welland an aqueduct had previously taken the earlier canals over the Welland River, but the site now required an inverted syphon to take the river under the deepened canal.

The locks, reduced from twenty-six to eight, halved the time of passage through the canal. Of the twenty lift bridges for highway and rail traffic, eleven were road bridges. Three of these carried interurban streetcar tracks, and five bridges carried railways only. Other crossings carried the high-voltage wires that radiated out from the hydroelectric power projects at the Falls and Queenston Heights, and some twenty submarine cables were laid either under the bed of the canal or were built into the walls and floors of the locks for use by public utilities. The canal, used in part at St. Catharines as a municipal boundary, also provided a bounding limit that restricted urban advance. Exceptions included Port Weller Dry Dock and General Motors, which had leapfrogged to industrial sites east of the canal and were later incorporated into the city's administrative limits.

Remarkable change occurred elsewhere. At Port Colborne, the commercial street with stores and banks along the east side of the

Four canals have crossed the Niagara Escarpment at Thorold. (*Left*) The First and Second Canals gave birth to the town, which developed on both sides of the waterway. (*Right*) The Third Canal followed an angular route east of the town. (*Center*) The Fourth Canal closely confined the growing town on its eastern side. (This aerial photograph A 19342-4 © 1965/09/26 Her Majesty the Queen in Right of Canada, reproduced from the collection of the National Air Photo Library, Ottawa, with permission of National Resources Canada)

canal was removed to make room for the widened canal. At Welland where the Third Canal already divided the commercial core into separate units, the widened canal further increased the divide between the two centers. At Port Weller, the new northern port of entry on Lake Ontario, material excavated from the locks and channels to the south became breakwaters constructed for 2.5 kilometers (1.4 miles) out into Lake Ontario, and the intervening channel 121.9 meters (400 feet) wide was excavated to form the harbor entrance. At Thorold the new canal curtailed the eastern growth of the town, isolated the town's cemetery, and caused the relocation of several buildings and the town's reservoir. Impacting on all communities along the canal, most vessels now passed through the canal without stopping, which limited the servicing of vessels to the entry ports and curtailed the remaining en route features.

The volume of water diverted into the

The Flight Locks of the Fourth Welland Canal were constructed at the northern edge of the Niagara Escarpment. The excavated materials were transported by rail to Port Weller, where they were used to provide protective breakwaters at the entrance to the canal. The Flight Locks, a triple tier of double locks, permitted the two-way passage of vessels. Their independent power system was supplied from the generating station (*bottom right*) through pipes laid in the upstream lock walls. (The St. Lawrence Seaway Management Corporation [both])

Vertical lift bridges, an intrinsic part of the scene along the Fourth Canal, provide priority to canal overland traffic. A highway and a railway bridge existed side by side at Port Colborne until the 1990s. The railway bridge was removed with the closure of the line rather than saved as a heritage-tourist feature, as in Welland, where a highway lift bridge was saved to remain a significant landscape feature of the downtown area. (John N. Jackson)

canal at Port Colborne varied according to water levels in Lake Erie and canal requirements. About 10 to 15 percent of the volume was used at the locks; when a ship is lowered, about 95.5 million liters (21 million gallons) of water are drained, an amount then used consecutively at each lower lock. Ontario Hydro, the largest user of canal water, diverts about 198.2 m^3/sec (7,000 cfs) to the Decew Power Plant in St. Catharines. A further volume of 9.9 m^3/sec (350 cfs) is used in the Seaway's powerhouse below the Flight Locks. Water is

Marine landscapes along the Fourth Welland Canal. A container vessel from Manchester, England, in the Flight Locks (**above left**), two vessels meet in the bypass channel at Welland (**below left**), and nautical distances from Lock 3 in St. Catharines are a reminder of the Canadian Frontier as the water gateway between Europe and the North American continental interior (**right**). (John N. Jackson [all])

Port Colborne underlines the significance of the Fourth Canal for industrial location. The harbor entrance, constructed on land reclaimed from Lake Erie (**top**), attracted grain elevators and other industrial activities. The artificial harbor (**center**), excavated inland from the shore of Lake Erie, attracted the heavy industry of Algoma Steel. The Robin Hood Flour Mill (**bottom**) is located on the abandoned Third Canal where crossed by the Fourth Canal. (John N. Jackson [all])

also taken from the canal to supply municipalities along its length and areas north of the Niagara Escarpment. Industry also draws heavily to supply major companies, including General Motors in St. Catharines, Atlas Steels and Union Carbide in Welland, and the paper industry along the Thorold-Merritton industrial strip. The canal, an engineering feat of magnitude and an international trading artery, has had further repercussions across the Canadian Frontier.

The flow of marine traffic increased rapidly after the new Fourth Canal opened, from 8.2 million tonnes (9 million tons) by 1933 to 19.5 million tonnes (21.5 million tons) by 1958.[10] When the operation of the canal was turned over by the federal Department of Transport to the St. Lawrence Seaway Authority in 1959, 48.6 percent of the tonnage was mine products; iron ore and then coal dominated this movement. Agricultural products came second at 32 percent of the total tonnage; here the dominant grain, Canadian wheat, was followed by American corn, Canadian barley, American barley, and American wheat.

The canal remained the core economic, visual, and historic feature for its several urban communities.[11] Advantages for the location of manufacturing plants included water for industrial uses and cooling purposes, the import of coal for power, and import-export links with European and other foreign markets. The range of activities included shipbuilding and ship repair at Port Weller Dry Docks and the production of vehicle parts at General Motors in St. Catharines. The pulp and paper industry had located next to the canal in Thorold, where the Ontario Pulp and Paper Company had docks on the canal; company vessels brought in timber supplies from Quebec and then carried exports to Chicago. In Welland the canal-associated operations included Plymouth Cordage, Union Carbide, Page/Hersey, Stelco, and Atlas Specialty Steels. And at Port Colborne were grain elevators, International Nickel (Inco), and the export of stone from the Onondaga Escarpment.

THE ST. LAWRENCE SEAWAY AUTHORITY ASSUMES CONTROL

In 1951 the Canadian government established the St. Lawrence Seaway Authority to construct, maintain, and operate a deep-draft waterway between Montreal and the Upper Great Lakes. In 1954 the United States Congress authorized the St. Lawrence Seaway Development Corporation to build corresponding navigation facilities on American territory. After nearly sixty years of political dispute, costly and controversial studies, and steady negotiation between rival commercial, industrial, transportation, federal, and provincial-state interests, there was agreement to proceed.[12] In an area of increasing power use and demand, the hydroelectric power potential along the International Rapids section of the St. Lawrence carried considerable weight in the decision. In 1954 the first sod was cut, five years of construction followed, and on 26 June 1959 the Seaway opened with locks that were the same size as those on the Welland Canal, the older waterway but not part of the construction works for its modern successor. The first vessel to enter the St. Lambert Lock was an icebreaker on 25 April 1959. The royal yacht *Britannia* sailed into this lock on 26 June carrying Queen Elizabeth II and President Dwight D. Eisenhower for the official opening. This event was followed by a royal review on Lake St. Louis and a ceremony at the Cornwall-Massena powerhouse where the president's place was taken by Vice President Richard M. Nixon.

Promoted as "the greatest engineering achievement of our time," which it was, incredible human costs were also involved. Landscape was reshaped. Seven communities were flooded, some 1,100 farms were inundated, about 20,000 acres of farming land were lost, and over 6,000 people lost their homes. The Long Sault Rapids were dammed and lost their former visual glory; churches and pioneer graveyards were submerged. Communities were created specifically to receive transplanted houses. These events took place outside the Niagara Frontier, but they underscore—as earlier with both the Welland and the Erie Canals—that the human landscape is structured by the technology of engineering and by the related political-economic decision-making processes that are involved.

The immediate commercial success of the St. Lawrence Seaway, the upsurge in tonnage, and the introduction of larger vessels then required a series of further construction works on the Welland Canal. The channels were dredged to the Seaway standards of 7.8 meters (25.5 feet). Pondage areas were separated from the navigation channels, and television cameras aided the speedier handling of vessels. Transit times were reduced from twenty-four hours in 1964 to less than fourteen hours by 1969. To increase vessel capacity, smaller-sized engines reduced the size of the engine room, and the width between the hold and the hull was diminished. The permitted beam of vessels allowed to pass through the locks was extended from 22.9 meters (75 feet) in 1959 to 23.2 meters

(76 feet) by 1976, and the maximum depth of vessels passing through the canal was increased from 7.6 meters (25 feet) to 7.8 meters (25.75 feet), and then to 8 meters (26.3 feet) by 1992. These changes in vessel design resulted in a smaller number of large-sized vessels carrying higher cargo volumes.

New administrative offices required by the Seaway were constructed in 1964 on the west side of the canal in St. Catharines at the Flight Locks, which displaced the historic location of the canal offices in the downtown area of that city. A service center with engineering and maintenance yards was added to this new location in 1971. At Port Colborne, the Marine Training School located on an abandoned section of the Third Canal to train ship's personnel on how to cope with on-board fires and emergencies. In the meantime, traffic flows in the new canal more than doubled, from 25 million cargo tonnes (27.6 tons) to 61 million cargo tonnes (67.2 tons) over the fifteen-year period from 1959 to 1973.[13]

This growth in canal traffic seriously diminished the function of Buffalo as a transshipment point. Having lost the Erie Canal and its through trade by water, there was now little reason for inbound or outbound vessels of the size permitted by the Seaway to dock at this city. While Buffalo remained the largest flour-milling center in North American, oceangoing vessels from the Upper Lakes with wheat bound for foreign ports now moved via Port Colborne and the Welland Canal. Thus, in the age of the automobile, only the Welland Canal remained a viable commercial waterway route of international importance at the Frontier.

A CHANGING CANAL LANDSCAPE

With increasing flows of highway traffic across the Fourth Canal, high-level bridges or tunnels were proposed. In 1968 a twin-tube, four-lane divided-highway tunnel 31.5 meters (2,400 feet) long under the canal at Thorold replaced two bascule highway bridges across the canal, a construction which improved highway traffic flows and eliminated traffic delays when the bridges were raised. This tunnel was constructed on a cost-sharing basis, two-thirds by the Ontario Department of Highways and one-third by the St. Lawrence Seaway Authority. A duplicate highway bridge at Port Colborne followed in the 1980s. Designed to avoid delays where Highway 3 crossed the canal at Lock 8, a bridge at one or the other end of this lock is always open to traffic.

Another change was that, with steadily

When the Welland Canal Bypass was constructed east of Welland, this restricted the town to the east and placed most of the established urban area on an island between the old and the new channels. All east-west railways were diverted to a new railway-highway tunnel (**above right**), and Main Street was taken under the new channel by a highway tunnel (**below right**). (J. N. Jackson [both])

expanding traffic volumes on the Fourth Canal, only the Flight Locks had been constructed to allow the two-way passage of vessels. The remaining single locks caused delays. To improve navigation, the twinning of the other lift locks was approved in 1962, when 129.5 hectares (320 acres) of land were purchased. This scheme was canceled in 1965 and a more grandiose project then announced. Nearly 810 hectares (2,000 acres) of land were acquired between Thorold and Lake Ontario for a new northern channel with larger and fewer "super-locks," to eliminate the single, one-way locks across the Ontario Plain and displace the Flight Locks. Bridges across the canal, including the Garden City Skyway on the Queen Elizabeth Way, would be replaced by highway and railway tunnels. A deep channel at the level of Lake Ontario would cross the Ontario Plain, superlocks with a lift of at least 25 meters (82 feet) would take ships across the Niagara Escarpment, and an extensive new pondage area would be developed on the edge of this escarpment to serve these lift locks. Land for this megaproject was appropriated by the federal government, but the project was deferred because traffic through the canal dropped by more than half between 1979 and 1993. The canal was no longer a congested waterway that required immediate new works to accommodate an increasing flow of vessels.

The start of construction on the Welland Canal Bypass east of the city of Welland. Note the grander scale of the new works when compared with the surviving channel in the center background. (John N. Jackson)

A second megaproject, to avoid the narrow channel and bridge through the city of Welland, involved construction of a canal bypass east of that city.[14] Contracts were awarded in 1966, and construction began next year. This channel, 13.4 kilometers (8.3 miles) long, had a navigable width of 91.4 meters (300 feet) and a depth of 9.1 meters (30 feet) so that two vessels could pass. Welland, which had grown around its earlier canals, now became situated mostly on an island between the new channel and the now abandoned Fourth Canal.

Changes to the landscape from the Welland Canal Bypass were massive. Over 49.7 million cubic meters (65 million cubic yards) of earth, clay, rock, and silt were excavated and then placed in predetermined landforms on both banks. These hills rose 18.3 meters (60 feet) above the level of the canal and provided a windbreak for passing vessels. The intention, to landscape the bare slopes with over two million trees and to create a new provincial or national park, resulted in only limited topsoiling and grass seeding until in 1993 a paper company announced that this barren landscape would be rehabilitated under a twenty-year project using nutrient-rich biosolids left over from its papermaking operations; about 60 hectares (148.3 acres) a year would be planted with spruce and hardwood trees.

Where the bypass crossed the Welland River at Port Robinson, a syphon culvert took this river under the canal. Completed in 1971, this structure contained four tubes and was 115.8 meters (638 feet) long. Construction required a new channel for the Welland River east of Port Robinson.

Highway and rail crossings were taken under the bypass channel by two tunnels. East Main Street was carried under the canal by a four-lane highway tunnel 220.7 meters (724 feet) long and 22.9 meters (75 feet) wide. Townline Road to the south carried two lanes of highway traffic and three lines of rerouted railway track. This tunnel had an approaching gradient of 0.75 percent, which required an open cut 4 kilometers (2.5 miles) long on both sides of the bypass and was itself crossed by a series of highway and railway bridges. These tunnels and their approaches required more excavation work than for the bypass channel. The cost of the East Main Street Tunnel was borne equally by the Ontario Ministry of Transport and Communication and the St. Lawrence Seaway Authority. The cost of the Townline Tunnel, because it involved rerouting the railway network, was carried by the Seaway Authority.

Other changes included the construction of a dock east of Welland that could hold two of the largest lake freighters and the loss of the city's central rail passenger terminal and the adjacent yards. Replacement yards, a station, and freight yards were constructed west of the city. Within the city many lines of track that had previously carved the city into segments were removed. In short, a city that had grown and been shaped by the canal since 1829 was again being radically reshaped through an external decision-making process to improve navigation between Lake Erie and Lake Ontario.

On the upgraded canal, the maximum trading flow of 66.2 million tonnes (73 million tons) was achieved in 1978 with 3,310 vessel transits.[15] Then came economic recession, changing patterns of trade such as the export of wheat via the west coast to China, the decline of traditional exports to the United

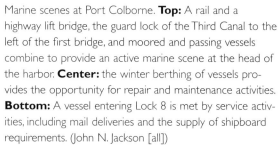

Marine scenes at Port Colborne. **Top:** A rail and a highway lift bridge, the guard lock of the Third Canal to the left of the first bridge, and moored and passing vessels combine to provide an active marine scene at the head of the harbor. **Center:** the winter berthing of vessels provides the opportunity for repair and maintenance activities. **Bottom:** A vessel entering Lock 8 is met by service activities, including mail deliveries and the supply of shipboard requirements. (John N. Jackson [all])

Kingdom, and reduced demands for ore through changes in the location of the North American steel industry. Tonnage reduced to a nadir of 31.8 million tonnes (35.1 tons) and 2,927 vessel transits in 1993. Subsequently, a slender but important increase has been achieved, with tonnage hovering at about 40 million tonnes (44.1 million tons) and some 3,300 vessel transits into the new century.

The cargo carried over the years has fluctuated considerably.[16] Between 1979 and 1998 agricultural products had increased from 29.7 percent of cargoes to 32.4 percent, and mine products decreased from 45.2 percent to 40.2 percent. Manufactured and miscellaneous cargo, mostly steel products, had increased from 14.4 percent to 27.4 percent. American wheat and corn had decreased in proportion and as total cargo tonnage, whereas Canadian wheat had diminished in total tonnage but increased as a proportion of the total traffic. Iron ore, coal, and coke had each decreased in total volume and as a proportion of the total trade. Gasoline and fuel oil had both decreased; manufactured iron and steel, pig iron, and cement had increased, and container traffic had virtually disappeared. Such data stress the commercial role of the Seaway as a major international waterway in a global economy, and again underscore how affairs at the Frontier often depend on distant, external, and foreign circumstances.

As with the Erie Canal but less seriously, the Welland Canal as a major contributor to economic development, urban growth, and industrial progress has diminished in relative importance as a transportation artery since its heyday of traffic volumes and tonnage carried in the late 1970s. Even so, the waterway remains of considerable local importance for employment, for the supply of water to industries and municipalities, and for the expanding tourist industry.

By 1999 Niagara's marine industry employed almost two thousand people, including winter employment in servicing, maintenance, and repairs in Port Colborne, and more than 125 marine industries along the Welland Canal.[17] The canal remained the shortest and cheapest route to the heart of North America for shippers from European markets, with marine transportation more pollution free and energy efficient than truck,

rail, or air. In the meantime, an important change in canal management had taken place. The Canada Marine Act of 1998 permitted the federal Minister of Transport to enter into a long-term management agreement with a consortium of users. These changes, described as "commercialization," removed over 150 years of direct government control over the waterway and forty years of management by the St. Lawrence Authority.

The new board, the St. Lawrence Seaway Management Corporation, has one representative each from the federal government and the Ontario and Quebec provincial governments; one representative from the shipping companies and the shippers of wheat, iron ore, and coal; and a president. The former Seaway head office has been transferred from Ottawa to Cornwall, Ontario, but the regional office in St. Catharines continues to manage the Welland Canal and its approaching navigation systems on both lakes. The prime objectives of the new corporation are to "promote a commercial approach to the operation of the Seaway, [and to] protect the long-term operation of the Seaway as an integral part of Canada's national transportation infrastructure."[18] Secondary considerations, to "protect the rights and interests of the communities adjacent to the Seaway,"[19] include the domestic and industrial supply of water from the canal, the encouragement and promotion of tourism, and the achievement of a parkway system of drives and trails along the full length of the historic and modern canal systems.

Future trade includes uncertainties about the proportion of Canada and American imports and exports via the east and west coasts and the Gulf of Mexico, and the production and demands from distant trading nations. Already the canal dimensions, as throughout history, are too small to accommodate the largest trans-Atlantic vessels that enter the St. Lawrence River. The new grandiose system of superlocks would require similar downstream provision along the St. Lawrence and probably an upstream lock at Sault Ste Marie. Currently, the land purchased east of St. Catharines for the potential superlocks remains under federal ownership to permit this eventuality, now envisaged about the year 2030.

NOTES

1. *Address of Stephen M. Allen, Esq. on Occasion of the Opening of Navigation to Niagara Falls* (Niagara Falls, N.Y.: Pool and Sleeper, 1857).

2. N. E. Whitford, *History of the Canal System of the State of New York*, 2 vols. (Albany, N.Y.: State Legislative Printer, 1906). For the ongoing history see R. Garrity: *Recollections of the Erie Canal* (Tonawanda, N.Y.: Historical Society of the Tonawandas, 1971), and *Canal Boatman* (Syracuse, N.Y.: Syracuse University Press, 1977); A. Muller Jr., *Looking Back So That We May Move Ahead: 150th Anniversary of the Grand Erie Canal* (Lakeport, N.Y.: Goding, 1975); C. D. Lewis, *The Erie Canal 1817–1967*, Occasional Contributions of the Niagara County Historical Society (Lockport, N.Y.: Niagara County Historical Society, 1967); and J. W. Percy, *The Erie Canal: From Lockport to Buffalo* (1979; reprint, Buffalo, N.Y.: Western New York Heritage Institute, 1993).

3. W. B. Dittmar, *Yesteryears in the Tonawandas*, Publication no. 3 (Tonawanda, N.Y.: Historical Society of the Tonawandas, 1968); and North Tonawanda Golden Jubilee Committee, *North Tonawanda Golden Jubilee* (North Tonawanda, N.Y.: North Tonawanda Golden Jubilee Committee, 1947).

4. C. A. Kaiser, *The Streets of Lockport*, with notes on the early history of the city, Niagara County Historical Society, Occasional Contributions no. 1 (Lockport, N.Y., 1949); H. M. Nicholls, *The Twilight Years of My Native Town* (Lockport, N.Y.: Niagara County Historical Society, 1958); and Lockport Chamber of Commerce, *Lockport— To the Canal and Beyond: A History of Lockport's Settlement and Growth* (Lockport, N.Y.: Lockport Chamber of Commerce, 1980).

5. J. P. Heisler, *The Canals of Canada*, Canadian Historic Sites: Occasional Papers in Archaeology and History no. 8, National Historic Sites

Service, National and Historic Parks Branch, Department of Indian Affairs and Northern Development (Ottawa, 1973); J. N. Jackson, *The Welland Canals and Their Communities: Engineering, Industrial, and Urban Transformation* (Toronto: University of Toronto Press, 1997); and R. M. Styran and R. R. Taylor with J. N. Jackson: *The Welland Canal: The Growth of Mr. Merritt's Ditch* (Erin, Ont.: Boston Mills Press, 1988), and *Mr. Merritt's Ditch: A Welland Canal Album* (Erin, Ont.: Boston Mills Press, 1992).

6. When excavating across the crest of the Niagara Escarpment, the bodies of sixteen American soldiers were discovered on the site of the Battle of Beaverdams, fought during the War of 1812.

7. "Welland Canal Industries," *Thorold Post*, Fair Edition, 1886.

8. R. F. Legget, *The Seaway* (Toronto: Clarke, Irwin & Co., 1979), pp. 41–42.

9. The major engineering appreciation is P. J. Cowan, *The Welland Ship Canal between Lake Ontario and Lake Erie, 1913–1932* (Ottawa: Department of Railways and Canals, 1935); reprinted from articles in *Engineering*, 1929–1931.

10. For data about traffic flows, see M. C. Urquhart, ed., "Canals, Tonnage Through the Welland Canal, 1867–1960," in *Historical Statistics of Canada*, Series S 189–199 (Toronto: Macmillan Company of Canada, 1956).

11. C. Aloian, *A History Outline of Port Dalhousie 1650–1960* (Port Dalhousie, Ont.: Port Dalhousie Quorum, 1978), and Welland Canals Preservation Association, *A Guide to Historic Port Dalhousie* (St. Catharines, Ont.: Welland Canals Preservation Association, 1986). For St. Catharines, see G. B. Balbar, *St. Catharines: Images of a City* (St. Catharines, Ont.: Vanwell Publishing, 1987); J. N. Jackson, *St. Catharines, Ontario: Its Early Years* (Belleville, Ont.: Mika Publishing, 1967); J. N. Jackson and S. M. Wilson, *St. Catharines: Canada's Canal City* (St. Catharines, Ont.: St. Catharines Standard, 1992); and R. Shipley, *St. Catharines: Garden on the Canal* (Burlington, Ont.: Windsor Publications, 1987). Thorold is covered in Thorold and Beaverdams Historical Society, *Jubilee History of Thorold, Township and Town* (Thorold, Ont.: Thorold Post, 1897–1898); *Township of Thorold 1793–1967: Centennial Project* (Toronto: Armata Associates, 1968); F. W. Harvie, *Town of Thorold Centennial 1850–1950* (Thorold, Ont.: Town of Thorold, 1950); and P. M. Orr, *A Tour of Historic Thorold and Historic Buildings in the City of Thorold: A Study of Thorold's Past and Its Buildings* (St. Catharines, Ont.: Department of Geography, Brock University, 1975). For Allanburg, see Mrs. H. Vanderburgh, *A History of Allanburg and Area* (Allanburg, Ont.: Allanburg Women's Institute, 1967); and B. Michael, *Port Robinson: Welland Canal 150th Anniversary, August 24th, 25th and 26th, 1979* (N.p., 1979). For Welland, see J. N. Jackson, *A Planning Appraisal of the Welland Urban Community Trends-Transition-Potential*, prepared for the Disposal of Lands Surplus to Canal Requirements by the Department of Public Works, Ottawa (St.

Catharines, Ont.: Brock University, 1974); F. A. Sayles, *Welland Workers Make History* (Welland, Ont.: W. Sayles, 1963); and G. B. T. Sawles, *Hometown: Historical Sketches* (Welland, Ont.: G. B. T. Sawles, 1959). Studies of Port Colborne include W. A. Smy, *Looking Back* (Port Colborne, Ont.: Port Colborne Historical Society, 1978); and R. Caperchione, *Historical Buildings of Port Colborne* (Port Colborne, Ont.: Citizen's Press, 1979).

12. Studies from different perspectives include L. Chevrier, President of the St. Lawrence Seaway 1954–47, *The St. Lawrence Seaway* (Toronto: Macmillan, 1959); D. D. Husband, Series Director, *The St. Lawrence Seaway and Its Regional Impact*, Cat. No. CP 46-3/6 (Ottawa: Ministry of Supply and Services, Government of Canada, 1979); G. A. Lindsay, Engineer-in-Charge, *The Great Lakes-St. Lawrence Deep Waterway* (Ottawa: General Engineering Branch, Department of Transportation, 1949); G. W. Stephens, *The St. Lawrence Waterway Project* (Montreal: Carrier, 1930); and W. R. Willoughby, *The St. Lawrence Waterway: A Study in Politics and Diplomacy* (Madison: University of Wisconsin Press, 1961).

13. Data from the annual *Traffic Report* (Ottawa: St. Lawrence Seaway Authority).

14. J. N. Jackson, *Welland and the Welland Canal: The Welland Canal By-Pass* (Belleville, Ont.: Mika Publishing, 1975); and St. Lawrence Seaway Authority, *The Welland By-Pass* (Ottawa: St. Lawrence Seaway Authority, 1975).

15. *Annual Report* and *Traffic Report* (Ottawa: St. Lawrence Seaway Authority), published annually. The local impact of this recession is examined in Niagara Region Seaway Task Force, *Niagara Jobs in Jeopardy* (Thorold, Ont.: Niagara Regional Development Corporation, 1988).

16. St. Lawrence Seaway Authority, *1998 Annual Report*.

17. Niagara Economic and Tourism Corporation, *Niagara Region—1999 Economic Development Highlights* (Thorold, Ont.: Niagara Economic and Tourism Corporation, 1999), p. 5.

18. This act came into operation on 1 October 1998; see Bill C-9, Statutes of Canada 1998, First Session, Thirty-sixth Parliament, 46-47 Elizabeth II, 1997–98, *An Act for making the system of Canadian Ports Competitive, Efficient and Commercially Oriented . . . for the commercialization of the St. Lawrence Seaway, Part 3, Seaway*. The process of change is described in President's Message and Performance Review, in St. Lawrence Seaway Authority, *1998 Annual Report*.

19. Ibid., ¶78(c).

CHAPTER EIGHT

MANUFACTURING AND SERVICE ACTIVITIES

The infrastructure of canals, railways, power resources, and highways have combined with population size, technology, and regional situation to create employment and job opportunities, which are the engine of economic growth on which much else depends. Manufacturing activities have expanded greatly and despite serious recent decline remain significant for productivity, trade, and employment on both sides at the Frontier. In the meantime, the trend for expanding employment in service activities for residents and tourism has become increasingly important.

INDUSTRIAL COMPARISONS

A comparative study undertaken by the Buffalo Chamber of Commerce indicated that, by 1927, five specialized manufacturing concentrations existed on the Canadian Frontier: St. Catharines-Port Dalhousie, Niagara Falls-Chippawa, Welland, Thorold-Merritton, and Port Colborne-Humberstone.[1] By industry, the automotive parts industry had located in St. Catharines, the electrochemical and abrasive industries in Niagara Falls, the electrometallurgical and high-grade steel industries in Welland, nickel refining in Port Colborne, and the paper industry in Thorold and Merritton. With some 12,630 employees and 261 establishments, these Canadian circumstances were dwarfed by the American Fron-

Tonawanda and the lumber trade are synonymous. Supplied by vessels from the Upper Lakes, stacks of lumber and berthed vessels from the Upper Lakes occupied the frontage of the Niagara River to provide a unique and distinctive marine-industrial scene at the American Frontier. (John Burtniak [both])

tier, where Buffalo and manufacturing concentrations in both Erie and Niagara Counties contained over 2,900 establishments and almost 105,100 employees.

The 1927 Census of Manufacturers recorded twenty-nine plants in Buffalo producing motor vehicles, bodies, and parts, and four producing aircraft and parts, with a total employment of 7,511. The largest steel producers—the Bethlehem, Donner, Wickwire-Spencer, and Seneca Steel Corporations—together employed about 13,000 persons; with smaller companies, about 2.7 million tonnes (3 million tons) of steel were produced annually.[2] The key industries were steel, lumber, grain, and rubber. The city had about 70 percent of the approximately three hundred industrial classifications that existed in 1927.

Manufacturing on both Frontiers had increased steadily during and immediately after the Second World War. On the Canadian Frontier employment increased from a labor force of 39,626 in 1961 to 46,250 in 1981, but declined as a proportion of total employment over that period from 37.9 percent to 30 percent.[3] About two thousand fewer manufacturing jobs were available in 1984 than in 1981, and small businesses were the main generators of new jobs. Plant closures, the loss of jobs in manufacturing, and the resulting adverse impact on the service economy were most severe in Port Colborne and Welland.

On the American Frontier manufacturing reached a peak employment of over two hundred thousand workers in 1954. By the early 1980s manufacturing employed three times more people on the American Frontier than in comparable activities on the Canadian Frontier. Transportation equipment and primary metal industries then ranked first and second on both Frontiers. Metal fabricating, paper and allied products, food and beverages, nonmetallic mineral products, machinery, and chemical and allied products followed on the Canadian side. Machinery (excluding electrical), fabricated metal products, electrical and electronic equipment, and chemicals followed on the American Frontier.

MANUFACTURING INDUSTRIES BY THE EARLY 1980s

The Automobile and Auto Parts Industries

Despite auspicious starts, the Niagara Frontier was not destined to become Detroit. On the Canadian Frontier, St. Catharines had Canada's first auto plant.[4] Oldsmobiles were manufactured by Packard Electric from 1905 to 1907, before production moved to Toronto. The factory, sold to the REO Motor Company of Lansing, Michigan, expanded production to twelve hundred cars a year by 1912. Regarded as a significant engineering achievement of or for that time, a locally made REO became the first car to make the journey across Canada from Halifax to Victoria.[5]

McKinnon's of St. Catharines began in 1878 to manufacture and sell buggy hardware on St. Paul Street, using power from the hydraulic raceway of the Second Welland Canal.[6] This company, the largest employer on the Niagara Frontier by 1907, in 1908 formed McKinnon Chain with plants in St. Catharines and across the boundary in Tonawanda. During the First World War, military harnesses, hardware, and munitions were produced, changing after hostilities to auto components, radiators, and rear axles. The firm pioneered the manufacture of differential and transmission gears in Canada. In 1929 General Motors assumed control of the plants in St. Catharines and Tonawanda and added the production of starting motors and generators.

Hayes-Dana, started in 1865 in Merritton, produced wagon wheels and then forgings for the emerging auto trade. After a series of takeovers, the Hayes Wheel Company was formed in 1922.[7] In 1929 the Dana Corporation of Toledo, Ohio, acquired an interest in the Canadian company. The Thompson Products Division of TRW Canada, a Canadian subsidiary of an American company from Cleveland, Ohio, located in West St. Catharines in 1931 to produce cast-iron and aluminum pistons. In 1937 the production rights of Drag Link, a manufacturer of auto-steering components, were purchased.

On the American Frontier Buffalo was the home of the Thomas Flyer, in 1908 the first car to go around the world.[8] "America's finest car," the Pierce Arrow was produced in a plant on Elmwood Avenue on the belt line of the New York Central, which delivered raw materials and the finished automobiles. This plant employed ten thousand workers at its peak during the First World War.

Ford started manufacturing in Buffalo at the J. R. Klein steel plant in 1910, and later moved to an assembly plant designed for the production of the Model T Ford. Located on

The automobile industry has developed on both Frontiers. **Above:** The General Motors Plant next to the Fourth Welland Canal in St. Catharines. **Below:** The Stewart Motor Corporation, East Delavan Avenue, Buffalo. (John N. Jackson [above], and M. H. Hubbell, *The Industrial Empire of Niagara, Pictorially Portrayed, 1918–1919* [below])

Main Street where the New York Central belt line crossed, in 1931 assembly operations moved to the Buffalo waterfront with its advantage of direct delivery from Detroit by water.

The Harrison Radiator Division originated at Lockport in 1910. Dunlop Tire and Rubber selected a site near River Road in Tonawanda for producing rubber products in 1919. A Chevrolet assembly and body plant began in Buffalo in 1922 on East Delavan Avenue; axles and other products were later added to the firm's output. In 1937 General Motors added another huge plant on a 65-hectare (150-acre) site on River Road in Tonawanda to make six-cylinder engines.

These manufacturing developments were related closely to the growth of the Lackawanna Steel Company plant, which made Buffalo a major steel-producing center.[9] The plant was acquired in 1922 by the Bethlehem Steel Corporation and modernized and expanded with a rolling mill and coke ovens to meet the needs of the expanding automobile market. In 1949 this plant, the sixth largest in the world, was capable of producing over 2.7 million tonnes (3 million tons) of steel a year; nearly twenty thousand workers were employed in 1965.

Much has changed in automotive manufacturing. Pierce-Arrow closed its facility during the Depression, the assembly of Chevrolet cars in Buffalo ceased in 1941, and Ford ceased assembly production on Fuhrmann Boulevard in 1958 when the assembly plant was replaced by one in Lorraine, Ohio.

Ford's Main Street plant became part of Trico, which manufactured windshield wipers. Emphasis changed from the production and assembly of vehicles to that of motor vehicle parts and accessories on both Frontiers and to the consolidation of the American auto industry into large international headquarters elsewhere than at the Niagara Frontier.

More recently the Auto Pact agreement of 1965 has encouraged the duty-free shipment of vehicle parts, as well as finished autos, to and from both countries.[10] Through this enactment, which favored the "Big Three" North American automakers (General Motors [GM], Ford, and Chrysler [now DaimlerChrysler]), the boundary at the Frontier became irrelevant for the automotive industry. As American manufacturers were required to maintain a proportion of their production in Canada, American-owned corporations established branch plants in Ontario, and the large-scale production of many automotive components was undertaken by several local firms on the Canadian Frontier. Another change occurred in 1984 when the Canadian Auto Worker's Union separated from the American union. Negotiations with the leading auto producers were also different because of the low value of the Canadian dollar and, because Canada has more advantageous federal and provincial health

Industrial landscapes in
Buffalo at the end of the
First World War. (M. H.
Hubbell, *The Industrial
Empire of Niagara, Pictorially
Portrayed, 1918–1919*
[both])

and social insurance schemes and benefits, companies did not have to pay for expensive medicare benefits.

By 1981 the manufacture of automobile parts employed about twelve thousand workers on the Canadian Frontier and some twenty thousand in the Buffalo metropolitan area.[11] GM, the largest employer on both sides, owned plants in St. Catharines, Buffalo, Tonawanda, and Lockport. In St. Catharines a new suburban plant was developed after the Second World War next to the Fourth Welland Canal. Supplemented by expanded operations in the northern suburbs, rear axles, front suspensions, disc brakes, spark plugs, fuel pumps, transmission components, and V-6 and V-8 engines were produced by this company.[12] On the American Frontier GM produced engines, forgings, and metal castings in a Tonawanda complex along the Niagara River.

A plant in Buffalo made axles, springs, and forgings, and the Harrison Radiator Division produced climate-control and engine-cooling equipment.

On both Frontiers, after a decline in employment at the company's engine plants, it was announced in mid-2000 that a new line of V-6 engines would be produced in St. Catharines. Earlier the company had announced its investment in a new engine plant at the company's powertrain facility in Tonawanda, a development believed to be the largest private sector, industrial investment on the American side of the Niagara River since the Second World War. Both Frontiers were perpetuating their reliance on the auto-making and parts industries through these decisions.

The Ford Motor Company operated plants on both sides of the boundary. Their Ontario glass plant opened in 1961 next to the QEW in Niagara Falls to produce windshields and safety glass. Ford's Woodlawn stamping plant south of Lackawanna, New York, opened in 1957; it employed about four thousand persons by 1983 to supply autobody stampings and panels, and by 1997 stamped daily some 1,542.2 tonnes (1,700 tons) of steel into doors, pans, and other assemblies for distribution by railcar to assembly plants across North America.[13]

Many smaller automobile parts industries also employed considerable numbers of workers. By the 1980s Hayes-Dana had a drive-train and chassis products division at Thorold, a forge division at St. Catharines, and a head office in downtown St. Catharines. The Thompson Products Division of TRW operated two adjacent plants in West St. Catharines for the production of valves, front and rear suspension parts, steering arms, and linkages. Dunlop in Tonawanda manufactured tires, and Trico Products in Buffalo produced windshield wipers, wiper arms, and blades until production moved to Mexico in the mid-1980s.

The Aerospace Industry

Emerging from the engineering expertise of firms such as Sterling Engine and Buffalo Gasolene, which produced marine and industrial engines beginning in the early 1900s, the American Frontier became a center for the manufacture and development of aircraft.[14] The Curtiss Aeroplane Company moved from Hammondsport, New York, to Buffalo in 1915 and expanded in a large plant on Elmwood Avenue. Described as the largest aircraft manufacturing establishment in the world, it produced airplane engines, JN-4 (Jennie) training aircraft, and flying boats. At the end of the First World War, Curtiss operated the Curtiss Aerodrome, a commercial airport in Tonawanda. Here air shows were held from 1920 to 1926, which included parachuting with chutes manufactured by the Irving Air Chute Company of Buffalo. The early development of aerial photography also introduced the new perspective of bird's-eye views of the landscape.[15]

Merging after the First World War with other companies to become the Curtiss-Wright Corporation, the company produced the P40-Warhawk plane in Tonawanda. Consolidated Aircraft also operated from the former Curtiss plant on Elmwood Avenue in Buffalo from the mid-1920s to the mid-1930s, until operations moved to San Diego. A new company, Bell Aircraft, used the plant on Elmwood Avenue and constructed a new building in Wheatfield, New York, close to Niagara Falls Airport.

Aircraft were produced in prodigious numbers during the Second World War. Curtiss-Wright built a new plant next to Buffalo Airport. Three shifts of mostly female employees turned out over 16,000 P40s, over 3,000 transport planes, and over 300 P-47G Thunderbolts; some 25,000 employees were employed at the peak of production in the two plants at Tonawanda and Buffalo. Bell Aircraft produced nearly 10,000 P-39 Airacobras and the P-63 Kingcobra, as well as the first American jet fighter-planes; the labor force grew to over 36,000 by 1943.[16]

At the end of hostilities, when military contracts ended, the automobile industry changed

The Sterling Engine Company manufactured the two 300-horsepower engines that powered this government patrol boat. Sterling engines held all world speed records for motorboats over several years. From such achievements, the American Frontier graduated to become a center for the aircraft industry. (M. H. Hubbell, *The Industrial Empire of Niagara, Pictorially Portrayed, 1918–1919*)

to the production of civilian vehicles to meet expanding home-based demands, whereas the aircraft industry either diminished or moved away as the wartime markets waned. Curtiss-Wright, after attempting to produce a civilian aircraft, left the Buffalo area and consolidated in Columbus, Ohio. Bell advanced the use of helicopters, but moved these operations to Texas in 1951. Its plant, acquired by Textron of Providence, Rhode Island, closed.

Across the boundary in Fort Erie, Fleet Aircraft of Canada was formed in 1930. During the mid-1930s the company specialized in the design and manufacture of airplanes for military training and civilian flying. Wartime production included fuselages and wings for the Lancaster bomber; nearly four thousand workers, mainly female, were employed. Genaire, established in 1951 at the Niagara District Airport, produced aircraft components including aircraft skis.

Metal, Chemical, and Other Manufacturing Industries

The manufacture of primary metals had a Canadian focus along the southern length of the Third and then the Fourth Welland Canal. In Welland, Atlas Specialty Steels, established in 1928, produced stainless, tool, and alloy steels, and the Page-Hersey and the Welland Tube works of Stelco (later Stelpipe), established in 1956, manufactured tubular products and large-diameter, arc-welded pipes. Inco Metals, established in 1918 in Port Colborne, once refined nickel, but, like its neighbor Algoma Steel, its production had declined or ceased by the 1980s. A variety of specialty steel products were also produced by over thirty smaller companies within the Niagara Region.[17]

On the American Frontier labor in the primary metals industry diminished drastically from 33,600 in 1960 to 11,300 by 1983.[18] With recession, a crippled auto industry, and less demand for its products, Lackawanna's Bethlehem Steel plant reduced its payroll to 8,500 workers by the mid-1970s; only several hundred personnel remained by 1990. Republic Steel at the same time failed to open its rebuilt plant, which was eventually torn down.

As heavy industry used large quantities of raw materials, location was related closely to low-cost water and rail transportation. The change to modern and cheaper transportation meant that smaller, newer mills in various locations could use scrap for raw materials and bring in low-cost iron ore from foreign countries. The same competitive product could now be manufactured in many different world areas to meet the demands of a global market.

A rather different picture emerges for metal fabricating and electrical products manufacture. Employment in these activities on the Canadian Frontier by the 1980s tended to be stable or increasing, and many small companies in most urban centers had diversified to produce an array of products. The larger companies included Newman Structural Steel in Welland for steel fabrication and erec-

The INCO smelter with its dominant smokestack and railway access at Port Colborne. (John N. Jackson)

tion, E. S. Fox in Niagara Falls and Port Robinson for custom fabrication, and Foster Wheeler in St. Catharines for boilers and heating equipment. John Deere produced agricultural implements at Welland, General Signal electrical appliances at Thorold, and Ohio Brass high-voltage electrical hardware at Niagara Falls. In a business park at Niagara Falls, Edscha of Canada produced metal fabricated door hinges, and Kuester-Magna Cable Controls manufactured cables for brake and clutch assemblies, and window-

regulator systems. Uri-Quatro Industries Canada produced photo-documentation systems and assembled medical cameras, and NETP was a research and development center for plastic products.

Also by the 1980s the Buffalo metropolitan area was gaining a reputation for high technology. American Optical made microscopes; Leica, the Swiss company, produced magnifiers; and Comtek Research in downtown Buffalo was engaged in research-oriented high technology. Fisher-Price, one of the world's largest toy makers, had headquarters and plants in East Aurora and nearby small towns; and sporting goods were produced by Dunlop Tire in Tonawanda.

The forests of Canada nurtured a considerable paper industry centered on the Second Welland Canal in Thorold and St. Catharines. The leading companies were Beaver Wood Fibre, Domtar, Kimberly-Clark, Provincial Paper, and Ontario Paper, producing vanillin as a by-product. The Niatec tissue plant was located in Niagara Falls, International Paper in North Tonawanda, and Continental Can produced paper drums in Tonawanda.

The chemical, electrochemical, and abrasive industries were important on both Frontiers. In Canada, Carborundum Canada and Norton at Niagara Falls, together with Exolon-E.S.K. at Thorold, produced abrasives and refractories; Union Carbide in Welland made carbon graphite electrodes for electric furnaces and graphite anodes; and Cyanamid Canada, the largest employer in Niagara Falls, produced a wide range of chemicals at two plants.

The larger chemical concentration in Buffalo and Tonawanda included Airco-Speer, carbon and carbide products; Carborundum, abrasive and graphite products; DuPont Chemicals, rayon and cellophane; National Aniline, petroleum-based household cleaners; Occidental (Hooker) Chem-

ical, electrochemicals; and Union Carbide, carbon and ferro-alloys. Research advances during and after the Second World War included oxygen bleaches, cellophane, rubber-compounding chemicals to make tires, organic peroxides, plastics, food and drying oils, detergents, and a quinine substitute. Ashland Oil Company in Tonawanda and Mobil's Socony plant in Buffalo refined oil.

After the Fourth Welland Canal opened, marine engineering on the Canadian Frontier became centered on shipbuilding and repairs at Port Weller Dry Docks, a division of Upper Lakes Shipping where self-unloading bulk carriers, tankers, icebreakers, and ice-strengthened ships were built and repaired at Lock 1 of the Fourth Welland Canal.[19] Other ship repair and maintenance activities were located at Port Colborne. Yachts were designed and produced for the recreational boating industry in Niagara-on-the-Lake. On the American Frontier American Shipbuilding closed its plant at the end of the Second World War, Buffalo Dry Dock did heavy repair work on Great Lakes cargo vessels, and Richardson Boat Company converted to peacetime production. As with the aircraft industry, decline in shipbuilding since the Second World War has been severe; it has become cheaper to buy ships built in foreign countries such as Korea, Japan, and China.

Shipbuilding and ship repair have a long history of close association with the Welland Canal and lake navigation. Port Weller Dry Docks, the only surviving shipbuilding and ship repair yard on the Welland Canal, relocated from Port Dalhousie on the Third Canal when the Fourth Canal opened. (John N. Jackson)

Shipbuilding and ship repair have a long history of close association with the Welland Canal and lake navigation. Port Weller Dry Docks, the only surviving shipbuilding and ship repair yard on the Welland Canal, relocated from Port Dalhousie on the Third Canal when the Fourth Canal opened. (John N. Jackson)

The food and beverage industries are dominated by wine production on the Canadian Frontier, an activity that relates closely to the Niagara Fruit Belt though imported juices are also used. Familiar names from long-standing cellars include Brights and Chateau-Gai in Niagara Falls and Barnes and Jordan & St. Michelle in St. Catharines. Cottage wineries producing premium wines have expanded in number and reputation since the 1970s. Hillebrandt, Reif, Inniskillin, Konzelman, Stonechurch, and Willowbank operated within Niagara-on-the-Lake; Chateau des Charmes in nearby St. Davids; and Henry of Pelham in St. Catharines.

Food production on the Canadian side also included dairy and ice cream products, fruit canning, and fruit juices. Flour milling at Port Colborne was represented by the Government, Maple Leaf, and Robin Hood elevators next to the Welland Canal and by Canada Starch, which arrived in the early 1980s. Greaves Jams and Marmalades preserved fruit in Niagara-on-the-Lake, and Nabisco (later Triscuit crackers) produced Shredded Wheat in both cities of Niagara Falls. The food and beverage industries, an expanding activity, employed about three thousand persons in 1981 on the Canadian Frontier.

On the American Frontier Rich Products was a Buffalo-based artificial creamer and food-processing manufacturer, and Freezer Queen Foods had a large plant on the Buffalo lakefront. Buffalo, producing over 907 million tonnes (1 million tons) of flour per year, was still the largest center for flour milling in North America by 1980 despite production declines. Breakfast cereals, including those made by General Mills, were produced in Buffalo and Niagara Falls.

Small players in the overall industrial situation, but important for their respective communities and the employment of a female labor force, textile manufacturers employed nearly one thousand people in the Niagara Region by 1981. Lincoln Fabrics in Port Dalhousie produced drapery and industrial cloth. Canada Hair Cloth fabricated canvas interfacing, lining, and stiffeners in downtown St. Catharines, and Warren Knit in the same city produced men's knitted outerwear. Wabasso in Welland manufactured denim and yarns, and the leather industry included Sunbeam Shoes in Port Colborne. On the American Frontier Buffalo manufactured clothing, including the famous Johnny Carson suits made by M. Wile.

THE BOUNDARY AS A FACTOR IN INDUSTRIAL LOCATION

After Confederation in 1867, the new Canadian national awareness created a demand for the domestic production of manufactured goods rather than reliance on imports from Great Britain and the United States. Tariffs of 20 percent, imposed in 1879 to protect infant Canadian industries, were not changed significantly until 1936.[20] To avoid these tariffs, American firms established Canadian subsidiaries. Products manufactured in Canada also had access to preferential tariffs of up to 15 percent on trade with Great Britain and its dominions. Furthermore, because abrasives and newsprint were permitted to cross the boundary at Niagara tariff-free, these industries were encouraged to locate at Niagara Falls and Thorold on the Canadian Frontier.

In the late 1920s, when Canada surpassed Britain as the United States's best customer, and Canada and the United States became primary trading partners, the Niagara Frontier was by far the greatest point of exchange between the two nations. In 1928 over one-quarter by value of shipments from the United States to Canada passed through the Niagara area, and about one-third by value of the Canadian shipments to the United States. Often the same companies operated on both sides of the Niagara River. As one economic unit under one executive head, American plants locating in Canada could combine senior staff when the two plants were close and accessible to each other. The Canadian Frontier, considered a "typical location" for these new enterprises because of proximity and accessibility, received more than its share of branch plants, a change described as from a "Frontier of conflict to one of contact."[21] The two Frontiers, separated by the boundary, were now linked economically for many purposes.

Both Frontiers emphasized their location on main transport routes between the two countries, advertised their access to markets on the other side, and attracted industries from the other nation. American companies operated on the Canadian Frontier, and Canadian companies on the American Frontier. Considerable and increasing volumes of trade crossed the intervening boundary; by 1983 Ontario's trade with New York State was $5.8 million, and imports to Ontario from New York State were $4.1 million.[22]

Many of the best-known industrial names on the Canadian Frontier were American companies. In 1983 these businesses included: General Motors, Hayes-Dana, Ontario Paper, TRW (Thompson Products), Foster Wheeler, and Exolon in St. Catharines and Thorold; John Deere and General Signal in Welland; Robin Hood Multifoods in Port Colborne; and Cyanamid, Ohio Brass, Carborundum Canada, Norton, Ford, Provincial Crane Division of AMCA, Nabisco, Oneida, American Can, and Unit Rig in Niagara Falls.[23] Fort Erie in particular had many small American-owned plants; the 1978 town directory listed thirty, including one company with about three hundred employees.[24] Their total employment of thirteen hundred persons contrasted with the thirty-four Canadian-owned plants with about eleven hundred employees.

In 1971 a consultant indicated that American companies chose locations in Niagara Falls, Ontario, because of administrative contact, the availability of parts and materials from the parent company, and close links with the corresponding American industry.[25] The report concluded that a location in Niagara Falls, Ontario, suited both American firms serving Canada and Canadian firms serving the United States. Easy access to markets in the other country was a reciprocal factor. Canadian companies had penetrated the American Frontier, with Buffalo and its environs distributing goods throughout the eastern United States. Conversely, goods destined for southwest Ontario were brought together at Buffalo to cross the boundary.

Buffalo, taking advantage of this two-way flow, had attracted Toronto bankers and businessmen with the advantages of conducting their American business in that city.

By 1977 some 175 Canadian firms had subsidiaries in the Buffalo-Niagara Falls metropolitan area.[26] They employed thirty-two hundred persons, manufactured a wide range of products from paper boxes to books, and had an estimated payroll of $30 million. In 1976 a Foreign Trade Zone established on the Buffalo waterfront attracted Canadian firms. Like a bonded warehouse, Canadian goods could be imported without going through customs entry procedures for storage, manufacture, or assembly. These goods became dutiable only when shipped out of the zone for American consumption. Toronto-based Harlequin Enterprises, a publisher of paperback romance novels, was one company that used the Foreign Trade Zone as its American distribution center. Canadian firms were welcomed by the local Chamber of Commerce and assisted by the Canadian Consulate in Buffalo. The attraction of Canadian industry to Buffalo-Niagara Falls was an industrial strategy developed by local civic and commercial interests. Moore Business Forms of Toronto built on Grand Island, and the Peter Schmitt Company, a major Buffalo food distributor, became a subsidiary of Weston Foods in Toronto.

A 1971 study of the Niagara Region indicated that foreign investment by American parent companies varied considerably by type of industry: low in total employment in textiles and in the iron and steel industries; less than dominant in food and beverages and in the nonmetallic mineral industries; and predominant in automobiles and parts, rubber, electrical apparatus, and chemical industries. [27] Of the 246 firms interviewed, 65 percent were Canadian owned, and 34 percent American owned. American-owned companies were larger, employed nearly twice as many people, and had a larger percentage of value added in manufacturing. This proportion was greater than in other regions of Ontario.[28] Parent plants and company headquarters were located in Buffalo, Cleveland, Detroit, and Chicago. The Niagara Frontier was described as an area of "intervening opportunity" between these locations and the primary market in Southern Ontario.[29]

THE CHANGING STRUCTURE OF ECONOMIC ACTIVITY ON THE CANADIAN FRONTIER

On the Canadian Frontier unemployment rates have been high.[30] They reached a peak of nearly 16 percent in 1983, dropped to a low of 6.5 percent in 1988, and then rose steadily to another peak of 13.9 percent in 1993. There has also been considerable change from full-time to part-time positions and much enforced and voluntary early retirement to reduce the numbers employed.

The annual list of company closures makes sad reading.[31] Welland in 1983 lost Newman Structural Steel, then Wabasso the next year. In 1985 Carborundum Bonded Abrasives left Niagara Falls, followed in 1986 by Hayes Dana from St. Catharines. Closures of well-known, long-established companies included Welmet Industries and Welland Iron and Brass in Welland in 1984, Barnes Wines in St. Catharines in 1988, and Sunbeam Shoes in Port Colborne in 1989. Hinterhoeller Yachts of St. Catharines succumbed in 1990, and next year C & C Industries of Niagara-on-the-Lake, Interlake Steel Products of Thorold, Burnstein Castings of St. Catharines, and Provincial Crane of Niagara Falls closed their doors. During 1992 Bradshaw-Stradwick left Welland and Monenco Consultants departed from St. Catharines to Greater Toronto.

By 1998 the ten largest manufacturing companies (with the number employed in parentheses) were:[32]

* General Motors, St. Catharines: rear axles, front and rear suspensions, and disc brakes (5,200)
* TRW Canada, St. Catharines: automotive parts, front and rear suspension parts (1,700)
* E. S. Fox, Welland: custom fabrication in stainless steel and aluminum (1,150)
* Atlas Specialty Steels, Welland: stainless steel (1,000)
* Dana Canada, Thorold: automotive parts (996)
* Acres International, Niagara Falls: planning, consulting engineering, and project management (850)
* Gencorp Vehicle Sealing Division, Welland: custom rubber-mixing and extruded products for automobiles (790)
* Donohue (formerly Ontario Paper), Thorold: newsprint (640)
* John Deere, Welland: agricultural implements (600)
* Stelpipe, Welland: seamless and welded pipe and tubular products (540)

The manufacturing sector of the regional economy reduced from 45,290 to 41,096 from 1987 to 1997, that is by 9.1 percent over this recession-dominated decade. The largest manufacturing sectors by employment by 1997 were transportation equipment (12,142), fabricated metals (6,596), primary metals (3,069), food (2,988), printing and publishing (1,938), chemical and chemical products (1,433), and beverage industries (1,068).

At the company level, between 1990 and 1998 General Motors reduced from 9,500 to 5,200 employees, Atlas Specialty Steels from 1,350 to 1,100, and Stelpipe from 1,109 to 540. Hayes Dana was static, and TRW increased from 1,000 to 1,700. Transportation equipment, the largest manufacturing group, declined, as did companies large and small and in most sectors. These losses were not offset by the arrival of several new but small companies despite vigorous promotional campaigns by the regional and local municipalities.

Manufacturing as a proportion of the total labor force declined to 21.3 percent by 1996. The active automotive-parts industry by the late 1990s[33] included TRW (Thompson Products), which produced suspension and steering systems; frames for Ford vehicles were produced at two Dana (former Hayes Dana) plants; and at General Motors an investment in new facilities produced the Gen III V-8 engine. The German-owned Ronal plant in Fort Erie produced aluminum wheels for the Volkswagen Beetle. Magna International through Venest Industries built a new manufacturing facility in St. Catharines.

The many small components and parts that are produced include battery warmers and chargers; rubber and plastic parts; stamping, castings, and forgings; dump truck bodies, and trailers; piston assembly; wiring harness; various joints, levers, and connecting rods, among others. Over thirty companies were involved in a production that reflected the Canadian-U.S. Auto Pact and the free-trade agreements of 1984 and 1994, the changes to manufacturing through just-in-time deliveries, and a transition to the independent production of parts rather than their manufacture by the automobile companies.

Even so, the economy of the Canadian Frontier remains vulnerable to recession, as when in 1998 a distant GM strike at Flint, Michigan, created unemployment for parts suppliers across North America within a few days. International trade remains extremely competitive. For example, the Auto Pact agreement of 1965, which allowed the Big Three automakers to import cars and their parts duty-free, was opposed by the Japanese and European Union automakers. They had built assembly plants in North America and faced a 6.1 percent tariff. The blow was that in 1999 the World Trade Organization ruled that this trading advantage had to be eliminated, with consequences that are as yet unknown but with an expected adverse role on some or all of the Big Three plants and their suppliers.

In the aerospace industry at Fort Erie, MBB Helicopter Canada arrived in 1984. Fleet Industries obtained contracts to build flaps and ailerons for the Boeing 717, Eurocopter Canada constructed helicopters, and Aero-Safe Technologies manufactured precision-machined components for the aerospace, defense, satellite, and medical equipment industries. At Thorold Donohue Paper (formerly Quebec and Ontario Paper) used recycled materials, less costly in power than working with wood chips, to produce the *Chicago Tribune*.

An interesting industrial survival is illustrated by Atlas Specialty Steels. Purchased by Sammi Steel of South Korea in 1989, the parent company went bankrupt, but the production of stainless, tool, mining, aerospace, and engineering steels recommenced under new management from within the company, and was then again sold to produce stainless steel. In 1998 Welland Pipe secured a contract to supply large-diameter transmission pipes for the Sable Offshore Energy Project. Biolyse Pharma moved from Quebec to Welland Vale in St. Catharines, the site of a former campus for Niagara College of Technology and originally the site of the Merritt mill that inspired the First Welland Canal, to produce pharmaceutical ingredients from botanical sources.

In the shipping-marine industry, employment has been reduced by about a third within the St. Lawrence Seaway Authority and its new management; Algoma Central Marine has moved its offices to St. Catharines; and Port Weller Dry Docks, after a difficult period of low employment, has been revived by several large contracts for the construction and repair of vessels.

Telemarketing, described in 1998 as "one of the fastest growing sectors of Niagara's diverse economy,"[34] has grown considerably in Welland through the ability of its bilingual English-French population to supply French-speaking operators, and the Canadian Niagara Frontier has become a major transboundary gateway on the expanding fiberoptic communications corridor between the United States and Canada.

The service-business sector of the Frontier's economy has grown, headed by architectural/engineering services, legal services, accounting, customs brokers, and computer services.[35] The average company size is small, offices exist in every urban center, and a high-rise cluster of office developments has arisen in downtown St. Catharines.

By 1998 the top ten nonmanufacturing-service sectors of the economy (with the number of employees in parentheses) were:

1. Casino Niagara (3,600)
2. District School Board of Niagara (2,184)
3. Regional Municipality of Niagara (2,141)
4. Brock University (1,578)
5. Niagara Parks Commission (1,550)
6. St. Catharines General Hospital (1,200)
7. Hotel Dieu Hospital (979)
8. Greater Niagara General Hospital (900)
9. Welland County General Hospital (900)
10. Niagara Regional Police Force (761)[36]

Service activities are not exempt from declining employment. Hospitals, a major employee in most urban centers, have been "downsized" with beds closed and staff reduced. In 1998 they faced the threat of further possible closures and reductions in employment to physicians, nurses, technicians, and administrative and service staff. The province argued that "restructuring" would reduce escalating costs through changing from costly hospital beds to cheaper home-care services, and that the closure of hospitals in the smaller communities would be offset by the expansion of specialized facilities in the larger centers.

Police, employees in the conservation authorities and the Niagara Parks Commission, and teachers and their administrators have also suffered from downsizing. Teaching, once presumed a "secure" profession, has been reduced, the number of school boards halved, and primary and secondary schools closed under the rationale that only the larger units are viable. In the reverse direction of expansion, in the mid-1990s the Ontario Ministry of Transport dispersed offices from Toronto to downtown St. Catharines. The city gained a new high-rise office building, a central bus station, and a contribution toward the regeneration of downtown, but after the transfer the number of provincial employees was reduced.

THE CHANGING INDUSTRIAL WORLD ON THE AMERICAN FRONTIER

Using data from the Greater Buffalo Partnership for 1988 and 1998 about companies with the largest number of full-time employees,[37] it is clear both that manufacturing industry remains an economic activity of considerable importance and that a greater number of the top employers are now engaged in service rather than manufacturing activities.

In 1988, of the top fifteen major employers on the American Frontier only four were manufacturing enterprises: General Motors Corporation (14,460), including Delphi Harrison Thermal Systems (6,000), and Powertrain Group (4,000); Ford Motor Company (3,145); Fisher-Price (2,600); and Dresser-Rand (2,450). A decade later the top four manufacturing companies had reduced from 22,655 employees to 17,400, a loss of 23.2 percent. The surviving companies were General Motors (10,100), American Axle and Manufacturers (2,800), Dresser-Rand (2,400), and Ford (2,100).

In 1988 the top service sectors with over three thousand employees were Erie County (8,858), Marine Midland Bank (5,005), Board of Education (4,349), U.S. Postal Service (4,002), City of Buffalo (3,865), State University of New York at Buffalo (3,832), and Buffalo General Hospital (3,131).

Ten years later the expanded service activities with over five thousand employees included the State of New York (18,839), the United States Government (13,000), Erie County (7,532), CGF Health System (6,768), Buffalo City School District (6,205), and the Catholic Health System (5,502).

Economic reliance in the Greater Buffalo area had changed remarkably from its established, long-term dependence on heavy-manufacturing industries to lighter manufacturing and service activities. This change within manufacturing industry includes more than twenty "high-tech" industries described by the Greater Buffalo Partnership as "tech-nologically advanced," "innovative," or "world leaders" in their respective fields.

An overall comparative assessment for 1999 is that: "For most of the decade, job growth rates in the Buffalo-Niagara Falls metro area have been at best one third of the nation overall. Between May 1995 and May 1999, the Buffalo-Niagara Falls metro area gained jobs in three sectors: construction (3% growth); . . . finance/insurance/real estate, or FIRE (up 5.4%); and services (up 6.5%). . . . Both the government and trade industries (wholesale and retail combined) declined slightly over this period . . . , while manufacturing's drop was significantly larger: down 3,100 jobs or –3.4%. . . . Over the same period, Southern Ontario (the Canadian Frontier plus Hamilton) saw gains of over 10 per cent in construction, transportation, and trade, and growth in all sectors except for FIRE, which posted a 9% decline."[38] The Frontier's economy had changed and was still changing rapidly.

NOTES

1. Data interpreted from W. N. Kessel, "Niagara Area Yardsticks," in Buffalo Chamber of Commerce, *The Niagara Area: Agriculture, Industry, Commerce*, Special Edition of the Buffalo Journal of Commerce (Buffalo, N.Y., 1930), p. 253.

2. Census statistics supplemented by data from the Buffalo Chamber of Commerce, *The Niagara Area*, pp. 49, 93, 121.

3. A caution is that employment may fluctuate considerably over short time periods. Also, as definitions and the period of coverage vary as the boundary is crossed, comparisons between the two nations are not specific. Primary sources include census data on labor, employment, and industry at the federal and provincial/state levels of both countries. This data is assembled and reviewed regularly on the Canadian Frontier by agencies such as the Planning and Development Department of the Regional Municipality of Niagara (Thorold), and the Niagara Region Development Corporation (later Niagara Economic and Tourism Corporation); and on the American Frontier by the Buffalo Area Chamber of Commerce (later The Greater Buffalo Partnership) and the Erie and the former Niagara Counties Regional Planning Boards.

4. "Modern Manufacturing Plants," *Canadian Machinery* (1905): 457. For early automobile production in St. Catharines see R. E. Ankli and F. Frederiksen, "The Packard Electric Company of St. Catharines, Ontario," *Automobile History Review* (fall 1983): 567–68; and H. Duraford and G. Baechler, *Cars of Canada* (Toronto: McClelland and Stewart, 1973), pp. 276, 310. For the American Frontier see "The Pierce-Arrow Motor Car Company," *Niagara Frontier* 25, no. 3 (1978). For the development of industry in the Niagara Peninsula see J. N. Jackson and C. White, *The Industrial Structure of the Niagara Peninsula* (St. Catharines, Ont.: Department of Geography, Brock University, 1971); J. T. Davis, *Pricing the Environment for Industrial Development* (Downsview, Ont.: Department of Geography, York University, 1968); and Special Research and Surveys Branch, *Economic Survey of the Niagara Region* (Toronto: Ontario Department of Economics and Development, 1963).

5. J. D. Nicol, *Jack Haney (The Canadians)* (Toronto: Fitzhenry and Whiteside, 1989).

6. McKinnon Industries, *The McKinnon People* (St. Catharines, Ont.: McKinnon, 1944).

7. Hayes-Dana Limited, *Fiftieth Anniversary, 1922–1972* (St. Catharines, Ont.: Hayes-Dana, 1972).

8. For the development of industry on the American Frontier, see W. S. Dunn, ed., *History of Erie County, 1870–1970* (Buffalo, N.Y.: Buffalo and Erie County Historical Society, 1972). Other accounts include Buffalo Chamber of Commerce, *Buffalo Area Market Information* (Batavia, N.Y.: Batavia Times, 1934); R. C. Brown and B. Watson, *Buffalo: Lake City in Niagara Land: An Illustrated History* (Buffalo, N.Y.: Windsor Publications and Erie County Historical Society, 1981); *Buffalo and Niagara Frontier from the Air* (Buffalo, N.Y.: Ronne and Washburn, 1924); and S. Eberle and J. A. Grande, *A Pictorial History: Second Looks of Buffalo and Erie County* (Norfolk, Virginia Beach, Va.: Donning, 1987). For the automobile industry see R. Squire, *Manufacturer of Wheels and Motors*, Adventures in Western New York History, vol. 15

(Buffalo, N.Y.: Buffalo and Erie County Historical Society, 1969).

9. T. E. Leary, *From Fire to Rust: Business, Technology and Work at the Lackawanna Steel Plant, 1899–1983* (Buffalo, N.Y.: Buffalo and Erie County Historical Society, 1987).

10. "Inquiry into the Automotive Industry," in *The Canadian Automotive Industry: Performance and Proposals for Progress* (Ottawa: Ministry of Supply and Services, 1978), pp. 3, 26–30, 219.

11. Niagara Falls Business and Industrial Growth Agency, *Regional Niagara Industrial Directory, 1983* (Niagara Falls, Ont., 1984) (later the *Niagara Business Directory*); and publications of the Buffalo Area Chamber of Commerce.

12. Niagara Falls Business and Industrial Growth Agency, *Regional Niagara Industrial Directory, 1983*.

13. P. Nyhuis, *Niagara Attracting the World* (Montgomery, Ala.: Community Communications, in cooperation with Greater Buffalo Partnership, 1997), p. 54.

14. J. S. Spragge, "It Happened in Hammondsport: How Glenn Curtiss Brought the Aviation Industry to the Niagara Frontier," *Niagara Frontier* 26 (1979): 59. For wartime developments, see *American Warplanes* (New York: Crescent Books, 1980).

15. See *Buffalo and Niagara Frontier from the Air*, which might be compared with *Views of Buffalo*, published for S. H. Knox, Buffalo (Portland, Me.: [L. H. Nelson Company, 1900]).

16. North Tonawanda Board of Trade, *The Tonawanda of To-Day* (Tonawanda, N.Y.: North Tonawanda Board of Trade, 1907).

17. Canadian data from the Niagara Regional Development Corporation (later the Niagara Economic & Tourism Corporation), an agency funded by the Regional Municipality to advance the economic prosperity of the Niagara Region. As most municipalities also have Economic Development Offices, industrial and tourist promotion has become an area of considerable overlap between the region and its municipalities.

18. American data from the Buffalo Chamber of Commerce.

19. W. Macht, *The First Fifty Years: A History of Upper Lakes Shipping, Ltd.* (Toronto: Virgo Press, 1981); and E. B. ("Skip") Gillham, *Niagara's Shipbuilding Heritage 1828 to Port Weller Dry Docks* (Vineland, Ont.: Glenaden Press, 1999).

20. A Reciprocity Treaty in 1854 between Canada and the United States provided a list of natural products that could be exchanged between the two nations. In 1911 a Reciprocity Agreement provided for free trade in natural products and a reduction of duties on many other products. A further treaty in 1935 was suspended when both countries participated in GATT (General Agreement on Tariffs and Trade).

21. J. W. Watson, "Urban Developments in the Niagara Peninsula," *Canadian Journal of Economics and Political Science* 9 (1943): 463; and "The Changing Industrial Pattern of the Niagara Peninsula," *Ontario Historical Society* 37 (1945): 49–59.

22. Trade Research and Analysis Section,

Ontario's Exports and Imports 1982 (Toronto: Ministry of Industry and Trade, 1984).

23. Niagara Falls Business and Industrial Growth Agency, *Regional Niagara Industrial Directory, 1983* (Niagara Falls, Ont., 1984). See also J. N. H. Britton, "Influences on the Spatial Behaviour of Manufacturing Firms in Southern Ontario," in *Contemporary Industrialization: Spatial Analysis and Regional Development,* ed. F. E. I. Hamilton (London: Longman, 1978), pp. 110–21; and J. H. Bater and D. F. Walker, "Foreign Ownership and Industrial Linkage," in *Industrial Development in Southern Ontario,* ed. D. F. E. Walker and J. H. Bater (Waterloo, Ont.: University of Waterloo, 1974), pp. 101–25.

24. Greater Fort Erie Chamber of Commerce, *Town of Fort Erie: Industrial Listing* (Fort Erie, 1978).

25. Batelle Institute, *Final Report on Industrial Development Opportunities for Niagara Falls, Ontario* (Columbus, Ohio, 1971), p. 2.

26. F. P. Taylor, *International Investment in Western New York* (Buffalo, N.Y.: Buffalo Area Chamber of Commerce, [1977]).

27. J. N. Jackson and C. White, *The Industrial Structure of the Niagara Peninsula* (St. Catharines, Ont.: Department of Geography, Brock University, 1971), p. 66.

28. D. A. Scorrar and M. Williams, "Manufacturing Activity and the Urban Hierarchy," in *Canadian Urban Trends: National Perspectives,* ed. D. M. Ray (Toronto: Copp Clark, 1976), 1:103–40.

29. D. M. Ray, *Market Potential and Economic Shadow: A Quantitative Analysis of Industrial Location in Southern Ontario,* Department of Geography, Research Paper 101 (Chicago: University of Chicago, 1965); and D. M. Ray, "The Location of United States Manufacturing Subsidiaries in Canada," *Economic Geography* 47 (1971): 309–400.

30. Niagara Economic and Tourism Corporation, *Fact Sheet: Niagara Region Statistics* (Thorold, Ont., May 1998).

31. Niagara Economic and Tourism Corporation, Niagara Region Business Directory, *Summary Report for Company Closures* (Thorold, Ont., various dates); *Niagara News* provides a continuing account of new economic circumstances.

32. Niagara Economic and Tourism Corporation, *Fact Sheet H: Niagara Area—Largest Public Private Employers* (Thorold, Ont.: Niagara Economic and Tourism Corporation, 1998). As employment may vary markedly over short periods of time, the number of employees provides only a general indication of the situation.

33. Niagara Economic and Tourist Corporation, *Fact Sheet E: Niagara's Business Community* (Thorold, Ont.: Niagara Economic and Tourist Corporation, 1997); "Niagara at Work: Manufacturing Industry, and Service and Technology," *The Standard* (St. Catharines, Ont.), 27 April 1998, pp. C1–C16, D1–D14; and Niagara Economic and Tourism Corporation, *Fact Sheet Q: Niagara's Automotive Sector* (Thorold, Ont.: Niagara Economic and Tourism Corporation, February 1998).

34. Niagara Economic and Tourism Corporation, *Fact Sheet L: Niagara's Call Centre and Telecom-*

munications Centre (Thorold, Ont.: Niagara Economic and Tourism Corporation, July 1998).

35. Niagara Economic and Tourism Corporation, *Fact Sheet B: The Niagara Region—An Overview* (Thorold, Ont.: Niagara Economic and Tourism Corporation, May 1997), p. 2.

36. Ibid., p. 2.

37. P. Nyhuis, *Top Fifty Area Employers* (Buffalo, N.Y.: Greater Buffalo Partnership, 1988 August 29 and 26 October 1998). This partnership, formed in 1993 by merging the Buffalo Development Corporation and the Greater Buffalo Chamber of Commerce, covers the eight counties of Western New York and the Niagara Peninsula of Ontario. The purpose is to expand business activity and enhance community vitality throughout this region. Manufacturing industries are covered in pp. 172–99, and High Tech in pp. 200–17. For an earlier study see Center for Regional Studies, *The Buffalo Economy: A Social and Economic Overview* (Buffalo, N.Y.: State University at Buffalo, 1987).

38. J. B. Sheffer, *State of the Region: Performance Indicators for the Buffalo-Niagara Region* (Buffalo, N.Y.: Institute for Local Governance and Regional Growth, University at Buffalo, 1999).

CHAPTER NINE

THE SETTLEMENT PATTERN, ITS POPULATION, AND GOVERNMENT

A complicated and varied pattern of settlement had arisen across the Niagara Frontier by the early twentieth century. The towns, no longer independent entities, had become interlocked and intertwined in an extended and expanding regional unit. This settlement pattern, the emergence of a new urban dimension, its population characteristics, the varied structures of local government on the two Frontiers, and the ethnic and housing characteristics of Buffalo as the Frontier's major urban community are introduced in this chapter.

CONTRASTING PATTERNS OF SETTLEMENT

By the 1990s the different patterns of historical evolution had created two contrasting and divergent patterns of settlement. The Canadian Frontier had distinct clusters along the Niagara River centered on Niagara Falls, Niagara-on-the-Lake, and Fort Erie; an inland line of towns along the Welland Canal; a number of smaller market towns and service centers across the agricultural areas; and a recreational-residential emphasis along the shore of Lake Erie. These urban centers with their several distinct units of settlement were separated by areas of open space that were mostly rural areas of productive agricultural land.

A more continuous urban agglomeration existed on the American Frontier around the eastern end of Lake Erie, north along the Niagara River, and east to Amherst, Lancaster, and West Seneca. The major centers were Buffalo and Niagara Falls. Only Lockport, relatively isolated, and East Aurora, to a lesser extent, were peripheral to this urban concentration.

Buffalo, a center of continental importance historically and today, has no precise comparison on the Canadian Frontier until Hamilton and Toronto are reached. The city expanded during the twentieth century to absorb small centers on its urban fringe and to spread out extensively like many other North American cities. This peripheral growth exists, but is less pronounced on the Canadian Frontier where more of a rural-urban division has been maintained.

Along the Niagara River next to the boundary, the town of Fort Erie faces the continuous industrial frontage that extends from Buffalo to Tonawanda along the now abandoned Erie Canal. The Canadian frontage of the two-lane, tourist-oriented Niagara River Parkway, backed by a line of residential development and a rural backdrop, faces the heavily trafficked, four-lane Niagara section of the New York State Thruway (I-190) and its riverside inland areas of intense urbanization and industrialization.

The two cities of Niagara Falls are non-identical twins that face each other across the Middle River. On the Canadian side the Niagara River Parkway that includes the landscaped Queen Victoria Park follows the river along the edge of the gorge to the edge of the Niagara Escarpment. There is more public open space, and more tourist attractions overlook or are close to the river than on the American side. Inland, both cities spread beyond their bounding multilane highways, the QEW on the Canadian Frontier and the I-190 (Niagara Expressway) on the American Frontier.

When the Lower River is reached, to the north of the Niagara Escarpment the Canadian centers of Niagara-on-the-Lake and Queenston face the American centers of Youngstown and Lewiston. All are peripheral to the more concentrated areas of population and settlement to the south on their respective Frontiers, and all are primarily residential-tourist localities. The Canadian side, more rural, lies at the eastern end of the Niagara Fruit Belt; orchards, farms, and fruit stalls stand next to the river. On the American Frontier residential development lines the river frontage, the former agricultural areas to the rear have gone, and the two urban centers are more closely connected along the river frontage with urban development than on the Canadian side.

Clearly the settlement pattern varies considerably as the boundary at Niagara is crossed, and a strong Canadian-American dichotomy exists. Two distinct worlds of landscape evolution have emerged over time. Technological advance has followed the same general paths, but the many variations between the two sides in the character and form of development have together contributed to major differences in the areal characteristics of settlement between the two sides.

Viewing this settlement pattern within the wider purview of the location within the Great Lakes region of North America, Niagara can be interpreted as the "settlement fulcrum" where the concentration on settlement changes from a downstream Canadian emphasis to an upstream American emphasis. Downstream along the Canadian northern bank of Lake Ontario are Toronto, Kingston, Cornwall, Montreal, Quebec, and other centers. No such concentration exists along the American southern shore. Upstream, a contrasting set of circumstances exists. The Canadian north shore is relatively underpopulated compared with Erie, Ashtabula, Cleveland, and Toledo on the American south shore of Lake Erie. This fundamental contrast in settlement around the Niagara Frontier even applies to the Niagara River, with the middle river separating two contrasting patterns of settlement. Downstream in Canada, Queenston and Niagara-on-the-Lake offer more intense urbanization than do Lewiston and Youngstown in the United States, and upstream, Canadian Chippawa and Fort Erie are less significant than the urban-industrial sequence south from Niagara Falls through the Tonawandas to Buffalo.

SUBURBAN MOVEMENTS

Both nations have had and continue to have strong suburban movements, but their impact and severity varies considerably. On the Canadian Frontier where municipal annexation and regional government have been encouraged, suburban expansion now mostly takes place within the same administrative area. On the American Frontier the outward movement of people carried with it tax dollars and services, including the movement of industry and shopping centers to suburban locations. The former political power of the two core cities, Buffalo and Niagara Falls, that had previously commanded the political and economic scene has been reduced. The suburbs created by the streetcar, paved roads, the automobile, and the provision of services became not "bedroom" communities but independent units with substantial investments in their infrastructure, a situation exacerbated as annexation was successfully resisted through laws passed by New York State that stressed the principle of municipal "home rule" in domestic affairs.

The inner city on the American Frontier, which once contained a diverse mix of upper, middle, and working classes living in close proximity within its administrative extent, became more divided into "enclaves of relatively different citizens surrounded by increasing percentages of ethnic poor."[1] This outward movement, described as the "White flight" to the suburbs, took advantage of an opportunity that was virtually closed to the Black population and led to an increasing proportion of its residents remaining in the confined inner cities of Buffalo and Niagara Falls. The more affluent White groups were drawn outward by the attractions of a cleaner environment and the preference for an individual detached house on a sizeable lot in a more open setting—an opportunity available only to those who were better educated and more financially secure. As the middle class moved out, the urban poor were housed in poorer-quality urban housing on the fringe of downtown.

These differences between the inner and the outer city were exacerbated by financial/mortgage policies. National policy favored private home ownership with government programs guaranteeing loans to veterans for the purchase of homes and tax benefits through the allowance of income tax deductions for interest payments on home mortgages, an advantage not available to Canadian residents and presenting a considerable difference between the two sides at the Frontier. The policies of real-estate developers and financial institutions also supported suburban spread, as did the social factor of clustering by which households with similar housing needs and social and economic characteristics grouped together in the same area.

"Buffalo residents resented paying county taxes for services that were used primarily by suburban and rural residents. The extensive county highway system was maintained by taxes from all county residents, while city streets remained strictly a city responsibility even though suburban commuters used them daily. The science and historical museums, the zoo, and the art gallery were supported by city taxes, yet were heavily attended by non-city visitors. The county sheriff's department patrolled the rural and exurban county, yet its costs were paid by all county taxpayers. On the other hand, suburban and rural residents complained loudly about the increased costs of welfare, a county responsibility, even though most welfare recipients lived in the city where housing was less expensive."[2]

A NEW URBAN DIMENSION

New words have been coined to explain the expanding urban phenomenon across former rural landscapes. In 1915 Patrick Geddes used "conurbation. The neighbouring great towns are rapidly linking up by tramways and streets no less than railways, while great open spaces which might have been not so long ago cheaply secured as unrivalled lungs of life are already all but irrecoverable. . . . To focus these developments, indeed transformations, of the geographic tradition of town and country in which we were brought up, and express them more sharply, we need some little extension of our vocabulary. . . . Some name then for these city regions, these town aggregates, is wanted. ["Constellations" and "conglomerations" were considered, then] what of 'Conurbations'? That perhaps may serve as the necessary word, as an expression of this new form of population-grouping, which is already, as it were subconsciously, developing new forms of social grouping, and of definite government and administration."[3]

The concept of conurbation applied to each Frontier at Niagara separately and to both units together. It applied to the Canadian Frontier where the communities along the Welland Canal were interlinked and interconnected by road, rail, and streetcar and by canal traffic and shipping services. Niagara Falls, separated from this line of canal settlements by only a short distance of intervening agricultural land, was connected thereto by road, rail, and streetcar and also linked by railway along the Niagara River south to Fort Erie and north to Niagara-on-the-Lake. With transboundary links by ferries, railways/streetcar networks, bridges, wires, and conduits, a continuous grouping of interrelated urban centers was even more evident in the expanding metropolitan areas centered on Buffalo and Niagara Falls on the American Frontier.

From conurbation, terminology has changed to "metropolitan," with both sides at Niagara being recognized as within this category within their respective national censuses.[4] As the streetcar was displaced by the automobile, as cheaper land on the fringe was made accessible by this new mode of transport, as mortgage policy favored new homes on external sites, and as utility companies and the communications industries encouraged an outward movement to former agricultural properties, population growth in the former inner core areas leveled off while the new suburban and out-of-town areas expanded. Spread-eagled outward growth, more evident on the American than the Canadian Frontier with its larger population size and more vigorous urban centers, was better recognized on the Canadian side where a form of regional government was established in 1970 by the province of Ontario over the array of small and large, urban and rural communities that comprised the Niagara Region.

From metropolis there has been increasing decentralization, encouraged by strong public investment in highways, electric utilities, waterworks, sewage works, and location policies. Terminology has become confusing and uncertain: "postindustrial," "modern" and "postmodern," "megalopolis," "megalopolis unbound," "the exploding metropolis," and "cosmopolis" have each been used. The only certainty is that of steady and continuing urban advance with multilane highways, extensive service grids, external regional shopping centers, and now isolated superstores and service centers with extended commuting lines, social-recreational journeys intertwining any defined urban area, and the enormous challenge of change to be found in the former inner cores of the once central cities. Put bluntly, it is a repetitious, ubiquitous, all-prevailing, and formless urban growth, very different from the emerging and distinctive forms and patterns that prevailed up to 1914 and the First World War or, with the intervening Depression, even up to the Second World War.

The whole structural basis of society has changed from the dominance of industrial production in large building complexes to service and knowledge industries with global connections to international economies. It is a new city with socially and cultural diverse characteristics that are widely and loosely dispersed and used over an extensive landscape in contrast with the laboring immigrant working-class districts close to the more prosperous, better-serviced, more healthy, better-educated, and politically more respected middle- and upper-class neighborhoods. This sea change in the urban condition remains reflected in urban form with its historical roots because of the time lag between old realities, new circumstances, and their interpretation.

The old core cities are losing, or have lost, their traditional dominance to become but one of several urban centers in an extensive urban region. Within this new polynuclear form the external centers may be larger or more important than the originating centers. Examples at the Niagara Frontier on both sides of the boundary include the dispersal of universities, hospitals, office complexes, and shopping centers to ex-urban locations. Previously these functions were all centrally located.

The new settlement reality at the Frontier, with its deep and still-surviving Native and pioneer roots in the landscape, had become an unbounded metropolitan area with increasing decentralization and multiple centers of growth, often in administrative and political conflict one with the other for funding, services, prestige, and advancement. Residents are no longer restricted to one municipality, but may enjoy facilities in a multitude of jurisdictions as part of their active life. A family can live in municipality A, with husband and wife working in B and C, shopping in D, attending a health clinic in E, their two children being educated in F and G, and with sporting and cultural interests in H and I. Administrative lines no longer combine many activities, and which agency provides services such as garbage collection, water supply, hydro, and road repair has become less important to most households than their costs and efficiency and the channels for personal involvement and the resolution of complaints.

POPULATION STRUCTURE AND CHARACTER

The Canadian and American Frontiers together contained a census population of slightly over 2.1 million by the late 1990s. The American Frontier had about three times the population of its Canadian equivalent, with Buffalo having a population that was slightly smaller than the total population living within the Niagara Region,[5] or rather less than Hamilton further west in Ontario. The sequence of urban places was Buffalo (300,717 estimated in 1998), St. Catharines (130,926 estimated in 1996), and then the American towns of Amherst and Cheektowaga with about 100,000 population. The two cities of Niagara Falls had a population of almost 77,000 in Ontario and less than 60,000 in New York State, and Welland had a population of nearly 50,000 by 1996. Centers outside the major cities had smaller populations. A caution of interpretation is that population refers to an area within municipal boundaries, with more changes to this structure of government on the Canadian than the American Frontier.

Employment rates in the two metropolitan areas astride the Niagara boundary over the 1990–1997 and 1997–2000 periods were higher on the American than the Canadian

Frontier.[6] The percentage increase was 1.2 and 0.5 respectively in the St. Catharines-Niagara area, against 1.8 and 1.9 over the Buffalo-Niagara Falls area. New job creation on the Canadian Frontier added 250 new workers in the blue-collar industries and 1,530 in the white-collar industries. Such data has to be compared with a loss of 1,952 blue-collar workers and a gain of 14,554 white-collar opportunities on the American Frontier. On both Frontiers the change is manifest away from manufacturing toward service activities, with the threat of unemployment being average on the American Frontier and higher on the Canadian Frontier. On both Frontiers the change is on average from the better-paying to the lower-paying jobs.

Comparing the age structures of the two populations using 1990/1991 census data, a surprising fact is that both Frontiers are almost identical with some 19 percent in the youthful 0–14 age groups, about 65 percent in the middle age group from 15–64, and about 15 percent in the elderly or retirement group of age 65 or over. The 25–34 age group was the largest on both Frontiers, and the numbers diminished successively for each five-year age group from 0–4, 5–9, and 10–14, then increased over the 15–19 and again over the 20–24 age groups. The proportion of youth in the total population has fallen steadily, and

seniors form an increasing proportion of both populations, with the Canadian Frontier becoming a significant retirement locality through the individual purchase of private homes, including condominium developments, and in planned retirement communities. The national increase of births over deaths has added population to both Frontiers. Net migration has remained in balance or with a slight inward movement on the Canadian Frontier, whereas the American Frontier has had an outward movement.

Ethnic cultural differences between the two sides of the river are substantial. United Empire Loyalists, immigrants from Britain, French Canadians, and southern European and Mennonite groups have settled on the Canadian Frontier. Blacks from the southern states, immigrants from southern and eastern Europe, and more recently persons of Hispanic (mainly Puerto Rican) groups have been drawn to the American Frontier.

A major difference factor between the Frontiers is that the United States restricted immigration in the 1920s, an action of paramount importance to Buffalo and other major industrial centers that had built up their industrial labor force with new entrants into their economies from the various nations of southern and eastern Europe. The acts of 1921 and the Johnson Immigration Act of

1924 not only cut off the supply of new labor from these countries, but recent immigrants were now unable to bring over other family members as continued to be the case on the Canadian Frontier where population expanded considerably after the Second World War with immigration from war-torn Europe. Consequently, a higher proportion of the population now living on the Canadian Frontier was born outside Canada, and a lower proportion in the Buffalo metropolitan area were foreign born.

By ethnic group, the primary population on the Canadian Frontier was British (English, Irish, Scottish, Welsh), and then came Italian, French, German, Polish, and Ukrainian groups by mother tongue, and smaller Dutch and Hungarian groups. This cultural diversity is evident at ethnic and folk art festivals and in the variety of church denominations, social groups, newspapers, and ethnic restaurants. Many European languages can be heard in the open-air markets at Welland and St. Catharines. The Folk Arts Council in St. Catharines has thirty-three different member groups, and there are about the same number in Welland. Even so, ethnic differences are less important politically than on the American Frontier, and ethnic neighborhoods in the urban centers on the Canadian Frontier are not as clearly differentiated

as in Buffalo. While the Niagara Region by the 1990s was adding European immigrants to its population, Buffalo's older European ethnic populations were moving from the inner city to the suburbs.

In the Buffalo-Niagara Falls metropolitan area in the 1990 census, Blacks formed 10.3 percent of the total population. In Buffalo, including the Lower East Side, the proportion was 30.7 percent. Other heavy African American concentrations existed in Niagara Falls and Lackawanna. Germans exceeded 25 percent of the population in Lockport and North Tonawanda, Poles had their highest concentrations in Cheektowaga and North Tonawanda, and Italians were an important group in the population structure of Niagara Falls.

By 1991 religious identification on the Canadian Frontier was primarily Protestant, followed by Roman Catholic. The largest centers on each Frontier, St. Catharines and Buffalo, were seats of Roman Catholic dioceses, and on the Canadian Frontier since 1998 regional public and Catholic school boards administer the educational system. On the American Frontier, according to a census undertaken in 1971, nearly half of the population of Erie County and over a third in Niagara County were Roman Catholic.[7] Catholicism, culturally strong in the Buffalo area, is reflected in its churches, schools, and institutions of higher education and results from the large Irish, German, Polish, and Italian immigrations over past decades. Six out of the nine private four-year colleges were founded by or are currently administered by Catholic orders.

The greatest loss of population has taken place in Buffalo, in 1890 the eighth-largest city in the United States.[8] Population peaked at about six hundred thousand in the mid-1950s. Then the eleventh-largest industrial center in the United States, the largest inland lake port, first in flour milling, second as a railroad center, and third in steel production, the city had a 23.6 percent loss in population between 1960 and 1975, 14.8 percent of the population with incomes below the official poverty level, and 85.7 percent of housing units predated 1940.

Since 1857 Buffalo has occupied roughly the same area, and after the Second World War population expansion has taken place beyond the city limits in the towns of Tonawanda, Amherst, Cheektowaga, West Seneca, Orchard Park, and Hamburg. Buffalo had become the classic example of an "underbound" city; the city's administrative extent had not changed despite the massive changes in population, technology, and industrial growth since the mid-nineteenth century.

Older incorporated centers, within or on the edge of the Buffalo metropolitan area, have also lost functions and population since the 1950s. Lockport, home of General Motors's Harrison Radiator Division, Tonawanda with its volatile aircraft and automobile industries, Niagara Falls with its chemical plants, and Depew with its railway shops have all declined. They have also been disrupted internally as their downtown retail functions were attracted to suburban malls. The highways that linked the malls and connected the workplaces with the residential areas created a metropolitan area, as in many other North American cities, joining together a series of former distinct and separated urban centers.

The Buffalo region maintained the eighth ranking in American manufacturing centers into the 1920s and grew as a steel and automobile manufacturing center until after the Second World War. Functionally, the city of Buffalo was the undoubted focus of a major metropolitan area, but people, commercial activities, and employment dispersed over adjacent municipalities. Beginning in the 1950s, the outward movement to shopping centers further weakened the downtown retail core, and new suburban malls located beyond the administrative boundary and the taxing authority of the inner city.

The size of this outward growth is expressed by the fact that "in 1950 the Buffalo-Niagara Falls urbanized area was 123 square miles centered around Buffalo, Niagara Falls, and the Tonawandas. . . . By 1990, the urbanized area had more than doubled to 286 square miles (133% increase) taking in most suburbs of Amherst, Cheektowaga, and West Seneca, and portions [of the outer townships]. . . . Most urban expansion occurred in the 1960s and 1970s when the urbanized area grew by over 30% (129.5 square kilometers; 50.0 square miles) each decade. Growth in the urbanized area has been much slower in the post two decades. The region added 20 square miles [51.8 square kilometers] to the urbanized area in the 1980s, and an estimated 11 square miles [28.5 square kilometers] through 1997."[8] The dichotomy of both urban expansion and population decline had become a peculiar if not ironic circumstance.

MANAGING THE URBAN ENVIRONMENT

When the expanding city decentralized outward over its limiting municipal boundaries, a severe challenge was presented for the historic local systems of government and the services which they provided. The two Frontiers responded very differently to this urban-administrative challenge (fig. 9.1). "Overbound" communities with urban cores and surrounding rural areas in each municipality and a coordinating structure of regional government emerged on the Canadian Frontier. "Underbound" administrative units with the boundary confining the urban area and with suburbs overlapping into an adjacent authority developed on the American Frontier.

On the Canadian Frontier twenty boundary alterations involving many municipalities had taken place in the Niagara Region between 1952 and 1964. In 1960, faced with threats of amalgamation from all sides, the politicians of Grantham Township decided that their best defense was a good offense. They applied to the Ontario Municipal Board (OMB) for the amalgamation of St. Catharines, Grantham, Port Dalhousie, and Merritton. Opposed by Port Dalhousie and more strongly by Merritton, an amalgamation hearing was held, with the outcome later that year being the end of the smaller units, their amalgamation into St. Catharines, and the birth of the now multinodal city that was to survive into the twenty-first century.

Even more extensive in its area coverage and the political and policy implications, in 1970 the Province of Ontario established the Regional Municipality of Niagara to achieve

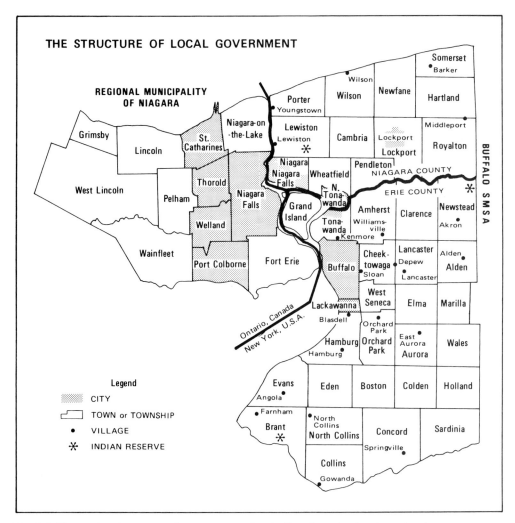

Fig. 9.1. The municipal structure of government varies significantly as the river boundary is crossed. The units are smaller, and greater in number on the American Frontier. The two-tier regional-municipal system on the Canadian Frontier faces the small-scale, traditional system of the American Frontier. (Prepared by the Department of Geography, Brock University)

unified action on regional problems. The regional municipality combined the historic counties of Lincoln and Welland and reduced the twenty-six municipalities to twelve. Regional responsibilities included planning, the production and wholesale distribution of water, bulk sewage collection and treatment, police, regional roads, health and welfare, and finance.[9] Local responsibilities included urban planning, roads, the retail distribution of water, the local collection of sewage, storm drainage, fire protection, transit, parks, recreation, libraries, and the collection and disposal of garbage. This dual regional-municipal system of government, at first well supported by the majority of authorities, was endorsed in 1977 and again in 1990.[10] Tensions then arose as the three largest cities (St. Catharines, Niagara Falls, and Welland) became foes of the regional system and stressed their desire for local autonomy.

With the "downsizing" of costs, facilities, and services from the federal to the provincial levels of government, in 1995 the Ontario Minister of Municipal Affairs and Housing announced the establishment of an Advisory Group on Municipal Government Reform to change the legislative framework under which municipalities operated and to amend responsibilities. A bill to amalgamate six municipalities into a new exapanded city of

Toronto followed in 1996, and some two hundred amalgamations in Ontario had resulted by 1997. In 1999 the provincial department of urban affairs launched new initiatives for municipal reform which included that Niagara should devise its own solution.

Under pressure either to reform its structure of government or to have a new structure imposed by the province, the regional municipality appointed a consultant to advise on the options. The options considered ranged from one city that incorporated all of Niagara's towns, cities, and the region into one unit; to three relatively self-sufficient cities based on St. Catharines, Welland-Port Colborne, and Niagara Falls; to the status quo that retained all centers as single units, except that Thorold was divided between St. Catharines and Welland.[11]

The final report argued that Niagara's regional government should be dissolved and that the twelve area municipalities might be reorganized into three urban units centered on north-south orientations along the Niagara River, the Welland Canal, and a rural western entity. A "Joint Planning Board" with representatives from the three cities would provide coordination.[12] As the Welland Canal provided the boundary for "Canal City," all cities along the canal lost land to the "River City," a proposal that caused immediate consternation. Over the next two years the existing municipalities, at odds one with one another, were expected to seek out voluntary partnerships and to amalgamate with or work out local servicing arrangements, with the new structure to be in place by 2004. The report stated that Canal City will act as the "Consolidated Municipal Manager" over public health and social services for all the cities, with water and sewage plants jointly owned by all three cities. This assessment was shelved in 2000 by the Provincial Government, which no longer requested immediate action.

Changing boundaries had become a politically tense activity. Localism and the cherished values of small communities with two centuries of history remained important to many citizens, whereas greater administrative efficiency and control was espoused by the senior levels of government. To the general public, it is the activities themselves that are important. People increasingly live in one place, work elsewhere, shop and enjoy leisure activities in other communities. "Snowbirds" may spend long winter vacations in warmer climes, and cottagers long periods by a lake, all of which reduces responsibility to and interest in hometown events. People have become more mobile through the ease and ubiquitous use of the private automobile that

has devalued the role of each local community and favored dispersed travel patterns to different centers. This new mode of living and a decreasing interest in local affairs may be reflected in the St. Catharines municipal elections of November 2000, where only 24 percent of the eligible public voted.

Whichever model emerges on the Canadian Niagara Frontier, the administrative situation on the American Frontier is very different and not in the immediate future likely to change. Here, a large number of small municipal units dominate the political landscape, and there has been only a limited metropolitan approach to the provision of urban services and the resolution of issues.[13] By 1991 Western New York contained 8 counties, 11 cities, 164 towns, and 77 villages, a total of 260 distinct units. The American Frontier also contained 101 school districts, 95 independent fire districts, and 79 special-purpose governments including housing authorities, library districts, industrial development agencies, and soil and water authorities.[14]

Buffalo itself had grown within a confined 108-square-kilometer (42-square-mile) area, an administrative structure that dates from the mid-nineteenth century even though considerable suburban growth had taken place outward beyond these restrictive administrative boundaries. Niagara Falls is likewise restricted. As in both instances the outlying suburban townships and villages have not always been able to "keep up" with the provision of new services, these functions have often been provided by the counties.

Regional organizations have had but a limited life. The Erie and Niagara Counties Regional Planning Board survived only a few years. The best-known metropolitan-wide function, the Niagara Frontier Transportation Authority, operates the Buffalo International Airport, the harbor, and Buffalo's Light Rail Rapid Transit service; a subsidiary, Metro Bus, administers the transit routes. There are a host of cooperative agencies and a large number of joint service agreements; for example, water from the Porter Avenue treatment plant in Buffalo is supplied to the Erie County Water Authority, and the Buffalo Sewer Authority receives waste from several adjoining sewer districts.

Administrative status on the American Frontier is based on neither population size nor the ability to implement guidance over development.[15] The Towns of Amherst and Cheektowaga are larger than the Cities of Niagara Falls, North Tonawanda, Lackawanna, and Lockport. The Town of Tonawanda is larger than the City of Tonawanda. Populous villages like Kenmore and Lancaster have entirely urban popula-

tions, yet "village" is defined as "a small group of dwellings in a rural area, usually ranking in size between a hamlet and a town." These administrative inconsistencies make area-wide problems difficult to overcome, even though many issues including land-use planning, transportation, unemployment, economic vitality, and waste disposal clearly demand overall regional definition and resolution.

A summary and comparative appreciation of government on the American Frontier is that in 1999, "Many issues, including environmental quality, transportation, economic development, utility services, and land use go beyond municipal borders. . . . Regional planning is more developed in Southern Ontario than in Western New York."[16] At the Niagara Frontier, regionalism versus localism provides a point of striking difference when the river boundary between the two distinct national territories is crossed.

With active debates on how best to govern the evolving metropolitan areas on both sides of the Niagara River, it is as well to appreciate that on both Frontiers there is a massive number of volunteer groups and charitable organizations that undertake community work and raise funds for their successful achievement. These citizen groups are perhaps most active in fields such as conservation and the preservation of land and historic buildings, in the prevention of pollution, and in family assistance when poverty, unemployment, ill health, or other disability strikes. They have concerns in strengthening the arts and in work with deprived children and the elderly. They are community strengths beyond the formal structures of government that add considerably to the quality of life at the Frontier.

At a superior level to the government agencies within the Frontier are the various provincial/state, national/federal, and international/global organizations with powers of control and direction over the local environment way beyond those which exist locally. We note, for example, the First and Second World Wars, when both sides at the Frontier advanced industrially; the causes were national and international, but with an immense local impact. A further example is provided by the contrasting legal, financial, health, and education systems between the two nations; the buildings and their several activities exist locally, but their important decisions are made mostly outside the local Frontier region. A truism is that the American federal government, with its greater population, resources, and financial basis, plays a far greater role in urban affairs, including housing, urban renewal, and transportation policies, than the Canadian equivalent where cities are the responsibility of the provinces. A Canadian federal department of urban affairs had but a brief life in the early 1970s. The same argument applies to the large national and international corporations, where again the major decisions are not made locally, but they exert their considerable impact at the Frontier through employment expansion and decline and the volume and direction of trading movements. In the continuing debate on how local municipal government is best structured and how functions are best distributed between the agencies that exist, the Frontier is not and never has been either an independent or an isolated unit. It is often the recipient that has to respond to a now world-based external decision-making process that includes technological advances and international political rivalries.

HOUSING AND ETHNIC NEIGHBORHOODS IN BUFFALO

Despite the serious decline in population, many parts of Buffalo remain attractive as residential environments and for private improvement. Middle- and upper-class people have moved into once-neglected houses and buildings and upgraded them,

Housing clearance and renewal next to the city center of Buffalo provide a mixed repertoire architecturally, socially, and visually. (John N. Jackson [both])

remodeling their interiors and restoring the exteriors. A substantial middle-class community now lives in the once-elite areas north from the central business district. While the larger homes between Linwood and Richmond Avenue have never deteriorated, much rebuilding has taken place on the Lower West Side. New houses in the Victorian style have been built between the

Federal Building on Huron Street and Elmwood Avenue and the gentrified brick houses on Whitney Place and Prospect Place.

Victorian cottages in the Allentown area of Buffalo have been renovated into comfortable city homes. Local firms specializing in the restoration of century-old buildings are producing a landscape that recalls former wealth and elegance. In the neighborhood where the Allentown Art Festival takes place, a strong community organization has helped guide and rebuild residences and shops.

Delaware Avenue, itself a designated National Historic District, and nearby streets contain opulent, stately homes built during the period of prosperity from 1860 to the First World War when the city expanded north from Niagara Square to Delaware Park. They reflect the industrial wealth and the political power of a city that sent two presidents, Millard Fillmore and Grover Cleveland, to the White House. Nearly all of these homes have been converted to businesses and now serve as prestigious office space for national or regional organizations such as the American Red Cross, the corporate headquarters for Niagara Trading, and the Computer Task Group. Even so, their visual impact and historic importance continues to grace the urban scene, enhance the quality of city life, and remain significant for urban tourism.

In the City of Buffalo most of the housing stock is over fifty years old and a high percentage are two-family homes. Each dwelling has a yard, however small. When immigrants arrived in great numbers, additions were built on or small frame houses erected in the backyard. The oldest houses in Buffalo, such as those once inhabited by Jewish immigrants on Hickory Street, were one-and-a-half-story, wood-frame houses, often with storefront shops on the main streets.

The most typical middle-class Buffalo home is a tall frame two-and-a-half-story, two-flat unit on a narrow lot with a two-story porch on the front. The lower porch has often been enclosed to provide additional space for the lower unit, often owner occupied. The upper flat will be rented, perhaps to relatives. Characteristically wood frame, well kept, and neatly painted, they are distinguished by brick on the lower front porch and by small additions at the rear. This type of house, the "next step up" socially and historically for many, is more common in Buffalo's housing stock than the single-family home.

The stability of working-class communities has sustained the visual quality of streets in industrial areas. As Banham has observed: "the houses may not be great architecture but the residential charm of these well maintained little streets is undeniable. . . . Almost

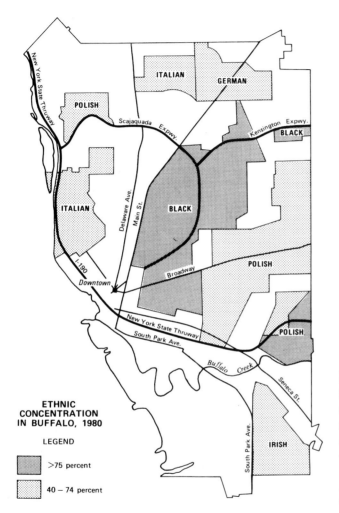

ETHNIC
CONCENTRATION
IN BUFFALO, 1980

LEGEND

>75 percent

40 – 74 percent

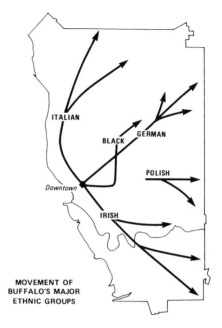

MOVEMENT OF
BUFFALO'S MAJOR
ETHNIC GROUPS

Fig. 9.2. Buffalo, a city of ethnic neighborhoods, is enlivened culturally and socially by the diverse composition of its population. The tendency is strong for the different ethnic groups to move outward within the city and to suburbs beyond the city's limits along the same migratory paths. (Gregory P. Stein, prepared by the Department of Geography, Brock University)

every possibility of nineteenth century domestic architecture was explored in Buffalo. Nearly all of it was uncommonly well made."[17] German carpenters with their out-standing craftsmanship have made Buffalo "a city where elaborate carving in native and exotic woods abounds."[18]

The housing stock never contained a

Typical Buffalo "two-flat" housing on Polonia of Buffalo's East Side. Twin Roman Catholic church spires provide visual and ethnic identification. (Gregory P. Stein)

great percentage of high-density tenement apartments; yet Buffalo from the late 1930s to the 1960s participated actively in urban renewal programs, with their disruptive social implications. Neighborhoods perceived as "slums" were torn down in a process described as "clean-sweep planning," and then replaced by unattractive, inferior low-rent apartment buildings. The authorities assumed that little, if anything, was worth saving, and this included buildings, the lots, the road pattern, and any social centers that might have existed. Displaced without much thought for their welfare, the poor and recent immigrants were forced into adjacent older neighborhoods. More recently attitudes have changed. Clearance has been replaced by rehabilitation and improvement, resulting in almost entirely new neighborhoods of middle-size, single-family homes as on

William Street from Michigan to Hickory Streets.

Today, ethnic neighborhoods are seen nostalgically as a source of stability and strength in "The City of Good Neighbors." Originally defined by barriers such as railway lines, they provide continuity and security for traditional beliefs; the parish for religion; and familiar faces in taverns, shops, clubs, and workplaces. South Buffalo is traditionally Irish; the East Side, Polish, now becoming Black; the West Side, traditionally Italian, now Puerto Rican; only "newer" North Buffalo is inherently ambiguous (fig. 9.2).

German immigrants who came to Buffalo from Pennsylvania, Alsace, and western Europe were the city's largest foreign-born group during the mid-nineteenth century. By the mid-nineteenth century the city was nearly half German, and though the population increased with other immigrants, by the 1880s the population remained two-fifths German. More prosperous than the Irish, the hard core of tradesmen and craftsmen was unified by language. Several German-language newspapers and singing groups thrived, and a German-American bank (later Liberty Bank) was founded in 1882. The German East Side area consisted of one-and-a-half-story frame houses interspersed with tall Catholic or Lutheran churches. The Germanic legacy was echoed in church and place names, fraternal organizations, and that unique Buffalo food roast beef on Kümmelweck. In a 1976 ethnic census, nearly 13 percent of the sample identified themselves as German.[19] From their area of highest concentration between Main and Genesee Streets, they have moved northeast in Buffalo and beyond to the suburbs.

Irish Catholics settled first near wharves that provided stevedore work in the Canal Street area between the Erie Canal and Lake Erie. They held some of the lowest-paying jobs, aggravated by seasonal unemployment when handling grain and freight ended as the lake froze. Irish residents expanded south and east to include the Hydraulics District and South Park Avenue, and had strong associations to companies such as Buffalo Forge. They occupied the neat frame houses of "The Ward," the old First Ward in the shadow of grain elevators along the Buffalo River, and narrow, two-flat frame houses in the 1920s and 1930s.

East and South Europeans made up the "new" immigration to Buffalo which began about 1870. Polish groups settled on the East Side and replaced Germans as the dominant ethnic group.[20] Joseph Bork, a German realtor, worked with John Pitass, a Polish priest,[21] to attract and retain Polish peasants who might otherwise have traveled west. Bork donated land to St. Stanislaus Church, established in 1874, and sold whole areas of frame houses to Polish immigrants. Polonia extended roughly from Fillmore Street on the west to Genesee in the north, Clinton on the south, and east to the city line.[22] Later immigration extended east of Fillmore, south of Genesee (north of Broadway), and to suburban Cheektowaga. Secondary centers began in the Black Rock area of North Buffalo and southeast of the original East Side settlement. This immigration helped to satisfy the enormous demand for unskilled labor. The difficult transition from peasant village to iron foundries and the clothing industry was eased by the large community with a common language and religion, parish churches, and parish schools.

Buffalo is an acknowledged North American center of Polish society. A Polish newspaper, the *Ampol Eagle*, has a circulation of twenty-five thousand, and most campaigning politicians still visit Buffalo's Polonia. Broadway Market, a visual and gastronomic delight, is especially crowded as later generations return to the old neighborhood at Christmas and Easter. The Polish community is also visible in the many large Roman Catholic churches. Other Polish communities, with neighborhood churches and "Dom Polski" halls, are to be found in Niagara Falls, Lackawanna, and North Tonawanda. After several generations, Polish ethnicity in Buffalo remains strong despite the movement of younger middle-class Polish families to the suburbs. As a result, by the 1980s the inner Polish areas had a large elderly population, and their churches, church schools, and local Polish businesses had lost much of their support.

Italians, the second-largest European group in Buffalo after the Poles, settled in city neighborhoods according to village and province of origin in southern Italy.[23] Often people from the same village would do heavy labor in the same industry or in the many construction projects such as roads, bridges, and laying sewer and water mains. The greatest number of Italian immigrants, mostly from Sicily, occupied the West Side. Other Italian groups settled in their own neighborhoods on Buffalo's East Side. Immigrants from Campobasso grouped around the Ferry-Moselle and Lovejoy Street areas, those from Abruzzi clustered north of Delavan Avenue, and Calabrians and Campanians on the near East Side. Other Italians, employed at Bethlehem Steel, lived in South Buffalo. Italian neighborhoods have changed hands more readily than the Polish areas. There is an ongoing northward movement of

West Side Italians. The annual Italian festival takes place on Hertel Avenue as increasing numbers of Italians have moved to North Buffalo. Since the Second World War, Italians have contributed greatly to the suburbanization of Tonawanda and Kenmore.

Jewish immigration began in association with the German community, the first permanent Jewish settler arriving in 1835 to teach German.[24] The major influx from 1880 to 1924 originated in Poland and Russia. Jews first located on lower Main Street and then moved to the East Side centered on William Street where community houses, a Jewish library, and synagogues were founded. In decline by 1905, many frame houses were removed over the 1930 to 1950 period. Replaced by the Willet Park project, the area became almost exclusively Black. The Jews dispersed up Humboldt Parkway into the Delaware-Richmond corridor and to North Buffalo and Kenmore in the 1910s and 1920s, and more recently to Amherst.

Buffalo's Black communities, about 50 percent of the city population, have roots at the corner of William and Michigan Streets, just east of the central business district. As racial discrimination and housing costs made the suburbs an unrealistic location, growth took place in the inner city east of Main Street.[25] These tracts are 75 percent or more

Black, a higher proportion than other ethnic concentrations.

Another recent large-scale migration is Puerto Rican. American citizens since 1919, this ethnic group reached the Niagara Frontier about 1952 as the extended families of migrant field laborers in southern Erie County. They later moved to Myrtle Street on Buffalo's Near East Side and to the West Side, replacing Italians.

Since the Second World War, Hungarian and Ukrainian populations have grown in Riverside in Northwest Buffalo. Slovaks no longer live near their St. Rita's Roman Catholic Church on the East Side. Swedes, remembered in a few Lutheran churches, have virtually disappeared as an entity. The City of Lackawanna contains more recent Yemeni neighborhoods which sustain their own mosque. Croatians have moved their church from next to the Bethlehem Steel plant to the extreme east of that city. Foreign immigrants came to work in the expanding factories of Buffalo, and when the decline in blue-collar work hurt these communities, their children had to move elsewhere to find work. More recently, Buddhist Vietnamese have located in the Broadway-Fillmore area.

By 1990 homeowners included two-thirds of the households on the American Frontier but, as home ownership reflected both income and housing discrimination, only 34 percent of the Black population and 33 percent of the Hispanic group owned their own homes. Mortgage denial rates were also highest for the Black and Hispanic groups. Minority Western New Yorkers were also underrepresented in the region's labor force and occupations. They "were significantly underrepresented among the region's officials and managers, and slightly underrepresented among office/clerical workers. . . . The same was true among professionals for all groups except Asian Western New Yorkers. . . . Disproportionately more Black and American Indian workers held typically low-paying service jobs, while disproportionally more American Indians and Hispanics were laborers."[26]

Politics in Buffalo still feeds on ethnic neighborhood and group identification. Irish, Polish, and Italian voters have had "their" mayors in the past, and the needs of the different ethnic groups are recognized by government[27] as when in 1967 the city commissioned an ethnic census by aldermanic district. Many residents of Buffalo live within their neighborhood and do not venture into the wider metropolitan area. They frequent their own neighborhood, the immediate workplaces, familiar centers, and recreational areas and know the main through routes in the city but not the intervening areas. Ethnicity in Buffalo is more than cultural differences; it is the identification of place with certain groups of people, but with ethnic churches losing population to nonethnic parishes, a trend since the Second World War.

NOTES

1. J. Percy, "The Niagara Link—The Niagara Region's Special Connection—Geography's Influence on History in Western New York and the Niagara Peninsula" (Buffalo, N.Y.: Western New York Heritage Institute, 1997), chap. 24.

2. Ibid.

3. P. Geddes, *Cities of Evolution* (1915; reprint, London: Williams & Norgate, 1949), pp. 14–15. The word *conurbation* later received general acceptance through its use by West Midland Group of Post-War Reconstruction and Planning, *Conurbation: A Planning Survey of Birmingham and the Black Country* (London: Architectural Press, 1948), p. 14.

4. J. W. Simmons and L. S. Burne, "Defining Urban Places: Differing Concepts of the Urban System," in *Systems of Cities: Readings in Structure, Growth and Policy*, ed. L. S. Burne and J. W. Simmons (New York: Oxford University Press, 1978), pp. 31–35. A change introduced in the mid-1980s to the U.S. Census definition makes Buffalo, Niagara Falls, and their respective counties more autonomous than previously.

5. Census data is used for these comparisons, but direct comparisons must be treated with caution as dates, definitions, and the administrative structure vary as the boundary is crossed. As the Canadian Frontier has "overbound" and the American Frontier "underbound" units, Canadian centers have developed suburbs within their municipal jurisdictions, whereas on the American Frontier this external form of urban growth is typically into adjacent municipalities.

6. W. Zelinsky, "An Approach to the Religious Geography of the United States; Patterns of Church Membership in 1952," *Annals of the Association of American Geographers* 51 (1961): 156, 170. D. W. Johnson et al., *Churches and Church Membership in the United States: An Enumeration by Region, State and County* (Washington, D.C.: Glenmary Research Centre for the National Council of Churches, 1974), pp. 140, 142. See also U.S. Bureau of the Census and Manpower Administration, *Urban Atlas, Buffalo* (Washington, D.C.: U.S. Government Printing Office, 1974).

7. A select bibliography is K. T. Whittemore, "Buffalo," in *Geography of New York State,* ed. J. H. Thompson (Syracuse, N.Y.: Syracuse University Press, 1966), pp. 407–22 (Supplement, 1977); M. Goldman, *High Hopes: The Rise and Decline of Buffalo, New York* (Albany: State University of New York Press, 1983); and W. S. Dunn, ed., *History of Erie County, 1870–1970* (Buffalo, N.Y.: Buffalo and Erie County Historical Society, 1972). See also the publications by or through the Buffalo Chamber of Commerce (now Greater Buffalo Partnership), such as J. Bisco, *A Greater Look at Greater Buffalo* (Northridge, Calif.: Windsor Publications, 1986); and P. Nyhuis, *Niagara Attracting the World* (Montgomery, Ala.: Community Publications, 1997). Circumstances by the early 1960s are examined in H. W. Reynolds, ed., *Urban Characteristics of the Niagara Frontier: An Inventory* (Buffalo, N.Y.: Committee on Urban Studies, State University of New York at Buffalo, 1964).

8. J. B. Sheffer, *State of the Region: Performance Indicators for the Buffalo-Niagara Region* (Buffalo, N.Y.: Institute for Local Governance and Regional Growth, University at Buffalo, 1999), p. 10-1. *Moody's Municipal and Government Manual* (New York: Moody's Investors Service, 1980); published annually.

9. Planning and Development Department, *Some Information on the Niagara Region and Its Planning* (St. Catharines, Ont.: Regional Municipality of Niagara, 1978).

10. W. L. Archer, *Niagara Region: The Report of the Niagara Regional Study Review Commission, 1975–1977* (Toronto: Ontario Ministry of Treasury, Economics and Intergovernmental Affairs, 1977), pp. 14–15; and H. Kitchen, *Niagara Regional Review Commission: Report and Recommendations* (Toronto: Queen's Printer for Ontario, 1989).

11. Berkeley Consulting Group, *Niagara Governance Options*, Options Paper #2 (Markham, Ont.: Berkeley Consulting Group, 2000), pp. 7–13.

12. Berkeley Consulting Group, *Good Governance for the Future: Niagara Government Review—Final Review* (Markham, Ont.: Berkeley Consulting Group, 2000).

13. J. Hyman et al., "Government in Western New York," in *Urban Characteristics of the Niagara Frontier: An Inventory*, ed. H. W. Reymonds (Buffalo, N.Y.: State University of New York at Buffalo, 1964), pp. 53–75.

14. Sheffer, *State of the Region*, p. 4.

15. T. H. Reed and D. D. Reed, *The Niagara Falls Industrial Community: A Study in Government Relations* (Niagara Falls, N.Y.: Multigraphing Letter Service, 1953).

16. Sheffer, *State of the Region*, p. 10-9.

17. R. Banham, *Buffalo Architecture: A Guide* (Cambridge, Mass.: MIT Press, 1981) p. 7.

18. Ibid.

19. R. G. Smaberg, *Report of 1976 Ethnic Sample Census and Management Information Study of the City of Buffalo* (Buffalo, N.Y.: City of Buffalo, 1977), p. 67. See A. F. Yox, "Bonds of Community: Buffalo's German Element," *New York History* 66 (1985): 140–63. For the development of ethnicity, see D. A. Gerber, *The Making of an American Pluralism: Buffalo, New York, 1825–1860* (Chicago: University of Illinois Press, 1989); and S. Eberle, "Neighbors: The People of Erie County," in S. Eberle and J. A. Grande, *Second Looks: A Pictorial History of Buffalo and Erie County* (Norfolk: Donning Co., 1987), pp. 73–102. A major earlier presentation of the German community is *Geschicte der Deutschen in Buffalo und Erie County* (History of the Germans of Buffalo and Erie County) (Buffalo, N.Y.: Reinecke & Zesch, 1898).

20. D. Niedzwiecka, "The Poles of the Early East Side," *Niagara Frontier* 5 (1958–1959): 47–49; and C. L. Bucki, "The Polish Immigrant, Buffalo, and the Church," Buffalo and Erie County Historical Society Archives.

21. C. Buczkowski, "Seventy Years of the Pitass Dynasty," *Niagara Frontier* 24 (1977): 66–72.

22. S. Gredel, *People of Our City and Country*, Adventures in Western New York History, vol. 13 (Buffalo, N.Y.: Buffalo and Erie County Historical Society, 1971), p. 10.

23. V. Yans-McLaughlin, *Family and Community: Italian Immigrants in Buffalo, 1880–1930* (Ithaca, N.Y.: Cornell University Press, 1977). See also S. Adler, *From Ararat to Suburbia: The History of the Jewish Community of Buffalo* (Philadelphia: Jewish Publication Society of America, 1960).

24. M. Plesur, "The Jews of Buffalo," *Niagara Frontier* 3 (1957): 29–36; Adler and Connolly, *From Ararat to Suburbia*.

25. C. M. Barresi, "Racial Tensions in an Urban Neighborhood," *Growth and Change* 3 (1972): 16–22.

26. Sheffer, *State of the Region*, p. 274.

27. Goldman, *High Hopes*, pp. 196–223.

CHAPTER TEN

QUALITY AND DISGRACE IN THE REGIONAL ENVIRONMENT

The quality of the environment applies to its natural and human characteristics. Amenity includes anything that is pleasant, agreeable, or provides physical or material comfort. The opposite to this wealth, a word that originally combined "weal" (well-being) and "th," is "illth" (ill + th) or negative wealth defined as "anything which diminishes the usefulness of the earth to man. Thus smog, soil erosion, water pollution, the destruction of scenic places, and noise pollution might all be considered forms of illth."[1] These varied features of the environment are here discussed for the agricultural base, the adverse characteristics of severe pollution, the urban heritage, and the high qualities of the rural landscape.

THE AGRICULTURAL BASE

As the automobile and urban growth dispersed cities, former farmland was developed, agricultural acres held vacant in anticipation of development, and independent villages absorbed into the urban matrix.[2] St. Catharines has taken over once-rural Grantham Township, and the city of Niagara Falls both Stamford and Willoughby Townships. As places like Getzville, Swormville, Clarence Center, and Bowmansville on the fringe of Buffalo have been engulfed by urban developments, their historic centers now house fewer people than the adjacent subdivisions.

The land base under agriculture has declined. On the Canadian Frontier the

The Niagara Fruit Belt once extended across the Niagara River, but only remnants now survive on the American Frontier. **Left:** A farm fruit stand in New York State. **Below left:** a description of a farm in Clarence, New York, in 1909. (John N. Jackson [left], and *New Century Atlas: Erie County,* 1909 [below left])

CLARENCE

BODINE—The Maples—

Webster and Anna M. Bodine, owners. Postoffice address Clarence R. F. D. No. 1. It contains 53½ acres in lots 6 and 8 on Salt Road; with its nearest market at Buffalo. The soil is a rich sandy loam, producing the usual products grown in this section. The orchard contains a variety of small fruits, and the dairy supports eight graded Jerseys. The balance of the stock consists of four horses for ordinary work and three fine road horses. There are about 18 acres in oats, wheat, corn and potatoes, seven in timber, 28 in meadow and grazing land, and an excellent water supply from never-failing wells. The farm is appropriately named from the beautiful maples in front of the residence. The buildings are in good repair. Webster Bodine, farmer and station agent at East Clarence, branch of the N. Y. C. & H. R. R., was born December 6, 1888, and reared on his father's farm. He was appointed station agent June 18th, 1907, and has given entire satisfaction in this

period from 1941 to 1981 witnessed the removal from production of about 25 percent of the land under field crops, orchards, and market gardens, including almost 30 percent of the orchard acreage.[3] Change has continued. In the late 1980s, with the expected influx of cheaper American wines through the Free Trade Agreement, the grape acreage was reduced and the industry expanded through producing high-quality wines. The intensive livestock, mainly poultry, and greenhouse industries have risen to greater importance. The export of potted plants is mostly to supermarket chains in the United States.

On the American Frontier, by the 1990s farms no longer operated inland from the Lower Niagara River, once an important source of production.[4] Along the Upper Niagara River, only industry and extensive urbanization were evident. Low-density rural populations existed only in peripheral townships around the urbanized area, and agricultural land was more distant from the boundary than on the Canadian Frontier. The Buffalo-Niagara Falls metropolitan area had spread widely and loosely over its rural domain, losing some 30 percent of its farms and 22 percent of its acreage between 1977 and 1997. The urbanized area of Buffalo-Niagara Falls had expanded from 123 square miles (318.5 square kilometers) in 1950 to 286 square miles (740.7 square kilometers) by 1990, an increase of 133 percent.[5]

The early 1950s witnessed the last years of extensive commercial fruit production in Niagara County.[6] Markets reached by rail could not survive the more efficient growing, storage, and marketing of produce from larger new orchards in more southerly areas of the United States. Smaller quantities of fresh fruit were grown. Apples, important for commercial processing rather than to serve the fresh market, had to compete with production from the Hudson Valley for the New York City market, and apples from Washington State limited the distribution of Niagara apples in the rest of the country. Niagara County grapes could not compete effectively with the Finger Lakes area, Chautauqua County, or California.

Ontario's Niagara Peninsula is the center of Canadian grape and wine production and grows most of the nation's peaches and other tender fruits, including pears, apples, cherries, and apricots. The production of vegetables is also extensive, as is the area in greenhouses.[7] By 1996 in the Regional Municipality of Niagara 2,672 farms covered 93,010 hectares (229,832 acres). There were 1.1 million peach trees, followed by apples (365,648 trees), and then pears (246,661 trees). Plums and prunes, and sour cherries each had over 120,000 trees. The 253 greenhouse operations under glass and plastic produced primarily cut flowers with 1.3 million square meters (13.6 million square feet), and then cucumbers and tomatoes at one-fifth of this space. Vegetables, nursery stock, potted plants, and bedding plants were also produced in these units, which added significant new landscape features to the Canadian Frontier. Greenhouses, highly automated for temperature and soil conditions, were often initiated by Dutch entrepreneurs attracted by lower prices for land than in their home country.

Chapman (1994) has recognized three broad agricultural types:[8]

1. Fruit and grapes grown on farms with an average size of from 8–40 hectares (20–100 acres). Smaller than the grape farms, the farmers mostly own their own land. With imported seasonal labor, often from Jamaica, small farm size, and a minimal need for expensive equipment, many farmers are part-time operators. Marketing includes pick-your-own operations and fruit stands next to the road on individual farm lots.

2. Field crops, with a diverse array of crops that include grain and corn, occupy larger fields than in fruit farming. Low-intensity activities such as grazing and pasture systems, pork and poultry production, and intensive livestock operations are included.

3. Speciality crops that include a range of vegetable, soft fruits and berries, greenhouses, and nurseries. These are highly intensive uses on farms of relatively small size, with very skilled managerial requirements and imported labor for painstaking tasks such as pricking out seeds into small containers. The greenhouse industry, located mainly north of the Niagara Escarpment, takes advantage of the favored climate which reduces heating costs, the low value of the Canadian dollar, the less amenable continental climate which encourages exports to the south, and a border location with highway trans-portation facilities to move the product. With their higher land values, some greenhouses have displaced tender-fruit orchards, and some pressure exists to extend specialty greenhouses south of the Niagara Escarpment to help safeguard the Niagara Fruit Belt.

The loss of valuable agricultural land to low-density urban sprawl, one of the worst examples not just in Niagara but throughout North America,[9] was a major factor that spurred the formation of regional government in 1970.[10] The subsequent regional policy plan of 1973 recognized both the importance of agricultural land and the need to protect the best acres from urban encroachment. Each town was allocated a specific area in which to expand; beyond this, urban boundary land in the rural areas was reserved for agriculture.[11] This policy was hotly contested, with the outcome being the over-abundant provision of rural land for urban development. By the turn of the century regional and municipal policy, euphemistically called "Smart Growth," was to achieve more compact developments with high densities, less pavement, shorter pipes and mains, and less service maintenance.

On the American Frontier several studies have urged the preservation of fruit and veg-

The Niagara Fruit Belt, which grows most of the peaches, grapes, and other tender fruits produced in Canada, is subject to severe attrition as urban development advances across these fertile and productive acres. (John N. Jackson)

etable croplands south and southwest of the Buffalo areas,[12] and agricultural preservation districts in Erie and Niagara Counties have helped to slow urban spread. As authorities on both sides now see some necessity to preserve agricultural land, some hope exists that agriculture will remain an integral part of the Frontier landscape into the future.

All was doom and gloom on the Canadian Frontier when the North American Free Trade Agreement (NAFTA) was announced. It was anticipated that with the import of cheap wines from Europe and the United States, Ontario would no longer be a wine producer but, led by Inniskillin and then by Chateau des Charmes and by Hillebrand

Wines, the aim became to produce quality wines.[13] Over a period of six years 3,471.5 hectares (8,578 acres) of local domestic vines were removed, and vinifera and French hybrid vines using a smaller acreage were planted. Marketing was upgraded by the VQA (Vintners Quality Alliance) appellation for wines made wholly from Ontario grapes, a standard akin to French or German labels for superior wines. Ice wines harvested after the grapes had been allowed to freeze on the vine were added, with both VQA and ice wines winning major awards at Canadian, American, and European competitions.

The results have been dramatic. Sales of Ontario VQA Wines, including some from Point Pelee but mostly from Niagara, have risen by some 40 percent per year since 1989; Inniskillin's new vines were first planted in 1974. The number of small "cottage" wineries has increased from fifteen in 1989 to a still-expanding fifty in number ten years later. The production of ice wines has increased from some 8,000 half-bottle cases in 1993 to 30,000 cases by 1997. Brock University in St. Catharines, at the center of the wine region, has established a Cool Climate Oenology and Viticulture Institute which, coupled with research and in partnership with the local grape and wine industries, offers a four-year honors degree in vine growing and wine making.[14] Niagara College of Applied Arts and Technology has established vineyards on its campus east of St. Catharines and combines with Brock University to advance the skills of middle management in the tourism and hospitality industries.

Visits to wineries have expanded greatly, and restaurants added to the wineries hold special events such as gourmet dinners, vineyard barbecues, craft and art shows, tours with tastings, meetings with vintners, and fruit and wine evenings. These events represent a great turnaround and reorientation of the wine industry and provide substantial new links between the physical background of soils and climate, a major manufacturing industry, tourism, and local entrepreneurial initiatives.[15]

ENVIRONMENTAL DEGRADATION

With hydroelectricity aggravating the situation, chemical wastes from Niagara's manufacturing industries and domestic wastes from the towns have been dumped into the rivers, carried into the air, or buried in land that discharges to the natural drainage system (fig. 10.1). Fishing, once of prime importance in

the lakes and rivers at the Frontier, has declined drastically due to rising water temperatures, increasing pollution from industrial wastes, sewage, fertilizers, and overfishing.[16]

On the Canadian Frontier the canal valley next to downtown St. Catharines has been culverted to conceal unsightly and odorous waters, and the downstream lakeshore beaches at Port Dalhousie are often closed for swimming during the hot summer months due to high levels of coliform bacteria. When the Third Canal opened in 1887, the middle section of the Second Canal between Thorold and Port Dalhousie that retained its flow of water was used as an industrial waste disposal channel. The channel received mill wastes from the pulp and paper mills that lined its length and raw untreated sewage from the municipalities. Martindale Pond at Port Dalhousie became the receptacle for the solid deposits from 156 untreated sewage outlets, estimated as the equivalent from 450,000 people for sewage and waste combined.[17] When in 1903 this pond was used for the Royal Canadian Henley Rowing Regatta, the severity of pollution placed this international event in jeopardy and endangered Port Dalhousie's sandy beach, its recreational swimming, fishing in the lake, and the attraction of summer crowds to this resort. This pollution spread along the south shore of Lake Ontario

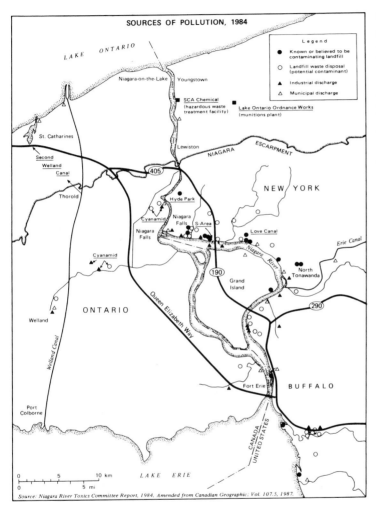

Fig. 10.1. Hydroelectricity introduced a range of manufacturing industry and added much urban growth to both sides of the Niagara Frontier. Their effluents and domestic wastes have in turn added serious pollution to the environment to the detriment of its air, water, and land resources. (Prepared by the Department of Geography, Brock University)

toward Rochester, with additional effluvia from the Niagara River.

Complaints about the disgraceful condition of the former Second Canal culminated in 1934, when municipal representatives forwarded their worries to the provincial Ministry of Health. An earlier solution—to drain the canal—had been suggested by the federal Department of Railways and Canals in 1929; a later proposal was that the channel might be filled and converted into a scenic highway. Remedial action came gradually, but never completely, as industries recognized that paper fiber in the canal represented an economic loss and installed "save-all" machinery.

Intercepting sewers and sewage treatment plants were also introduced, but these remedial actions did not materialize until after the Second World War. The first unit at Port Weller, which opened in 1951, was not followed by a more suitable secondary sewage plant at Port Dal-housie until some twenty years later. The canal, its industries, and its towns had left behind an unhappy legacy. Amenity and illth, both of profound importance to the community, were and still are unhappy bedfellows in a Frontier otherwise promoted for the high qualities of its urban life and for the attractive physical environments that provide the backdrop to urban development.

On the American Frontier by 1971, 870 million liters (230 million gallons) of water a day withdrawn from the Niagara River were returned through twenty-eight major industrial outfalls and thirteen municipal sewage outfalls.[18] The International Joint Commission then reported that Canadian waters in the Upper River "generally meet" their standards, but concentrations of coliform bacteria and phenols were excessive along the American bank of the Upper River and throughout the Lower River, and that objectionable discoloration was present close to the American discharge points.[19]

Severe pollution in the Buffalo River, by the 1950s a cesspool for receiving all types of industrial, municipal, and domestic wastes, was alleviated by the Buffalo River Improvement Project. Water pumped from Buffalo Harbor to various industries was used for cooling, diluting wastes, and augmenting low water flows. By 1972 enough oxygen was present to again support fish life. The Buffalo River, though still polluted, was then "no longer the oil covered, methane belching, stagnant pool that it was less than seven years ago."[20]

By 1978 only the Lower Niagara River, where Niagara Falls, New York, added industrial and municipal pollution to an already degraded river, was classified by the Great Lakes Quality Board as a problem area. Water-quality objectives had not been achieved because remedial programs were incomplete.[21] High levels of bacteria and phenols from sewage treatment plants in Lewiston and both cities of Niagara Falls and discharges into the Buffalo and Upper Niagara River were still present. The city upgraded its facilities to provide complete secondary waste-water treatment plus phosphorus removal, but this plant broke down within a year. Though eventually repaired, it was identified as having the worst discharge of toxins into the Niagara River.

A ghastly new landscape of fear and manmade folly emerged on the American Frontier with the Love Canal disaster of 1978.[22] Modern postwar homes and a school belonging to the Niagara Falls School Board in the LaSalle district of Niagara Falls, New York, were abandoned when the "impermeable" lining and clay cover of an aborted hydroelectric canal, used as a toxic chemical dump in the 1940s and 1950s, cracked open. Fumes, chemicals (mostly solvents), and pesticides, including lindane and deadly dioxin, leaked into the basements of suburban homes and the grade school. Over 50 percent of the children in the neighborhood were born with birth defects that included mental retardation, extra toes or fingers or fewer than normal, or an extra row of teeth; there were also rare blood diseases, epilepsy, asthma, and urinary problems.

After several official attempts to assure residents that no problem existed, and with an angry grassroots movement led by Lois Gibbs stressing the many health and genetic hazards, a federal state of emergency was eventually declared. Some 939 families were evacuated from the contaminated area, homes boarded up, the local school closed, and the area enclosed and isolated with a chainlink fence. By 1980 lawsuits had been filed against Occidental Chemical, successor to Hooker Chemical, the chemical company responsible for the dump, and the company in turn filed countersuits against the state, the city, and the school board.

Love Canal may be the tip of the iceberg. By 1984 the American Frontier had a large number of hazardous dump sites, including Hyde Park, S-Area, sixty-eight industrial disposal areas in Niagara Falls, as well as a county site used by several major industries. Also, a federal munitions site east of Lewiston known as the Lake Ontario Ordnance Works was used as a dump for radioactive wastes from the Manhattan Project, which produced the atomic bombs dropped on Hiroshima and Nagasaki in Japan at the end of the Second World War.[23] "The Niagara River is in

Residents of the Love Canal area in Niagara Falls, New York, were obliged to abandon their homes in a modern subdivision after buried toxic wastes percolated to the surface and caused severe health problems. (John N. Jackson)

crisis. . . . Within a 4.5-kilometer (2.8-mile) belt of land in New York State adjoining the Niagara River, there are 164 hazardous waste disposal sites."[24] The American Frontier had gained an unenviable reputation as one of the most environmentally contaminated areas in North America, and seepage from there into the Niagara River had severe repercussions for the Canadian Frontier, one being that Niagara-on-the-Lake no longer takes water from the river but is supplied from the Welland Canal via a reservoir at DeCew Falls.

Growing public concerns over the disposal of toxic wastes were manifest in a 1980 controversy over whether a chemical disposal company in the Town of Porter, New York, should be allowed to build a pipeline to discharge large volumes of treated chemical waste into the Niagara River upstream from the municipal water intakes of Niagara-on-the-Lake, Ontario. People were concerned whether the "cleaned" wastes would be harmless or cause further deterioration in water quality. And for her leadership and actions against the flow of toxic chemicals into the Niagara River, Margherita Howe of Niagara-on-the-Lake was awarded the Order of Canada in 1983 as the citizen largely responsible for the unprecedented agreement signed between the two countries to prevent this environmental abuse.

On the Canadian Frontier controversy was generated in the 1980s with the selection of a major site by the Ontario Waste Management Corporation for the disposal of hazardous industrial wastes.[25] The site proposed in Niagara Falls, Ontario, was rejected strongly by that city as completely incongruous and incompatible with a tourist-oriented locality; as the major growled, "What, a waste disposal site next to the world-famous Falls!" When a site in an agricultural area of West Lincoln was selected, strong objections arose from residents, farmers, and those living on the truck route to the site. An inquiry, which began conducting hearings in 1990 to resolve the conflict, was prolonged and eventually unsuccessful.

When stream and lake quality were assessed in 1999, "the majority of Western New York lakes, rivers, creeks, reservoirs and other water resources are considered sufficiently degraded to interfere with uses. . . . Common waterbody uses impaired or stressed throughout the region were fishing, fish consumption and propagation, bathing, and water supply . . . fish consumption advisories were given for . . . lakes in Erie and Niagara Counties, Lake Erie, and Lake Ontario."[26] Since the 1989–1990 season, Eighteen Mile Creek, the Barge Canal, and Buffalo's Delaware Park Lake had been added to the advisories list and, with regard to hazardous waste sites, the American Frontier "had 82 class 2 hazardous waste sites."[27]

The Frontier, with its historical background of heavy industry, has a considerable and unwelcome heritage of illth sites. The big question on both sides, in addition to the remedial measures that are required to redeem past mistakes, has become, where and how does an industrial society dispose of its wastes without frightening consequences to amenity, the health of the local population, and the quality of the tourist industry? The Niagara River and its catchment area in both countries has become a major problem at the global level of attention, with NIMBY (Not In My Back Yard) becoming an argument by the populace against *any* local site along either the river or inland.

A CONTINUING ROLE FOR ENVIRONMENTAL CONSERVATION

With the many thousands of Canadian and American dollars that have been spent on cleanup operations, it is easy to become complacent.[28] Pollution may not always be so obviously bad as in the past, but considerable dangers and the need for effective management policies remain. Air quality across the boundary presents the interesting fact that both sides blame the other in their weather and news reports. It all depends on the season and the way the wind is blowing, into Canada from the midwestern United States or into the United States (and the eastern Niagara Peninsula) from industries in Southern Ontario. Either way, major polluting factors include the exhaust emissions from road transport, coupled with fumes from industrial and energy production and domestic premises. Centers on both sides of the boundary record smog or fog, moderate to poor air-quality conditions for several days each year, and the occasional poor air-quality advisory warnings.

Water pollution still exists. The Second Welland Canal carries effluent from paper mills in Thorold. The waters of Lake Erie are not free of algae, but the warnings of the 1960s and 1970s that the lake was dying are no longer valid and certain species of fish such as muskie and pike are making a comeback here and in the Upper Niagara River. Along the shoreline of Lake Ontario sewage treatment and pollution controls have reduced the levels of raw human and industrial waste that once polluted the beaches, but recreational swimming throughout the summer months is often denied by closing the beach areas, the stench from rotting algae creates a severe deterrent to their passive recreational use, and after heavy rain sewage plants overflow to dump raw sewage into Lake Ontario.

The eggs laid by a colony of herring gulls on an island in the Niagara River above the Falls have become less contaminated with chemicals, and the fear that the entire species will vanish has gone as the colony is now flourishing. Residents have returned to the Love Canal disaster area, and passengers on the *Maid of the Mist* no longer float through a puree of brown froth and chemical spray. Even so, many concerns remain. The poisons stored in old dump sites along the American side of the Niagara River have mostly *not* been removed from their sites which have been capped and contained to prevent new poisonous additions and leakages. The sites remain fractured, further leaks are possible, and the designed life for the new structures is less than the period required for the chemicals to degrade into harmless residues.

A report by Regional Niagara has noted that although Lake Erie was cleaner by 2000 than it has been for fifty years, toxic chemicals that remain in the water and the sediments continue to affect fish and wildlife. Both "governments continue to advise the public to restrict consumption of fish and wildlife due to contamination by persistent toxic chemicals."[29] The same authority notes that in the streams and rivers that drain the Niagara Peninsula, except for Twelve Mile Creek from sand deposits in the Fonthill Kame, "water quality . . . is generally poor exhibiting high levels of phosphorus, suspended solids, and bacteria. . . . The poor water quality has resulted in significant degradation of fish populations and other aquatic life."[30]

Due to the outbreak in 2000 at Walkerton in Southern Ontario of E. coli bacteria in the town's water supply that caused hundreds of people in the area to become ill and several to die, great concern has arisen in the rural localities of the Canadian Niagara Frontier that depend on wells and groundwater for their domestic water supply needs. This resource is not mapped, and wells are not generally monitored on a regular basis as pollution is not anticipated. Furthermore, landfill sites in Niagara Falls and South St. Catharines have been described as "a string of environmental cancers slowly poisoning the delicate beauty of the Niagara Escarpment."[31] As landfill settles and slowly decomposes, its leachables may sooner or later leak out to pollute the underlying soils, groundwater springs, and wells.

On the Canadian side of the boundary, since 1995 the provincial government has changed, reduced, or not enforced standards for water purification and testing and the municipal and industrial discharge of pollutants into waterways. Budgets and staff at the province's Ministry of the Environment have been reduced considerably. Protection agencies such as the Niagara Escarpment Commission have received severe budget and staff cuts, which have limited their actions and placed their land-use controls more in the hands of development than conservation interests. The activities of the Niagara Peninsula Conservation Authority have likewise been curtailed and its influence limited by provincial political strategies, and the amenity arguments of the Niagara Parks Commission to protect landscape around the Falls have received less attention than the municipal promotion of expansion and development.

The threat exists that further upstream diversions of water from the Niagara River will take place, either to the water-hungry United States or to be sold to other countries. In 1999 an Ontario company known as the Nova Group gained permission from the Ontario Ministry of Environment to extract 600 million liters (27,276.5 million gallons) of water from Lake Superior for shipping to Asia. The serious threat to downstream activities, including shipping lanes, tourism at the Falls, municipal and industrial water supplies, and the like, was insufficient to deny

the sale. The sale abroad of water, the lifeblood of the Canadian environment, had official approval. Only after an enraged public outcry and the focus of national attention on this matter was the permit revoked by the Minister of the Environment. The threat of further requests remains, with the people of Canada as a potential exporter of water being more concerned than American interests as potential importers.

Environmental protection remains an important need for the health of everyone as the process of urbanization continues to advance at Niagara. As the Canadian regional municipality has stated, sustainable development "means ensuring that, in meeting our needs, we do not deplete nature's capital or degrade its life support systems. It means ensuring that the environmental legacy that we pass on to our children is as good as, or better than, the one that we inherited."[32] The issues are of increasing local and national concern, with environmental groups such as Greenpeace, the Council of Canadians, and the Sierra Club, among others, adding their weight of argument to those of local civilian pressure groups. Nor has trust in government been assisted by Toronto's desire to export its garbage by rail through numerous communities to the deep hole of an abandoned and fractured mine at Kirkland Lake in Northern

Ontario or to the rejection of an American site in Michigan which would use the heavily trafficked Highway 401 corridor and pass through communities like Sarnia en route.

THE URBAN HERITAGE

As landscape at the Frontier has emerged and changed through a series of phases and technological periods, every place has a substantial heritage from its roots through named achievements up to the present. Modern character at the Frontier is an accumulation over time. The past cannot be changed, the present is the starting point for the future, and how we use, save, or amend what has survived from the past has become our responsibility.

All communities on both Frontiers have lost much of their built heritage. In 1992 the St. Catharines Local Architectural Conservation Advisory Committee (LACAC) concluded: "Unhappily, St. Catharines has lost many architectural clues to its special identity as a hometown: The Carnegie Library, St. Joseph's Convent, the Wright House, the May-Clark-Seiler House, and the Niagara Jail are only the most recent of our losses. We are all the poorer for their demise."[33] And Banham, in 1981 writing about Buffalo,

stated: "Like other cities, Buffalo has lost a disquieting number of important buildings. Some were casualties of economic and social change, some of changes in architectural fashions, and others of our pragmatic penchant for measuring progress and quality of life almost completely by standards of utility and modernity."[34]

Only a few sites have been recognized by landmark designation. The Canadian Frontier has provincial plaques, national historic sites, and markers,[35] a system supervised by the Ontario Heritage Foundation, an agency within the provincial Ministry of Culture and Recreation. Most cities also have a municipal LACAC to advise councils about the merits of buildings and to indicate those suitable to be marked with a designation plaque. These committees often publish their findings and prepare detailed brochures for residents and visitors who wish to explore the city's architecture, traditions, and history on foot or by car.

The American Frontier likewise has its designated National Historic Sites and some buildings are listed in the National Register of Historic Places, the two highest categories. There are also National Historic Districts, and other landmarks have been listed by the Buffalo Landmark and Preservation Board. By 1986 Buffalo had seven designated historic preservation districts and sixty landmark

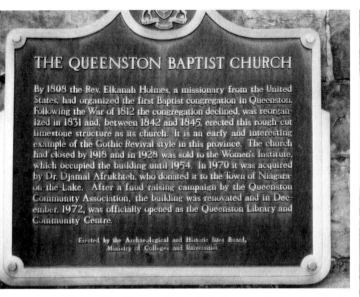

THE QUEENSTON BAPTIST CHURCH

By 1808 the Rev. Elkanah Holmes, a missionary from the United States, had organized the first Baptist congregation in Queenston. Following the War of 1812 the congregation declined, was reorganized in 1831 and, between 1842 and 1845, erected this rough-cut limestone structure as its church. It is an early and interesting example of the Gothic Revival style in this province. The church had closed by 1918 and in 1928 was sold to the Women's Institute, which occupied the building until 1954. In 1970 it was acquired by Dr. Djamal Afrukhteh, who donated it to the Town of Niagara-on-the-Lake. After a fund-raising campaign by the Queenston Community Association, the building was renovated and in December, 1972, was officially opened as the Queenston Library and Community Centre.

Erected by the Archaeological and Historic Sites Board,
Ministry of Colleges and Universities

Plaques identify many, but not all, features of interest on both sides at the Frontier. (John N. Jackson)

BERGHOLZ

GERMAN LUTHERAN SETTLEMENT

FOUNDED OCT. 12. 1843

THIS SITE OF
HOLY GHOST CHURCH AND
6 ACRES IN VILLAGE CENTER
DONATED BY
HON. WASHINGTON HUNT

PRESENTED BY
WHEATFIELD BICENTENNIAL COM.
1976

buildings,[36] but many were endangered because the city was now less prosperous, the costs of preservation were high, and federal grants were less available. The preservation districts of Allentown, Delaware, Linwood, the Joseph Ellicott Theatre District, and West Park were near neighbors along or close to Delaware Avenue, and other preservation districts covered the Olmsted parks. The economy is changing, yet a high regard remains for the city's cultural amenities, its rich architectural-historical heritage, and their strong appeal for tourists and residents.

The industrial heritage is usually neglected. Both Frontiers offer scope for industrial tours presenting the major industrial characteristics of their environments in terms of their employment history, the industries that have located on that site, and the products that have been produced. Of the once ubiquitous water-powered mills, only a few have survived at the Frontier. They include the Welland Mills in Thorold (**top right**), and the Canada Hair Cloth Mill (**bottom right**) next to the center of St. Catharines. Both mills were served by raceways from the Second Welland Canal, and both provide genuine reminders of how the early canals influenced and shaped the communities that grew along the waterways. (John N. Jackson [both])

On both Frontiers many public and private groups identify major features with plaques and signs. An example is the large number of designations introduced along the Niagara River Parkway by the Niagara Parks Commission. Together with signs authorized by government, all signs of identification help to achieve historical recognition and understanding for the feature that is presented. Signage provides credibility for place and helps to make the building or function being presented better known. It helps private citizens, councillors, and officials to recognize, preserve, and enhance the resource that has been identified as an integral part of that community.

But designation and signing do not prevent damage or loss. They are not complete or comprehensive, and they do not prevent either the private or the public property owner from altering or selling the property. On both

Frontiers the preservation laws are weak and the rights of property owners to do as they wish with their property, subject only to minimum safeguards, are strong. Heritage is viewed by some groups as a deterrent to development and progress. The material loss of important historical buildings and sites, including major architecture, has been high. It is rare for a developer to be stopped by history, slowed down perhaps, and maybe required to amend his plans. This attitude of disrespect could slowly be changing, in part through the publicity given to regrettable losses, in part through the commercial success of many restored buildings, and in part through an increasing realization that older buildings and historic districts are important components in the character and landscape of modern cities.

The push for preservation is usually through a small handful of dedicated volunteers under the leadership of some inspired individual and may not enjoy the active support of the local council. The movement is generally initiated when some local landmark is threatened, often too late as the endangered building may occupy a site that is no longer required, be of unsound structure, require considerable upgrading to meet modern standards, present a fire hazard, or lack suitable access or parking space. There may be conflict between civic pride and the development

process, legislative tools are weak, and it is often a David-Goliath process with a few active members of the public against the entrenched attitudes, power, authority, and financial strengths of government.

Neither conservation, preservation, heritage, nor the pursuit of amenity are easy processes to pursue. On the Canadian Frontier the Ontario Heritage Act can only defer for up to 180 days the demolition of a heritage building, and this in turn requires political support and the necessity to raise the required funding for the works necessary to safeguard the building or site. The process is slow, uncertain of success, and all too often buildings are demolished or placed on sale before the community knows about this decision. In 1995 the Ontario government canceled the program that offered matching grants to the owners of designated properties. Revisions to the Heritage Act, under review for several years, are not matters of high priority or the political agenda, and on the American Frontier less than 10 percent of municipalities have adopted historic preservation ordinances.

The dilemma of need versus opportunity is clearly expressed by Willowbank in Queenston, a 1,200-square-meter (3,937-square-foot) two-story mansion of 1834, considered one of the finest examples of colonial

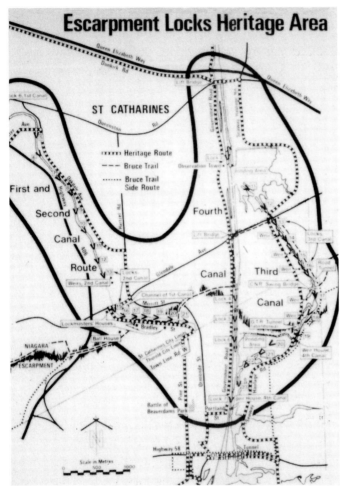

The historic canals have been viewed as a heritage resource through many postwar reports by consultants and government departments. Where the former canals and the modern Fourth Canal crossed the Niagara Escarpment has in particular been viewed for this potential. (Parks Canada, Ontario Ministry of Culture and Recreation, and Ontario Ministry of Natural Resources, 1980)

architecture not only in Canada but in North America, and recognized for this importance with a provincial historic plaque.[37] The estate covers 4.8 hectares (11.9 acres) of landscaped grounds with original roadside stone walls, gate, and grass-covered carriage track up to the house. The building, externally unchanged, has been used as a convent and as a school for boys with learning disabilities. Possible recent commercial uses as an estate winery and as a conference center have been contested by either the town council or the Niagara Parks Commission over concerns that traffic congestion on the Niagara River Parkway would be increased. Its use as an office complex by this commission has been proposed but rejected.

In 1999 over half of the estate was sold to a Toronto developer with plans to construct at least six homes on lots next to the mansion. In 2000 the proposal was for a twenty-three-room country inn with ten guest rooms in the mansion and thirteen in a building to be constructed nearby, and with a parking lot and swimming pool. The local community organization wishes to conserve the building and the estate but exclude the adjacent buildings and these other activities, but it does not have the funds or expects to be able to raise the money to preserve the estate. The Ontario Heritage Federation would probably be willing to maintain the estate, but only if it were donated to the people of Ontario. As the government of Ontario has priorities other than the purchase of historical properties, the future is likely to be decided by developers rather than by the public conscience.

Such uncertainties of action become more serious because heritage is mostly viewed as saving certain structures and to a lesser extent particular streets and selected areas, yet almost all inner-city areas prior to the First World War are in the heritage category. They contain the point of origin and the reasons for the emergence of that central place, and the buildings reflect the changing forces and functions that have operated on that environment over time. But heritage is also a cultural attribute. With the exception of Black History Tours, very few are the tours and pamphlets that introduce the contributions to urban life made by each ethnic group, their leading personalities, their important buildings, and that group's contributions to the arts, sports, and recreation, among others. As manufacturing industry has played such a

substantial role in the evolution of the Frontier's landscape, industrial tours might also receive much greater recognition; an example is that guides for the inland city of Hamilton include not only present and former industrial sites, but also working conditions in factories, buildings used for service activities, change in the types of machinery, workers' suburbs, and the development and contributions of trade unions.[38]

There could also be far greater appreciation of the diverse physical background and the human response to the differences in vegetation, relief, and drainage that have so influenced agriculture, transportation, the settlement pattern, hydroelectricity, and certain industrial developments. There could be a number of traverses that emphasize natural features along both sides of the Niagara River, inland across the Niagara Peninsula from Lake Ontario to Lake Erie, and across the American Frontier from Lake Ontario to the plateau area south of Buffalo.

Everything is potentially of interest. The Falls, the gorge, and the precincts of the Niagara River are undeniably of exceptional importance as tourist locales, but the total regional scene and how it has evolved are also of substantial interest. The environment for all who live and work there or visit is a vast repository of history that identifies the past and has become the unchangeable basis for the future. It is a landscape that has been constructed, changed, manufactured, and designed wholly by man. It has resulted from social, economic, religious, and technological determinants, of which some have been lost and others are relicts in that the human process of development and achievement has ended at some time in the past, but the memory remains and has become a continuing part of the modern Frontier landscape.

THE RURAL LANDSCAPE

The pioneer survey grid imposed over the landscape of the Canadian Frontier a regular, even-sized pattern of lots and concessions bounded by straight roads that remain clearly visible over rural areas with farm buildings on their original lots. This pattern was perpetuated when farmsteads were located close to these long straight roads and at right angles to the preexisting roads.[39] The track up to the farm from the road was at right angles to the road, and the front door of the house faced the road. The farm's outbuildings were then grouped in rectilinear fashion around the farm buildings, again at right angles to the road to provide a strong visual grouping that mostly survives to this day. The same lin-

earity applies when the lot and road frontages were divided into smaller units for perhaps a new farm, a store, a church or chapel, a cemetery, a firehall, a rural school, or a residential building (fig. 10.2). An exception to this persistent regular pattern of roads and buildings occurs in the Short Hills area south of St. Catharines where relief prevailed as a dominant factor. The grid pattern of straight roads is also discontinuous across the Wainfleet Marsh west of Post Colborne.

A second component, clearing the land of its forest cover, was never completely achieved.[40] Remnant forest areas, woodlots, lines of trees, isolated clusters, and individual trees survive to provide some 10 percent of the rural landscape on the Canadian Frontier. These areas include land along the Niagara Escarpment and its steep-sided reentrant valleys to the north, the Short Hills area between St. Catharines and Fonthill, Point Abino on the Lake Erie shoreline, and many woodlots in the southeast of the Niagara Peninsula where some reforestation has also allowed abandoned agricultural land to return to forest.

Most of the windbreaks around farm buildings, in fencerows along rural roads, and in hedgerows around the subdivided fields have been planted by the landowners, sometimes with government grants to plant trees

AN EXAMPLE OF LAND SUBDIVISION IN REGIONAL NIAGARA

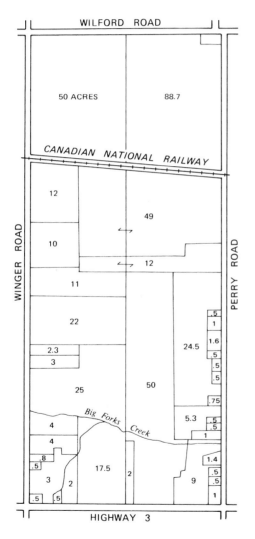

Fig. 10.2. The landscape, created in a regular pattern out of the forest cover to provide agricultural lots for pioneer settlers, has been divided and then subdivided again and again into smaller and smaller lots of varying shape and size as the land was parceled out to the next purchaser. (Prepared by the Department of Geography, Brock University)

on their properties to help restore a former forested landscape, but more often to meet individual requirements such as protection from wind or snow, to supply maple syrup, or to beautify properties with exotic rather than native trees.

Much of this former roadside planting has disappeared. With the automobile, the requirements of road construction with increased pavement widths and roadside drainage channels caused the loss of many trees. Trees were also placed farther away from the road. The advance of overhead wires and underground utility services caused further losses, as have salt damage and the natural factors of old age, floods, and windstorms to the older plantings.

The abundance of trees and woodland areas adds the significant three-dimensional, vertical component of height to the rural landscape. In addition, the Canadian Niagara Frontier is part of the Carolinian life zone and therefore "home to many species typical of areas further to the south. . . . It is one of the richest ecosystems in Canada, supporting an unusual variety of plant and animal life: 2,200 plant species, nearly 400 species of birds, and 47 species of reptiles and amphibians."[41] This abundance is also a resource in jeopardy. As Environment Canada concluded in 1996, "existing upland forest and vegetation cover along streams fell well short of what would be required for a healthy natural environment."[42] The deficiencies included inadequate habitat requirements for wildlife dependent on a forest environment, and the need to protect living conditions for fish and other aquatic life in streams and rivers including those used for sports fishing.

Further distinctive rural components are the photogenic barns used for storing grain, hay, and other farm products; for sheltering livestock; and sometimes as a communal center for local social events. In addition to ground-floor activities, a ramped approach may lead to a second internal storage area through a large opening. Often with vertical wood siding and a stone base, the square or rectangular bulk of height and width of the barn with a hipped gable roof, frequently surmounted by a cupola to provide light and ventiliation, embellishes the rural landscape with its distinctive architecture. Later, round silos, reflecting increased livestock production, may have added a further dominant and constrasting dimension of shape, height, color, and constructon materials other than wood to the changing rural backdrop.

New farming practices have continually changed the rural landscape. Horses and fields of hay were replaced by the tractor and power-driven machinery. Other changes have been brought about by the arrival of railways, the advent of rural power grids, and the use of the farm truck. Farm machinery has been steadily mechanized and improved. Engines have been attached to saws and water pumps; milking machines have replaced the hand milking of cows. Animals and crops have changed remarkably since the first clearance of forested lands.[43] As settlements grew, grain and livestock farming predominated. This changed after the 1870s when fruit and grapes increased in importance and as the railways promoted wheat production on the prairies. Apples, the most important fruit crop in the 1880s, had been replaced by peaches by the early 1900s. Grape production also spread rapidly after the 1880s. The geographical extent of agricultural land uses, greatest in 1911, declined as did the number of farms and the acreage under field crops and fruit trees, while the grape and wine industries expanded.

The rich diversity of the modern rural farming landscape is expressed through the tours organized annually by the Niagara Foundation of Agriculture.[44] These have included visits to vineyards and their associated wineries; to peach and apple orchards; to sheep, pig, poultry, goat, deer, emu, quail, ostrich, and dairy farms; and to various types of greenhouses. Open houses have been held to view the processing of specialty preserves from Niagara ingredients; a farm that demonstrated environmental initiatives to protect water quality, conserve soil, and preserve natural habitats; a reinstated water-powered gristmill with original machinery that produced stone-ground flour and cornmeal; a breeder of Egyptian Arabian horses; the production of culinary, medicinal, aromatic, and decorative herbs; a nut farm; and a farm with high-bush cultivated blueberries. This broad-ranging ensemble demonstrates the challenging yet changing nature of local agricultural patterns.

The rural landscape is a personalized one that may reflect the names of early pioneer settlers and their varied social, ethnic, and religious groupings.[45] The first to arrive, the United Empire Loyalists gave their name to many features in the landscape: to waterfalls (Ball's Falls), to small harbors (Port Davidson on the Welland River), to creeks (Lyons Creek), to the headlands on Lake Erie (Morgan's Point), to roads (Lundy's Lane), to "Corners" where two roads met and crossed (Shipman's Corner, which became St. Catharines), to small village settlements (Beamsville), and to mills (Burch's Mills, the first Canadian mill to use the waterpower of the Niagara River at the Falls). Roads, as in former Willoughby and Bertie townships, that are named after Willick, Weaver (Weber), Miller (Müller), Detenbeck, Bossert, and Sherk recall the early occupation of the land by German-speaking groups.

Almost every type of urban nonfarm activity has intruded upon the rural environment. The routes of railway track and their accompanying stations were followed by the hydroelectric lines of different power companies and by a network of overhead telephone wires and services that steadily removed the former social isolation of the countryside. The motor vehicle added the linear spread of urban residential and other activities along main and subsidiary rural roads, so that former gravel and earth roads became urban streets, and the former distinctions between "urban" and "rural" have become blurred. There is now an "urban fringe," a locality that lies within the "urban shadow" of higher than rural land values and which some authorities describe as "rurban," combining "rural" and "urban" into one graphic word.

However described, the surviving rural landscape contributes steadily to tourism through the visual character of its extensive production, and the ever-changing patterns through the seasons of different field, farming, and activity patterns. There are the ever-present attractions of rows of vines, the fruit trees in blossom, the patterns of wood-lots and fields, the grouping and spacing across the landscape of farm buildings, the farm-gate and pick-your-own purchase of fruit and vegetables, the barns and grazing animals, the nursery gardens, greenhouses, and the riding stables, which together with the varied physical landscape provide a rich variety of distinct and different experiences from spring blossoms to autumnal colors that bring tourists to the region, and residents out of the city through "runs-in-the-country" by automobile, bicycle and walking tours, eco-tours, and farm-visit programs.[46]

Areas of special attraction include the prominent forested landscape of the Niagara Escarpment. Now safeguarded by the Niagara Escarpment Commission established by the Ontario provincial government in the late 1960s to protect this linear physical and heritage resource from excessive quarrying and urban development,[47] and dedicated as a World Biosphere Reserve by UNESCO in 1990, this preserved rural landscape includes the earlier privately developed Bruce Trail system along the crest of the Niagara Escarpment. Other than the steady process of continuing urbanization has entered the decision-making process over rural concerns.

This new approach to the rural resource endowment also includes forested conservation areas in Willoughby Township, at St. John's in the Short Hills, the Short Hills Provincial Park, the Ball's Falls Conservation area, and a wetland area in the Wainfleet Marsh managed by the Niagara Peninsula Conservation Authority. On the American Frontier conservation areas include the old-growth forest of Reinstein Woods State Natural Preserve in Cheektowaga where lakes, wildlife, and marshes flourish in a metropolitan setting. A larger conservation area, the Beaver Meadow Nature Center, run by the Buffalo Audubon Society, uses a boardwalk to cross marshy areas. Buckhorn Island Park provides important nesting sites, and ducks and geese are an important aspect of the marine scene along the Upper Niagara River. State parks have been provided at Evangola, Four Mile Creek, Golden Hill, and Wilson-Tuscarora; another is named after Joseph Davis; and public open space has been reintroduced along the Niagara River and the surviving Erie Canal system.

Golf courses, public and private, must be added as a sporting provision for their valued extensive open space and as an expanding resource mostly on former agricultural land. Thirty-two public courses are listed in a 1998 regional directory for Canada's Niagara

Region,[48] and a few private clubs have to be added. All provide attractive areas of landscaped space and an open season from April through October, longer when the winter is mild. Most provide restaurants, club facilities, indoor sporting activities, and outdoor surfaced cart paths for summer and winter use. The Canadian season is longer than on the American Frontier, where there is a more limited availability and a lower landscaped quality for the public courses.

Some eighteen new courses were in the early stages of development on the Canadian Frontier by the late 1990s, including courses designed with houses and community facilities for retirement and adult-style groups. The Niagara Parks Commission is providing a major new international championship golf course next to the Niagara River Parkway in conjunction with a large hotel and historic recognition for the site where the Battle of Chippawa was fought during the War of 1812.

NOTES

1. O. P. Stankey, with J. L. Robinson, *The Anglo-American Realm*, 2d ed. (New York: McGraw-Hill, 1975), p. 8.

2. Farm data is covered in *Canadian Census of Agriculture*, Statistics Canada, and *Census of Agriculture*, American Census Bureau. Both report every five years, in years ending 1 or 6 in Canada, and 2 and 7 in the United States. Because the definition of a farm varies, Canadian and U.S. data are not directly comparable.

3. P. Chapman, "The Agricultural Industry," in J. N. Jackson, *The Niagara Region: Trends and Prospects*, Occasional Publication 4 (St. Catharines, Ont.: Department of Geography, Brock University, 1985), pp. 4–20. A Canadian study is K. B. Beesley and L. H. Russwurm, eds., *The Rural-Urban Fringe: Canadian Perspective*, Geographical Monographs no. 10 (Downsview, Ont.: Department of Geography, Atkinson College, York University, 1981).

4. Local History Committee, *The Town of Porter, 1776–1976: A Bicentennial History* (Porter, N.Y.: Historical Society of the Town of Porter, 1976).

5. J. B. Sheffer, *State of the Region: Performance Indicators for the Buffalo-Niagara Region* (Buffalo, N.Y.: Institute of Local Governance and Regional Growth, University at Buffalo, 1999), pp. 10.1–2.

6. Studies include U.S. Bureau of the Census and Manpower Administration, *Urban Atlas, Buffalo*, UA-SMSA 1280-1 (Washington, D.C.: Government Printing Office, 1974); J. F. Hart, "A Map of the Agricultural Implosion," *Proceedings, Association of American Geographers 2* (1970): 68–71; United States Department of Commerce, *1969 Census of Agriculture—County Data, Erie County, N.Y. and Niagara County, N.Y.* (Wash-

ington, D.C.: Government Printing Office, 1971); and J. P. Amato, "The Physical Environment Factor in the Analysis of Agricultural Land Use Patterns: A Case Study in Western New York" (Ph.D. diss., University of Toronto, 1976).

7. Fruit Belt studies include Canada Land Inventory, *Land Capability for Agriculture, Preliminary Report* (Ottawa: Lands Directorate, Environment Canada, 1976), pp. 8, 10; and W. Simpson-Lewis et al., *Canada's Special Resource Lands: A National Perspective of Selected Land Uses* (Ottawa: Lands Directorate, Environment Canada, 1974), map folio no. 4; D. Gierman, *Rural to Urban Land Conversion*, Occasional Paper no. 17 (Ottawa: Lands Directorate, Fisheries and Environment Canada, 1997); D. M. Gierman and J. Lenning, *Rural to Urban Land Conversions* (Ottawa: Lands Directorate, Environment Canada, 1980), map folio no. 5; W. K. Bond et al., *An Analysis of Government Programs on Canada's Fruitlands*, Annual Meeting, Canadian Association of Geographers, 1981, p. 5; and R. R. Krueger, "Urbanization of the Niagara Fruit Belt," *Canadian Geographer* 22 (1978): 188–89. The data in this paragraph is from *Agricultural Profile of Ontario* (Ottawa: Statistics Canada, 1997).

8. P. Chapman, "Agriculture in Niagara: An Overview," in *Niagara's Changing Landscapes*, ed. H. J. Gayler (Ottawa: Carleton University Press, 2000), pp. 282–83.

9. H. J. Gayler, "Planning for Our Future," *Downtowner* 16, no. 1 (2000): 25.

10. H. B. Mayo, *Report of the Commission: Nia-gara Region Local Government Review* (Toronto: Department of Municipal Affairs, 1966), p. 55.

11. Regional Municipality of Niagara, *Regional Niagara Policy Plan* (St. Catharines, Ont., 1973), pp. 3.2, 5.1, 6.2; and J. N. Jackson, "The Niagara Fruit Belt: The Ontario Municipal Board Decision of 1981," *Canadian Geographer* 26 (1982): 172–76. Provincial policy statements include Ontario Ministry of Food and Agriculture, *Food Land Guidelines: A Policy Statement of the Government of Ontario on Planning for Agriculture* (Toronto: Government of Ontario, 1978), pp. 4, 14. See also J. N. Jackson, "The Niagara Fruit Belt: A Resource in Jeopardy," *Contact: A Journal of Urban and Environmental Affairs* 9 (1977): 24–41.

12. See, for example, J. P. Amato et al., "Agricultural Land Use around an Expanding Urban Area: The Example of Erie County (Buffalo), N.Y.," Annual Meeting, Association of American Geographers, 1980; and "Area Plan Seeking to Halt Threats to Rural Balance," *Buffalo Courier Express*, 3 December 1979, p. 3.

13. The success of the Niagara wine industry has led to a plethora of publications, including *Wine Regions of Ontario* and *The Six Unforgettable Weekends of Summer: 1998 Calendar of Events*, funded by Agriculture and Agri-Food Canada, Canada's Adaptations and Rural Development Fund, and the Wine Council of Ontario (St. Catharines, Ont.). See T. Astler, *Vintage Canada: A Tasteful Companion to Canadian Wine* (Toronto: McGraw-Hill Ryerson, 1993); L. Bramble and S. Darling, *Discovering Ontario's Wine Country*

(Toronto: Stoddart, 1992); L. Ogryzlo, "Drink Locally, Act Globally," *Downtowner* 14, no. 4 (1998): 25–29; W. F. Rannie, *Wines of Ontario: An Industry Comes of Age* (Lincoln, Ont.: W. F. Rannie, 1978); J. Schreiner, *The World of Canadian Wine* (Vancouver, B.C.: Douglas and McIntyre, 1984); and D. J. P. Ziraldo, *Anatomy of a Winery: The Art of Wine at Inniskillin* (Toronto: Key Porter Books, 1995).

14. Niagara Economic and Tourist Corporation, *Fact Sheet P: Niagara's Agricultural and Horticultural Industry* (Thorold, Ont.: Niagara Economic and Tourist Corporation, July 1996). See also "Niagara at Work: A New Direction," *St. Catharines Standard*, 27 April 1998, pp. A6, A9, A12; and M. Boland, "One Cool Climate Institute," *Downtowner* 14, no. 4 (1988): 16–18.

15. Niagara Economic and Tourism Corporation, *Touring Niagara* (Thorold, Ont.: Niagara Economic and Tourist Corporation, 1998), lists twenty-seven wineries with on-site facilities and tours. See also Wine Council of Ontario, *Winery Tour Map* (St. Catharines, Ont.: Wine Council of Ontario, 1998); and H. J. Gayler, *Agritourism Developments in the Rural-Urban Fringe: The Challenges to Land Use and Policy Planning in the Niagara Region, Ontario*, paper presented at the International Rural Geography Symposium (Halifax-Truro, N.S.), July 1999.

16. H. C. Frick, *Economic Aspects of the Great Lakes Fisheries of Ontario* (Ottawa: Fisheries Research Board of Canada, 1965).

17. W. J. Bell and A. E. Berry, "Sanitary Situation in Sections of the Old Welland Canal," *Canadian Engineer* 68 (1935); and Gore and Storrie, consulting engineers, *Report on Disposal of Sewage and Industrial Wastes in Second Welland Canal Area* (Ottawa: Department of Transport, 1939).

18. Erie and Niagara Counties Regional Planning Board, *International Environmental Study: Environmental Enhancement of the Niagara River* (Buffalo, 1971), pp. iii–5.

19. Lakes Erie-Ontario Advisory Board to the International Joint Commission on Control of Pollution of Boundary Waters, *Summary Report on Pollution Abatement Progress in the Niagara River* (Ottawa and Washington, D.C.: International Joint Commission, 1971), pp. 1–2.

20. R. Q. Sweeney, "River on the Mend," *Limnos* 5 (1973): 13.

21. Great Lakes Water Quality Board, *Great Lakes Water Quality: Seventh Annual Report to the International Joint Commission* (Windsor, Ont., 1979), pp. 38–54. See also C. H. Chan, *Water Quality Surveys on the Niagara River, 1974* (Burlington, Ont.: Inland Waters Directorate, 1977). Standards are presented in R. N. McNeely et al., *Water Quality Sourcebook: A Guide to Water Quality Parameters* (Ottawa: Inland Waters Directorate, 1979), table 1B. Later studies include R. J. Allan, A. Mudrock, and M. Munawar, eds., "The Niagara River—Lake Ontario Pollution Problem," *Journal of Great Lakes Research* 9, no. 2 (1983): 109–340; and Niagara River Toxics Committee, *Report of the Niagara River Toxics Committee*

(Toronto: Niagara River Toxics Committee, 1984). The pollution of the Niagara River resulted in the expansion of the DeCew reservoir and water-control plant at DeCew south of the Niagara Escarpment in St. Catharines, and in the supply of water to communities, including Niagara-on-the-Lake, from these facilities.

22. L. M. Gibbs, *Love Canal: My Story* (Albany: State University of New York Press, 1982); W. L. T. Hang and J. P. Salvo, *The Ravaged River: Toxic Chemicals in the Niagara River* (New York: New York Public Interest Research Group, 1981); A. G. Levine, *Love Canal: Science, Politics and People* (Lexington, Mass.: Lexington Books, 1982); Saratoga Associates, *Final Generic Environmental Impact Statement for Love Canal Area Master Plan*, 3 vols. (Buffalo, N.Y.: Saratoga Associates, 1990); and R. P. Whalen, *Love Canal: Public Health Time Bomb* (Albany: State of New York Department of Health, 1978).

23. M. P. Zweig and G. M. Boyd, *The Federal Connection: A History of U.S. Military Involvement in the Toxic Contamination of the Love Canal and the Niagara Frontier Region* (Albany: New York State Assembly Task Force on Toxic Substances, 1981).

24. R. Malcomson, "Niagara in Crisis," *Canadian Geographic* 107, no. 5 (1987): 13.

25. The Ontario Waste Management Corporation, A Provincial Crown Agency, "is responsible for the development and implementation of a province-wide system for the treatment and disposal of liquid industrial and hazardous wastes"; see D. A. Chant, *Phase 3 Report Summary* (Toronto: Ontario Waste Management Corporation, 1984).

26. Sheffer, *State of the Region*, p. 2-3.

27. Ibid., p. 2-4.

28. D. Draper, "Water, Water Everywhere: Niagara's Cautionary Tale," and H. Tammemagi, "The Worth of Water," *Downtowner* 16, no. 3 (2000): 26–31.

29. Department of Planning and Development, *A Living Legacy: Towards an Environmental Conservation Strategy for Niagara* (Thorold, Ont.: Regional Municipality of Niagara, 2000), p. 11.

30. Ibid., p. 12.

31. H. Tammemagi, "Watching Our Wasteline," *Downtowner* 15, no. 5 (1999): 35.

32. Ibid., p. 5.

33. R. R. Taylor and the St. Catharines L.A.C.A.C., *Discovering St. Catharines' Heritage: The Old Town* (St. Catharines, Ont.: Vanwell Publishing, 1992), p. vii. For the loss of buildings, see also R. R. Taylor, *Touring St. Catharines in a REO circa 1910–1920* (St. Catharines, Ont.: St. Catharines Museum, 1992), p. 93. For Fort Erie, see A. M. Fox, "Our Built Heritage," in *Many Voices: A Collective History of Fort Erie*, ed. J. Davies and J. L. Felstead (Ridgeway, Ont.: Fort Erie Museum Board, 1996), p. 346. An American appreciation is N. F. Stafford, *Welcome to the Niagara Historic Trail*, Official Bicentennial Publication of Niagara County (North Tonawanda, N.Y.: Tonawanda News, 1976).

34. R. Banham, *Buffalo Architecture: A Guide* (Cambridge, Mass.: MIT Press, 1981).

35. Historical Heritage Branch, *Ontario Historic Sites, Museums, Galleries, and Plaques* (Toronto: Ministry of Culture and Recreation, various dates).

36. A. M. Fox, *Designated Landmarks of the Niagara Frontier* (Buffalo, N.Y.: Mayer Enterprises, 1986), pp. iv–v.

37. B. Burgess, "Queenston Residents Fear Estate Faces Ignoble Fate," *St. Catharines Standard*, 28 October 2000, pp. A1–2.

38. R. Kristofferson, *Made in Hamilton 19th Century Industrial Trail* and *Made in Hamilton 20th Century Industrial Trail* (Hamilton, Ont.: Made in Hamilton Heritage Project, 2000).

39. O. R. Scott, "The Rural Landscape of Southern Ontario," in *Agriculture and Farm Life in the Niagara Peninsula*, ed. J. Burtniak and W. B. Turner, Proceedings Fifth Annual Niagara Peninsula History Conference, Brock University (St. Catharines, Ont.), 1983, pp. 23–36.

40. M. R. Moss, "Forests in the Niagara Landscape: Ecology and Management," in H. J. Gayler, *Niagara's Changing Landscapes* (Ottawa: Carleton University Press, 1994), pp. 139–75.

41. Planning and Development Department, *A Living Legacy: Towards an Environmental Conservation Strategy for Niagara*, Publication 95–2 (Thorold, Ont.: Regional Municipality of Niagara, 2000), pp. 17–18.

42. S. Holland-Hibbert et al., *Evaluation of Upland Habitat in the Niagara River Area of Concern* (Burlington, Ont.: Centre for Inland Waters, Environment Canada, 1996), in ibid., p. 20.

43. P. Chapman, "Agriculture in Niagara: An Overview," pp. 282–83.

44. Sixteen farms were included in Niagara North Federation of Agriculture, *Rural Routes: An Agricultural Adventure* (St. Catharines, Ont.: Niagara North Federation of Agriculture, 2000).

45. J. N. Jackson, *Names across Niagara* (St. Catharines, Ont.: Vanwell Publishing, 1984).

46. This rural implosion of its historical context and regional setting is covered by H. J. Gayler, "Urban Development and Planning in Niagara," in H. J. Gayler, *Niagara's Changing Landscapes*, pp. 241–77.

47. Preliminary proposals in 1967 led to, L. O. Gertler, *Niagara Escarpment Study: Conservation and Recreation Report* (Toronto: Niagara Escarpment Study Group, Regional Development Branch, Treasury Department—Finance and Economics, 1968). The Escarpment Plan was approved in 1985 and then revised as the result of a review initiated in 1990. A later assessment is *The Niagara Escarpment Plan* (Toronto: Environmental Planning and Analysis Branch, Ministry of Environment and Energy, 1993).

48. Niagara Economic and Tourism Corporation, *Niagara Region Golf Courses 1998* (Thorold, Ont.: Niagara Economic and Tourism Corporation, 1998).

CHAPTER ELEVEN

THE EXPANDING TOURIST INDUSTRY

The tourist industry with deep roots at the Falls has expanded since the 1950s as a major economic opportunity and as a landscape feature on both Frontiers. Its wide-ranging ramifications extend from highway travel to overnight accommodation in hotels, motels, and caravan and camp sites. The industry includes retail expenditures in restaurants and stores, on entertainment, and at special events, festivals, and sport and recreational facilities. Underlain by the qualities of both the physical and the historical-architectural backgrounds and by the new mobility provided by the motor vehicle and the airplane, tourism in every municipality has become an intense promotional activity. The primary concern, attracting visitors in competition with other locales at home and abroad, has become a major part of the local and regional economies at Niagara. A range of travel and tourist features are introduced in this chapter: travel for shopping, recreation, and entertainment across the Niagara River; Buffalo as a tourist destination; marine facilities; former religious resorts; and the tourist character of the small towns on the banks of the Lower Niagara River. Themes at the Falls and their vicinity follow in the next chapter.

TRAVEL ACROSS THE NIAGARA RIVER

Bridge traffic includes an outward two-way weekday movement to work in the other country. Residents on both sides of the boundary live in one country but work across the river. The number and proportion of these regular transboundary travelers diminish by distance inland from the boundary, with the prime commuter links being between Fort Erie and Buffalo and the two cities of Niagara Falls.

The boundary, easily crossed for recreational and social journeys, enriches life at the Frontier considerably as the facilities of the other nation are now easily accessible to the residents of the other side, and most tourist attractions, recreational facilities, and cultural events enjoy support from the other side of the Niagara River.[1] Examples include these festivals and parades on the Canadian Frontier that regularly include American groups, particularly marching bands; the Royal Canadian Henley Regatta at Port Dalhousie attracts competitors from several rowing clubs in the United States, in particular from the Buffalo and Philadelphia areas; and the Shaw Festival Theatre in Niagara-on-the-Lake attracts many patrons from Buffalo.

A strong element of transboundary sharing exists. When medical facilities are inadequate or overburdened, transfers can be made to the other side. This applies when a severe snowstorm cripples one side more than the other; snowplows may then be moved to the other bank. Students may take courses on the other side of the Niagara River that are more suited to their needs, or more convenient in access or schedule from their home or workplace.

The list of interchanges between the two adjacent nations and their facilities is considerable. At Crystal Beach the Buffalo Yacht Club and the Buffalo Canoe Club have almost wholly American memberships. At the Bertie Boating Club most boats belong to American citizens, and in the Port Colborne Marina several slips are used by American boats. At Sherkston Beaches, a major camping-swimming area on the Canadian shore of Lake Erie, and at nearby Crystal Beach (until it failed in 1989) the majority of visitors are from the United States.

In Fort Erie activities such as hockey, baseball, soccer, and figure skating feature frequent games between Canadian and American teams, and residents of Buffalo play on the Canadian teams. At the Fort Erie Races over half the betting transactions are in American dollars, a fact which helps to explain why in 1998 the number of authorized gambling machines were nearly doubled. Restaurants at Fort Erie and Niagara Falls attract patrons from the Buffalo area, restaurants on both sides advertise across the boundary, and a two-way evening and weekend trade of importance to businesses on both sides of the boundary exists.

Advertising for Lewiston's Artpark draws customers from the Niagara Peninsula and Toronto. The Niagara Falls Arts and Cultural Center in Niagara Falls, New York, includes Canadian groups in its program and draws a proportion of its audiences from Ontario. The Niagara Falls Convention Center with large-scale sport and music events has a strong Canadian participation. Buffalo's Albright-Knox Art Gallery mails calendars to Canadian schools and colleges, Canadian galleries lend to exhibitions, and many Canadian groups take advantage of both facilities. Likewise many season ticket holders for the Buffalo Sabres are Canadian, and Canadian attendance for Buffalo Philharmonic concerts in Kleinhans Music Hall is high. The mutual boundary along the Niagara River is permeable. It carries a substantial two-way movement to enjoy the cultural, recreational, leisure, and sporting activities available in the other nation.

Shopping journeys differ substantially from travel to work, recreation, or a visit to friends "over the River." Much now depends on relative cost and the respective value of the Canadian and American dollars. In the early 1980s gas prices were less in Canada, and long line-ups of vehicles with New York license plates clogged the roads in Fort Erie and Niagara Falls. By the early 1990s this flow was reversed into the United States, where the lure of lower prices for many household goods was considerable. Weekend journeys were encouraged by different shopping hours (on Sundays most stores in Ontario were closed) and the differential sales tax (in Canada an 8 percent provincial tariff [PST] and a 7 percent federal Goods and Services Tax [GST] against a 4 percent state levy on the New York side).

American outlets advertise in the local Canadian newspapers, and the large shopping malls advertise their wares using full-page supplements with maps of their location. American shopping centers in Niagara Falls and Buffalo provide a bigger and different selection of consumer goods. They are also closer in time and distance to the towns on the Canadian Frontier, and often have easier access than a comparable journey to retail centers in Hamilton or Toronto.

A recreational journey across the boundary illustrates how the facilities in one country become the domain of the other. American residents, mostly from Buffalo, cross the Niagara River regularly during the summer season to their cottages along the Canadian north shore of Lake Erie (fig. 11.1). Lake Erie is shallow, its waters warm and

U.S. COTTAGE PROPERTIES ON THE CANADIAN SHORE OF LAKE ERIE, 1977

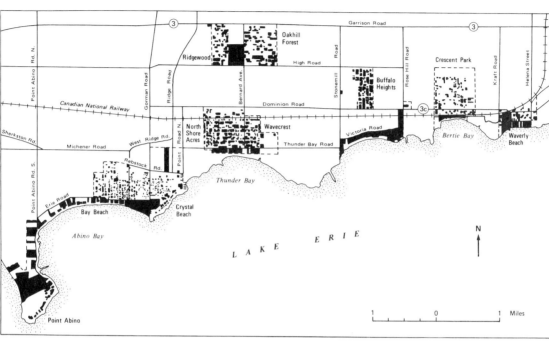

Fig. 11.1. American-owned summer cottage properties now extend west along the shore of Lake Erie from Fort Erie to Port Colborne. Disputes have arisen over whether the sand beaches are privately owned or part of the public domain. Original data by John N. Jackson from the Rating Register for each municipality, from John N. Jackson, *Recreational Development and the Lake Erie Shore* (1967). (Prepared by the Geography Department, Brock University)

inviting, and its beaches sandy and attractive. The Ontario shoreline also contrasts with the beachless waterfronts of Buffalo and Lackawanna where the recreational potential has been destroyed by industries and rail tracks, and also with the less pleasing shoreline of low bluffs along the American south shore of Lake Erie.

Lakeshore lots between Fort Erie and Port Colborne were purchased by Buffalo residents from the late nineteenth century onward, a penetration so effective that by 1945 "the region might almost be regarded as a suburb of the Gateway City."[2] Those who come to the lakeshore during the summer months may commute back to work in Buf-

Grand Island

General Interest

EDGEWATER PARK

WILLIAM VOETSCH, Proprietor

Dancing Pavilion, Six Bowling Alleys, Shooting Gallery, Doll Rack, Base-Ball Grounds, Rathskeller, Boating, Fishing, Bathing, Razzel-Dazzel, Merry-Go Round, Ferris Wheel

—RESTAURANT—

—You can make arrangements for special parties in advance—

NOTICE.—Take Yellow Car to the foot of the Buffalo & Electric Ry. Trestle which will connect with a fast and well equipped Ferry Boat. Trips every 15 minutes.

Left: The fringe of American Grand Island, accessible from Buffalo by streetcar and ferry, attracted recreational parks before the Canadian north shore of Lake Erie took over these activities. **Below right:** Many high-quality, American-owned "cottages" line the Canadian north shore of Lake Erie. **Below left:** Public access to the lakeshore beaches has been restricted severely by their American owners. (*New Century Atlas: Erie County*, 1909 [above], and John N. Jackson [both, below])

falo. Residents from Buffalo and its vicinity have created most of the resortlike atmosphere that exists; their currency and newspapers prevail, as do vehicles licensed in New York State. A subdivision named Buffalo Heights demonstrates this American predominance; street names such as Delaware Avenue and Bidwell and Chapin Parkways are taken from the city across the river.

The impact of seasonal transfer to the Canadian shore is immense.[3] The municipal assessment records in 1977 indicated that over 80 percent of the lakefront properties in the Town of Fort Erie were American owned, an ownership that diminished inland from Lake Erie, with the American proportion for the entire town being 43 percent, 4,490 lots out of 10,359. Over 13 percent of the total tax bill and over 20 percent of the residential taxes were paid by these "foreign" residents.

While the public "road allowance" beaches with their limited width are crowded in summer, the beaches in front of the adjoining American properties are almost empty. Access is restricted to the private owners and their guests. Canadians feel deprived of access to "their" beaches by the overwhelming American presence. Residents of the Niagara Peninsula feel they are "confined and pushed from our heritage of crown land which rightfully belong to each and every one of us. This problem . . . must be checked."[4]

American "cottage" ownership provides an excellent example of where movement across the boundary has caused strained relationships in the economy of an adjacent country. The word "cottage" is also a misnomer. Many are large, expensive mansions, family compounds on estate-sized lots with facilities that include tennis courts and swimming pools. The beaches are labeled with No Trespassing signs and other indications that the land and the beach are deemed private property, an American rather than a Canadian feature along the shoreline of Lake Erie.

BUFFALO AS A TOURIST CENTER

Buffalo does not always present a favorable image to Canadians. Winter snow, urban decline and decay visible from the major highways when driving from the Peace Bridge to the New York Thruway, derelict lines of rail track, and obsolete or decaying industrial buildings are all part of the scene. Reality is something different. The city has been introduced as a booming port, an expanding manufacturing city, the point of entry to the Erie Canal, and a center that grew through the sudden abundance of hydroelectric power. These economic features were expressed in the urban landscape through the rise of grand houses, opulent office buildings, and entertainment facilities that included art galleries, museums, and educational, social, and cultural services housed in notable buildings of historical and architectural merit. The modern city is striving hard to overcome past deficiencies and to use and reuse the finer remnants that have survived or may be reclaimed from the past.

A market analysis in 1980 found that both native Buffalonians and newcomers were well satisfied with Buffalo.[5] Natives were not inclined to move elsewhere; newcomers were pleased with the relative low cost of living and the many local amenities that included major-league sports teams. High among the recorded assets were the variety and quality of Buffalo's restaurants. Newcomers extolled the ethnic foods and the mosaic of ethnic neighborhoods. Buffalo, the home of chicken wings and "beef on weck," appealed to both groups.

Local cultural activities are held in high esteem. The Buffalo Philharmonic Orchestra, founded in 1935, attracts first-class conductors and performers to architects Eliel and Eero Saarinen's acoustically excellent Kleinhans Music Hall. A number of orchestras and other ballet, opera, and symphony groups complement this excellence, and for concert radio there is WNED-FM. The State University of New York at Buffalo, Buffalo State College, Canisius College, and the many smaller colleges also promote a variety of cultural events. Together with local and community galleries, they inspire a sizable artistic community.

The Albright-Knox Art Gallery, housed in a 1905 building designed by Green and Wicks, is regarded as among the ten best galleries of modern art in the United States.[6] The campus of Buffalo State College houses the Burchfield-Penney Art Center, a center for paintings by Charles Burchfield, who during the 1920s to 1940s specialized in local urban landscapes of houses and streets. Hallwalls Contemporary Arts Center, founded in the mid-1970s, and the Anderson Gallery with its changing exhibitions of post–Second World War art add artistic variety. The city is also a center of serious jazz with musicians of international reputation attracted to a number of clubs.

Buffalo's Theatre District includes Shea's Center for the Performing Arts. Built as a movie "palace" in 1926, bought by the city, and restored to provide an authentic and ornate 1920s three-thousand-seat movie and stage palace with a great Wurlitzer organ, here the great films of the day were introduced to a Buffalo audience. The Theatre District downtown includes the Studio Arena Theatre, the Irish Classical Theatre Company, the Market Arcade (designed in 1892 by Green and Wicks), and many restaurants. The University at Buffalo has built a theater on its Amherst campus and provides free Shakespearean plays in Delaware Park each summer. The renewal of the Theatre District, in large measure designed and promoted by the Department of Architecture at the University at Buffalo, indicates the direct involvement of the university community and highlights Buffalo's architectural assets.

In a 1999 assessment the most popular sports attractions were Buffalo's major- and minor-league professional sports teams, with much less enthusiasm for auto and horse racing at Buffalo Raceway and across the border at Fort Erie Racetrack.[7] Sports conventions held in the Buffalo Convention Center add to the high caliber of the region's athletic facilities. With audiences for arts and culture, live theater headed the list, then art and craft fairs, followed successively by the art museums and galleries, jazz and popular musical concerts, symphony and opera concerts, and then dance and ballet performances. There can be no doubt about the high performance levels in these several activities and their regular attraction of patrons from the Canadian Frontier.

The city's modern skyline silhouettes high-rise office buildings, a convention center, and several new hotels. The Buffalo Convention Center has become a community center for various trade shows and regional businesses. Buildings have been cleaned, the accumulated patina of soot and grime removed, air pollution mitigated, and water pollution in the Buffalo and Niagara Rivers reduced.

The industrial waterfront is being redeveloped for office space, stores, housing, and a naval park. A new bank complex has been completed by Toronto investors along Main Street. In 1996 Marine Midland Arena opened as a new sports and entertainment facility to house the Buffalo Sabres of the National Hockey League. This arena has also accommodated other sports teams, including baseball, the Buffalo Bandits (lacrosse), and the Buffalo Blizzard (professional soccer), and has hosted concerts. With the Buffalo Bills (football) and the Buffalo Bisons (baseball), sports and recreation are well represented in the city. Skiing is popular to the south, as is horse racing at Buffalo Raceway in Hamburg, at Batavia Downs Racetrack, and across the boundary at the Fort Erie Racetrack.

A light rail, public transit system supported by connecting bus services has been promoted as a major assistance toward revitalization.[8] Funded by the federal Urban Mass

Above: Buffalo's City Hall terminates a vista that was introduced by Joseph Ellicott. **Below:** The scene now lies within an urban renewal setting of office and residential buildings. (John N. Jackson [above] and Gregory P. Stein [below])

Transportation Administration and by the State Department of Transportation, the first phase of Metro Rail opened for service in 1985 from downtown to the South Campus of the University at Buffalo. The subway emerges in downtown Buffalo onto a six-block pedestrian mall named Buffalo Place that has been integrated with the renewed Theatre District. Rail ridership declined to a five-year low of some 6.3 million passengers by 1999, down 16 percent from 1995. Bus ridership declined to a low of about 19 million riders in 1997 and then increased to over 20.5 million riders by 1999.

The architectural heritage, considerable for a city of its size, reflects not only economic prosperity and population, but also the enlightened, cultural aspirations of the elite ethnic groups.[9] The baroque street plan is centered on the grand axis of Court Street between the McKinley Monument (1907), Lafayette Square anchored by the Art Deco City Hall (1929–1931), and Niagara Square. Though much of the former grandeur of Frederick Law Olmsted's extensive parkway system has been lost, Lincoln, Chapin, and Bidwell Parkways and Richmond Avenue retain their open character, and Elmwood Avenue reminds the observer that the grand avenues which graced and still grace the city once were lined with tall, arching elms until the trees were lost to Dutch elm disease.

The city boasts five houses designed by Frank Lloyd Wright, often described as America's greatest and most original architect. The Prudential/Guaranty Building (1895–1896), the most famous of Louis Sullivan's office buildings, has a lavish facade of dark red terra-cotta, ornate ironwork, and a Tiffany stained-glass ceiling inside. This building, an early steel-framed skyscraper designed by "the father of the American skyscraper," was the tallest building in Buffalo when built. Henry Hobson Richardson's Buffalo State Hospital (1870–1896), which became the Buffalo Psychiatric Center, is a massive Romanesque building of red sandstone walls set within parklike grounds designed by Frederick Law Olmsted and his partner Calvert Vaux to provide a fine example of late-nineteenth-century design incorporating both architecture and landscaping.

Daniel Burnham's Ellicott Square Building (1895–1896), for a time the largest office building in the world, is noted for its elaborate exterior and the intricate mosaic floor in its glass-covered central court. The Victorian-Gothic Post Office (1894–1901), with a dominating tower, has been rejuvenated as the central campus of Erie County Community College. The only survivor from the 1901 Pan-American Exposition, the New York State Building, now houses the Buffalo and

A light rail transit system has contributed to the urban renewal process in downtown Buffalo. (Gregory P. Stein)

Erie County Historical Society. The Art Deco style of the 1920s and 1930s is exemplified by the Rand Building (1929), the Liberty Bank Building (1921) on Lafayette Square, and Buffalo City Hall (1929–1931) on Niagara Square.

The International style is also well represented downtown. Skidmore, Owings and Merrill's (former Marine Midland) Center (1969–1974) terminates the vista down Main Street. Minoru Yamasaki's Manufacturers and Traders (M & T) Bank Building (1964–1966) at twenty-one stories was the first of the new high-rise structures, and the Erie County Savings Bank opened its new twelve-story building in the late 1960s.

The steeples and domes of many churches pierce the sky to provide commanding landmarks and identification across the city. The most impressive, Our Lady of Victory Basilica (1922–1926) in Lackawanna, has the grandeur of a great European cathedral. The First Presbyterian Church (1889–1891) on Symphony Circle, constructed of sandstone with a slender medieval tower, also emphatically terminates a vista. Further landmark examples include Temple Beth Zion (1966–1967) on Delaware Avenue; St. Paul's Episcopal Cathedral (1849–1851), designed by Richard Upjohn in

Buffalo, noted for its architectural heritage, is embellished by five houses designed by Frank Lloyd Wright. All were associated with the Larkin Company to provide a strong link between the industrial prowess of the city and its renowned domestic architecture. Above is the Darwin D. Martin House (1904–1905) at 125 Jewett Parkway. (John N. Jackson)

an Early English Gothic style; St. Joseph's Roman Catholic Cathedral (1851–1855, restored 1976–1977); St. Andrew's Evangelical Church (1885), which copied its Gothic brick style from a German church; and Blessed Trinity Roman Catholic Church (1923–1928), which is a North Italian Romanesque brick structure with a colorful terra-cotta entrance. Trinity Episcopal Church (1886) on Delaware Avenue is famous for its stained-glass windows by Louis Tiffany and John La Forge.

The Macedonia Baptist Church (1849) was the first Black church and an important underground railroad "station" for fugitive slaves. The Polish National Catholic Cathedral (1903) has three doors symbolizing the Holy Trinity, statue niches, and a stone cross at the apex of the church.

Many other buildings add depth to Buffalo's architectural heritage. Environments rich in such features are more pleasant as places in which to live,[10] preservation groups urge that

Invented in Buffalo in 1843, monumental grain elevators provide a commanding feature along the waterfront of the Buffalo River. (John N. Jackson)

their character be guarded carefully as the city advances into the future, and an environment rich in such assets helps to draw tourists and visitors. Even so, restoration and renewal of some buildings may endanger others, as in the redesign of Stanford White's Butler mansion (1895–1898) on Delaware Avenue for a business headquarters while a lesser White structure was demolished for a parking lot to make this conversion possible. The Larkin Administration Building (1904–1906), an office structure designed by Frank Lloyd Wright, was demolished in 1950, and the Erie County Savings Bank Building (1890–1893) in 1967. As regretted by Banham in a chapter headed "Lost Buffalo," "Any vanished building designed by a famous architect or architectural firm should be included as part of local and national architectural history. Buffalo has lost buildings by Frank Lloyd Wright, H. H. Richardson, and McKim, Mead and White."[11]

Not to be forgotten is the power, the quality, and the grandeur of the monumental grain elevators that line the Buffalo River upstream from the Michigan Street Bridge. As Banham has argued elsewhere: "They need to be brought back among the canons of giant architecture, and they deserve far more respect and honor than they commonly receive in America, for they represent the triumph of what is American in American building art."[12] The building housing the Buffalo Gas Light Company (1848) might also be noted; its facade reflects the former importance of this public utility, and its location on the Erie Canal and Lake Erie is a reminder of easy coal imports from both routes. And the railway era, recalled in the great railway stations that have survived from the past, includes the Art Deco New York Central Terminal (1928) that continues to tower over its neighborhood. Although use and activity have changed drastically, the Pierce-Arrow Motor Car Company and its factory complex (1906–1907) might also be recalled for its early automobiles and the role of this plant in the development of this industry.

In a 1997 composite rating that included the arts, theaters, museums, ballet, opera, symphonies, and libraries, the Buffalo-Niagara Falls metropolitan area was rated twenty-four out of the 351 North American metropolitan areas, a favorable position but lower than Toronto, ranked at fifth place. Buffalo, however, was also ranked higher than the St. Catharines-Niagara metropolitan area (eighty-fifth place) and, being closer than Toronto, helps to explain the transborder traffic that has been introduced.[13]

THE EXPANSION OF MARINE ACTIVITIES

With the Frontier's setting on two of the Great Lakes and its long history of canal and harbor development, it is not surprising that marine facilities have become a vital part of leisure activities. Since the Second World War, marinas, often with associated marine services, restaurants, and condominium projects, have located on sites that include the banks of the Upper and Lower Niagara River; the shorelines of Lake Erie and Lake Ontario; in or next to the Welland Canal harbors at Port Colborne, Port Dalhousie, and Port Weller; and in the lakeshore vicinity of Buffalo.

At the southern entrance to the Welland Canal, Port Colborne celebrated its twentieth Annual Canal Days in 1998. At the northern entrance, the Royal Canadian Henley Rowing Regatta on Martindale Pond continues to expand to include national and international rowing events; in 1995 FISA (Fédération International des Sociétés d' Aviron), the governing body for world rowing, awarded this site the World Rowing Championships that were held in 1999. Expansion at Port Dalhousie includes a walkway around the lower harbor that has been completed on the west side and is expected to eventually connect the two sides.

Boat cruises have been introduced in and out of the harbor at Port Dalhousie, around Buffalo Harbor, and along the Upper Niagara River. At Lockport narrated cruises depart from a restored 1940 warehouse to "lock through" two locks of the Erie Canal system;

Commercial shipping activity at Port Dalhousie has been replaced by the Royal Henley Rowing Regatta in the Upper Harbor (**left above**), and by marina activities in the Lower Harbor (**left below**). Note the setting next to the first lock of the Second Canal, left foreground. (John N. Jackson [both])

a walking tour of the former water-power tunnel is included in this tour. And in the late 1990s there have been attempts using fast motorcraft to restart the long tradition of the tourist links across Lake Ontario from Toronto to the destinations that have included Port

Dalhousie, Niagara-on-the-Lake, and Queenston on the Canadian Frontier, and Youngstown and Lewiston on the American Frontier. In 1999 international air-lake cruises recommenced on the Great Lakes, the revival of a popular pastime during the 1920s and 1930s, but one that had almost died out by the 1960s; the itinerary included the Welland Canal, with shore visits.

A Recreational Waterway has been created along the abandoned Fourth Canal at Welland. The banks, designed as open space, have been developed as a linear park for active and passive recreational purposes, which has encouraged condominium and high-rise residential projects in a landscaped, open-space setting next to the water. Pedestrian walkways have been added to both banks, and Merritt Island between the Welland River and the former Fourth Canal has become a public park. Boating, water skiing, and rowing championships have been introduced, including the South Niagara Rowing Club in Welland, which hosted the Regatta of the Americas prior to the World Rowing Championships in St. Catharines. A former commercial-industrial waterway and its vicinity have been transformed, and in the city center colorful Giant Murals have been added to building facades as a contribution toward inner-city improvement. The first

mural was commissioned in 1986; by 1999 the number had increased to twenty-eight, almost all in the downtown area.

Progress toward achieving recreational routes along the old and present-day Welland Canals has been slow and inadequate. [14] When the Fourth Canal was constructed, roads were provided on both sides of the channel to service electrical installations and to provide emergency access to vessels. Nurseries were established and trees planted at points along the canal banks to prevent erosion and to provide windbreaks against the predominantly westerly winds for vessels passing through the canal. Visitor centers have been provided at Lock 3 in St. Catharines and at Lock 8 in Port Colborne, with the canal and its historical associations gradually becoming a major tourist attraction second only to the Falls on the Canadian Frontier.

However, despite many strongly supportive post–Second World War planning studies by all levels of government, the major idea of a continuous parkway for automobile and associated trails for pedestrians and cyclists between the two lakes has not reached fruition. The intention had been to link a whole range of historic features in the canal communities by a parkway of the same caliber as the Niagara River Parkway. Progress has included the partial construction

Large-sized murals painted on the bare walls of buildings have been introduced to downtown Welland, after the commercial strength of the town center was prejudiced by decline through the proliferation of out-of-town shopping centers. (John N. Jackson [both])

Top: Landscaping was introduced during the completion phases of the Fourth Welland Canal; a boulevard along the canal was then envisaged, but not completed. **Middle:** A private lake-to-lake trail was completed along the old canal system during the 1980s. **Bottom:** The grand idea of a continuous Welland Canals Parkway between Lake Erie and Lake Ontario along the present and former routes of the Welland Canal has been advocated in several major post–Second World War planning studies, but it remains that canal service roads, ideal for public open space-recreational purposes, are closed to the public. A pedestrian footpath system along the canal and linking as a circular route with the trail along the Niagara River Parkway was under construction by the year 2000. (The St. Lawrence Seaway Management Corporation [top], and John N. Jackson [middle, bottom])

Above right: The Erie Canal followed the east bank of the Niagara River between Tonawanda and Black Rock-Buffalo. Filled in after closure, this abandoned route offers a high amenity potential for recreational open space. To the south in the vicinity of the Peace Bridge, the canal route has been converted to Highway I-90. **Below right:** The lower scene shows a pleasure boat in the Black Rock Channel against the backdrop of an older industrial building. (John N. Jackson [top], and Gregory P. Stein [bottom])

of a canalside hiking-cycling-jogging trail along the modern Fourth Canal in St. Catharines, with extensions through Thorold and Welland to Port Colborne that were subject to steady but slow completion during the year 2001. With the emphasis on a multiple-use trail rather than the grander concept of a Welland Canals Parkway linked with the Niagara River Parkway as a river-canal circular tour, it is sad to note that many lengths of the inviting canal banks remain closed to recreation with No Trespassing and No Access signs. Recreational, open-space progress has been far less than along canals elsewhere, including the Lachine Canal in Montreal, or along the Rideau Canal, the Sault-Ste Marie Canal, and the Trent-Severn Waterway in Ontario. Despite its dual routes, the

Welland Canal system across the Niagara Peninsula of Southern Ontario has been designated as neither a Canadian National Park nor as a Historic Site.

On the American Frontier a system of open space with recreational opportunities and heritage preservation is being achieved along the former Erie Canal inland from Tonawanda. As reported in 1995, "A new vision has emerged for the system, a vision to conserve its history and environment, to make it a gathering place for leisure-time enjoyment, and to re-energize adjacent communities, bringing new benefits and prosperity."[15] Waterfront parks also either exist or are in the process of development along the Upper Niagara River, an attempt to redeem the blighting impact of the Robert Moses Parkway, and to provide an environment comparable to the Niagara River Parkway and its recreational trail. Isle View Park in Tonawanda, River Walk between this city and Buffalo, and recreational trails along Scajaquada Creek and the Erie Canal may also be noted.

At Buffalo several reports seek to redevelop the Inner Harbor, the port where trade generated by the Erie Canal made Buffalo into a major nineteenth-century city. These proposals by the Empire State Development Corporation, a state agency, include the restoration of former commercial slips and cobblestone streets, the re-creation of old buildings, and a major interpretative center. These developments would be in conjunction with the existing naval and military parks, with perhaps the Erie Canal being designated a National Heritage Corridor as recommended by the National Park Service. The promotional push for these developments is the expanding tourist industry; the political issues to be resolved are whether state or federal agencies should fund and have the authority to manage this new venture when the Erie Canal was once a state venture separate from federal initiatives.

FORMER SUMMER RECREATIONAL RESORTS

Three former religious campgrounds survive in the urban landscape on the Canadian Frontier. Their distinctive circles, radiating roads, and religious street names now form part of the residential environment (fig. 11.2). All were served by railway and steamer access. Crystal Beach Amusement Park, conceived as a religious assembly-ground, had become a recreational resort for Buffalo residents by 1890; Queen's Place in the village, with six roads radiating out from its central meeting-place, survives from this period. A

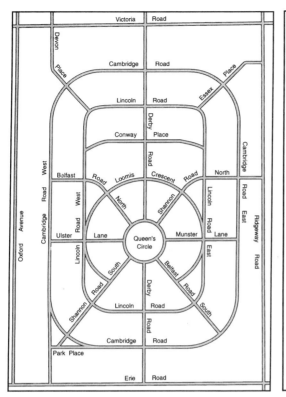

Crystal Beach

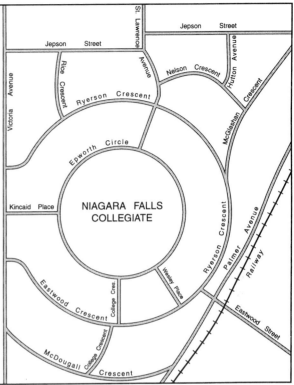

Niagara Falls

Fig. 11.2. A reminder of former religious campgrounds on the Canadian Frontier are circles and radiating roads, with accompanying streets named after religious leaders. (Prepared by the Department of Geography, Brock University)

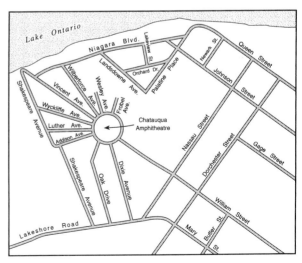

Niagara-on-the-Lake

Crystal Beach developed as a major summer recreational resort on the Canadian north shore of Lake Erie. (John N. Jackson [both])

Methodist summer resort with cottages, auditorium, and gardens for meetings and missionary and temperance conventions was established at Wesley Park in Niagara Falls, Ontario, in 1885; with a station on the Michigan Central and staircase access to the river below, its form survives in the circular streets around Epworth Circle.

The Michigan Central and passenger vessels from Toronto brought people to a third resort, the Canadian Chautauqua west of Niagara-on-the-Lake. Named after the institution southwest of Buffalo, this center was inaugurated in 1874 as a summer school with an educational and recreational assembly and a program that included lectures and concerts. By 1890 the grounds held a three-story frame hotel, cottages, a four-thousand-seat amphitheater, and a railway station. A central circle, a few homes, and radial streets survive from this venture, which lasted until 1909.

A bygone recreational feature, Erie Beach Amusement Park at Fort Erie, a resort founded in 1885, on summer weekends attracted crowds of up to twenty thousand from Buffalo to its park, swimming pool, zoo, and casino.[16]

Nearby, private summer cottage resorts along the shore of Lake Erie enjoyed rail access from Buffalo to their select vacation facilities.[17] Solid Comfort west of the canal at Port Colborne was served by a flag station on the Grand Trunk (former Buffalo and Lake Huron), and Tennessee Avenue in the present city recalls former frequent visitors from this southern American state. Lorraine, established in 1898 on the sand dunes east of Port Colborne, became an exclusive resort for Buffalo businessmen. Served by a special passenger train, daily commuting to Buffalo was provided during the summer months.

A racetrack at Fort Erie, established in 1897, developed in conjunction with rail access across the International Bridge for Buffalo patrons.[18] The railway also promoted St. Catharines as "The Saratoga of Canada." Visitors, many from the southern United States, came by train to drink curative waters and relax in the baths of the mineral springs. The Welland Hotel, close to the town center, and the Stephenson House overlooking the canal valley of Twelve Mile Creek were centers of spa activity by the 1850s. Followed within a decade by the Springbank Hotel,[19] these spa hotels survived until the end of the century, when pollution destroyed this earlier asset.

Niagara-on-the-Lake, appreciated as "a fashionable suburb of Toronto" by the late nineteenth century, attracted weekend steamer excursions from Toronto across Lake Ontario, and visitors by rail from Buffalo to the Queen's Royal, Chautauqua, and Lakeside hotels.[20] In addition, a Canadian military camp, established in 1871 on the Commons near Fort George, was used for summer training.[21] Parades, drills, and tattoos attracted crowds of spectators. Troops, camp supplies, and visitors were brought in by the Erie and Niagara railway.

At Port Dalhousie steamer services operated in conjunction with the Welland railway carried a seasonal tourist flow from Toronto to Lakeside Park with its attractive beach, or carried passengers to the Falls who then enjoyed evening entertainment at the port before returning. As the railway also served the communities along the canal to the south, Port Dalhousie expanded as a local recreational site for excursions from across the Niagara Peninsula.[22]

On the American Frontier Grand Island was served by steamer from Buffalo and by ferry from the mainland. Exclusive clubs and summer homes were built there by the 1850s, followed by country estates and lines of summer villas, hotels, and amusement parks.[23] By the 1890s cottagers and amusement operators favored the Canadian beaches of Lake Erie with their easier direct access by rail and steamer. A different type of recreational amenity was the discovery of mineral water with supposed therapeutic powers at Alden on the American Frontier, where hotels with baths and a sanitorium were established before the end of the century.

THE TOWNS OF THE LOWER NIAGARA RIVER

Four small now-residential communities on the banks of the Lower Niagara River offer significant historical and architecturally important assets that attract a considerable number of annual tourists. Niagara-on-the-Lake and Queenston on the Canadian Frontier and Youngtown and Lewiston on the American Frontier are each associated closely with the earliest days of Frontier settlement, and each contain significant buildings and memories from these formative years when the river and its portages provided the main route of entry to the continental interior. All lie on the fringe of their respective national territories and have restricted hinterlands because of the intervening river and its boundary. All were bypassed when the canals encouraged the inland expansion of settlement, and all became quiet, off-the-beaten-track "cul-de-sac" communities, which by

the accident of isolation helped to preserve their character and identity. All, as reemergent centers in the later eras of the motor age, now face the severe and persistent clash between residential expansion, tourism, and the high amenity qualities of their respective environments. In each the number of visitors far outweighs the resident population.

In **Niagara-on-the-Lake**, acclaimed as "one of Canada's most charming communities" and "the prettiest village in Ontario,"[24] the business district dates from the earliest history of the Niagara Frontier. Queen Street, the main shopping avenue, is lined with impressively restored old buildings retailing high-quality goods from around the world. Hotels, inns, and restaurants have arisen along or close to that street. A memorial clock tower unveiled in 1922 serves as a focal point in the street scene and as an important urban landmark. Open space includes Simcoe Park at the center; the Commons, the open space surrounding Fort George, and the Niagara River Parkway to the south; Fort Mississauga within the grounds of the Niagara Gold Club to the west; and Queen's Royal Park where the Niagara River meets Lake Ontario on the site of a former hotel.

Fort George, built by the British when Fort Niagara on the opposite bank was about to be passed into American hands, then pro-

The National Shrine of Our Lady of Fatima is graced by life-sized statues, a domed chapel, and an avenue approach to provide a major attraction east of the Lower Niagara River on the American Frontier. (John N. Jackson)

minology as a "stabilized ruin," a memory of the defended border but now isolated within the incongruous but pleasant setting of a golf course.

Modern residential developments to the south and west of the old town prejudice the integrity of Niagara-on-the-Lake as "the Birthplace of a Province (Ontario) that breathes history, culture and elegance."[25] Tourists now greatly outnumber permanent residents during the season, causing pedestrian congestion in the town center at peak periods, and the parking of vehicles has spread into the nearby quiet residential streets.[26] Some inhabitants feel this influx disrupts a pleasant and peaceful place in which to live; others see it as a benefit because of expanded business and employment opportunities, the greater range of services and shops, and the availability of high-quality entertainment and restaurants. Recognizing a greater potential for growth than had previously existed, a Chinese lady entrepreneur has purchased the best of the town's hotels, a popular restaurant, and prime

tected the Niagara River as the major Canadian water route to the continental interior. Captured by the American army during the War of 1812, the fort, reconstructed and restored by the Niagara Parks Commission in the late 1930s, became a National Historic Site that was placed under the jurisdiction of Parks Canada in 1969. Parts of the adjacent Commons have been encroached upon to provide senior citizen apartments, car parking at Fort George, and the Shaw Festival Theatre. Fort Mississauga, constructed in 1814 of rubble after the town was burned by American forces during the War of 1812, was occupied until the 1840s. It survives in official ter-

Top right: The high urban quality of Queen Street, the main street of Niagara-on-the-Lake, is dominated by the Clock Tower, a memorial to those who fell in the First World War, to provide a significant focal point in the town's urban structure. This street is lined with a series of important historic buildings, which provide a continuous urban facade and includes the renovated Court House (**bottom right**) now used as a theater by the Shaw Festival. Most buildings along Queen Street house high-quality retail outlets that serve the tourist crowds. The contrast with the effervescent gaiety of Clifton Hill in Niagara Falls is remarkable. (John N. Jackson [both])

downtown land, and created a small, high-class plaza; her small-scale landscaping schemes have added color and vitality to an already attractive downtown scene.

In Niagara-on-the-Lake the aura of historical and architectural greatness is enhanced by the Shaw Festival with performances held in three locations: the Festival Theatre built in 1972, the Court House Theatre where the festival started, and the Royal George Theatre in a restored former cinema.[27] Focusing on the plays of George Bernard Shaw and his contemporaries, the festival enjoys an international reputation, plays to full houses, and attracts over three hundred thousand visitors per year.

Interesting is the upscale contrast between Niagara-on-the-Lake and Niagara Falls, Ontario, its upstream urban neighbor. The former has shaped its character around forts, old buildings, burial grounds, and historical markers, "quite consciously shaping the tourist gaze around education and history rather than

High-quality domestic architecture within spacious grounds makes a remarkable contribution to the urban quality and character of Niagara-on-the-Lake. (John N. Jackson [both])

amusement. . . . The difference between the two towns, ten miles apart, remains jarring and is a testament to the continued significance of class to the tourist gaze."[28]

The combination of residences, often architecturally important, and their surrounding landscaped gardens set within the tree-lined streets of a small-scale grid together contribute much of quality to the urban scene. If the stately estate homes are allowed to incorporate commercial facilities, then the open space would be diminished or lost, yet these spacious homes and landscaped gardens have become too expensive to maintain as family residences. One outcome is that a large number of B & B (bed and breakfast) accommodations have arisen over recent years, which helps to satisfy the tourist demand; the large homes are more fully used and their attractive settings within landscaped open space have been retained.

Lewiston, the former river port at the northern end of the Niagara Portage, faces the same residential and amenity dilemma through the expansion of tourism.[29] The historic portage, with buildings dating back to the 1820s and 1830s, makes the town center "the most historic square mile in America." Designated historic districts in and about the center with pioneer homes, churches, inns, and the Lewiston Museum in a former church help to preserve the inherited character of this Frontier town. Even the McDonald's hamburger chain has taken over a pioneer hostelry, maintaining the character of this mid-1820s stone building that was built as a stagecoach terminal, and excluding the symbolic golden arches. The tourist influx is reflected in the range and type of stores along the main street and intrusions such as parking signs and tow-away zones.

The Earl W. Brydges Artpark, a major contributor to pressures for change, holds a summer festival of the performing and visual arts on part of an 80.9-hectare (200-acre) state park located at the northern end of the Niagara River gorge. Developed in part on fill from the Robert Moses Power Project, the site has destroyed the epic climb up the Niagara Escarpment of the original portage. Visitors pass through the town's residential areas to reach the lower entrance of the park. In 1983 about 40 percent of the 145,773 theater-goers had meals and snacks at Lewiston's restaurants, making "the total value of just the meals served to Artpark visitors . . . an estimated $501,879. . . . Add on the value of Artpark employment, tourist-related services, sales of other goods, and one begins to appreciate the economic value of Artpark."[30] A nearby major attraction is the National Shrine Basilica of Our Lady of Fatima, an outdoor cathedral with over one hundred life-size statues. With Artpark, the shrine, and the village each visited by numerous tourists, as at Niagara-on-the-Lake Lewiston's heritage is saved by tourism but the qualities of townscape have been changed drastically by the influx of tourists and the provision of facilities for them.

Queenston, facing Lewiston across the Niagara River where the Iroquois Trail once crossed, "has more points of historic interest than any other place in Canada. Laura Secord lived here, General Brock died here [at the Battle of Queenston Heights in 1812] . . . and had four burials, three of them in Queenston."[31] William Lyon Mackenzie's house, where he published the radical *Colonial Advocate*,[32] and which was completely rebuilt in the 1930s, now functions as the Mackenzie Heritage Printery featuring early letterpress equipment. The village also houses the Laura Secord Homestead, where this heroine of the War of 1812 lived and started on her famous trek to DeCew to warn the British commander about the pending American attack that became the Battle of Beaverdams.

Queenston contains the homes of William Lyon MacKenzie (**left**) which now houses printing exhibits, and the home of Laura Secord (**below**) who walked from Queenston to DeCew Falls to warn of an impending American attack during the War of 1812. (John N. Jackson [both])

Close by, the private Samuel E. Weir Collection and Library of Art focuses on Canadian historical art in the owner's former home next to the Niagara River; Weir, a lawyer from London, Ontario, collected paintings, drawings, prints, sculptures, and books. As noted previously when discussing heritage, Willowbank, a pillared colonial building with an eight-columned portico constructed on top of a high bank in 1834 for the sheriff of Lincoln County, provides an admirable example of Classical Revival architecture.

Nearby, the Sir Adam Beck Generating Complex has not recognized its high tourist appeal. The raised banks that surround the power reservoir remain as bare rock; they have not been landscaped. The water is not used for recreational purposes, a museum of historical electrical appliances has been discontinued, and public tours of the generating station have been terminated. By contrast, the nearby Floral Clock with some twenty-five thousand blooms and intense landscape gardening is a major attraction managed by the Niagara Parks Commission. The mechanical operation of the clock, modeled on the one in Princes Street Gardens, Edinburgh, Scotland, remains the responsibility of Ontario Hydro. Important scenically is the Observation Overlook across the gorge from the American Robert Moses Niagara Power Plant, where thirteen penstocks feed the generating station at the base of the gorge from the forebay and pump storage reservoir above.

Queenston Heights Park crowns the southern end of the inspiring parkway length along the Middle River. Here the Battle of Queenston Heights was fought in 1812, and the park entrance at a stop of the former Niagara Park and River Railway focuses in splendid Renaissance fashion on the monument dedicated to General Sir Isaac Brock, who with his aide-de-camp is buried in a vault at the base. Nearby is the smaller monument erected in 1910 by the Canadian government in memory of Laura Secord. Forts Drummond and Riall, named after British generals, are part of the popular picnic park and recreation grounds; the ramparts of Fort Drummond now contain a wading pool for small children.

Youngstown's claim to tourist fame is Old Fort Niagara, which occupies the headland between the Niagara River and Lake Ontario. Active under French, British, and now American flags, the fort, constructed by the French to guard the northern entrance to the Niagara River, has preserved fortifications and stone buildings.[33] As a major center of the fur trade, the fort is the oldest and most important building at the Frontier and the oldest on the Great Lakes.

This stone castle, surrendered to the British by the French in 1759, was used for British raids into American territory during the American Revolution, but was not attacked during that period. Eventually ceded to the United States, Fort Niagara remained in British hands until 1796, and was a major location for the immigration of Empire Loyalists to the new territory that became Canada, the pioneer survey of those lands, and the allocation of land to these incoming settlers and disbanded troops. Captured by the British during the War of 1812, the close of that war ended the military importance of a fort no longer required for defensive purposes. In 1927 the complex was restored and furnished to recreate an eighteenth-century atmosphere, and the Old Fort Niagara Association was formed to maintain the fort which has become a major destination for visitors to the Frontier.

Access to the fort is via the multilane Robert Moses Parkway to the large parking area. As this access bypasses the village of Youngstown, this historic center is isolated and separated from the fort. Niagara-on-the-Lake on the Canadian bank offers a greater degree of unity. Here the town center, its historic buildings, and the preservation areas are major attractions. The Commons are visually part of the town, as are Fort George, Butler's Barracks, and Navy Hall. All are part of the same community, whereas the smaller village of Youngstown has become a residential locality and a marina resort divorced from the fort as its major attraction.

NOTES

1. This study of movement from the American to the Canadian side was undertaken by J. N. Jackson in 1978 with financial support from a Canada Council grant. S. E. Davies and R. Lemon were the research assistants. The data has been interpolated to the 1990s from a range of personal sources and further enquiries.

2. W. Hatcher, *Lake Erie* (Toronto: Bobbs-Merrill, 1945), pp. 362–63.

3. J. N. Jackson, *Recreational Development and the Lake Erie Shore* (Grimsby, Ont.: Niagara Regional Development Council, 1967).

4. Mayor of Port Colborne, *Welland and Port Colborne Evening Tribune*, 11 August 1966.

5. D. R. Hetzner commenting on research for the "Talking Proud" media campaign, in collaboration with B. J. Gorbaty for Healty-Schutte Advertising (Buffalo, N.Y.), 15 July 1980, and capitalizing on the success of a major-league sports team.

6. *Smithsonian* 12 (December 1979).

7. J. B. Sheffer, *State of the Region: Performance Indicators for the Buffalo-Niagara Region* (Buffalo, N.Y.: Institute for Local Governance and Regional Growth, University at Buffalo, 1999), pp. 11-2, 11-4, 11-8.

8. C. T. Lanigan, *The Buffalo-Amherst Corridor: Technical Report* (Albany: Office of Planning Coordination, State of New York, 1969), pp. 11–14; and Wallace, McHarg, Roberts and Todd, *The Regional Center: A Comprehensive Plan for Buffalo* (Philadelphia: Wallace, McHarg, Roberts and Todd, 1971). Traffic data from Sheffer, *State of the Region*, p. 10-6.

9. The primary source is R. Banham, *Buffalo Architecture: A Guide* (Cambridge, Mass.: MIT Press, 1981); the dates and the details of buildings are acknowledged to this source. See also M. Headrick and C. Ehrlich, *Seeing Buffalo* (Buffalo, N.Y.: n.p., 1978); A. Heckscher, *Open Spaces: The Life of American Cities* (New York: Harper and Row, 1977), pp. 205–206; J. Quinan, *Frank Lloyd Wright's Larkin Building: Myth and Fact* (New York: Architectural History Foundation, 1987); and M. L. Quinlan, "Spanish Revival Homes in Buffalo," *Niagara Frontier* 28 (1981): 1–16. Commercial growth and prosperity, and the rapid rise to fame and fortune of Buffalo, are expressed statistically in P. Becker (mayor), *Statistics Relating to the Government of Buffalo* (E. W. Beck, 1896). Vessels arriving at and departing from the City of Buffalo increased from 100 in 1832, to 2,739 in 1855, to 5,515 by 1893. Cargo burgeoned from 8,000 tons

in 1832, to 1,484,406 tons in 1854, to 4,758,966 tons by 1893.

10. K. Lynch, *What Time Is This Place?* (Cambridge, Mass.: MIT Press, 1972), p. 30.

11. Banham, *State of the Region*, p. 263.

12. R. Banham, *A Concrete Atlantis: U.S. Industrial Building and European Modern Architecture 1900–1925* (Cambridge, Mass.: MIT Press, 1986), pp. 19–20.

13. D. Savagean and G. Loftus, *Places Rated Almanac* (New York: Macmillan Travel, 1997), pp. 282, 307, 311.

14. J. N. Jackson, *The Welland Canals and Their Communities: Engineering, Industrial, and Urban Transformation* (Toronto: University of Toronto Press, 1997), pp. 458–71. Major studies include M. Greenwald, A. Levitt, and E. Peebles, *The Welland Canals: Historical Resource Analysis and Preservation Alternatives* (Toronto: Historical Planning and Research Branch, Ministry of Culture and Recreation, 1976); Marshall Macklin Monagham Limited, *Welland Canals Corridor Development Guide*, prepared for the Regional Municipality of Niagara (Thorold, Ont.: Marshall Macklin Monagham Limited, 1988); *Welland Canals Parkway and Trails Master Plan*, prepared for the Planning and Development Department, Regional Municipality of Niagara (Cambridge, Ont.: IMC Consulting Group, 1996); Burke and Associates, *Welland Canals Parkway and Trails: Capital Campaign Feasibility Study* (Burlington, Ont.: Burke and Associates, 1998); and Bill Hallett and Associates, *Campaign Plan for the Welland Canal Parkway and Trails* (Toronto: Bill Hallett and Associates, 1998).

15. Beyer Blinder Bello Consortium, Consultants to the Canal Recreational Way Commission, *Executive Summary: New York State Canal Recreationway Plan* (Canal Recreational Way Commission, 1995).

16. P. C. Andrews, *The Canadian Shore from Pt. Abino to Erie Beach*, Adventures in Western New York History, vol. 14 (Buffalo, N.Y.: Buffalo and Erie County Historical Society, 1966), pp. 8–10; and F. Petrie, "Picnickers Covered by Cinders," *Niagara Falls Review*, 14 March 1970.

17. E. F. Ott et al., *A History of Humberstone Township* (Port Colborne, Ont.: Humberstone Township Council, 1967), pp. 112–13. See also *The History of the County of Welland* (Welland, Ont.: Welland Tribune Printing House, 1887), p. 275.

18. M. F. Campbell, "Race Track Sixty Years Old," *Fort Erie Times-Review: Fort Erie Centennial, 1857–1957* (1957), pp. 22–23, 31.

19. C. Duquemin, *The Spas at St. Catharines*, Outdoor Studies Pamphlet 113 (St. Johns West, Ont.: St. Johns Outdoor Studies Centre, 1984); and S. M. Wilson, *Taking the Waters: A History of the Spas of St. Catharines* (St. Catharines, Ont.: St. Catharines Historical Society, 1999).

20. *St. Catharines Journal*, 27 October 1859.

21. E. A. Cruikshank, *Camp Niagara* (Niagara Falls, Ont.: Frank H. Leslie, 1906).

22. C. Aloian, *A History Outline of Port Dalhousie, 1650–1960* (Port Dalhousie, Ont.: Port Dalhousie Quorum, 1978), pp. 17–24.

23. R. R. Macleod: *Cinderella Island* (Grand Island, N.Y.: R. R. Macleod, 1950), pp. 37–43; and "Two Chapters of Grand Island," *Niagara Frontier* 1 (1953–1954), pp. 90–94.

24. G. Roland, ed., *Explore Canada* (Montreal: Reader's Digest, 1974), p. 247; and G. Cantor, *The Great Lakes Guidebook: Lakes Ontario and Erie* (Ann Arbor: University of Michigan Press, 1978), pp. 22, 24.

25. P. J. Stokes, *Old Niagara-on-the-Lake* (Toronto: University of Toronto Press, 1971); and G. Balbar, *Niagara-on-the-Lake: The Old Historical Town* (Belleville, Ont.: Mika, 1990).

26. Proctor and Redfern Limited, *The Economic Impact of Tourism Development Proposals in Niagara-on-the-Lake: Summary of Findings*, prepared for the Management Subcommittee of the Parks Canada Study Group (Niagara-on-the-Lake, Ont.: Proctor and Redfern Limited, 1977).

27. The Shaw Festival, conceived in 1962, performs the works of playwright George Bernard Shaw and his contemporaries; B. Doherty, *Not Bloody Likely: The Shaw Festival, 1962–1973* (Don Mills, Ont.: J. M. Dent, 1974).

28. K. Dubinsky, *The Second Greatest Disappointment: Honeymooning and Tourism at Niagara Falls* (Toronto: Between the Lines), published as *The Second Greatest Disappointment: Honeymooners, Heterosexuality, and the Tourist Industry at Niagara Falls* (New Brunswick, N.J.: Rutgers University Press, 1999), pp. 242–43.

29. M. D. Robson, *Under the Mountain* (Buffalo, N.Y.: H. Stewart, 1958); Sesquicentennial Committee, *Lewiston Sesquicentennial, 1822–1972* (Lewiston, N.Y.: Sesquicentennial Committee, 1971); and H. B. Kimball, *Helen Kimball's Lewiston* (Lewiston, N.Y.: Edwin Mellen Press, 1987).

30. Community Services Research and Development Program, *Artpark: A Market Survey and Analysis* (Buffalo: State University of New York at Buffalo, 1983), p. 27. See also Arts Development Association, *Artpark and Its Constituencies—1979: A Report on Surveys* (Minneapolis, Minn.: Arts Development Association, 1979).

31. E. A. Huggins, *An Address Given at the Unveiling of the Historic Plaque Commemorating the Founding of Queenston, October 28, 1973* (St. Catharines, Ont.: Niagara Regional Library Service, 1973). See G. A. and O. M. Seibel, *The Niagara Portage Road* (Niagara Falls, Ont.: City of Niagara Falls, 1990), pp. 131–204.

32. *Colonial Advocate*, a journal that criticized the elite group of gentlemen known as the Family Compact, who ruled Upper Canada and helped to end colonial rule by Britain in favor of independent self-government.

33. B. L. Dunnigan: *History and Development of Old Fort Niagara* (Youngstown, N.Y.: Old Fort Niagara Association, 1985); and *Siege—1759: The Campaign Against Niagara* (Youngstown, N.Y.: Old Fort Niagara Association, 1986). For the village, see E. L. Howard, *The History of Youngstown, N.Y.* (Lockport, N.Y.: Niagara County Historical Society, 1951); and V. M. Howard and E. L. Howard in J. T. Blixt, *Youngstown Centennial, 1854–1954* (Youngstown, N.Y.: Centennial Committee, 1954).

CHAPTER TWELVE

THE FALLS AND THEIR VICINITY

A CHANGING LANDSCAPE

The Falls entered the public conscience as a prodigy of nature, a sublime cataract, a rocky precipice, and a picturesque tumbling torrent.[1] As the scene was changed by improved accessibility, hydroelectricity, hotels, and entertainment, the area lost its wild grandeur as developers tried to make it both a fashionable resort and an industrial site. Ironically, as more people flocked to view the great "natural" wonder at Niagara, it became more and more a man-made artifact, whether by sensitive design or by rapacious industrial and commercial intrusion. As noted by one author, "To many, it seemed as if Niagara Falls had been saved in 1885 through the establishment of the New York State Reservation and authorization of Ontario's provincial park. . . . In truth, however, the battle for Niagara Falls had only just begun."[2] The changing scene at the Falls, expanding tourism, and the design problems associated with how to retain and enhance the magnificent scenic setting provide the finale for discussion.

THE PROVISION OF PUBLIC OPEN SPACE AT THE FALLS

Visiting the Falls began primarily as an élite journey for gentlemen.[3] The Erie Canal, and to a lesser extent trans-Atlantic steamers and then vessels on Lake Ontario, brought in more of the middle class, including women. Grand hotels such as the Canadian Pavilion and the American Cataract House were constructed soon after the War of 1812, and were the prelude to many others, grand and not so grand. Stairways were built from Table Rock and Prospect Point to the edge of the river, with trails to "caves" (overhangs) behind the sheet of falling waters. The Burning Spring, the Lundy's Lane and Queenston Heights battlefields, and a stone observation tower built in 1833 at Terrapin Point on the brink of the Horseshoe Falls became major attractions. Access to view the Falls was over private property, and visitors paid for the privilege.

Carnival acts and sensational entertainments were added to lure the tourist. In 1827 some fifty thousand people watched as the schooner *Michigan* was sent over the Falls with a shipload of live animals. The natural landscape changed as trees were felled to open up views of the river and overhanging ledges blasted away to attract and please the crowds. Dufferin and Goat Islands were developed with bridges, roads, gardens, and vantage points. Thomas Barnett's Museum at Table Rock featured deformed animals, live snakes, and Egyptian mummies. The *Maid of the Mist*, a tourist boat introduced in 1846, brought loads of passengers close to the Falls. Tourist promotion included boosterism as the "Honeymoon Capital of the World."[4]

When Charles Dickens, the English novelist, arrived at the Falls in 1842, the scene was still idyllic: "To wander to and fro all day, and see the cataracts from all points of view; to stand upon the edge of the Great Horse Shoe Falls, marking the hurried water gathering strength as it approached the verge, yet seeming, too, to pause before it shot into the gulf below; to gaze from the river's level up at the torrent as it came streaming down; to climb the neighbouring heights and watch it through the trees, and see the wreathing water in the rapids hurrying on to take its fearful plunge; to linger in the shadow of the solemn rocks three miles [4.8 kilometers] below; watching the river as, stirred by no visible cause, it heaved and eddied and awoke the echoes, being troubled yet, far down beneath the surface, by its giant leap; to have Niagara before me . . . ; to look upon it every day, and wake up in the night and hear its ceaseless voice: this was enough."[5]

By 1897 the scene had changed. Lines of railway tracks now approached the Falls from all directions (fig. 12.1). Stations and yards accumulated where the narrow gorge was crossed. Railways on the Canadian Frontier followed the top of the gorge, their stations overlooked the scene from the high land west of the Falls, and the streetcar followed the edge of the gorge. On the American Frontier the railway also followed the top of the gorge,

The original, natural scene at the Falls has been subject to considerable change over the years, as seen in these postcards. **Top:** Vegetation has been cleared, a large hotel added, and visitors view the scene from a horse carriage with road access along the crest of the gorge. **Bottom:** on the American Frontier, visitors might cross a narrow wooden bridge to climb the viewing platform at Terrapin Point. Note also the start of intrusive skyline development on the Canadian Frontier. (John Burtniak Collection [both])

and stations and lines backed up to the American Falls.

As described in the Rand McNally guide of 1897: "Niagara Falls is one of the points of easiest access in the world. It is fifteen hours' ride from Boston, twelve from New York, fourteen from Chicago, and one hour from Buffalo. Travellers by the Grand Trunk crossed the river on the Railway Suspension Bridge. . . . Travellers by the Michigan Central cross the river on the Cantilever Bridge. . . . The New York Central reaches the Falls direct from Rochester, and also by a line from Buffalo. . . . The promoters of two electric-car lines between Buffalo and the Falls promise they will be running 'electric trains' within a few months. . . . The Falls, never so accessible as now, will soon be yet easier to access."[6]

Horsedrawn carriages met all trains, nearby hotels lured the visitors to their doors,[7] and amusements proliferated as the railway companies provided fast excursion trains and cheap fares. Hotels and entrepreneurs promoted tightrope walks across the Whirlpool Rapids and barrel trips over the Falls and through the rapids.[8] Commercial and industrial greed had taken over "much of the grandeur from the spectacle of the cataract. No longer sublime, Niagara was quickly falling into disrepute, suffering from what one journalist called 'the disastrous results of a bad name.' "[9] The Falls, now in competition with the new coastal summer resorts that had arisen, was tawdry, disfigured, and the hotels old and costly.

A notorious "front" had developed on the Canadian side at the Falls by the 1860s and 1870s.[10] Tourists visiting the Horseshoe Falls were rewarded by tawdry museums, freak exhibitions, and sensational sideshows. Pickpockets and a carnival atmosphere prevailed. The American side had ugly stone dams, a gristmill, a hotel promenade with laundry hanging out to dry, and a "mammoth Bazaar" of cheap goods for tourists. Bath Island between the mainland and Goat Island had walls covered with advertising, a lumberyard, shanties where "Indian" goods were offered for sale, and a pulp mill with heaps of sawdust. Prospect Park contained fancy wooden structures, gaudy lights, and an enormous brightly painted tunnel for visitors to enter the Cave of the Winds. A stream of tar ran down the banks below the Falls at the gasworks. All favorable points of observation around the Falls had been fenced so that a charge could be made to view the Falls. The banks swarmed with sharpers, hucksters, and peddlers vying with industrial works.

Named "The father of the International Parks at Niagara Falls," Lord Dufferin Gov-

Fig. 12.1. Railways provided both towns at the Falls with greatly improved access, and promoted industry, tourism, and urban growth on both sides of the gorge upstream from the Falls. (From *A New Guide to Niagara Falls*, Rand McNally, 1897)

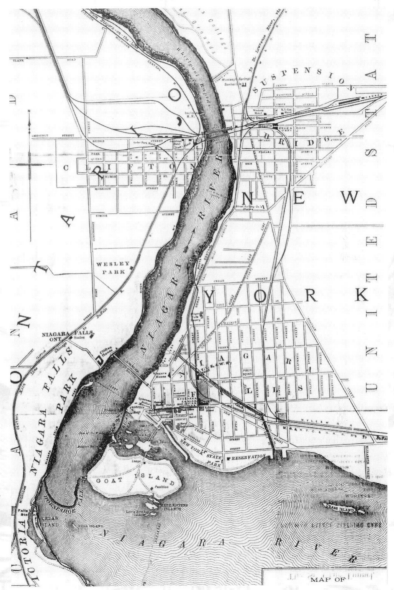

ernor General of Canada made the first public suggestion and took the first public action toward the betterment of conditions. In 1878 he wrote to the governor of New York and urged that the governments of Canada and the State of New York join together "to acquire whatever right might have been established against the public, and to form around the Falls a small public international park."[11] After years of constant pressure and lobbying, and in the face of violent opposition from industrialists and the upholders of private enterprise especially on the American side, in 1883 the New York State Legislature passed an act to

No longer "the sublime spectacle of nature," the Falls fell rapidly into disrepute as the railways brought in more and more visitors to view the now disfigured scene. (*The Graphic*, 9 October 1880)

preserve the scenery at the Falls. Some 167 hectares (412 acres) along the bank of the river, including 121 hectares (300 acres) under water and all of Goat Island, were purchased to become the first state park in the United States (fig. 12.2). Goat Island—the last remaining forested estate—was itself seriously threatened by development: it was being viewed for purchase and development as a palatial private hotel on private grounds.

A larger area along the rim of the gorge, from south of Goat Island to the Suspension Bridge across the Whirlpool Rapids, had been recommended for purchase in a State Survey of 1879, but the high cost of acquiring private land for romantic and sentimental reasons was considered prohibitive. A bond issue passed in 1885 when commissioners were appointed to control the newly acquired property, the state *reservation* (not "park") at Niagara. The preservation of scenic beauty had become a public purpose that warranted the expenditure of public money, a move without precedent

Fig. 12.2. The river scene at the Falls, despoiled by tawdry developments on both banks, was saved by the provision of public open space, a "park" on the Canadian bank and a "reservation" on the American bank. (Prepared by the Department of Geography, Brock University)

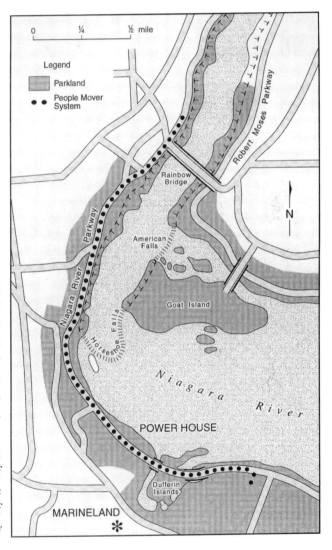

PARK AREAS AND ROAD ACCESS AT THE FALLS

in the United States. A fourfold increase in the number of visitors was soon recorded, an influx which in turn soon led to the provision of hotels and tourist-trap lures away from the immediate vicinity of the Falls.

Fences, signs, and gatehouses were removed; some 150 buildings and structures cleared; and the area redesigned using "back to nature" principles. Native trees and shrubs were planted, bridges and retaining walls constructed with facings of rustic stone, electric lights at night were banned, the reservation was closed at dusk, and scenery was safeguarded by restoring and protecting the banks from erosion. Monuments and memorials were excluded; sales and solicitations within the park were prohibited. Free public access was encouraged with charges levied only for the use of the elevators at Prospect Point to the foot of the American Falls, the use of carriages, boat rides on the *Maid of the*

Backed by a ridge that now carries an increasing number of towers and high-rise hotels, Table Rock House and the open space of Queen Victoria Park have replaced the hodgepodge of ugly commercial ventures that formerly lined the Canadian bank of the Niagara River at the Falls. (John N. Jackson)

Mist, and visits to the Cave of the Winds. These actions at the State Reservation refurbished the tarnished image that had prevailed, and placed Niagara among the nation's and the world's great parks.[12]

On the Canadian Frontier, after failure to involve the Dominion government, the Ontario Legislature passed comparable legislation in 1885, namely "An Act for the Preservation of the Natural Scenery about Niagara Falls." Some 62 hectares (154 acres) of land from above the Horseshoe Falls at the current Dufferin Islands to below the Falls at Clifton House were acquired, plus a water area of 128 hectares (317 acres) (fig. 9.2, p. 345). The whole of the upper slopes and north to the railway suspension bridge had been included in this plan, but again because of high land values these areas remained under private ownership. The property line was drawn along the Michigan Central (Canadian Southern) railroad just below the edge of the Niagara Escarpment where the park was backed by a steep wooded slope. Critical for the future, the commanding upper views were not placed under the commission's control.

The line of unsightly buildings and undesirable structures along the edge of the river was removed, and the area, suitably landscaped with trees, new roads, and paths, was opened as the Queen Victoria Niagara Falls Park in 1888. A new macadamized road was constructed through the park. Visitors were charged to cross the bridges to Dufferin Islands, to enter the tunnel behind the Horseshoe Falls, and to ride through the park in carriages. The park was also extended north along the gorge to Brock's Monument at Queenston Heights, where the Military Reservation with military, provincial, dominion, and private ownerships was placed under the control of the commissioners in 1895.

Important distinctions now emerged between the two parks. In the United States, where industry had flourished along the river, the commissioners controlled only a small extent of property. In Canada public land extended farther along the river front, but the bond issue had to be repaid by revenues from the park. As entrance fees, a restaurant, and franchises provided insufficient income, solvency depended upon the sale of waterpower privileges from the Niagara River to generate hydroelectricity within the park boundaries. These power rentals saved the park financially, but the power stations depleted the flow of water in the river and lowered the level of water where it crossed the Falls. The construction of the power plants, including the numerous excavations to lay underground conduits, destroyed scenic characteristics south of the Falls until filling and surface restoration was completed in 1918.[13]

To many it was intolerable that private works should be constructed in a public park. Hydroelectric stations conflicted with the public recreational-open space mandate. In 1908 the plant of the Ontario Power Company below the Falls was described as "especially Offensive" and "a most striking obstruction of the gorge,"[14] but controversial decisions had necessarily to be made by the commissioners to ensure survival of the park. Except for the Ontario Power plant, the stations were upstream of the Falls. Their grand architecture reflected both pride in the new achievements of electricity and proved worthy tourist attractions. Also, no alternative existed. Since the park surrounded the Falls on the Canadian Frontier, power facilities had to be located within its confines. The American Frontier did not have this dilemma; its power stations lay outside the park boundaries.

The principle of "natural scenery" enunciated by Frederick Law Olmsted and applied to the Niagara Reservation on the American side of the river meant that "nothing of an artificial character should be allowed a place on the property, no matter how valuable it might be under other circumstances and no matter for how little cost it may be had."[15] His plan for Goat Island involved an extensive system of walks to take people through the scenery and a series of stone seats to view the cascading water.

On the Canadian Frontier, in 1914 Olmsted was involved in the location and design of Table Rock House. In 1916 he urged that the administrative offices be located outside the park boundaries at the top of the bluff and protested against a shelter over the Spanish Aero Car cableway at the Whirlpool because it had "been executed with a deplorable lack of intelligent regard for the scenery."[16] Olmsted also urged strongly that Niagara Glen, later designated a Nature Reserve, be preserved for posterity because of its distinctive vegetation and scenery.

MANAGING THE NIAGARA RIVER

Not only the land but also the river had to be controlled and managed by the actions of humans. From 1842 to 1906 the Horseshoe Falls had receded at an estimated annual rate of 1.2 meters (3.8 feet) a year (fig. 1.5, p. 81). This diminished after the power diversions to 0.7 meters (2.3 feet) a year. Even so, erosion continued to cause concern. A rock fall in 1954 dislodged tons of rock from Prospect Point, and a notch in the center of the Horseshoe Falls was eroding rapidly.[17] With the decreased flow in the river, rocks were exposed through the veil of falling water at the American Falls. These problems were met by the construction of a submerged weir above the upper rapids, which raised the level of the Grass Island Pool, resolved the scenic problem at the American Falls, and increased the flow past Goat Island to the Horseshoe Falls.

Provisions for further remedial work were made in the Niagara River Treaty of 1940 and undertaken between 1954 and 1957 as a joint project between Ontario Hydro and the American Corps of Engineers. The bed of the river was deepened on both sides at the Horseshoe Falls and a thirteen-gate international control dam at the south end of the

Grass Island Pool replaced the earlier underwater weir to divert water from mid-channel. A five-gate extension was added in 1963. This spread the flow of water more evenly across the river, reduced the rate of erosion in the notch at the center, and provided an unbroken crestline at the Horseshoe Falls. At Terrapin Point—the area that had once accommodated the tower—the land was drained and then backfilled during the 1970s to create a large viewing area. The modern scene across the river at the Falls is therefore an amalgam of natural erosive forces and human controls including engineering structures, supervised excavations, the diversion of the river's flow to hydroelectric plants, and international decisions over the amounts of water that may be diverted. The natural river had become a managed phenomenon.

To offset concerns that the American Falls might degenerate from a vertical waterfall to a series of cascades, as part of an international study in 1969 the American Falls were drained by constructing a coffer dam across the top of the channel between Goat Island and the mainland. It was as if a human tap had turned off the river, the purpose being to examine the implications of further intervention.[18] Should the river scene be designed as a vast sculpture for the greatest visual effect or should the natural process of irregular rock falls continue? The report indicated that the removal of talus from the base of the Falls was technically feasible. Scale models demonstrated that a clear fall would heighten the dramatic effect of the Falls, particularly if the water level in the pool was raised by a downstream dam. Removal, however, was not recommended. It "would disrupt the local scene and . . . create, on a grand scale, an artificial waterfall in a formal park. It would interfere with the geologic process and would be contrary to the recent emphasis on environmental values."[19] The Falls would become static and unnatural. As no action has followed, the American Falls will continue to retreat gradually but steadily upstream as its rocks and those on Goat Island continue to erode and fall. Humanity had changed the course of nature, but nature on this occasion was allowed to prevail.

THE TWO PARK SYSTEMS

On the Canadian Frontier a continuous system of landscaped public open space now extends along the Niagara River for 56.3 kilometers (35 miles) from Old Fort Erie to the town of Niagara-on-the-Lake. World recognition has been obtained for the outstanding provision of formal and informal open space, the design of buildings, and a continuous Niagara River Parkway and recreation trail along the Upper, Middle, and Lower Niagara River. Renowned floral displays are to be found at Ontario Hydro's Floral Clock near Queenston, in Queen Victoria Park at the Falls; at the School of Horticulture next to the gorge; and at various golf courses, restaurants, parks, and historic sites along the parkway. A greenhouse with tropical birds near the Falls, a nearby fragrance garden for the blind, and the recent Butterfly Conservatory north of the Whirlpool provide colorful year-round attractions.[20]

On the American Frontier state reservations have expanded from Goat Island to the northern and southern ends of Grand Island, the Whirlpool, Devil's Hole, and Fort Niagara, but, except for Goat Island, the extent of open space is discontinuous and less evident. Goat Island separates the Canadian Horseshoe Falls from the American Falls and, as the island is wooded, its natural character helps to recall the original forested setting of the Falls. The outer circle of roads provides access to several exciting viewpoints that offer inspiring views of the Niagara River cascading down to the Falls, the Three Sisters Islands are set directly within the rapids, and Luna Island lies between the American and Bridal Veil Falls. Many small islands in

the Upper Rapids between Goat Island and the American Falls add scenic value to this attractive stretch of rushing water. In Prospect Park, close to the Rainbow Bridge, are the Observation Tower for viewing the scene and elevators that take the visitor close to the river where the *Maid of the Mist* boats can be boarded.

The Canadian side had retained the historic Chain Reserve, the strip of land next to the river that became part of the Niagara Parks Commission in the early 1900s, whereas New York State sold its One Mile Strip to private developers in the 1800s (fig. 3.3, p. 143). New York State had also to contend with the earlier and more intensive development of hydroelectric sites next to the river and the attendant development of heavy industry attracted to the river frontage, both factors that worked against a comparable system of open parkland along that bank.

Further, Ontario's Queen Victoria Park is backed by the escarpment ridge which separates the scenic vicinity of the Falls from the tourist areas behind it. The park with its wooded slopes allows visitors to enjoy vistas, to look over the river, and to take pleasure in gardens and landscaping at the edge of the Falls. Vantage points along the edge of the gorge also provide uninterrupted views of the American Falls. The layout and the relation-

The Niagara River Parkway, a resplendent commitment to high-quality landscape design, follows the river frontage on the Canadian Frontier from Fort Erie to Niagara-on-the-Lake, in stark contrast to the high-speed, multilane Robert Moses "Parkway" on the American side. (John N. Jackson)

ship of the Horseshoe, American, and Luna Falls can be appreciated as an entity, highlighting the scale, the grandeur of the scene, and the mighty erosive power of the wide, fast-flowing river.

The view from the New York State Reservation is more oblique to the Falls. With less engagement in the total scene, wooded Goat Island here provides the major scenic focus. There are splendid views of the rapids and across to the Canadian side, and pedestrian access to view the Luna and American Falls. Birds wheeling over the Falls are also part of the visual scene, as are the many colonies of ducks along the shores of the Upper River.

Several east-west roads on the Ontario side connect to the heavily used Niagara River Parkway for easy access to the Falls, which are clearly visible from the parkway. Traffic counts by the early 1990s indicated some 3.5 million vehicles with about 12 million passengers from April to October, excluding motorcoach passengers. On the American side the Robert Moses Parkway has intervened next to the Falls. Access to Goat Island from this parkway has been rebuilt, though entry to the island is unclear because of parking lots, old streets, and redevelopment. On the island the access bridge even terminates in a highway-oriented, clover-leaf

junction, and parking lots have displaced some of the woodlands and trails designed by Frederick Law Olmsted for contemplative appreciation of the natural scene.

The Robert Moses Parkway follows the Niagara River from Grand Island to Lewiston. As a multilane, limited-access, high-speed highway, it intrudes into the landscape bordering the rapids and separates the Niagara State Reservation Park from the nearby town and its visitor facilities. Recognized as an expensive mistake, its traffic has been diverted into the business district of Niagara Falls, and the roadway removed and replaced with grass. Tree planting to the east along the river above the Falls attempts to hide the extent of heavy industry, but places to stop and view Grass Island Pool and the broad, cascading river are few. Landscaping extends north from the Falls, where the parkway separates residential areas from the scenic gorge and its attractive fringe of open space.

The one-way road around Goat Island and the West River Drive on Grand Island are the only roads on the American Frontier that even begin to approach the scenic qualities of Ontario's Niagara River Parkway. Considerable contrast also exists where the two parkways cross the edge of the Niagara Escarpment, with panoramic views of the gorge, the lower Niagara River, and across the Ontario

A Viewmobile system from a parking area above the Falls has replaced the idea of massive road proposals and has helped considerably to retain a pedestrian environment. (John N. Jackson)

Plain to Lake Ontario and the skyline of Toronto. On the Canadian Frontier the two lanes of the Niagara River Parkway wind pleasantly through wooded Queenston Heights Park, and a scenic overview provides the opportunity to study the vista of the Lower Niagara River and its surrounds. On the American Frontier scenic character has been displaced by the four lanes of the Robert Moses Parkway and another four lanes for NY 104. The visually important scene has been subordinated to an inappropriate clutter of highways with their negative and distracting visual impact on the landscape.

The Canadian road network at the Falls was only narrowly saved from such destructive development. To cope with increasing traffic volumes, in 1966 a traffic consultant for the Ontario Development of Highways proposed high-speed freeways and a tunnel approach to the Horseshoe Falls.[21] A one-way traffic system planned along the river eliminated intersections, and a new riverside road carried up to seven traffic lanes (fig. 12.3). Parking facilities included multistory garages and surface parking lots close to the Falls. A two- and three-level promenade-viewing area was envisaged at the Falls, with pedestrian walks separated from the lines of traffic by overpasses. These grandiose, automobile-oriented proposals were rejected by the Niagara Parks Commission: "Informal development should be the general rule. . . . We must protect the green turfed and pleasant planted areas."[22] Instead, a "people-mover" system of buses, recommended by landscape consultants, came into operation in 1985, at first running from a southern parking area near Chippawa to the Rainbow Bridge and later expanded to Queenston Heights. This system and the elimination of most roadside parking spaces helped to retain the significant areas next to the Falls as landscaped pedestrian environments.[23]

Subsequently, several studies have focused on scenic quality, amenity, and the provision of open space along the river frontage. In 1988 the Niagara Parks Commission prepared a twenty-year plan that emphasized the need to relieve visitor pressures next to the Falls by extending activity along the Niagara Gorge to Queenston Heights and by increasing the length of stay and the visitor season with more themed attractions such as landscaped gardens and opening the gorge. "Gateways" for the reception of visitors and as centers of attraction in their own right were proposed at Fort Erie, Niagara Falls, and Niagara-on-the-Lake, and a linkage to a Welland Canal Parkway would connect the Niagara Parks System with the trail and parkway system expected along the Welland Canal.[24]

On the American Frontier reports have stressed the need for action to improve the deteriorated environment along the river frontage.[25] *Niagara Waterfront Master Plan, 1992* studied the economic and recreational potential that existed along the gorge between the Niagara reservation and Lewiston. With a major goal being to increase the usage of open space along the gorge, a trail system was proposed along the edge of the Upper River. A group organized by the Niagara Falls Area Chamber of Commerce advocated priority for the waterfront between Wheatfield and Fort Niagara and that projects be started in the area which they named "Niagara the Park."

A later report urged the need for action "to integrate an understanding of Niagara Falls USA and Niagara Falls Canada as one

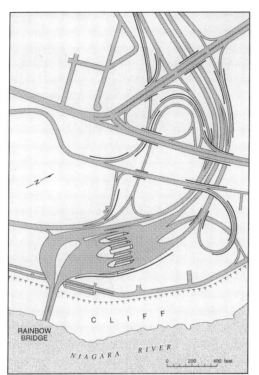

RAINBOW
BRIDGE

C L I F F

N I A G A R A   R I V E R

0   200   400 feet

Fig. 12.3. A Conflict Situation: A Multitude of Highways or Scenic Quality at the Falls? A severe conflict between highways and the high-amenity quality of the scene at the Falls on the Canadian Frontier was averted in 1966 when the Niagara Parks Commission opposed grandiose provincial highway proposals, and then introduced a Viewmobile people-mover system from a parking area south of the Falls. (Prepared by the Department of Geography, Brock University)

city in two countries; the complementary assets on both sides of the River; existing and future plans and projects; the environmental and development opportunities; and priority actions to stimulate economic development, protect and enhance a cultural heritage, and ideas for the future of Niagara Falls and region."[26] And when in 1998 the same consultants studied the southern end of the river, they argued for "seamless crossing" at the Peace Bridge and an international zone around the two communities that would allow Americans to act and operate on the Canadian side as they

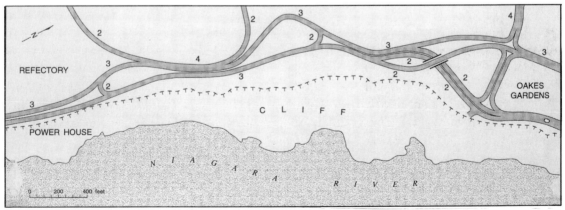

REFECTORY

POWER HOUSE

C L I F F

OAKES
GARDENS

N I A G A R A   R I V E R

0   200   400 feet

would under American law, and Canadians to do the same on the American side.[27] As with the international achievement of the St. Lawrence Seaway, an international approach to tourism at the Falls and along the Niagara River could become an item on the political agenda for mutual consideration between the two nations.

THE RECREATIONAL-SCENIC CONFLICT

As Carver (1975) has stated, in the vicinity of the Falls exceptional natural beauty vies with honky-tonk blare and glare as vendors compete for the tourist dollars: "Niagara Falls is the classic example of man's capacity to smother and tarnish the very places he most admires. It is a place of majestic beauty, and also a scene of humiliating follies. It is a prodigy to be spoken of in superlatives: the biggest, the ugliest, the most extraordinary."[28]

The exciting river scene can be viewed from tunnels behind the Horseshoe Falls, boat rides on the *Maid of the Mist*, the Spanish Aero Car over the Whirlpool, and in tours via Viewmobile, helicopter, coach, and taxi. Pedestrian walkways have been placed along the banks of the river, in the gorge, and on the international bridges. Elevators and inclines

carry passengers up and down the cliffs to the *Maid of the Mist* landings and to and from the higher levels at Table Rock. At night during the summer the Falls are illuminated with colored lights, which helps to extend the viewing period and also the operating hours in the commercial-entertainment establishments. A winter success is the Festival of Lights once held simultaneously on both sides, but recently on the Canadian side only.

Along Clifton Hill in Niagara Falls, Ontario, extending into Ferry Street-Victoria Avenue and along the ridge overlooking the Falls, and spurred by Louis Tussard's English Wax Museum of 1959, a circus atmosphere has emerged with the honky-tonk blare and glare of flashing lights, advertisements, and tourist facilities. The carnival atmosphere includes several daredevil and wax museums, souvenir stores, and amusement complexes, which together with hotels and motels provide a range of tourist attractions that cater to large tourist crowds and are as much a part of the landscape as the adjacent protected environment of Queen Victoria Park.

This tourism on the Canadian side is dispersed to several locations across the landscape. Several distinct tourist districts exist. Downtown Niagara Falls is associated closely with the railway era and the railway bridges across the gorge. At the Falls the primary attraction of Queen Victoria Park extends to above the Niagara Escarpment via Clifton Hill, which spreads in three directions: south to the Fallsview area overlooking the Falls; west via Victoria Avenue to the tourist area along Ferry Street-Lundy's Lane, which includes the Lundy's Lane battlefield site; and north via the farther tourist area of Victoria Avenue to Downtown Niagara Falls. There are other tourist districts centered on the Marineland Theme Park, north along River Road to the Whirlpool, and south along the Parkway to Chippawa. The Niagara Square Shopping Mall, an associated motel, and the Niagara Falls Art Gallery/Kurelek Collection may be added as tourist locations. Streetscaping within and between these areas and improved circulation between the different tourist districts have both to be improved if tourists are to be encouraged to move between the various attractions.

The range and the variety of attractions at the Falls may compare with a Disneyland, but with the substantial difference that Disneyland, centrally owned and controlled, is designed and organized as a recreational theme park. Niagara Falls has no central management. The attractions, dispersed across the landscape, are only in part controlled by public agencies with amenity interests such as the Niagara Parks Commission and the New York State Reservation. Tourism across the Canadian-American boundary does not function as a unit as with other industries; rather, responsibility is spread across many different types of public and private agencies and lacks any central, controlling mechanism. The industry has also grown piecemeal through numerous public and private decisions, and most are fitted into the urban landscape wherever a place can be found and often in competition with other urban functions and activities.

Observation towers described as "space needles" and high-rise hotels providing magnificent views of the Falls together with entertainment, shopping, and dining facilities have burgeoned in the Fallsview area above the Falls. The Seagram (now Minolta) Tower, built in 1962, which rises 99.1 meters (325 feet) above ground level, was followed by the Oneida Tower (now Casino Niagara), constructed in 1964. The tallest of all, the slender Skylon Tower, built in 1964, rises 160 meters (525 feet). In 1966 the high-rise developments on the crest were linked to Table Rock next to the Falls by an incline railway. They face on the American side the ungainly Prospect Point observation tower next to the American Falls. This tower, 85 meters (259.1 feet) high, takes people to the top to view the Falls and to the gorge for the

Maid of the Mist sightseeing vessels.

The Canadian towers were at first viewed favorably by the Niagara Parks Commission as "distinctive landmarks" but, as their number increased and new proposals arose, attitudes changed and commercial tourism was again perceived as a threat that would destroy the quality of the environment.[29] There was concern that the Falls would become localized within a forest of surrounding towers that would overshadow the dramatic features of the river. The offending towers, located outside the protective jurisdiction of the Niagara Parks Commission, lay within the City of Niagara Falls, where tax assessment, employment, tourist expansion, and the promotion of development were and still are deemed more important aspects of the municipal decision-making process than the quality and amenity aspects of the landscape.

Clifton Hill in Niagara Falls, Ontario, provides a garish but convivial scene of tourist gaiety that competes with the Falls as a natural attraction.
(John N. Jackson [both])

By the 1980s municipal zoning regulations in Niagara Falls, Ontario, required that buildings be set back 24.4 meters (80 feet) from the westerly limit of the commission's lands. The maximum height of buildings at this line should not exceed 19.8 meters (65 feet) above ground level, and beyond this distance an additional 0.3 meters (1 foot) in height might be added for each additional 1.2 meters (4 feet) from the setback line. Even so, tall structures have continued to accrue: Casino Niagara, using its height to incorporate a high, cascading waterfall, has replaced the Maple Leaf Village amusement area and the Oneida Tower where an enormous Ferris wheel had revolved since 1979 within clear view of the Falls; Pyramid Place (now Imax Theater) housed within its six stories "the largest movie screen" in Canada; high-rise hotel blocks have been constructed on the skyline close to the towers; and at Marineland it is anticipated that the artificial mountain will be crowned with a turretted medieval castle. The attractions continue to expand and compete with each other for the tourist dollar.

In 1974 the American Falls International Board recognized that visual attractiveness included "all that comes within the direct view of the Falls on both sides of the river."[30] The protective park belt was "no longer an effective method of achieving the original purpose of the Parks. If unchecked, the steady build-up of new construction on the skyline [would] result in an artificial environment that [would] overshadow . . . the Falls."[31] The International Joint Commission urged an international study to set priorities for future development and recommended that the two federal governments discourage the local governments "from undertaking or permitting future developments that would detract from the visual enjoyment of the Niagara Falls."[32] As no such action has followed, the skyline has been dominated increasingly by large-scale prestigious hotels.

On the American side tourist developments are more subdued. In 1974 the City of Niagara Falls, New York, built a convention center. Other developments have included an enclosed Winter Garden filled with tropical plants, a Native Indian Center for the Living Arts in the shape of a turtle (now defunct) and the Rainbow Centre mall (also defunct), and several major hotels to redevelop a deteriorated landscape. A landscaped pedestrian walkway and visitor center have also been completed. At the edge of the gorge the Schoellkopf Geological Museum and the Aquarium of Niagara Falls have replaced power plants and industry, while Goat Island, managed by the state, has retained its extensive area of public open space and the popular Cave of the Winds trip.

High-rise structures of tourism at the Falls by the 1980s. (John N. Jackson [all])

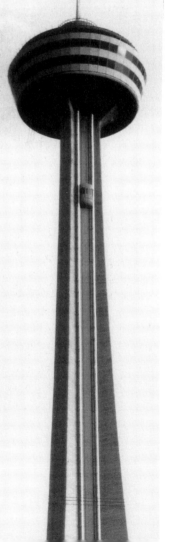

By 1981 it was estimated that 12.5 million visitors a year came to the Canadian side and some 5 million to the American side at the Falls.[33] By 1997 tourism had increased greatly: to 1.6 million people at the *Maid of the Mist*, 1.1 million at the Journey Behind The Falls, and some 662,000 at the Falls Incline Railway. On the American Frontier in the same year, an estimated 4 million people visited the Niagara Reservation State Park at the Falls. Peak visitor periods at both parks were in July and August on weekends and during Canadian and American holidays. Stopovers might be for a day or weekend visit from nearby places, part of a North American holiday by automobile or coach, or a brief stop-off during an aircoach tour with groups from across the world.

By 1994 a regional *Accommodation Survey* indicated 14 million annual visitors came to Niagara Falls, Ontario: 44 percent from the United States, 27 percent from Ontario, 18 percent from overseas, 8 percent from Quebec, and 3 percent from the rest of Canada.[34] Direct spending on accommodation was $72.5 million in Niagara Falls (74 percent), out of $98 million in the Niagara Region; Niagara-on-the-Lake followed at 10.8 percent and then St. Catharines at 8.5 percent. Motels and hotels had developed close to and overlooking the Falls, in the Center Street-Ferry Street area, and in a linear strip extending along Lundy's Lane (Highway 20) almost to the Welland Canal on the Canadian Frontier, and to a lesser extent along Pine Avenue (US 62) and Buffalo Avenue in New York.

Tourism at the Falls and in adjacent areas along the river had certainly become a feature of considerable magnitude, drawing an annual influx of tourists from the vicinity and around the world, in strong competition with other national and international locations. The industry had become big business, the principal issues being how to retain and improve the quality of the environment at and around the Falls, how to extend the length of visitor stay, how to spread the tourist load and its dollars more evenly across the Frontier, and how to extend the tourist season from its limited, six-month May-October high period.

MAJOR NEW TOURIST DEVELOPMENTS

Designed, constructed, and maintained by the Niagara Parks Commission, a Niagara River Recreation Trail has been completed along the Niagara River Parkway from Old Fort Erie to Fort George in Niagara-on-the-

Lake. Walkers, cyclists, joggers, and roller-bladers use this continuous paved and land-scaped route between the two lakes. Small bridges separated from the parkway span the creeks and ravines en route, and markers and plaques have been added to explain historic features along this trail.[35] Links have been provided with the Bruce Trail that extends from Queenston Heights to the Bruce Penin-sula, and the Niagara River Recreational Trail will become part of a Lakeshore Trail that is being extended from Toronto via Hamilton along the south shore of Lake Ontario, and then along the river to cross the anticipated replacement Peace Bridge into Buffalo.

Another achievement by the Niagara Parks Commission is that since 1996 the grounds of the Niagara Parks Botanical Gar-dens have featured the Niagara Parks But-terfly Conservatory. Over two thousand but-terflies with over fifty species are housed within a 1,022-square-meter (11,000-square-foot), climate-controlled tropical environ-ment. Over seven hundred thousand visitors were attracted during 1997, making this attraction second only to the *Maid of the Mist* cruise and to the Journey Behind The Falls. Open throughout the year, the conservatory has helped end the image of tourism as a sea-sonal, summertime-only activity that ends on Labor Day and restarts in the spring.

The most important new tourist develop-ment, Casino Niagara, described as "interim," opened in late 1996. The 8,918.4 square meters (96,000 square feet) of gaming space included more than 2,700 slot machines; 144 gaming tables for blackjack, baccarat, roulette, poker, and other card games; and a special high-limit gaming room. Craps was added in 1999, after being made legal along with blackjack and baccarat. Open for twenty-four hours a day throughout the year, with restaurants, bars, lounges, and food courts, the complex soon employed more than 3,500 persons and was larger than any other employer on the Niagara Frontier except General Motors. From 27,000 to 48,000 patrons were attracted daily, or close to ten million visitors during the first year of operation. The casino had become the single most visited tourist attraction in Canada, and Niagara Falls the nation's third major destina-tion for tourism after Vancouver and Toronto.

The urban impact, immediate and signif-icant, included zoning for fourteen new hotel developments, including three five-star hotels,[36] and the expansion of existing hotel, dining, entertainment, and retail space. New retail outlet malls were also approved. The casino has estimated that 83 percent of the wages paid to employees are spent in the community, mostly on housing and furniture and then, in descending order, on transportation, food and beverage, apparel and services, local restaurants and bars, and entertainment. The casino pays to lease off-site office space and purchases locally items such as flowers, articles for its gift stores, and supplies for its restaurants. The estimated spin-off into the region is three thousand jobs, and a further number of this magnitude are employed in indirect jobs throughout Ontario.[37]

A major new tourist facility and catalyst for development had been achieved, with high expectations for the future. At the start of the new century, the big questions are whether gambling will prove an ephemeral success or a permanent change to the economic climate of Niagara Falls and the neighboring region, the latter being anticipated. And will a competing type of venture or ventures be constructed on nearby American territory in Buffalo or Niagara Falls, New York, perhaps under Native auspices such as the Seneca nation?

In 1994 the Canadian casino became part of the provincial initiative known as the Niagara Gateway Project, which had as its objectives: "to facilitate the development of a tourism development strategy which would position the Niagara Region as a high-yield, year-round, world-class tourist destination. . . . Niagara's tourism industry is considered underdeveloped. Typically, visitors stay for a short period of time and spend only a little money. The Niagara Gateway Project, it was hoped, would inspire a turn around."[38] Though anathema to many,[39] but as an Ontario provincial emphasis on gambling to raise revenue seems unlikely to change, this money-spinning aspect of tourism can be expected to provide an important new economic base for the Canadian Frontier.

The issue of particular concern, the overshadowing of the river scene by encircling the Falls with high-rise hotels, was addressed in a 1998 Tourist Area Development Strategy which acknowledged that "Niagara Falls is a tourist icon. . . . Yet, the importance of Niagara Falls as a national symbol and its significance as an economic generator for the Niagara Region, the Province of Ontario and Canada has not yet been fully recognized."[40] The multiple recommendations then included a major landscaping and greening program to more closely connect the area above the Falls and Queen Victoria Park with the city. There was also the possibility of converting the existing Canadian Pacific track at the top of Clifton Hill to a Grand Boulevard with a public transit system that would integrate the different tourist areas, but that depends on the reorganization of the rail system and the future of highway-rail crossings over the Niagara River.

On the vexing question of more high-rise hotel developments hemming in the Falls, the consultant argued rather belatedly and perhaps with tongue in cheek that: "High-rise buildings can add to the beauty of Niagara Falls if they are designed with excellence in mind. Therefore, it is important to conscientiously plan the emerging skyline. This requires a regulatory approach which is focussed on built form and careful consideration of each development. . . . Each development needs to be well designed, carefully sited and massed to avoid overshadowing the Park and other parts of the Tourist Area; to ensure a solid wall is not created at the top of the escarpment and to enhance the pedestrian environment by maintaining sunlight standards, ensuring skyviews and mitigating wind impacts."[41] With amenity and commercial expansion again in severe conflict, policy had changed from height restrictions and setbacks at the edge of the Niagara Escarpment to the creative design of new buildings within settings of landscaped open space. "The intention is to permit tall buildings to be built but to reduce their impact by having them become smaller and to provide for appropriate gaps between high-rise buildings."[42]

These thoughts were followed in late 2000 by the announcement that a permanent casino would be located on the Murray Hill site above the Falls. The site covers 8 hectares (19.8 acres). Gaming space will be doubled. Expected are a thirty-story, 368-room hotel; a shopping area; a theater; a parking garage for three thousand cars; walkways; and a large glass dome as the centerpiece of the design. Some five thousand permanent full- and part-time jobs are anticipated, with about the same number indirectly created. All will be financed by private enterprise, with ownership upon completion resting with the Ontario provincial government. The interim casino will remain in active use until the expected completion date in 2004, but whether in the future there will be one or two casinos is as yet unknown.

The permanent casino as a megaproject is expected to be linked by monorail along the existing Canadian Pacific track to an all-season amphitheater housing 3,500 people during the colder months, and with a summer capacity of 15,000. The amphitheater would be located next to Marineland, which opened in 1961 and in 1998 added Friendship Cove, a new whale pool billed as one of the largest facilities of its kind to provide a new habitat for killer whales. Ground was broken in late 2000 for expanded whale facilities with three new aquariums south of the present facilities, including a 5-kilometer (1.9-mile) raft ride on a man-made river through River Country with wildlife exhibitions and aquariums, and walk-through attractions where fish and aquatic animals may be viewed from glass tunnels in Shark Encounter and Ocean Aquarium.

The expansion of tourism at the Falls involves more than Casino Niagara and Marineland. CyberPort Niagara offers hands-on exhibits that entertain and educate through various interactive displays, including optical illusions. Ripley's Entertainment has announced the construction of a large acquarium on a yet to be determined site, and across the river a new aquarium has been announced by Aquafalls as a major contribution to redevelopment in Niagara Falls, New York. A Niagara Film Festival, introduced in 1998, featured fun and nostalgic classic movies, one of which starred Marilyn Monroe, who in 1952 in the film *Niagara* took advantage of the city's reputation as Honeymoon Capital of the World. The annual Winter Festival of Lights has in some years attracted 1.5 million spectators. The People-Mover transportation system on the Ontario Frontier has been extended from the Falls to Queenston Heights. The Toronto Power Station that ceased operation in 1974 is expected to be used for some form of commercial space, possibly combined with a museum, as a collaborative project between private enterprise, Ontario Hydro, and the Niagara Parks Commission.[43]

Tourism on a grand scale, now based on international capital, major large-scale high-rise hotels, artificial entertainment, and amusement rather than the grand river scene of the pre-railway era, has become the seemingly endless catalyst for tourist growth and economic expansion at the Falls and its vicinity.

THE TWO CITIES OF NIAGARA FALLS

Complex and contradictory relationships have developed within and between the two cities.[44] Both cities evolved in close association with the grand natural scene of the Falls, but as later features in the landscape than the two portages that had previously bypassed the Falls. Both cities lie on the extreme fringe of their national territories, and both rely on industry, the natural environment, hydroelectricity, transportation, and tourism for their strengths. Hydroelectricity provided a clean, abundant, and relatively cheap source of power for domestic and industrial purposes. The new source of power also attracted heavy industry, including unsightly chemical and electrometallurgical plants close to the Falls and along the Niagara River to the south, which reduced the flow of water across the Horseshoe, Luna, and American

Falls; greatly diminished their quality and tourist potential; and added the severe impact of industrial air and water pollution.

Tourism at the end of the nineteenth century with excessive commercialism and daredevil stunts then nearly destroyed the pleasures of a visit to the Falls. Today, as more and more visitors arrive, more and more facilities are required next to and in the vicinity of the scenic climax that dominates both Frontiers. The difficulty of locating these facilities and amenities in pleasant surroundings, without damaging or destroying the very landscapes that the visitors have come to enjoy, has become a task requiring careful foresight and planning in a money-driven economy. The expansion of tourism, primarily an external force, is based on larger Canadian, American, and worldwide populations; their rising real incomes; and their ability to travel by car, coach, and airplane to distant locations. The natural scene, previously the prime attraction, has become backdrop.

Both cities at the Falls have dual downtown areas, old central business districts that grew close to the gorge in conjunction with the railways, and a more recent clustering of tourist facilities near the Falls. Both have heavy stakes in the traffic flows over the highway and railway bridges that cross the river. Both have parkland next to the river managed by provincial or state agencies. Important differences reflect the change in direction of the river as it crosses the rock outcrop at the Falls and makes a sharp right-angle turn, a physical phenomenon that influenced the development of portage routes longer and inland on the Canadian Frontier and shorter across the elbow of turn on the American Frontier, and of hydroelectric canals which could more easily divert water on the American side of the river.

With the expanding new industry of tourism, the advantages of situation and location at the Falls accrued on the Canadian Frontier. Here, at the edge of glacial Lake Tonawanda, the river was set within a gorge, and the flat land along the banks of the river was backed by the steep rise up the Niagara Escarpment to the Fallsview area above the Falls. The American side had no such advantage. Flat inland from the river, it enjoyed no elevated terrain. Both sides enjoyed the majestic river scene, but the Canadian side had the advantage of direct views toward all the Falls, the ability to see the scene along and next to the river from the heights, and though long since fallen into the gorge, the initial advantage of Table Rock that was soon appreciated as the best vantage point for viewing the extraordinary scene.

Both sides had to be saved from the ravages of railways, industry, and the obscene commercialization of tourism and hydroelectric power plants. This extensive process of reclamation has been more extensive and carried to a greater degree of success on the Canadian Frontier, where Queen Victoria Park has been extended into a lake-to-lake riverside parkway designed to high visual standards. The Niagara Reservation State Park on the American Frontier was restricted. It did not extend to the Upper and Lower Niagara Rivers, where the One Mile Strip facing the river had been sold, and was later spoiled by the construction of a high- speed, multilane highway along most of the river's length. The contrast is marked between the quiet, noncommercialized, continuous, two-lane, scenic Niagara River Parkway along the Canadian bank, and the high-speed, multi-lane, heavily travelled traffic route of Highway 190, River Road, and the Robert Moses Parkway on the American bank.

Expanding tourism with its auto-based clientele has presented a different set of problems and opportunities for the two cities. There are dissimilar foci of attention. On the Canadian Frontier the current emphasis is on Casino Niagara, the expansion of hotel and amusement facilities, and the concern that high-rise developments will rim and mar the high caliber and quality of the scene at the Falls. Architectural and landscape judgments have been presented as the answer to this critical dilemma but, through the sheer volume of increasing demand, the Falls are likely to become overshadowed by further high-rise developments on the Canadian side.

The American focus is different. Although reasonable progress has been made, there remains the need to renew the outmoded urban and industrial areas that grew with the railway, before the automobile transferred the emphasis on tourist activity away from the stations and the bridges across the gorge to the vicinity of the Falls and Goat Island. This island, more so than on the Canadian Frontier, is backed on the mainland by the confusion of old with modern developments, by the regular grid of an urban street pattern that carries through and local traffic, and by a closed section of the Robert Moses Parkway that awaits redesign with landscaping.

Today, the two cities of Niagara Falls are linked across the gorge by a combined railway-highway bridge, a railway bridge, and a highway bridge. The new highway bridges with direct access to multilane provincial and state highway systems have encouraged new patterns of urban growth, including industrial developments, the location of major shopping centers in the suburbs, and the decline of former central business and tourist districts. Away from the river, both cities are unassuming, mundane environments that require landscaping and much civic improvement. On the Canadian Frontier land next to the QEW has attracted light industrial plants and new residences, and there are chemical and glass plants in outlying areas. The inner residential areas contain dispersed industrial plants and strips of commercial development along the major routes, especially Lundy's Lane on the Canadian Frontier. On the American side industrialization is more prominent. Sprawl and suburbanization have taken place to a greater extent, often outside the city's boundaries in the Towns of Niagara and Wheatfield to the east. The Canadian side is less confined administratively than its American neighbor, and development does not overspill into adjacent jurisdictions, as is commonplace on the American Frontier.

Heavy manufacturing industry expanded greatly when the river was harnessed for power, especially on the American side where a sequence of electrochemical works along Buffalo Avenue (NY 384) follows the river. Notorious toxic waste sites that detract from the tourist image lie within and outside the city boundaries. The industrial complex and the tracks that once lined the top of the gorge have been replaced by the high-speed Robert Moses Parkway, but this inglorious highway

route also separates the inland urban residential areas from their river frontage. How to more successfully take advantage of the gorge, its turbulent river, and its limited fringe of open space have become important to Niagara Falls, New York. Though industrial buildings next to the gorge have been cleared, traces and still-functioning outlets for waste tunnels and sewage carrying contaminated material to the river remain in the side of the gorge.

Among the noted dissimilarities between the two cities is that the Canadian side has attracted American hydroelectric companies, but not the reverse. Niagara Falls, New York, has a more intensive industrial area to the south than was ever achieved on the Canadian Frontier. Traffic across the Rainbow Bridge has direct multilane access through an attractive pedestrian-free streetcar cutting lined with stone to the QEW in Ontario; in New York State the same traffic feeds directly onto the streets of the city with its many junctions through local and cross traffic.

After a century or more of tension between tourism and manufacturing in both countries, tourism has more closely occupied the vicinity of the Falls, and hydroelectric generation has moved to the Niagara Escarpment. As much manufacturing has also moved away, both cities face severe problems of industrial decline and urban obsolescence, aggravated by the transition from rail transport to the dominant movement of goods and passengers by truck and automobile. Both also face urban change and reorientation as the industrial city changes to its postindustrial counterpart. And as the two cities advance inexorably into the future, extensive landscaping and civic design are required for the renowned areas around the Falls to compete successfully with other world locations as tourist, living, and work environments in the postindustrial world. The quality of the environment has to be stressed continually, since both cities sit astride a major world tourist attraction. They seek both to attract tourism and to keep their manufacturing functions. Tourism plays a larger role in the Canadian city, but the American city having to cope with toxic dumps must also make a considerable number of improvements.

NOTES

1. E. McKinsey, *Niagara Falls: Icon of the American Sublime* (Cambridge, Mass.: Cambridge University Press, 1985). See also J. E. Adamson, *Niagara: Two Centuries of Changing Attitudes, 1697–1901* (Washington, D.C.: Corcoran Gallery of Art, 1985).

2. A. Runke, "The Role of Niagara in America's Scenic Preservation," in Adamson, *Niagara*, p. 125.

3. For the development of tourism on the Canadian Frontier see G. A. Seibel, ed., *Niagara Falls, Canada: A History of the City and the World Famous Beauty Spot* (Niagara Falls, Ont.: Kiwanis Club of Stamford, 1967); and *Ontario's Niagara Parks: A History* (Niagara Falls, Ont.: Niagara Parks Commission, 1985). For the American Frontier see M. F. Williams, *A Brief History of Niagara Falls, New York* (Niagara Falls, N.Y.: Niagara Falls Public Library, 1972).

4. K. Dubinsky, *The Second Greatest Disappointment: Honeymooning and Tourism at Niagara Falls* (Toronto: Between the Lines), published as *The Second Greatest Disappointment: Honeymooners, Heterosexuality, and the Tourist Industry at Niagara Falls* (New Brunswick, N.J.: Rutgers University Press, 1999).

5. C. Dickens, *American Notes For General Circulation* (London: Chapman and Hall, Cheap Edition, 1850), p. 133.

6. *A New Guide to Niagara Falls and Vicinity* (Chicago: Rand, McNally, 1893), pp. 8–9. The transition from the sublimity of nature to Niagara as the quintessential natural landscape of America is covered in W. Irwin, *The New Niagara: Tourism, Technology, and the Landscape of Niagara Falls, 1776–1917* (University Park: Pennsylvania State University Press, 1996).

7. For a history of hotels, see G. A. Seibel, "The World's Most Famous Address," in Seibel, *Niagara Falls, Canada*, pp. 48–59.

8. K. S. Brong, *The Niagara Daredevils* (Newfane, N.Y.: New York Star Printing, 1955).

9. P. Berton, *Niagara: A History of the Falls* (Toronto: McClelland and Stewart, 1992; paperback ed., 1997), p. 174.

10. G. A. Seibel, "River of Pleasure," in G. A. Seibel, *Niagara Falls, Canada*, pp. 261–67.

11. R. L. Way, *Ontario's Niagara Parks: A History* (Niagara Falls, Ont.: Niagara Parks Commission, 1960), p. 15. Frederick E. Church, landscape artist, and Frederick Law Olmsted, landscape architect, with Henry Hobson Richardson, the Romanesque architect, and William Dorsheimer, district attorney for northern New York State, started the movement for public parks. Lord Dufferin initiated the public action.

12. For actions on the American Frontier see J. T. Gardiner, *Special Report of New York State Survey on the Preservation of the Scenery of Niagara Falls 1879* (Albany, N.Y.: Charles Van Benthuysen, 1880), p. 8; T. V. Welch, "How Niagara Was Made Free: The Passage of the Niagara Reservation Act in 1885," *Buffalo Historical Society, Publications* 5 (1903): 325–59; and T. Evershed, "Map of Land Proposed to Be Taken by the Commissioners of the State Reservations of Niagara, 1883," *Science* (15 May 1885).

13. For park developments on the Canadian Frontier see *Annual Report of the Commission for Queen Victoria Niagara Falls Parks, 1895* (Toronto, 1896), pp. 6–24. The centennial publication is G. A. Seibel, *Ontario's Niagara Parks: One Hundred Years* (Niagara Falls, Ont.: Niagara Parks Commission, 1985).

14. J. W. Spencer, "Spoliation of the Falls of Niagara," An Address before the American Association for the Advancement of Science, *Popular Science Monthly* 72 (1908): 291, 304.

15. S. H. Olsen, *The Distinctive Charms of Niagara Scenery: Frederick Law Olmsted and the Niagara Reservation* (Niagara Falls, N.Y.: Buscaglia-Castellani Art Gallery, 1985), p. 7.

16. F. L. Olmsted, "Report on Table Rock House," 10 July 1914, in *Twenty-Ninth Annual Report of the Commissioners for the Queen Victoria Niagara Falls Park* (1915), pp. 34–36; and "Report of Frederick Law Olmsted," 5 May 1916, in *Thirty-First Annual Report of the Commissioners for the Queen Victoria Niagara Falls Park* (1917), pp. 31–33.

17. Regular Veterans Associations, *The Collapse at Niagara* (Buffalo, N.Y.: Dougan Press, 1954).

18. American Falls International Board, *Preservation and Enhancement of the American Falls at Niagara*, Final Report to the International Joint Commission, Appendix B, Aesthetics, 1974, p. 3. See also J. T. Johnston et al., *The Preservation of Niagara Falls: Final Report* (Ottawa: Special International Niagara Board, 1930), p. 17 and Appendix C.

19. International Joint Commission, *Preservation and Enhancement of the American Falls* (Ottawa and Washington, D.C., 1975), p. 15. For earlier statements see *The Preservation of Niagara Falls: Final Report of the Special International Niagara Board* (Ottawa: Ministry of the Interior and Mines, 1929); and *Preservation and Improvement of the Scenic Beauty of the Niagara Falls and Rapids* (Washington, D.C.: United States Printing Office,

1937). A recent statement is Goals and Objectives Committee, Erie and Niagara Counties Regional Planning Board, *International Environmental Study: Enhancement of the Niagara River* (Buffalo, N.Y.: Erie and Niagara Counties Regional Planning Board, 1971); and J. E. Adamson, *Niagara: Two Centuries of Changing Attitudes, 1697–1901* (Washington, D.C.: Corcoran Gallery of Art, 1985).

20. Many parkway features can be attributed to Thomas B. McQuesten, chairman of the Niagara Parks Commission from 1934 to 1994; see R. Barnsley, *Thomas B. McQuesten* (Markham, Ont.: Fitzhenry and Whiteside, 1987), pp. 45–52.

21. De Leuw, Cather and Company, *Functional Planning Report: Proposed Roadway in the City of Niagara Falls* (Don Mills, Ont., 1966).

22. Niagara Parks Commission, *Eighty-first Annual Report, 1967* (Niagara Falls, Ont., 1968), pp. 38–39.

23. Richard Strong and Associates, *The Niagara Parks Commission— Long Range Comprehensive Planning Studies 1969* (Toronto: Richard Strong and Associates, 1969), pp. 16, 19.

24. Moriyama & Tashima Planning Limited, for the Niagara Parks Commission, *Ontario's Niagara Parks Planning The Second Century. A One-Hundred-Year Vision* (Toronto: Moriyama & Tashima Planning Limited, 1988).

25. These reports are introduced in Waterfront Regeneration Trust, *Niagara's Future: A Citizens Vision for Niagara Falls and Region* (Toronto: Waterfront Regeneration Trust, 1997).

26. Ibid.

27. Waterfront Regeneration Trust, *Buffalo-Fort Erie International Waterfront Gateway Strategy* (Toronto: Waterfront Regeneration Trust, 1998); quoted in the *St. Catharines Standard*, 14 November 1998. This study was financed jointly by the Town of Fort Erie and the City of Buffalo.

28. H. Carver, *Compassionate Landscape* (Toronto: University of Toronto Press, 1975), p. 223. Carver was chairman of the Advisory Group, Central Mortgage and House Corporation, Ottawa.

29. Niagara Parks Commission, *Ninety-Second Annual Report, 1978* (Niagara Falls, Ont., 1979), p. 4.

30. American Falls International Board, *Preservation and Enhancement of the American Falls at Niagara*, Appendix B, pp. 37–38.

31. International Joint Commission, *Preservation and Enhancement of the American Falls at Niagara*, pp. 19–20.

32. Ibid., pp. 20–21.

33. According to M. J. Piraston, Regional Manager, Niagara Frontier State Park and Recreation Commission, Niagara Falls, 17 December 1979. Data updated on the Canadian Frontier from the Niagara Parks Commission, Annual Reports.

34. Niagara Economic and Tourism Corporation, *Fact Sheet N: Niagara's Tourism Sector* (Thorold, Ont.: Niagara Economic and Tourism Corporation, 1977), p. 2. See Tourism Market Analysis Section, *Tourism Statistical Handbook*, Ontario Ministry of Industry and Tourism (Toronto, various dates), and Planning and Devel-

opment Department, *Tourism in the Niagara Region, Report No. 1, Economic Impact—Tourist Characteristics* (St. Catharines, Ont.: Regional Municipality of Niagara, 1983), p. 3.

35. B. Wilson, *Plaques along the Niagara River Recreation Trail* (Niagara Falls, Ont.: Niagara Parks Commission, 1993).

36. City of Niagara Falls, Canada, *Niagara Falls, Canada: Community Profile 1997* (Niagara Falls, Ont.: City of Niagara Falls, 1997).

37. Casino information is from Casino Niagara, *Casino Niagara—Facts* (Niagara Falls, Ont.: Casino Niagara, 1998).

38. R. S. Veley, Executive Director, *Toward a Tourism Master Plan: A Blueprint for Sustainable Tourism Development* (Toronto: Ontario Casino Corporation, 1997), p. 4. Advisory Committee on a Tourism Strategy, *Ontario's Tourism Industry: Opportunity-Progress-Innovation* (Toronto: Ministry of Culture, Tourism and Recreation, 1994), p. 36.

39. A critical appreciation of the gambling ethic is D. Cushman, *Whereof the Pawns Are People: A Report on Casino Niagara* (St. Catharines, Ont.: Missions Committee for Niagara Presbytery of Hamilton Conference, the United Church of Canada, Niagara Presbytery, 1996).

40. F. Lewimberg and G. Dark, *Niagara Falls Tourist Area Development Strategy* (Toronto: Urban Strategies Inc., 1998), p. 5.

41. Ibid., p. 15.

42. Ibid., p. 60.

43. Sandford Fleming Foundation, *Engineerium: Executive Summary— Planning Report for an Energy Museum and Science Centre at Niagara Falls* (Niagara Falls, Ont.: Sandford Fleming Foundation, 1982). See also J. Carr, A. J. Fisher, and K. D. Srivastava, *Feasibility Study for the Sandford Fleming Engineerium* (Waterloo, Ont.: Sandford Fleming Foundation, 1980), summarized with other studies in *Consultants' Reports Used in the Feasibility Study for the Sandford Fleming Engineerium* (Waterloo, Ont.: Sandford Fleming Foundation, 1980).

44. The major studies of the Canadian Frontier are G. Seibel, *Niagara Falls, Canada*; and G. A. Seibel and D. M. Seibel, *Niagara Portage Road*. The American Frontier is covered by H. B. Mizer, *A City Is Born—Niagara Falls—A City Matures— 1892: A Topical History 1932*, Niagara County Historical Society, Occasional Contributions No. 24 (Niagara Falls, N.Y., 1981); Niagara Falls Area Chamber of Commerce, *Then & Now— Niagara Falls, New York—1892–1967: The Eternal Wonder* (Niagara Falls, N.Y.: Chamber of Commerce, 1967); N. F. Stafford, *Welcome to the Niagara Historic Trail*, Bicentennial Publication (Lockport, N.Y.: Niagara County Development and Planning Department, 1976); and the Local History Committee of the Bicentennial Commission of the Town of Porter, *The Town of Porter 1776–1976: A Bicentennial History* (Youngstown, N.Y.: Historical Society of the Town of Porter, 1976). A photographic appreciation of the Falls is P. Berton, *A Picture Book of Niagara Falls* (Toronto: McClelland & Stewart, 1993).

CHAPTER THIRTEEN

THE NIAGARA BOUNDARY

A RETROSPECTIVE APPRECIATION

An international boundary is a fundamental geographic division that separates and divides two countries, even though physical and human similarities prevail on both sides. This book has tried to explain landscape at the Niagara Frontier as the cumulative record of past uses, with the physical background, transportation, and technological change being fundamental shapers of the emerging scene, and introducing new phases through which the development process has progressed. We conclude by asking what the situation would have been had no boundary been located along the Niagara River, which leads into a short statement about the changing meaning and role of the boundary at Niagara.

AS IT MIGHT HAVE BEEN

Our account has pursued the development of the area on both sides of the Niagara River since 1783, when the river was divided between two nations. At that time the British anticipated an Indian reserve to the east along the south shore of Lake Ontario, a supposition that would have resulted in either a considerable expanse of land in Western New York remaining under British control or the creation of an Indian "state" friendly to the British east of the Niagara River. In either circumstance, the British would have retained the Niagara River as their critical line of water communication via the St. Lawrence and Lake Ontario to the Upper Lakes, and the old province of Quebec would not have lost its western extent to American domination.

Given the feasible scenario of the boundary *not* following the Niagara River and with British territory on both sides of the river, how might the river and its precincts developed?[1] With the boundary somewhere to the east, the Loyalist outflow in the 1780s from the United States may be presumed to have settled along both sides of the Niagara River. Newark (now Niagara-on-the-Lake), located on the principal route to the continental interior and central within the area being settled, might well have retained its status as the capital of Upper Canada. Its administrative functions need not have moved to the more secure location of York (Toronto). In these circumstances the town at the northern entrance to the river could have remained the center of trade, social, and government activities as the British colony expanded.

A new portage on the west bank of the Niagara would not have been necessary, and there would have been no later need for both an Erie and a Welland Canal. One route between Lake Erie and Lake Ontario around the Falls would have sufficed, perhaps with the addition of an Oswego Canal to Albany and New York should a second outlet to the Atlantic Ocean been required. A Welland Canal would not have been needed. Sailing vessels on Lake Ontario could have taken the Niagara River to Queenston and then locked around the Falls to Chippawa, a shorter distance than along the present Welland Canal, and a route that would have taken advantage of the Lower Niagara River as a commodious potential harbor within protected banks.

At a later date as the size of vessels increased, the entrance to the Niagara River from Lake Erie might have been transferred west to avoid winter ice and to extend the navigation season, and this route might reasonably have followed that of the present Fourth Welland Canal between Lake Erie and the Niagara Escarpment, then a route across the Ontario Plain to the Niagara River, thereby perpetuating the retention of Niagara-on-the-Lake as the major urban and marine center.

Buffalo, arising as a port at the eastern end of Lake Erie and as the head of navigation for the Upper Lakes, would still have grown as a port at the head of the canal that bypassed the Falls, at the head of navigation for Lake Erie and the Upper Lakes, as a service center for its inland hinterland area, and then as a major rail transportation center because of the need to cross the Niagara River en route from New York to the Detroit and Chicago areas of the expanding American economy. Should Buffalo have been initiated and expanded under the auspices of British colonial rule, it would have developed under the different land practices of government control rather than under the private auspices of the Holland Land Company, and the Erie Canal would not have been required to foster its growth.

St. Catharines would have grown as a local market center subordinate to Niagara-on-the-Lake, towns would not have evolved along the now nonexistent Welland Canal, and the centers along the Niagara River would have assumed greater importance. Tourism would still have centered on the Falls, and hydroelectricity under the same national ownership might well have been used to promote industrial development along both sides of the river rather than unilaterally as now on the American side.

AS IT IS

As the boundary is crossed, some differences are immediate and obvious. The Canadian side has introduced the metric system of measurement. Gasoline is purchased in liters and not gallons, and speed limits are measured in kilometers rather than in miles. Canadian and American dollars have different values and a changing relationship one to the other. Two so-named parkways parallel the Niagara River; a two-lane Canadian scenic

route lies within a continuous linear park system, while the American parkway is a high-speed, four-lane, through route that carries heavy traffic. The Canadian side incorporates mass planting and floral bedding; on the American side the smaller amount of open space is landscaped mainly with clipped grass, trees, and shrubs.

The British tradition in Ontario, reflected in names and titles such as the *Queen* Elizabeth Way, the *Sir* Adam Beck Power Station, and the crown on motor vehicle license plates, has played an important role in settlement evolution. With American independence in 1783 and then the influx of United Empire Loyalists, land in Canada was available from the colonial government in varying amounts based on military rank and civic status of the settler. The division and sale of land on the American side took place later, through a private landholding company, and was purchased according to the means of the settler. The units of land subdivision were smaller and the number of survey roads greater on the Canadian side.

In both instances the pioneer division of the land into townships provided the basis for the correct municipal form of government, but the American side more so than the Canadian Frontier has retained its historically large number of small, long-established administrative units of local government organization. Their traditional boundaries have been less changed by annexation and reorganization, and no system of regional government such as the Regional Municipality of Niagara, created in 1970, has occurred.

Many consequences stem from the different political situations on the two sides as the boundary is crossed. The Canadian Frontier emerged by evolution within the British Empire, the American Frontier by revolution against its British antecedents. Most trade on the Canadian Frontier was initially with Britain, but links to the United States expanded through proximity, after the repeal of British laws in the 1850s, and when railway bridges crossed the Niagara River. The first treaty to control the diversion of boundary waters was between Britain and the United States. Capital to achieve the Welland Canal and the Canadian railways was in part raised in Britain and New York. American involvement in the First and Second World Wars was later than in Canada, which followed Britain immediately into these two wars.

Rail transportation began earlier on the American side, played a larger role in urban and industrial development, and was significant in transforming Buffalo into a major national railway center, with a number of competing lines adding to its industrial and port activities for lake and canal commerce. Both cities of Niagara Falls also benefited, but to a lesser extent, from tourist and industrial developments. The towns along the Welland and the Erie Canals also advanced considerably through the impact of railways.

Hydroelectricity, first developed on both sides by American private interests, was used extensively near its source in Niagara Falls and Buffalo to foster industrial development. Later managed on the Canadian Frontier through a public agency, in contrast with its American use at source, it was then transmitted inland to the advantage of centers throughout Southern Ontario. Pollution of air and water resources from its new industrial activities created a severe problem along the Niagara River and its environs.

As surfaced and graded highways evolved from dirt roads on both Frontiers, the interurban multilane highway for fast-moving vehicles was introduced on the Canadian Frontier when the Queen Elizabeth Way between Toronto and the United States at the Peace Bridge ushered in an extensive system on both sides of the boundary. This novel creation, a form destined to alter the urban situation across North America, transformed the pattern of Frontier settlement from a series of small communities plus Buffalo into a two-nation metropolitan complex.

The two parts of this international urban grouping had different links within their respective nations. The Canadian Frontier lay on the fringe of expanding southern Ontario and was an integral part of the "Golden Horseshoe" around the western end of Lake Ontario, whereas the Buffalo-Niagara Falls metropolitan area was more isolated from neighboring metropolitan areas in that nation. This is also the reverse of the situation that existed until the Second World War, when Buffalo was dominant on the Frontier.

The two patterns of settlement differ markedly. The Canadian Frontier has a greater number of small centers. It is a multinodal region, with independent centers emerging along the Welland Canal, along the Niagara River, and across the agricultural landscape. Although some amalgamation of adjacent jurisdictions has taken place, the urban centers remain mostly separated by intervening areas of agricultural land. The American settlements have a larger total population. They are more fused into one urban-industrial agglomeration, more dominated by a single major city, and occupy more land. Lewiston, the Tonawandas, and Buffalo are connected along the frontage of the Niagara River and inland by railways, highways, and continuous development; only Lockport to the east is reasonably separate.

Manufacturing concentrated at Buffalo because of its great transportation advantages. The city grew to be a leading North American metropolitan center through the combined forces of rail, lake, and canal transport. When first railway and then highway bridges spanned the Niagara River, and as Canadian nationalism sought industrial expansion, economic links were forged across the boundary. American industrial plants located branches in Canada. Larger than the local Canadian industries, they promoted much employment and considerable urban expansion on the Canadian Frontier. Though Canadian-owned industries and activities occur east of the Niagara River, they are fewer and more recent. The two industrial structures are similar, though more subdued on the Canadian than the American Frontier; the tendency is to carry similar industries based on automobile parts, chemicals, and metal-working activities. With manufacturing in relative decline since the 1980s, and with service activities expanding as a proportion of total employment, both Frontiers remain important centers of production. More American plants have moved to the Canadian Frontier than in the reverse direction, and the boundary itself with two-way trading flows has provided an important factor in industrial location at the Frontier.

Canals crossed the Niagara Escarpment at Thorold-St. Catharines and at Lockport. They increased the availability of hydraulic power and added considerably to urban impetus and industrial expansion. Both canals were enlarged and expanded during the nineteenth century, but the Erie Canal as a state enterprise then waned and was in part removed, whereas the Welland Canal expanded to become an international waterway under the auspices of the federal St. Lawrence Seaway Authority, but is now managed by its commercial users with federal ownership of the land required for a future Fifth Welland Canal.

The broadly based industry of tourism has grown considerably, with popular new attractions of a butterfly conservatory, a continuous riverside trail, a casino, and an expanded Marineland on the Canadian Frontier, but also through the addition of marina facilities, golf courses, and across the Niagara Fruit Belt with the expansion of high-quality wineries and associated service activities. Of the urban centers outside the immediate vicinity of the Falls, Niagara-on-the-Lake and Buffalo have gained considerably from expanding volumes of tourist traffic.

The land on both sides of the Niagara River has been used wisely, but also seriously abused. There has been a lack of compatibility between industrial growth and the amenity qualities of the landscape; between tourism, the increasing number of visitors and commercial developments to meet their demands; and between the increasing demands of urban growth and the need to retain the best areas of agricultural land. As the natural waterways have become seriously polluted with industrial and municipal affluents, safeguarding their quality has become an important item on the agenda of both Frontiers. There is also a strong need to save and reuse significant historic buildings and to conserve those of architectural importance. Both Frontiers have been negligent about conserving heritage resources, and the continuing need for environmental conservation remains of critical importance.

Over recent decades, sharp and important changes in emphasis have taken place. The Canadian Frontier has continued to expand in terms of population growth. Population decline is evident on the American Frontier, especially in the city of Buffalo where the situation is marked by steady suburban expansion into adjacent out-of-town administrative districts. On both Frontiers the population structure of the urban centers is multiethnic and multicultural, through large-scale immigration of often low-income groups from eastern and southern Europe during the heyday of urban expansion in the late nineteenth and early twentieth centuries, and continuing more so from abroad on the Canadian than the American Frontier.

Until the First World War, the city was the prime focus of population and industrial concentration, but the current trend is toward the diffusion of industry, services, and housing, leading to decreasing population size and densities in the older inner-city areas, to urban renewal and steady redevelopment in these localities, and to a greater spread into extensive new suburban and exurban developments. The arrivals of the motor vehicle and then of multilane highways are major contributors to this new urban scene, as are the freedoms in location introduced through hydroelectricity and a range of power resources including piped oil and gas. The traditional roles of site and situation influencing the course and form of urbanization have been diminished substantially by these many new circumstances and forces and by the technological ability to change rather than to depend upon landscape quality.

Both Frontiers face the complex issue of rural-urban land conversion. Public policies to protect agricultural land are stronger on the Canadian than on the American Frontier, but both countries have permitted high levels of land consumption and urban dispersal. The rights of property owners and developers have been placed on a higher plane than conservation and the public interest in land.

The status and relative importance of settlements have also varied considerably over time. In 1783 when the boundary was formed, Fort Niagara and the river passage between the two lakes were then of supreme importance. This changed as Niagara-on-the-Lake developed on the Canadian bank as the first capital of Upper Canada, a position lost to York (Toronto), and then as Buffalo became the rising commercial center at the head of navigation for the Upper Lakes.

The introduction of the Erie and then the Welland Canals radically changed the focus of settlement attention. On the Canadian bank the transition was inland from the river to the line of settlement that arose along the Welland Canal between Port Dalhousie on Lake Ontario and Port Colborne on Lake Erie, with St. Catharines becoming the dominant city along this lineal strip. On the American side, after the Erie Canal connected Lake Erie with the Atlantic Ocean, Buffalo expanded magnificently with industry, services, and transportation services as a terminal and exchange port between expanding lake and canal systems of navigation. The city, the dominant center on the American side, extended its sway into a regional hinterland that extended into the Canadian Frontier.

The railway with bridges across the Niagara River more closely connected the two riparian communities, with industrial growth and commercial expansion being strong on both banks but prevailing most actively on the American side. On the Canadian side St. Catharines was bypassed by this now-prevailing mode of transport in favor of Merritton; Welland with canal and railways to serve manufacturing industry advanced to greater importance; and Thorold with no through east-west lines of track declined. On the American side railways concentrated attention on Buffalo, and on the Tonawandas and Lockport to a lesser extent, and on Niagara Falls for its tourist attributes. Lewiston yielded to Lockport, and Lockport in turn to Niagara Falls as communities expanded along the Niagara River rather than inland from the boundary.

The electric streetcar then served to more closely interlink the communities on both sides of the Niagara River, assisted their growth, and emphasized the centrality of the downtown centers that had now emerged on both sides. It should be noted that the Canadian system centered in St. Catharines could not expand west from that city because of ravines in the landscape which curtailed the expansion of that city with western communities along the Ontario Plain transferring some

allegiance to the expanding Hamilton urban system, whereas the area east of St. Catharines was connected directly with Niagara Falls and Buffalo on the American Frontier. Tourism at the Falls also expanded greatly with the availability of this new form of local transportation, and the Great Gorge Route became one of the most popular tourist attractions in North America until this scenic route was usurped by hydroelectric developments at the base of the gorge.

With the automobile era, the Queen Elizabeth Way linked the Canadian Frontier into the rapidly expanding greater Toronto region, the epicenter of Canadian manufacturing and a major service center for shopping, sports, recreation, leisure, and entertainment. The Canadian Frontier became urban fringe to this dominating metropolitan complex. In the meantime, Buffalo and its vicinity were bypassed by the New York Thruway on land and by the St. Lawrence Seaway for marine traffic. The Erie Canal became a historical-recreational resource rather than the commercial waterway that initiated prodigious urban and industrial growth during the nineteenth century. Tourism, too, although of expanding significance to both Frontiers, favored the Canadian rather than the American scene at the Falls. Also the inland areas on the Canadian

Frontier had higher rural, agricultural, and landscape values than their counterparts in the more urbanized American environments.

This changing and challenging process of long-term and continuing urbanization returns us to the physical background of the land, air, and water resources that introduced this narrative and provided the basic incentive for the human settlement of the Frontier region. Nothing has remained as it was. Everything has changed. Rivers have been diverted to mills, industry, hydroelectric plants, and water-supply reservoirs; some rivers have even had their directions of flow reversed. Marshland has been drained to encourage agriculture. Ports and harbors have been established to modify the shorelines of both lakes. The barrier of the Niagara Escarpment to through navigation has been foiled by portages along the Niagara River and then by the construction of two canals. Quarries and pits have been dug into the land to provide road and construction materials, and underground gas has added pumping stations, a distribution system, and industrial activities to the landscape. The land, originally heavily forested, has become the scene for a multitude of different urban, industrial, transportation, and rural-agricultural activities, causing pollution and leading to the ecological management of former natural resources.

CONCLUSION

Geographers seek to understand a varied and complex landscape that contains many subtleties of meaning and opportunity. As we all live, work, and enjoy recreation and leisure opportunities in this environment, its characteristics are matters of great practical, academic, and public concern. A deep human need exists to understand the roots, the quality, and the associations of place. These features are primarily of our making, and we alone have the responsibility for the future character of our living landscape. The Niagara Frontier is a significant place. It deserves to be treated as such and not squandered.

The Niagara Frontier began as a human division of the earth. From its inception it gave different meanings to the two sides of the Niagara River. In contrast with the previous Native periods of occupation, the boundary immediately became a fundamental international discontinuity, in time also a discontinuity of administration as provinces and states, municipalities, and the laws they invoked were added. The boundary also often coincided with the areas established for administration by church, business, and service organizations.

Though changing from the midpoint of the Niagara River to the line of the deepest channel, the boundary has always followed the majestic Niagara River. It has, however, changed drastically in meaning and purpose. It was drawn through territory that was largely unknown, without regard for either the affinities that existed across the Niagara River or the regional position of the area on a major route of transportation to the continental interior. It was a primary division of part of the Great Lakes Basin previously under British control, between rival British and American nations. The boundary meant much to the first Canadian settlers who sought to escape tyranny and retribution in their former homelands, but less to later waves of immigrants on both sides searching for homestead and living opportunities.

After both sides had been settled, mutual destruction during the War of 1812 and emerging nationalism on both banks caused the boundary to harden. The boundary became an incontrovertible fact which has influenced and continues to influence many decisions. It softened and eased as a boundary when bridge connections, industry, and travel across the Niagara River increased. This has been the story told in this book. The boundary separates and divides; it also links and associates the respective banks and will continue to exercise this contradictory effect as today gives way to tomorrow. The lines writ by nature are deep; the lines writ by man, even in swift-flowing river waters, also leave their indelible impression on the earth's surface.

NOTE

1. The assistance of Dr. H. J. Gayler, Associate Professor of Geography, Brock University (St. Catharines, Ont.) is appreciated in compiling these conjectures.

INDEX